A HOSTEL ODYSSEY

Text copyright © Domenico Napolitano, 2021

The right of Domenico Napolitano to be identified as the author of this work has been asserted by himself.
ISBN 9798520587194

All rights reserved. No part of this publication may be reproduced, distributed, or transmitted in any form or by any means, including photocopying, recording, or other electronic or mechanical methods, without the prior written permission of the publisher, except in the case of brief quotations embodied in critical reviews and certain other non-commercial uses permitted by copyright law.

This is a memoir. The events are portrayed to the best of my memory. While all the stories in this book are true, some names and identifying details have been changed to protect the privacy of the people involved.

Introduction:

This diary covers three years of my life, starting and ending in September, from 2014 to 2017.

Before proceeding with reading the story, I want to point out that a substantial difference in style exists between the first year and the following two.

It is right at that point in fact, that the scenarios, characters, nature of choices, pace and variety of events will experience a sharp change and give birth to what I consider an odyssey.

However, no matter the different dynamics, my first year had to be inserted in the book both for its crucial role in shaping the future events, and for the story to be better comprehended.

A HOSTEL ODYSSEY

To all the people who
were part of this story

I landed in London in the night of the 22nd of September 2014.
I had previously stayed in a hostel in Inverness Terrace, near Hyde Park. I knew the place already and the atmosphere in there was perfect for me, it was all I needed to be happy, literally.
My plan was to find work somewhere in London and live in the hostel, sharing my life with tourists from all over the world. I knew that London was going to take a lot from me, and I didn't want to be deprived of a social life by a routine that would have put me into a state of forced loneliness and constant mild depression.
At late night, I had finally made it to the venue just to find out that my prepaid card was not accepted by the reception nor by cash machines.
-We can't let you in, you can rest for a few minutes by the sofas while you try to sort that out though- a receptionist told me.
The very first problem with my new life. It was too late to call anyone and to be fair I didn't think anyone could have helped me in that case.
I had just started worrying when I noticed that a friendly-faced guy who looked my age was smiling at me.
-Is everything ok?- he probably noticed that something was wrong in my smile of polite response.
-Well, it's a long story I guess, although it just happened, basically, my card wouldn't work so...- I realised he wasn't getting much of what I was saying.
-I'm sorry, my English is very bad- he said with a thick French accent which made me smile for real.
-You look very French with that dark spot near your nose- I tried to say in French. He laughed, then asked me to try and explain what had happened to me in his language. I slowly managed to finish my story to see him suddenly standing up, taking his wallet from his jeans pocket, counting 140 pounds and giving them to me.
-Are you serious?- I asked him. Who did something like that? Why did he trust me if he didn't even know me at all? I didn't like to take any help from others, never, but I didn't really have any other options.

-You are so kind, wow, I mean, you really are the best, and I promise I will give you everything back tomorrow morning- I slowly moved my hand towards his and grabbed the notes.
-No worries, take your time- he said and smiled to me again.
I checked in, wished the kind guy good night, then moved to room 90, put my stuff into my top bunk bed and finally got to sleep for a few hours.

The next day I rushed to try my card in every cash machine around Bayswater area, but I couldn't find any that worked. I didn't have any time to waste so I walked back to the hostel to get my laptop out and send applications for work, all while hoping not to see the French guy around to avoid the embarrassment.
Well, I can't work without eating first, I thought whilst approaching the stove. A big plate of pasta with tomato sauce was all I needed to get going, and also the only thing I could cook.
-You must be Italian- someone behind me said. A red-haired guy opened a plastic bag and took out some pasta and various sauces from it.
-My name is Leonardo, nice to meet you- he said.
-Dom, pleasure-
-Hi, I'm Valentin- a guy that was apparently with him introduced himself as well. He was a bit chubby with some short brown hair. His clean shaved face, a suit without a tie and shiny black shoes gave me the impression that he was overdressed for a hostel, but he looked kind of cute.
-Yeah, I know what you're thinking, he's gay and so proud of it- Leonardo joked. Valentin slapped his arm, looking complacent.
We sat down to eat together and by the time we were done I realised that Leonardo had already befriended a bunch of people, good score since it was his first day there just like me.
-I need to get work as soon as possible or I'll have to go back home, my parents told me- Leonardo sounded worried.
-Same, and I have no idea how to apply for work, but I think my girlfriend will help me, she's good with computers and all that stuff. I think I just grew up in the wrong generation- I

2

said. My girlfriend was in Russia, but she did commit to helping me find work through accessing my accounts.
-I have an interview today already though, waiter position- Leonardo chewed his last bites of pasta.
-I want to live in London so badly. In my area, you have to know someone already or wait for someone to introduce you to someone while here you just talk to strangers and I love it- I said.
-What do you mean?-
-You see, I want to make friends with new people everyday and not talk to people I already know, just in case they get to know too much about me and they start becoming judgemental-
-That doesn't make sense- Valentin said, then blinked at me.
-You didn't seem very friendly at first- Leonardo cut me to the quick.
-I'll show you how to apply for work- Valentin smiled.
By the end of the day, I had sent about at least fifty different applications, mostly on catering jobs, even though I had no experience on such whatsoever, but I was ready to lie in case.
From that moment though, I spent every minute with Leonardo and Valentin, my two new friends. Sometimes I saw Davinia, a cute Spanish blonde girl to which I had introduced myself on my second day in the common room of the hostel, although apart from a walk together in Hyde Park, I hadn't managed to spend more time with her due to the fact that she was already fully employed.
I became more anxious with the passage of time, but on the third day, I received my first phone call. At least, I was going to have a chance.
A recruitment agent told me he could have found me a job very quickly and all I needed to do was show up by their office in Hammersmith, pay them ten pounds for a two hours training and get a certificate that would have got me started straight away. Did I really have a choice?

I was in a better mood when I left the building that late afternoon and got into the tube on my way back to Bayswater. The agency looked too professional to actually be

some sort of swindle agency that tricked desperate migrants with no contacts in town like me.
Funny though, how many different ways there were to serve a plate on a table, who would have ever thought about that? The training wasn't too hard, and it seemed like they really needed staff.
Whatever, I'm ready to take anything just to make some money, even if ten per cent of my minimum wage is apparently due to them, but with my current money situation I can't afford to check if that's even legal.
A message from them arrived the same night as I was sitting at the step outside the hostel with the two guys and some other random tourists.
-You are requested at the Thames Hotel, Tower Bridge for an early shift week, starting tomorrow until Sunday, please confirm as soon as you can-
-YES- I replied, just in case lower case letters weren't good enough.

My first shift was scheduled for 4 am and was going to end four hours later.
-I didn't know it was part-time- I told my manager, a woman in her forties with an eastern European accent when I met her at the hotel near Tower Bridge.
-You don't have enough experience to work a full shift, but we'll see what we can do after this week-
Fine, I thought, I just need to show them I'm a very hard worker and they'll like me for sure.
By the end of the week, almost everyone liked me as they realised that they just needed to tell me what to do and I would have done it without questioning.
-The guy just moved here, he told me- a waiter commented out loud while I was running through the tables.
-I can see that, but give him some time and you'll see- I heard another waiter responding to him.
The head waiter, a Turkish guy called Oman, who showed me around first liked me a lot, unlike the manager, who thought I was disorganised and needed to calm down a bit on the floor.

-Dom, you're just supposed to take dirty plates back to the kitchen and polish some more cutlery, you're not allowed to take the orders, I told you already- she was getting annoyed now, but I couldn't focus much on what she was saying because of her dress.
-You have to just ask them if they want tea or coffee, and also fill up the jars with more milk by the way- she added.
-Yeah sure, sorry- I said, glad and also disappointed to realise that I had a pathetic role in that place.
-Dom, do you want to take orders at that table?- an Italian guy, a bit older than me asked me as soon as the manager was gone for a break.
-Sure, I'm just scared I won't understand the customers well-
-You'll be alright young man, come on- he smiled and gave me his pen and notepad.

I can't go on like this for a long time though, I thought after the second day of work. My shift was ending when the morning had just started. Waking up at 3 am forced me not only to go to sleep much earlier than I wanted to, but also deprived me of the social life I was mainly aiming at getting. What was the point of living in a hostel if I couldn't hang out with people? Tourists had just started drinking and going out right when I had to go to sleep.
I thought about this while I walked on Tower Bridge on my way back to the tube station when I saw I had received some voice mail.
-Hello, Mr Domenico? My name is Evan, I'm calling from Cote restaurant, Sloane Square. We saw your cv and would like to call you in for an interview. Could you come in for a trial shift at 4 pm tomorrow? Please call us back whenever possible, thank you very much- I had to listen to this voicemail message about four times to make sure I understood each word.
It must have been her. I don't remember sending an application to any place called Cote in fact. It was going to end soon because of the distance between us, but she was still doing me favours.

October 2014

On the first of October 2014 I had my trial shift in Cote Restaurant in Sloane Square, lovely looking area in Chelsea. The French manager asked me a bunch of questions and literally told me, at the end of the interview, that Italians have a passion for food and would be good members of staff in a restaurant by default. He ignored the fact that I had learnt how to cook pasta through YouTube just a few days before, but I was grateful to my country for carrying a name and a reputation that helped me get that job without proving anything.
I tried to learn as much as possible from my trainer that day, a runner from Bangladesh, a real character. Unlike many others, he literally cared about nothing. He would sometimes drink during the shift, do the minimum necessary for his duty to be considered done by the managers, exploited the sympathy he had from the guys of the kitchen and the time he had been working in that place in his favour to never be in trouble or being monitored by anyone. They all trusted him and didn't ask him any questions and he clearly enjoyed it.
I did my very best. Getting that job would have ended my anxiety, allowed me to start getting paid properly, and given me confidence and signals that I could have made it for real in my new life.
By the end of the shift, everyone had tried to offer me a break several times. They were impressed by my hard work and most of them liked me. Now I just had to ask them if I was hired but I was too shy and humble on my first day to actually interrupt the managers in a busy moment.
Eventually, an attractive young manager from Poland told me to wait a minute, made a phone call to someone and came back to me to tell me I got the job. I suspected they didn't really care about listening to the opinions of my colleagues about me but just hired me because staff was needed as Christmas time was approaching and it was going to get very busy.
I left the restaurant and took the tube the way home, satisfied and excited about it.
Some of my hostel friends were already working, some of them didn't have a good time at the trial shift and were not

hired. We all acted nice to them and encouraged them to keep trying. Everyone needed to leave the hostel and move to a room somewhere in London to start a normal life. Everyone but me though. I was happy to be there in the hostel, and even if I felt like all I needed was new people all the time, I couldn't deny I was getting closer and closer to my very first friends.

My job, a runner, consisted of a bunch of duties, all of them quite simple and repetitive, but also hard on the long run which was perfect for me so that I could avoid spacing out and daydreaming.
Duties consisted of polishing cutlery, folding napkins, which was also the favourite activity of some waitresses in the moments they were feeling particularly lazy and wanted to have some chats with each other. They would sit together at the corner of the floor and talk either about their boyfriends, complain about the management or about colleagues who were not around.
-The environment for the newcomers in this restaurant is very nice at the beginning. Everybody treats you with respect and with a smile for everything they ask you to do. After ensuring you have signed a contract with them, their way to talk to you would suddenly change- said the head runner Ripon whilst we were polishing cutlery. I guessed this was based on a few specific fears that people that just moved to a new country probably feel. This is also the reason why they usually employ young people that just moved to London. Young people have no idea, no expectation nor understanding of what London can offer them if they at least try to make their projects come true.
Runners' top priority was the word "service", usually screamed very loud by chefs who were scared not to be able to deliver their courses in the quickest possible time, which was their top priority.
Moreover, runners had to take all dirty crockery downstairs to the kitchen porter, pick them up again when they were clean and set them back on the shelves near the coffee machine, where the waiters would use them to make coffees and all sort of stuff.

I usually volunteered to be the drop off guy, the one that runs up and down the stairs. I once counted doing this more than 200 times during a shift. Hard job, but it gave me that sense of usefulness I wanted to feel so to know that my position was appreciated and I was wanted by the rest of the staff.
This kind of behaviour had its consequences though. Some members showed me appreciation, asked me if I needed help or sometimes even tried to do part of my job without being caught by me.
On the other hand, some members showed a very self-orientated attitude when dealing with others. They would let their selfish and protective instinct prevail over the ideal of kindness.
Runners were on the lowest step of the pyramid, then there were waiters, assistant managers, managers, head managers and then some other people in upper positions, the ones that usually showed up in a suit and a big smile, shook hands with everyone and sat with a humble look on a table to do stuff on their laptops while sipping some tea. I enjoyed observing how the staff reacted in such moments. One thing I noticed was that the most selfish members were extremely toady towards those people while the nicest ones would treat them with the due respect but nothing more than that, and I loved to see that every time I made this correlation in my head I was right.
Anytime the head manager came over, one of the managers had kept a cup of tea, a cup of coffee, a tea pot and a tea spoon clean to the point of shining somewhere behind the drawer, ready for any request of the guy in higher position. Another manager would warn the entire staff about the visit of the head manager and a wave of anxiety hit some of us even if we were doing just fine. Some managers would start having quick talks to everyone, like a teacher preparing his kids before the school exams. If you didn't get scared and ready to do your best he would have seen it in your face and he wouldn't have been happy about it.
Anxious people in charge want their insecurities to feel justified by perceiving you had some as well and if they

didn't, they would believe you just weren't caring at all about your job.
-Domenico, clean the bottom of every wine metal holders-
-It's 10 in the morning, he's not going to order wine and I'm going to do this later again anyway when we set up for dinner...?-
-Do you want to go home Domenico?-
I felt like anytime an order I was given was unnecessary I was entitled of doing it faster. The manager was mostly focused on checking whether his shirt was properly ironed or not, he wouldn't pay attention to me.
If a promotion at work were to be promised to me in exchange of a few days of toady behaviour I might have accepted only according to the size of the reward.
The general manager in our restaurant was always stressed but wasn't really toady by nature. He would heavily walk up to the stairs from his office saying "gonna have to go and talk to this retard now... oh hi Daniel! How are you doing today? So nice to see you". The expression on his face changed suddenly and the vein on his forehead pulsed out of impatience, muscles next to his lips contracted as strong as he could so that an actual big smile would appear on his face. I liked him, I liked it that he didn't freak out and just acted with them the way he acted with everyone.

Days started going by and I was learning a lot of new things about food and catering I had never thought I would be needing to know, but there I was, working in a restaurant against every expectation considering that the only job I ever did was in the clothing industry with my father.
The team of runners that worked with me alternatively was made of Ilaria, Angelo, Lena, Ripon, Damien and Clotilde. What I didn't know back then, was that the staff was going to constantly change. In fact, in just a few weeks, two waiters and one runner left. I wondered if only the toady ones were the ones that survived longer.
I asked a fit waitress from Slovakia for her phone number the day she was leaving but she turned it down saying it wasn't a good idea.

My shift usually started at 4 in the afternoon and ended with the closing of the restaurant. Everyday I was getting faster and better, I needed to consolidate my position and I wanted the approval of everyone. I wasn't happy if even one person there wasn't happy about me, a sign of insecurity which pushed me to do more and more for everyone. The result was that all others started taking it easy and getting lazier, knowing that I would have done what was needed to be done no matter what my actual duties were.

As a drop off guy, I was the number 3 on the runner team. Number 1 was the service runner. It was most of the times girls doing this. It was the lightest of the duties that we had, and it consisted of carrying a big tray with plates on top of it so that the waiters would put them on the tables. The chefs would only want to see girls doing the service as they wanted to flirt all the time and make compliments over the way they moved their bodies while taking the tray. The girls would smile even without having any intentions of ever going on a date with them, but they knew their staff food would have tasted better if they smiled back at their comments.

Number 2 was the station guy. He was there to polish cutlery and glasses as soon as I took them upstairs from the kitchen porter area. They were the ones to get free food all the time. The service ones were always on the floor, I was always running up and down, therefore the numbers 2 were having generally a good time. Sometimes we also had a number 4, an extra runner to just go around the floor and clean the tables when the restaurant was too busy.

The kitchen staff was a hell of different characters, it somehow looked like it might have been a place where the government would put convicts to work in order to discount their sentences and reach freedom a bit quicker. They were swearing and insulting each other all the time, words of rage and frustration with threats of violence were constantly filling up the kitchen. Silence was set to calm things down only by the sous-chef, a Jamaican man who spoke disrespectfully to everyone except girls. Out of fear of being sent home they would just stop talking out loud but keep muttering between their teeth.

There was only one guy that seemed to be careless about everything, even about the sous-chef.
His name was Salvatore, a tall guy with bushy, long, dark curly hair from Sardinia. In his opinion, the region where he came from was a country itself, not part of Italy, and even though reality spoke differently, I didn't deny him the pleasure to feel he was right.
We often talked for hours outside of the restaurant. Besides very different views we had on nature and religion, I got to be very fascinated by him in general.
He would always laugh out loud and never put pressure on anyone, acting very respectful with all. I was happy to talk to him and we became friends very quickly.

November 2014

The beginning of November was eventless. I wanted to work and save money so badly that I asked one of my managers to let me work seven days a week, to which she calmly replied that even if I wanted to, I couldn't have made it without running out of energy at some point. Besides that, they put me on evening shifts only, most of the times doing closure. Coming back home after work meant no tube service. I had to take a bus from Sloane Square to Marble Arch and wait for another bus to take me home. I had no data service activated on my phone so sometimes I had to just wait and wait without knowing about any disruptions or lack of service on specific routes. I spent several nights waiting for what seemed to be more than an hour for my bus to come, sometimes so tired I would fall asleep for a few minutes at the bus stop and realised, when I woke up, that I had just missed it.
I usually got home between 2.30 or 3.00 in the night and had no one to talk to. A bread baguette I used to take home every time I could get one from the restaurant and a jar of chocolate cream to spread on it would often keep me company. Sometimes I would remember to buy four cans of beer and store them in the fridge in the kitchen, hoping to find them again when I would come back. Beer was becoming a daily thing for me.

This lifestyle led me to make a choice. Either I continued being exploited for the minimum wage, or I continued being exploited for the minimum wage after spending a productive morning at least.

I decided I would wake up everyday at 11 am no matter what, take my time for a proper breakfast and go for a run in Hyde Park. I would usually run around the big pond for about half hour and then head back to the hostel to have some quick food again before going to work, hopefully in time to ask for staff food as well before the start of my shift.

Within the first weeks of November, I finally got a bank account and a national insurance number, which meant I could finally start getting paid and reduce my anxiety caused by the fact I was running out of money.

I asked Iliana, my manager, to have Tuesdays and Wednesdays off so that I could watch the football, to which she accepted without problems.

Apart from the busy evenings in my days off though, I never knew what to do during the day.

I would usually go downstairs to the kitchen and make some food, take it to the common room next to it and see if there were people to talk to.

One night I met a guy with short black hair and a very nerdy aspect sitting next to an older woman with a thick English accent at a table in front of mine, keen on trying to solve chess puzzles from a book. After a little while I figured that they had been stuck on a problem for about ten minutes. When I approached them and asked if I could join, they answered back with a smile and welcomed me to their table. Fifteen minutes later, none of us had found the solution yet. Eventually, we went through the solutions page and found out that the right answer consisted of pushing a pawn to the edge of the board and promoting it into a bishop, which was quite unusual, but also the only good move since a promotion into a queen would have resulted into a stalemate.

I was terrible at chess, but I loved playing it. I never really played it in Italy if not for a very brief period of time on my computer, but other than that, football was the only socially accepted game in my area and the only one I happened to develop knowledge about.

In chess, I only knew how the pieces moved, but I knew no strategies at all. The nerdy guy, called Dean, beat me multiple times and also effortlessly. Sometimes I was ahead of him and my position was better than his, but he used his experience to remain calm and slowly regain advantage by the end of the game.
Dean was very skinny and tall, and looked pretty weird. He was studying physics in a university in London, he was completely broke and had no social skills whatsoever. He would sometimes show up like a ghost and just ask me for a game without even saying hi or saying good night when he went to bed.

Eventually, I found out that Leonardo had left London. After his unsuccessful trial shift, he decided to move back to Italy. Few days after, Valentine told me he was going to leave as well, although, not before flirting with me. Eventually, he suggested me to go to the bathroom with him so he could give me head. I thought about it for few minutes, then with the help of the third beer, I accepted the offer. When we were done, Valentine stood up and we both smiled to each other, both quite satisfied. A second later though, the smile disappeared from his face.
-Anyway, you have to know that I'm a slut- he said, then walked away.
I thought he was joking, but he wasn't. He would never talk to me ever again for some reasons. He left the week after.

Meanwhile, my friendship with Andrea, a guy from Lecce, was consolidating and we were hanging out everyday. He studied at some sort of cosmetics school and was planning to work as a masseur on his own. He told me about the money someone could make like that and the numbers were quite impressive. It made me wonder several times why I kept working in a restaurant, creating some frustration and jealousy inside of me.
I also realised that my pace with girls was too slow and that sounded like an alarm to me more than ever when I missed a good chance in mid-November.

ourselves and our countries, then some philosophical talks on what we liked about the hostel and how we could improve civil behaviour inside of it, up to saying hi each time and share conversations where Samir did his best to teach me stuff I didn't know.

-I see you here trying to introduce yourself to girls, and I like it that you do this. When I was your age, I was exactly like you, quite shy, but with a great desire to prove myself I could make it in life. Now, let me tell you something though. The time of fun has an end, regardless of whether you want it or not. At some point, you'll be too old for it, and the last thing you want is to let it pass past you. You see, the most important lesson I learnt when I was young was that it all depends on your choices and mindset. Nothing comes to you like if it's due, nothing happens just because you're getting older. You need to know, that every time you're sitting in that chair and let a girl pass by you and you don't say anything, you miss a chance. Yes, she might not be interested, but the fact you don't interrupt her walk to force her to look at you is a problem that will affect you forever if you're not careful-

Everything he said not only made sense, but also disturbed me a bit. He said things I had learnt to silence. I used to think that with the passage of time, things were just meant to happen no matter what, as if the book of life was already written, and at some point, the main character gets laid. But what that man was telling me that night, was that the choices shaped everything about a life's worth. A concept I wanted to deny, but that I couldn't really.

-You're right. I do my best to get to talk to them, although I recognise it's not enough, and also, I tend to plan the whole thing in my head before trying to get it started- I agreed with him not only because I had to, but also because I was hoping he would stop it. He was throwing truth bombs against me, hitting my weaknesses and making me feel uncomfortable.

-Ageing doesn't mean anything if you don't gain experience, and with girls, theories don't work that much. You need the practice, a lot of it so that you can navigate through the rapids. See, as I said, your twenties started, and they will also end one day, sooner than you think. By that time, you must be able to say you enjoyed every moment of them, otherwise, you miss it!- his voice got stronger and stronger by the time he ended his sentence, giving me the certainty that what I thought about him was true. He had gone through the same I was going through. The inhibition, the fear to fail and despise for rejection. I could tell he felt like that too in the past, and how glad he was for having overcome it, or at least that was what I assumed.

By Christmas, Samir's words were still echoing in my head, and they were helping me to deal with my breakup. In fact, Ivy, my girlfriend who lived in Moscow, declared herself tired of everything, especially of our arguments all the time. It was her that started them, but it was also because I wasn't paying much attention to her. Our everyday phone calls slowly became to happen every other day, and then gradually, both of us lost interest in each other, even though we just hadn't had the courage to talk about it up to those days.
I promised her that I would have visited her in Russia as soon as I could, to which she responded with no enthusiasm at all, telling me not to bother about it.
The restaurant was on fire before Christmas and I was given a few double shifts that not only killed my social life even more, but also started depriving me of enough sleep and I was suffering for this. I was 23, and I felt that my invincible body could be abused forever, but I slowly went on to realise this was damaging me physically and mentally.
I could wake up early in the morning, work the entire day, come back at night, sleep one or two hours before having another double shift, leave the restaurant, go to a club, stay up all night and then sleep all off the following day.
It was for this reason that I didn't manage to develop a deep friendship with the guys of the family. I only saw them a few times a week if I was lucky and always at night, when they were too drunk to stay awake or when they had already left for party.

The weather was still acceptably warm, my first winter in England was not at all what I expected, in fact, winter was way worse in Italy. It felt good to stay outside the hostel by the steps of the buildings next to it and drink cans of beer and just talk to people.

I met many people. Some of them even gave me the impression we would have become great friends if they weren't going to leave the very next day, which often made me a bit sad.

I spent Christmas working double shift as they said they would pay me double the amount of the minimum wage. A good deal to me at that time. I checked my bank account and saw I had over 3.300 pounds, the most I had ever had in my entire life. It cost a lot of work and a humble lifestyle which I didn't mind, as it was the first part of the plan in fact. I was doing fine, and if it wasn't for two very annoying co-workers, Emma and Lena, a waitress and a runner who just hated me for no reason and tried to make my life as hard as they could, I would have said I had absolutely nothing to complain about in my London life.

January 2015

By January, my relationship with a few members of the staff at work radically changed. At the beginning, they all acted nicely to me, but at some point, after I had proved how friendly and hard-working I was, somebody started taking advantage of me.

My relationship with Ilaria, who used to be often very emotional and complain about me all the time, finally improved when she became a waitress and didn't have to work with me anymore. The thing was, that I worked hard when she was there with me, but she exploited my lack of ambition in the restaurant to just speak at my back to the managers although some of them realised how hard I worked, just smiled at her and said they would do something about it. I concluded that the harder one worked, the more people took it for granted that he will do more than what he was initially asked for. Members of the staff tended to be more respectful towards the evil ones. It was all like a mafia film where everybody tries to captivate the sympathy of the higher ranks, constantly pretending to work harder when the

head manager was near them and preparing in their heads what to say about others that could have put them in a better position with higher chances to be promoted or to get a pay rise.
-Evan, did you see how that guy comes five minutes late everyday? I mean it doesn't matter that he works much harder than anyone else but did you see he is always late?- people asked trying to deflect the positive focus on my hard working and direct it to my punctuality flaws.
In that restaurant nobody talked to each other to discuss any issues. They all talked to the managers, and pretended to be your friends while smiling to you. In my most frustrating moments, I even thought that they would have been morally able to kill you if that had been necessary for them to be promoted. I was a bit depressed by the idea that people would do things like these only to get extra 0.50 per hour, I thought whilst putting the box of water bottles under the sink, getting them ready for the tables upstairs and carry that box up and down for the fiftieth time that night.
Damien, one of my first co-workers and one of the most chilled ones left the restaurant and went back to France to study. It was nice working with him, although I wasn't able to act like him. I used to get anxious about the work being done as fast as possible, whereas he didn't care about it much. I just couldn't work like him and I was slightly jealous about his quality. Clotilde, the young runner from France had become a waitress just like Ilaria and her attitude also changed. She was also a runner once and that's why she was nice to all of us, and besides, her frustration at work whilst she was a runner was annoying, which made me glad she left the runners' station for the floor. Sometimes she was great, sometimes she got angry at me because I allowed her to. I wasn't very happy about those times she got emotional, but now I was glad to play along and have a nice relationship with her.
The young Angelo was the best. He worked just as hard as me, but he also didn't really take it that seriously. He enjoyed laughing and I was very happy every time he was scheduled to work with me. Together, me, him, Pierre and Ripon were the best team. No sneaky behaviour, we worked

fast more than we worked hard when we were together and there were no complaints nor the fear of them. It really was all a matter of attitude, and too many people in that place had a bad one.
Meanwhile, I had to admit that working long shifts and coming back home way too late to properly enjoy the hostel life was costing me a lot, especially when I realised that the people in there were going through the natural developments that usually occur within people that hang out together a lot. I was feeling sorry for missing out on those moments, including the arguments they sometimes had. I wanted to be part of all of that, but I just couldn't.

February 2015

The weather in London started getting cold, but it was not that serious. It never was actually. I expected the weather to be colder the upper I looked on the globe map, but London was still a city in England, a country with maritime climate that borders with the Atlantic Ocean and gets current that brings warm water from the Gulf of Mexico, ensuring that temperature variations are relatively small. You didn't really enjoy all four seasons in England, you just had one relatively cold long season with slightly perceivable peaks of high and low over the year.
Back then, Manuel, a very extrovert Sicilian guy with dark skin and short dark hair was doing well in the hostel. He was flirty and successful a few times as far as I could see. He got rejected a lot too, but he always kept trying.
I waited for him in the basement one night, pretending to be doing something on my laptop. He passed by at some point, talking loud with his friend while going down the stairs with a happy expression on his face, bragging about the date he had the previous day, like if nobody else in the world had ever been on a date with anyone before. I did like him, so I said hi and smiled at him and his friend. He immediately shook my hand, he was friendly and easy going, but maybe he needed me to say something first. I guessed sometimes people want to receive a signal from someone so to know if it's the case or not. I would usually shape the conversation according to the

person I happened to be with. That was why I looked for people that were similar to me so that it would all go smoothly. If I were with a shy guy that had no interest in hunting girls I would end up talking about things that he liked and try to make him feel comfortable, although I found it painful.
-Lots of girls in here- I started it.
He smiled back and told me we should go see if someone was there who wanted to spend time with us. I agreed and felt a bit nervous. I thought I just wanted to make a good impression on him first, so to gain a potential wingman to help me out as a priority, then would come the girls.
We approached two young Swedish girls, both blonde, both looked very Swedish from the distance. They were very pretty and maybe I would have been a bit shy and would have made a decent type of approach if it were to depend on me. I used to be less confident the better a girl looked. Manuel had the same cheeky approach with anyone instead. He flirted without giving me the chance to start. I didn't hide behind him or acted like the good guy between the two of us. I stood next to him and said something fun while introducing myself.
They seemed happy to have met us and we sat at the same table. We talked a bit about our countries and ourselves as if we were two successful men with some mystery and eventually, we spotted them glancing at each other and smiling for a second.
About an hour later, we convinced them to go and grab drinks at the supermarket in Queensway.
It was late and we needed to rush, since the sale of alcohol in London after 11 pm was out. I knew that there were places that sold stuff under the counter, but I didn't know which ones and neither did Manuel.
I got some beers for me, Manuel got white wine, the girls got spirits. Good choice, I thought, and I felt like Manuel felt the same as me by the way his eyes looked when we heard they wanted something stronger than just beers.
We went back and started drinking in the basement of the hostel. The conversation was fun and eventually we started talking about sex. If we hadn't started this, they certainly

wouldn't have either. The louder they laughed, the better I thought we were doing.

By late night, we all agreed on going out for a walk, although before that, the two girls looked at each other serious and told us to wait a minute whilst they went to the toilet.

Manuel and I went far enough from the toilet to finally let a "YES" out and hugged. Good chemistry for a first night together.

The girls left the toilet and we pretended we were just talking and rushed to change our facial expressions. They looked better now. They had put some more make up on and fixed their hair. The plan was to take them out and sit down while smoking a cigarette on some steps near the hostel, far from people, where we could have got some privacy.

We went out but couldn't find anywhere comfortable for the girls, at least according to them.

I looked at them under the lights of the streets, a different type of beauty than the one I was used to see in the streets of my city. Their straight blonde hair and their pale skin was somehow very attractive to me.

The expression on their faces changed, looking a bit... disappointed?

-I'm totally swamped by thoughts of us flirting- I said the first thing that came to mind.

They laughed a lot and that changed everything. Did I just feel that they were getting turned off because we were taking it too slow?

I didn't hesitate any longer and I kissed Cecilia, hoping that my wingman was doing the same with the other so that she wouldn't take mine away out of jealousy. He was entertaining her to what I realised, but she didn't really fancy him, in fact she kept staying next to her friend while Cecilia just wanted to stay with me and keep it going.

Eventually, we made a move back inside the hostel. The plan was now to take them to our rooms on our own. Cecilia followed me, but so did her friend. Maybe she was jealous of the chemistry I had with her friend and the fact that I made her laugh a lot before that moment made my thing with her a more special thing than the one she was having with him. He was just looking for sex, while she was looking for that meaningful fun night to remember, maybe.

After talking Swedish with each other, they told us they weren't coming to our room, but they suggested the toilet instead.

-We are going to give you head in the toilet together- Cecilia whispered to me all of a sudden, giving me some mad heartbeat.

The idea of that happening was amazing, but I wanted to be a loyal wingman. I didn't want to leave him, but I did hope he would understand and accept it.

The two girls and I entered the toilet, and so did my man.

The girls didn't like it that Manuel came to the toilet too and left, their language now was the only one between them and the voices were getting louder. They were arguing.

We realised nothing was going to happen and we looked at each other disappointed. We were so close to a real life porn film to just see it disappearing right there, without being able to do anything about it.

I desperately tried to take Cecilia to my room. She followed me, leaving her friend angry, who ran to her room. I thought she wasn't a good friend to her, but there was no way to express this thought to them as the other girl was furious.

Anyway, Cecilia was finally coming with me to my bed. In the meantime, Manuel understood it and told me he would go downstairs to have another beer and wait for me, which I appreciated.

Cecilia looked sad though. She knew her relationship with her friend might have been ruined for the rest of the holiday and maybe longer. They came from the same city and had been friends for years.

I didn't want to be that guy that splits people apart, my night of pleasure wouldn't cost more than a friendship, even a toxic friendship made of fake support and convenience like theirs.

I told her we could go look for her friend and make things clear between them, and eventually if she got to calm down, I might have even got what I wanted.

We found her friend upstairs, loudly crying and swearing in her language. Cecilia approached her and got insulted, which eventually made her cry too.
I was in the middle of two girls crying and wished I was downstairs with Manuel having few more beers. That was the thought going on in my head and I was just about to finally admit my mistake and give up, wish the girls good night and leave that situation when Cecilia's friend took all the energy in her body and kicked me at the height of my thigh.
Suddenly, I rolled down a few steps and fell at the bottom of the stairs, confused and in pain.
For a few seconds, I panicked, hoping nothing serious was broken. I tried to stand up and found out I sprained my ankle, but the rest of my body was apparently fine, except for a general aching. I was lucky though, many stairs downfalls became mortal for so many people. Nothing serious happened, but I was shocked.
I looked up and saw that they were still arguing.
I left, defeated by some younger angry girls, and went to the kitchen to talk to Manuel for a bit, but I found him busy with another girl already.
I went to bed.

The next day work was harder. Having to go up and down the stairs carrying dirty cutlery and glasses wasn't easy because of my ankle. I explained what happened to my colleagues, but they all laughed. I wondered what their reactions would have been if they were to hear that a girl got thrown down the stairs in a hostel by an angry man out of frustration who kicked her without asking her how she felt after the fall and continuing his angry conversation with his friend like if nothing happened. I concluded that I just couldn't be bothered answering back and I just laughed with them.
It was quite late when I got back to the hostel. I was pleased to see the two Swedish girls having dinner with some white wine in the living room, smiling at each other. They wouldn't talk to me though. I made my way to the kitchen and chilled a bit.
They left the next morning.

March 2015

Days went on being pretty much the same. Waking up at noon, taking it easy to finally stand up, go to Hyde Park for a quick run and then back to the hostel for a plate of pasta with tomato sauce and some random toppings thrown in the pan, trying to spice it up as it was always the same course and I was fed up with it. As usual, even having four hours in total to have a quick run, a quick lunch and to make it to work, I was late. Getting on the workplace wearing the uniform, a black apron, black trousers, black shoes and a black t-shirt underneath it and ready to work at 4 pm was hard, and I realised it would have been like this all the time. I tended to spend as much time as I could doing my personal stuff with a speed that was proportionate to how much spare time I had. The more time I had, the slower I did whatever I needed to do.
So, there I was, on my day off, sitting in the hostel, talking to people in the living room and checking out the girls. Those blonde girls with tight clothes ready to party in London, the city people visited, took pictures and lived stories they would tell everyone back home and me, sneaking my way in the middle of all this.
Nothing special was happening down there in the kitchen area, maybe it was too early, it was late afternoon after all, so I made my way back to my room to chill a bit with my can of beer.
As I stepped into my room, I saw two good looking girls sitting on the floor, drinking a bottle of white wine together.
I said hi and put a half smile on my face. The girls said hi back to me with an enthusiast smile and I pretended I was going to do some stuff in my bed while I was actually just choosing a simple thing to say to start things out. Alcohol would have helped me out while the conversation slowly turned into where I wanted it to go through afterwards.
-You girls are Swedish, eh?-
-Yes!- They exclaimed together.
They were roughly the same age of the Swedish girls from the previous week. One had two long braids and the other one

blonde straight hair. Their skin wasn't as pale as the stereotyped Swedish though.
-Would you like some wine?- they asked, and kept tittering.
-Ah no thanks, but I'll take your company with pleasure, as long as you're ok with a beer drinker here-
-Ah... sure why not?- and they laughed again.
-So, are you girls just visiting? Or looking for work here?- I asked, knowing already what the answer was.
-No, we're just visiting and leaving tomorrow...- they said with the usual sad tone all tourists had.
We were drinking when Andrea entered the room.
I immediately looked at him and said, -Hey Andrea! Meet Linnea and Fanny, from Sweden-
The girls greeted him with a smile, but he was just not in the mood and quickly found an excuse not to join and went to bed.
Fair enough, I'll get going on my own, I don't need anyone, I thought.
They told me they weren't going through the living room to meet other people like I was planning. They were on their own and just wanted to go straight to the party area, Piccadilly Circus.
-Lucky coincidence, I was going there too tonight- I lied.
-Really?- the girls believed me.
Now, my rule was, don't wait too long before you kiss one of them and get it going. I was not going to spend a night in a club, maybe even pretending to like to dance while I absolutely hated dancing, just to see if I would succeed at the end of a boring night like a club night without chasing after other girls.
That was also why I didn't want to go to a club with a girl in general. I'd get stuck with her the whole time while some other girls might even show me availability and smile at me, probably appearing hotter than my girl for some reason I wasn't entirely aware of.
On top of that, not only I'd be stuck with her, but I might just lose her anytime, stolen from another guy, and then what was I going to do? Complain? Get mad?
None of these things would have helped. None of them would have made sense. I don't think I could have any rights of

complaining when a girl chooses someone else, but I also don't think I should have spent a night in a way I didn't want to. I needed to make a move as soon as I possibly could. The worst thing I could imagine would have been spending money to get into a club and losing sight of the girls, maybe spotting them getting with someone else. Money and sleeping time taken away from my life in exchange of nothing, and I couldn't allow it.

So there I was, walking on Bayswater Road with the two Swedish girls, hoping for a great night to be. Piccadilly was about forty minutes walk, but I didn't care about it. I was happy, they were tourists, the weather was good and the view of Hyde Park and the fancy buildings was excellent. Several car drivers probably thought the same, while they shouted and honked at Linnea, who now had her dress off and was pissing near the fences of Hyde Park, on the pavement.

She was dangerously drunk. The girls had drunk a lot, also because of me, as I bought a bottle of wine too much and got them to drink even more.

They were getting worse and were not able to walk properly. They were swinging more than walking on the pavement now and people started getting curious. I thought about what could have happened to me if a police officer were to see the whole thing.

It wouldn't have been a happy situation, but I definitely couldn't have been accused of any specific crime. The girls just had few drinks, but we had to interrupt the walk towards Piccadilly when I realised the girls weren't in an acceptable state.

That was it, another failed night.

I felt it was my responsibility to take them home safe, it was me that convinced them to drink more after all. They didn't know their limits though, which was silly.

We were walking the way back when Fanny apologised for this.

-Don't worry at all, these things happen, let's just go all home safe- I said with a smile, pretending it was just cool to me. In fact, I planned on working on Fanny as soon as her friend had fallen asleep. Fanny was drunk but at least still conscious.

She appreciated that and held my hand. Maybe not all hopes are lost, I thought.

Meanwhile, Linnea couldn't walk any further and started crawling on the ground, so I lifted her up and tried to speed up towards the hostel. She wasn't very light, but that was the only option, morally speaking and, why not, also a chance to show off to her friend.

We went through the hall and the Arab guys at the reception looked at me real badly, as I was helping out a drunk girl. In their opinion, there were many lines women were not allowed to cross, but I was living in that place, I liked it and didn't want to argue with them.

The three of us got to our room when Linnea started vomiting. We helped her out, brought her to the toilet for a few minutes, then helped her to bed which, by luck, was the middle one.

When I went off the step, Fanny was looking at me, but was also lost in her thoughts, pretty drunk but apparently doing better. I didn't wait any further and kissed her in the dark of the room, and she returned the kiss passionately.

I told her to follow me downstairs, outside the building. I was there in the room already, on an easy way to success, but still decided to take her out to find out if she was conscious or not. I didn't want to put myself in trouble with an unconscious person.

We went outside and I asked her some basic questions about life to make sure her brain was lucid.

If she proved me to be fully lucid, who was I to hesitate? Sometimes girls just pretend to be drunk because that would help shy guys make a move when they were taking too long.

I took her to the stairs and the kissing restarted. This time I started touching her everywhere, desperate after months of hard work and very few nights for myself. I was craving that feeling as never before.

I told her I was going to take her to my bed and she nodded her head yes.

Great, great! I thought, and carried the girl hand in hand to my room, realising the receptionists looked at me the whole time. Jealous of my conquest?

My girl looked quite good, and there was chemistry between us since the very beginning.

I jumped into Fanny's bed and helped her get naked. I was really excited, although I had to realise that slowly, but unrelentingly, my conquest fell asleep into my arms. The drunkenness had knocked her out right in that moment.

I stayed next to her, drunk too and not really able to stand up and reach my bed. Besides that, I still had her hand between my legs and no particular desire to take it off. She liked me, enjoyed talking to me, flirted along and I stopped touching her in the moment I realised she had lost consciousness.

I was just about to fall asleep when I noticed a man with a torch slowly walking in the room, looking inside people's beds one by one.

Out of fear, I quickly wore my trousers and closed my eyes, pretending to be sleeping.

The curtains of Fanny's bed were opened, and the light of the torch was directed straight into my face.

-What the hell is going on?- I pretended to be completely surprised.

-Follow me downstairs and take your key card with you- the receptionist said, rude as usual.

The bearded receptionist had a wildly satisfied grin on his face while he pretended to be angry with me for breaking the rules.

I tried to defend myself saying we were just sleeping next to each other, but he mentioned the fact my trousers were unzipped and accepted no replies. His colleagues approved whilst looking at me with very serious faces. Samir tried to say something in my favour in Arabic but, as far as I could tell, he got dismissed quickly.

I had to leave the hostel. They wanted to put me in the streets in the middle of the night.

I stayed silent for a minute, then I told them I was going to bed and just move out in the morning. At least, I was going to be off the next day.

I didn't sleep that night. I had to find a new place and buy another big suitcase to put all my stuff in it. I threw away

some of the things I didn't really need any more, then left the hostel without saying a word to anyone.
Two receptionists, the only nice ones, two tall and kind French and Spanish girls looked sorry to see me go. On top of that, I also lost about 200 pounds in deposits made for the following two months.
I stayed outside the hostel, looking at Inverness Terrace, then back at it. I was no longer welcomed in there and I still couldn't fully process it.
-Andrea?- I called the guy from Lombardy. He was nice and we had some degrees of friendship already, although I never really got fully integrated in the group of Italians that got there in November.
-Have you got somewhere to stay for me for a few days maybe? I'll pay you upfront for this- I said, somehow confident he would please my request.
-Yeah, sure, I'll be really happy to help you Dom. I'll send you the address now- he said. Nice guy, Andrea.
I was safe for a few more nights at least. I wasn't short of money after all, but I still didn't know how to feel about it.

April 2015

My new home was in Shirland Road, near Warvick Avenue tube station.
It was in a basement, by a corner next to a pub and a betting shop. A black gate and stairs to reach our place, a pretty big flat with a garden on the back, accessible for all.
A couple of weeks were gone, and I couldn't really deny I was enjoying sleeping longer and better.
I met Claudio, a guy from Sicily in his late thirties who worked as a mailman, polite and definitely not conflictual. He would usually mind his own business but was always open to conversation.
His roommate was a guy from Sardinia called Franco, not conflictual either but definitely not keen on conversing for too long. His spot on the red sofa in front of the tv was his thing apparently. The moment I stepped into that house, everyone rushed to tell me to not sit on that sofa. I thought he would be a bossy person with some domination issues, but

I didn't want to test him. I was the new guy after all, and even though I was paying rent since the very beginning, I did think that the best thing for me was to show I was not argumentative and was willing to respect the previously established order in the house. I did not like this though and I was ready to challenge this idea soon.

The way they described him to me made me think twice on what kind of impression I should have tried to make on him. Over the course of the first two weeks though, he proved to be just a totally nice and honest person. He was just the kind of guy that preferred to be on his own. He worked a lot and loved to sit in his dirty looking but comfortable sofa in the corner of the room, all whilst smoking weed and spacing out. He used to come back at night after very long shifts in the kitchen of a pub, and just found his peace on that specific spot. He would prepare some quick pasta with pesto, eat it from the hob so he didn't have much stuff to clean after getting high on weed, leave it for the next day and punctually clean it the next morning before going to work, which didn't bother any of us after all.

I once sat on that sofa while he wasn't there and fell asleep after coming back home at 5 in the afternoon from work, really tired from a shift that started at 6 in the morning. The noise of the door opening and his bag heavily falling down the floor woke me up. He smiled at me and told me to stay sit when I stood up.

I did not stand up to obey the sort of tradition that was going on in that house, or maybe I partially did, I have never been a conflictual person neither. But mostly, the reason why I was moving aside was because I thought it was his moment to rest. I had wasted an entire day again between work and sleep and had nothing else to do before the next morning, so I had to cause myself to sleep again if I wanted to be ready for another ten hours shift at work.

We had a joint together and tried to talk about football. At some point though, I realised he was trying to be on his own and noticed he had become less and less keen in talking, staying polite enough not to tell me to leave. The atmosphere got a bit weird, so I said good night and left. He did not reply.

The new house wasn't too bad, I thought. I was sleeping in a student room made for four people where we were staying in three, Andrea, Michele and I. They did enjoy the hostel life back in Hyde Park but wanted to leave sooner than I did, especially considering that I didn't want to leave the hostel at all.
Marco, our landlord, asked Andrea and Michele if I could have stayed with them in the same room so that he could make some extra money, being the owner of the place.
It was a good deal, for two working class people, to make a small sacrifice, hosting another guy they already knew and trusted like me in order to save about 60 pounds per month, I figured. The major benefits were for the landlord though, but we didn't argue with that. I was not in a position of complaining and I was just hoping that the two guys would agree with the plan.
Michele said yes straight away. He was the youngest and very easy-going. He didn't really care about anything but rap music, computers and weed. If he could have saved any extra money that would have bought him extra weed, it would have been just great for him. On the other hand, Andrea wasn't happy about it straight away, although Marco managed to convince him in private. He wanted to host me for a few days, not share the room with me apparently.
I didn't get any upset though. I had a feeling that Andrea and I were going to become good friends.
Andrea was a pizza chef in an American style bar with music and dance floor, packed with girls almost every night according to him. As for Michele, he was a kitchen porter in a restaurant near our place.
Unlike me, they would both come back from work just after midnight. By then, I was either already sleeping or just too tired to do anything since I had to wake up at 5 in the morning for work.
I used to try my best and wait for them to come back home to get some company, often failing at it.
Going to work and coming back to just sleep and get ready for another day of work everyday was slowly killing a part of my will to be alive. Most of the times I decided to wait for

my two roommates awake I ended up just falling asleep anywhere I was, no matter in which position. I fell asleep on the sofa, on the chair by the kitchen table, and even on the floor behind the door.
-Mate, what are you doing on the floor?- Michele was surprised and sorry for hitting me on the back when that happened.
-Sorry, just trying to wait for you guys and hang out, I am missing you even though we live together...- I muttered.
-Poor you! Wanna come to the kitchen for some food and a smoke?-
-Yeah!- I said, finally happy to be able to socialise with the people I shared my room with.
It didn't work though. The kitchen had two sofas. The one that belonged to Franco, untouchable, and the black one by the other side of the living room, bigger and better looking. I sat there while Michele and Andrea were setting a laptop ready for some tv series and a smoke. I fell asleep in a matter of seconds. The warmth of the kitchen and the comfort of the black sofa were a lethal combination.

Few hours later, I woke up to go to work. I walked up the stairs, exhausted before the day could even begin just to find out my bicycle was stolen. The thin padlock was cut in half and left on the pavement next to the gate where the bike was locked to. Those 20 pounds I decided to save not buying a proper padlock had cost me my bicycle.
On top of that, this caused me to be late for work too, since walking to the tube and reaching Sloane Square like that took longer than cycling.
Filip greeted me with an evil smile. He was one of those that aspired to become a manager through toady behaviour with them. Acting respectful while being fake, none of the managers were buying it. They didn't like him much. He could be evil with his colleagues and never wanted to take the blame for anything. Anytime he made a mistake with me he would just apologise by whispering to me, showing some degree of correctness, but when I made a mistake, he avoided the conversation with me and just started it when

the managers were around so that he could shout out loud what I did wrong.
He thought that by demeaning others, he could elevate himself in the ladder of the workplace.
-Good morning Mr. manager- he said to me while I walked past him and ignored him. I was no more than five minutes late after all.
-You are free to be late and not worry about your colleagues because you are the manager, right?- he went on.
-My bike was stolen and that's why I'm late- I said, just being totally honest.
-Sorry what?- he suddenly changed his voice tone, and from mocking he became angry.
Filip would first mock and provoke people until he got a reaction, a reply that was bad enough to get a manager to know about it. Some of them would believe him, but most of them got used to him and just said something like "Yeah I'll do something about it" or just turn their eyes high and keep going with the work. We were a terribly busy restaurant.
-How dare you talking to me like that?- he shouted, coming towards me with an angry face and his chest held up to try and scare me.
I stood up in the middle of the floor, contemplating two options. My instinct told me to knock him down, but my comfort zone told me to bear that moment, go on and keep working. I hated arguing with people and I had spent my entire teen years believing that if everybody was like me the world would reach perpetual peace.
My final reaction was something in between the two options. I looked at him in the eyes without speaking at all. I challenged him in a way that I wanted to prove him I was not submissive. I was being submissive just because I was afraid of losing my job and not being able to find another job, then run out of money and being forced to move back to Italy, but the fact of the matter was, that I had over 3k in my bank account and a cv that would have allowed me to find a job in hospitality within a few days. I had nothing to worry, basically.

I realised it in that moment. Was that the moment I was finally going to stop people from treating me in a disrespectful way in there once for all?
I didn't really do anything except staring at him with a serious face. This went on for few more seconds and, spotting no reactions, he came closer, breathing like a horse and hitting my chest. I remained firm, then started getting closer to him too.
-If you want to solve this outside, we can do it- he tried, in the last desperate attempt to scare me.
-Works for me- I replied.
Right then, the two Polish waitresses who worked on the front of the restaurant told him something in Polish which I didn't understand. He calmed down a bit and went to the staff table to just continue muttering in his language. I had no doubts he was swearing against me and I did the same in Italian as Angelo approached me and asked me what was going on.
For almost an hour, just before the restaurant would open to the public we kept going on without talking to each other and just swearing with the colleagues that spoke our own languages, subconsciously looking for support in a moment where the opinions and lies of a sick member of the group can lead the rest of it to burst their personal and working frustrations on you and blame you for everything, letting people eventually believe that you were the problem of every problem and giving them the chance to kick you out saying "Finally he's gone!". Another vision of me leaving Sloane Square with my head down the ground and my broken bag barely holding to my right shoulder and all the staff members by the door, celebrating as if the restaurant had finally lost the one and only problem they had and now all lives would have moved on the way they were supposed to. That was just one of such visions. I used to overthink, but some of these visions were justified by my anxiety.

May 2015

It was my second month in Shirland Road, and I was enjoying a few aspects of living in a house, although I also realised I was missing something.
Andrea was so kind he would give me a smile every time I entered the living room. He seemed he was doing nothing interesting, just rolling a joint. I sat down in front of him and huffed while looking somewhere else. Maybe it was my way to communicate to him that something was going on with me and I needed to talk to someone. I didn't really need to huff, I could have started my story straight away, but I firstly needed a sign of approval by him, meaning that I was entitled of going ahead. He was too kind and would never deny someone the possibility to open up. Nice people would usually listen to others, maybe as a way to develop the feeling of gratitude in them. Something like "do you remember when I heard you letting off steam? Now I would appreciate it if it could be my turn to do so too".
-Are you ok Dom?-
-Yeah, actually yeah- I started, so that he wouldn't feel the weight and negativity of what I was going to say already.
-You know, lately I've just been thinking how different life is when you live in a house from when you live in a hostel-
He laughed. He was happy to laugh all the time and was able to bear any kind of negative conversation and give me opinions on pretty much everything. He was also happy to get rid of the drama with laughing and changing topic when necessary. He was great.
I laughed too, trying to hide the drama and depression that was hitting me hard with the passage of weeks.
-Andrea, you may think it's weird, but it seemed to me that every life experience was intensified in the hostel. The timeline of events moves faster and with more things happening in the meantime. A week in a house and a week in a hostel would present different amount and type of events. When you live in a house, you spend your Monday at work, then you may go with some colleagues to the pub and have a pint. Same faces you have seen in the last six months of work. Usually, you have the guy who has to leave because he is arguing with his girlfriend who is mad at him for having a pint with his colleagues. The fact that he paid attention to

other living beings was unacceptable for her and she decided to talk about something bad he did a few months before for which he already apologised a few times, but he was too nice and anxious to deny her the pleasure of feeling in control of the relationship, therefore he had to leave.

Then you have the girl who is sitting in the corner, who just scrolls her social media platforms and checks messages and likes she got from other people, smiling every now and then, careless of the topics being discussed by the rest of the group.

Then, you had a few married guys who would go back home and there is basically just you and your favourite mate left, you would talk for a bit and then go back home. At the end of the day, you have given your Monday to work, a couple of hours of observing how all the people that are near you just have their things to care about, then sleep and get ready for Tuesday. Everyday would be the same. Some weeks, most weeks, would be literally the same, you are stuck in a one-way direction life in which the protagonist of the story is the increasing capital of the company you work for. Some weeks are just great, you receive some good news from your parents back home, get a pay rise at work, get lucky with a pretty girl you wish your friend has spotted you flirting with to boost your ego and improve your social position. People would look up to you for showing that you could achieve things that not really all of them could, and you would feel safe. That specific thing would keep your social position safe for the following weeks, even months if the girl was particularly attractive.

But the thing is, that most days of your regular life are regular days, boring in the long run.

I lived my whole life in a boring small town, and all I wanted to do was to enjoy as many types of moments and as intensely as I could. Regular stable life was something I didn't want as I always had it. Most people may be happy with a regular life since birth to death, but most people fail the way they live.

I think that the regular week of someone who lives in a house has just got a few hours of peak. The Friday night, as you are supposed to be off on Saturday, the day to party. You are

tired after work, but coffee and the excitement about a fun night to come is most of the times able to keep you up ready for fun. Then Saturday night, with a Sunday where you are supposed to be able to sleep as well and not go to bed too late as you have a whole week ahead.
Two days a week. Two out of seven. Five days out of seven are almost entirely submitted to who you work for. You own about a third of the day while the rest of it has be to given to your employer, the transport and rest, not to mention the psychological stress of knowing that any sudden plans you may have wanted to make about yourself has to go through the permission of your boss, who could decline it if it were to interfere with the best of the company, even though your working contribution to the company is what allows it to thrive in the first place-
I stopped there. I noticed how he looked at me. He let me rant all that time without interrupting me. I felt in some moments he was about to say something but respectfully did not. I would have obviously given him his turn to talk and prove respect back. I felt like I needed to let this out and wanted to know what he thought about it. I noticed he agreed with a few things I was saying by nodding his head and smiling. I did not want to give him that impression though. I never liked to be a victim, especially if a change of the situation was achievable, leaving me no excuses to just complain rather than start acting. But we were taking into account the condition of the working class people, in this case, immigrants.
It was not easy at all. Starting from fewer possibilities than others is not easy, and the road to success and financial stability is harder to get than it is for people born richer, and that is a fact. Complaining made sense then, but just up to a certain extent. I could never deny the fact that we lived in a place with no major problems of any kind and therefore plenty of chances, for literally anyone, to achieve their goals. It was our fault that we spent time hanging out on the sofa, watching tv, poisoning ourselves with beer and weed, the worst of all.
Sometimes though, a bit of complaining to let it out was helpful for me to recharge.

-Well yeah, but you don't really think of going back to the hostel, right?- said Andrea and fake laughed. He was nervous, he was afraid that I would leave and his rent expense would go up about 15 pounds more each week. Not a great amount of money but still, it wasn't good news after all.
-No- I lied, and pretended to believe that his fear was silly, so I fake laughed too.
-Of course not- I said, nervously, and the fact that I repeated myself had to have given him some reasons to fear an impulsive choice from me.
He laughed again but couldn't keep his eyes off from me, maybe trying to spot any reaction in me that could have confirmed his ideas about it.
He probably noticed some reactions as he suddenly stopped laughing and got serious.
He realised I was plotting to leave the house. I couldn't live there any longer than two more weeks without losing my mind.
Who was I, after all, to just spend my time reaching a perfect balance with myself, if humans are social beings anyway? Shouldn't I have tried to improve my social skills rather than my loneliness skills? Or at least give them some priority?
He read my mind. He figured out that my arguments were debatable, unusual but not easy to prove wrong. In fact, they weren't wrong.
It was not a matter of logic more that it was a matter of lifestyle choices. I had no reason to tell anyone what the best thing to do with their lives was, but all I could do was offer my arguments and show the interlocutor only the bright side while leaving out the downside of the situation.
-Don't you think that you can't smoke in bed if you go back to the hostel? You know... sitting down here.. no one bothering you, our table, nobody complaining about noise, no need to check in and check out when your booking comes to an end...- he kept going for another minute, but I wasn't really listening.
He had some fair points that I could not argue with, but he just missed to realise that my points were not better in quantity but rather in quality. It was the importance I gave to the presence of other people and especially, the number

of events happening on a daily basis to fulfil my need of escaping boredom that were undebatable. There was no way to argue as in fact we were both right, but we just wanted different things.
-Hey, you shouldn't worry, really, I'm here with you guys- I said, and felt guilty about the feeling of uncertainty I caused into him. I thought I might had even been able to stay longer just for him and for how kind he was, but I also had to care about my priorities and well-being. I felt like I needed to find a solution.
I made a move towards my room, the light of the sun hitting the floor from the window. We lived in a basement, but we could see the sunshine sometimes, less that we could have from an upper floor obviously, but still good for me anyway. I didn't really have great reasons to complain. The rent was cheap, the roommates were lovely and the location was good.
I sat down in my bed, thoughtful. If only it had been me, choosing to be there, things would have been different in my mind. I got kicked out from the hostel and it was a frustrating feeling. It should have been my choice to move into a house, whenever I would have been ready for it, and now I felt like I had an unsolved business with it.
There I was now, sitting in my bed, waiting for nothing to happen. I realised I hated days off because I had no projects going on in my life. Humans are not supposed to be doing nothing, it goes against all the instincts developed through the long struggle of evolution.
I needed to work on something. That was the solution. But what exactly could I do?
I had huge projects stored inside of me, but they had to wait a little bit more.
I jumped on my new bike on the way to my gym in Oxford Street.
The sunshine was a tricky one in England. Sometimes I could see the sun, and the sky looked good and cloudless, but it wasn't warm. I still needed a jacket and maybe a scarf sometimes. Those moments when the weather wasn't really that cold and I underestimated the danger of cold breeze hitting my neck were the ones when I usually got sick.

I cycled through Little Venice bridge, crossed Royal Oak station, passed by Queensway and then turned left before Hyde Park and cycled straight towards Oxford Street. It wasn't pleasant to cycle in what was the most overcrowded street in London, with pedestrians who seemed to have suicide tendencies. They all looked stunned by the shops and were keen on taking pictures while completely ignoring vehicles in the streets. Cars honking and angry drivers didn't scare the tourists apparently. It was not unusual to hear swear words from cab drivers who didn't want to miss the green light but had to miss it because they had to brake every few seconds and were upset when they realised that the other cab picked someone up who could have been their customer.

I used to mostly cycle on the pavement on the parallel street to avoid all that stress.

I parked my beautiful white and red bicycle in front of the gym and made my way in through the escalators of the mall underneath it.

So many fit men and women in that gym just made me feel a bit insecure sometimes, but a great shape had never been my main goal in life, although I envied how good somebody looked in there and wanted to get there as well, but I was too lazy for that. It required too much hard work for how much I cared about it.

I made my way to the biceps machines, the ones I was using the most, trying to find the closest one to some girls. It was not my fault that some of them just looked incredible after all.

I was relatively good at approaching girls, but it also depended on the environment. I was good at approaching in a library or in a hostel, but just too shy and intimidated in a gym. I simply recognised that the competition between me and the other guys was not even debatable.

In such situations, it was easy to call myself defeated before I even tried, but I wanted to believe I wasn't that kind of guy, a fearful one. As a matter of fact, so many of those guys with better looks and bodies than mine had their own fears that, like me, wanted to push away by working out and trying to feed their egos enough to dismiss their insecurities. Many of

those guys were confident and would talk to them, but many others would look at them and pretend to continue working out while scrutinising the entire scene. It all just looked very lame to me.
In my case it wasn't insecurity, but rather my awareness that in order to get certain bodies, I needed to show certain arms. I finished working out on my biceps and decided to take a few minutes break, making my way to the speed walk and aimed at spending a few more minutes there before going back to the arms machines.
Spacing out, I found myself staring at this guy with dark hair working out on the same biceps machine where I was.
He looked back at me as he realised I was staring at him. I looked away, a bit embarrassed, and got going towards the speed walk, but for some reasons I felt the subconscious need to look at him again to find out he was still looking at me. What was I doing? Why did I keep looking at him? He may be thinking I'm looking for trouble or something, I thought. Then I realised that I knew him, I had met him before, somewhere.
He smiled and said hi to me.
My legs were directed towards the other side of the room, but my upper body looked towards him. What to do? I decided to be polite. I couldn't just leave after someone said hi to me. Besides being rude, that would be another reason for him to believe that I was a creep.
-How are you?- he said.
He did recognise me, but I just couldn't.
-Hi, I'm good and you?- I replied.
-How is Juventus doing?- he asked, lighting a bulb inside of my head.
Everything came back to my mind very quickly. He was a guy I met in the hostel in Hyde Park who once gave me instructions on how to watch online football games. We had a chat about Italian football once and then I only saw him a few more times but never really got the chance to talk to him again properly.
-It's going great, we reached the final, we're soon going to play in Berlin for the glory- I replied, while still pretending I had recognised him from the very first moment.

-You deserved it- he said with a smile.
Now, that moment when I didn't really know what to say, if I should leave with a smile to cover lack of interest in keeping the conversation going or stay and say something else, running the risk of annoying him in case he wanted to be left alone and was just small talking to me.
-How is life going in the hostel?- these words came from my mouth without I even realised it.
-Oh, actually I have my own place now, my brother bought a flat here and I'm living with him now, saving some money and enjoying the privacy a little bit more- he ended with a laugh.
-Really?- I said, and then went on, -I kind of miss it to be honest, now I'm living in a house and the guys are great and so is everything else, I can't complain really, but I kind of miss it, I was kicked out and wasn't ready to leave. It was not what I wanted and it's a bit frustrating.- I was afraid I had spoken too much and he would think I was crazy.
-Oh do you? Well I understand you, there's a few things I miss from the hostel too so I see where you're at-
-Yeah...- I said, aiming at stopping the conversation so I put on my fake smile and was about to say it was nice talking to him after all when he continued.
-You know what hostel would be good for you then? The one in Russell Square, my brother spent some time in there with me some time ago...- he said, now removing his arms from the machine to sit more comfortable.
-What makes it a better place?- I asked him, curious.
-It's bigger, more people, more social life, it would suit you well because I remember how you used to talk to everyone in there, and that was a smaller one, much smaller, and the location is even better, you're few minutes away from everything-
-Oh, I see... well, that's interesting, I will definitely check it out- I said, meaning to do it straight away.
We went on for a little bit, but I couldn't focus on anything he was saying as I was excited by the idea of having found a new place to live and also, by the fact he happened to remind me that the football team I supported was going to play the biggest of all games. We wished each other luck with the body building and said bye.

I locked my bike outside my home and bought a bottle of white wine. I knew Marco loved it and he said he was visiting us that night. He could be annoying sometimes, but kind after all, and he would usually come to visit us bringing something with him. A bottle of white wine was the usual, but sometimes he would take chocolate or just random snacks and stay with us. The wine would serve him to start his conversation about politics, where the only one entitled of speaking was himself basically. We would need to ask to talk a few times before he would finally give us a say but as soon as one started, he would stop us right away, continuing on his topic like if nothing had happened. He just pretended that he wanted to listen just so we could feel on the same level, but he would just look somewhere else and nod his head and just say "yes" to show us he agreed with us even if we had said nothing that could have claimed a yes or a no. Me, Andrea and Michele would just look at each other and smile every time he did that. We liked to make fun of him. We would use a few of his typical lines between us and they would come out always fun to hear. We started repeating his words during his talks just to see if he spotted us.
-Well, anything else?- I said, even trying to imitate his voice and my roommates barely managed to hold laughs that seemed to be about to explode out of their chests.
Marco moved on like I hadn't spoken at all.
Franco couldn't care less of what was going on. He couldn't roll a joint with Marco there just next to him, but we noticed he was agonising.
Marco noticed this too and looked at him. He chuckled and said -Wanna roll a joint eh?-
Franco pulled on his good boy face and was just about to say something like "Why would you even think that?" with the biggest of all the fake smiles when Marco started shouting.
-I received complaints from next door! It's the second time it happens in a week! I am tired of you, I am tired of you!- he repeated, suddenly standing up and spitting everywhere around himself and on the table. I had to cover my plate with both hands to try and prevent his saliva from reaching my food.

He punched twice on the wall and we all jumped, caught by surprise. Marco was bigger than all of us and seeing him angry wasn't a good show.

Franco kept smiling, he wasn't used to be intimidated by anyone. He had a dominant behaviour and was only silent because his landlord was talking and he liked staying there, close to where he worked and didn't want to react and risk to lose the deal he had with him. I understood his situation perfectly.

Marco saw how nobody was reacting to that and took advantage of that moment to let his steam off even more. He punched the wall again and then threw the ashtray on the floor, imposing Franco to clean it up.

He was going too far. He walked around the room muttering some words in his dialect that only Michele could understand and then looked at us. We didn't have a happy face, nor were we satisfied about realising the fact that our landlord could have had some rage issues.

-Don't you agree with me?- he asked with a big smile, trying to get us from his side.

We didn't reply, still shocked about how fast the situation degenerated into that scene. Franco didn't deserve this.

When he left, I was still looking down, and so was Andrea. I had no idea what Michele was doing or thinking, but I preferred to just not do or say anything until Marco was out of the building.

We stayed silent one more minute after he was gone, then we said a few nice words to Franco and helped him clean the floor.

I went back to my room and took my laptop, brought it to the kitchen and started surfing the internet, looking for that hostel in Russell Square, ready to make a booking just to check it out. A weekend to be spent like a tourist in central London couldn't have killed me after all.

I had my usual plate of mushrooms, eggs and spinach next to me and got ready to look for availability when I started procrastinating as usual. I would usually set my duty online and promise myself to carry it out, but I only really started taking care of it after half hour of watching people's news on social media and a few online chess games.

That was when I saw an advertisement that promoted cheap flights with a company that was encouraging people to visit Berlin for the final game of Champions League. Internet spied on my activities and there was nothing that I had previously clicked and looked for in the net that wouldn't return to me with some news and info so to push me to buy more of whatever it was that interested me.

A cheap flight to Berlin was there, just a click away from me. I stared at the screen for a minute, then checked it out. I didn't think about it any longer than few seconds and impulsively bought a ticket. Who cared? It was just three days away from work, I could have asked for a weekend off and then a Monday off for the following week so to have three days in a row and this shouldn't have been a problem with my managers.

I was the hardest working man in there and never really asked much, especially weekends off, as I usually asked for Tuesdays and Wednesdays. I could have used one of my holidays off days just in case.

I gave a call to my restaurant to communicate them about the news and update my rota. No one replied, they were too busy I assumed.

Leaving that aside, I finally opened the hostel bookings site and checked the one in Russell Square.

The prices were acceptable although a weekend by the end of May would have cost me about 50 pounds. Whatever, I thought, today is the day of impulsive choices.

I made the payment and then finished my plate, which was cold and tasteless now.

I lifted my head up to find out everybody was still there, all high and incapable of having a conversation. Michele was on his phone, surfing the net. The other two were spacing out, God knows what was in their heads. I was not curious to find out at all and just felt more excited than before about the perspective of leaving soon. They had no idea I had just booked a short holiday and a weekend in a hostel in central London where I was going to decide if I was going to stay or leave that killer boredom. The only one I really liked was Andrea, but he would have understood me.

Days went by as usual in the restaurant, and I was just working better and smiling more.
-Are you in love?- Marc once asked me. My manager was a Barcelona supporter, he was cool and friendly, definitely my favourite to work with. Being on the floor with him meant harmony between all colleagues. He knew how to stop people from becoming argumentative.
-You either joke to distract them or just ignore them- he once said to me and winked.
He accepted my request to get days off when I needed them at the condition of buying something for him.
-Sure I will- I said, happy to do it for him.
-No, you don't have to, I was just kidding, enjoy your time there and be ready to get demolished very hard- he said, then laughed.
I was totally going to get him a gift from Berlin.

Friday morning arrived sooner than I thought. I jumped on my bicycle the way to Russell Square, just the usual way to the gym in Oxford Street with a few more minutes into Tottenham Court Road area, then making my way left, then right again passing by Russell Square Park, finally reaching Guilford Street.
I left my bicycle next to the entrance and locked it to a black gate. Number 71, there I was.
I stopped by the stairs and breathed the air I was so badly missing. The smell of socialisation was intoxicating. Different languages, faces and races were under the same roof and were talking loud and happy. The tourists I liked.
I immediately started checking out if some girls were there. It would have been good to start a conversation with someone even before checking in.
A Spanish receptionist greeted me, I tried speaking her language, in which I wasn't bad at all.
Russell Square hostel had to be a better place than the one in Hyde Park. It was just a little bit more expensive and the receptionists were mixed genders.
For some reasons, I was looking for excuses to believe that the place where I was now had to be better than the previous one. I had no reasons to be there otherwise. Even the fact

that I noticed the presence of girls at the reception made me feel like the treatment of guests was going to be better. I knew that people at work could be nice and permissive or rude and strict according to a lot of different factors, none of them involving their sex though.

This girl is friendly, I forced myself to believe, having no clue about what her name could be, as the sticker on her uniform was old and the name blurred away.

I made another big smile and thanked her again when she was explaining stuff I already knew. The hostel was managed by the same company that owned the one in Hyde Park. I hoped that she wouldn't go through some checks and find out I was on a black list or something like that. She gave a few pieces of information about how the hostel worked, and I pretended I was new to that.

All went good, no black list. I was in.

The living room was more than twice as big as in the previous hostel. It was very bright, there were twelve tables and twice as many benches that people were moving so to make more space for groups of tourists. I liked seeing tables stuck together and a big hob in the middle with hot food in it, surrounded by people who were distributing it in plastic plates of different colours. They all seemed happy, everyone was talking to someone, everyone was laughing. Some tables were loud, some were not. I saw a girl lost in a book by a table next to the wall, two girls drinking wine and laughing nonstop over something one had said to the other, an old black man with a big moustache reading the newspaper and apparently discussing politics with a younger man with glasses and a plate of roasted chicken for the older guy temporarily left on the side. The two seemed very passionate about something. I went past them so I could put my bag on the floor and just look at the whole room for one more minute before going to my room and put the sheets on my bed and maybe, if I was lucky, even put my tag on a bottom one. I disliked having to climb stairs to reach the top bunk bed every time I had forgotten something or simply had to go to sleep.

I decided to make a move to my room quickly so that I could go back upstairs and enjoy what I was seeing. My room was number 10, downstairs. I had just moved past a table of a German couple who was keen in analysing a map of central London when I saw a guy, alone at his table, apparently careless of all that was happening around him. He was on his red laptop, playing a chess game online.
I looked at his moves for few seconds and noticed he was higher rated than me. I couldn't help approaching.
-Hi- I said, and for some reasons I didn't know how to continue.
He didn't reply. He kept looking at the screen, focusing on his moves.
-Wanna play a chess game with me?- I said, not sure if it was right to ask, considering that my opponent didn't really look keen on talking to me at all.
-Yes- he said, without taking his eyes away from the screen. He didn't seem happy about that. I thought he was just being kind enough to please me with a game he didn't want to play.
-Fine, then I'll just go to my room to leave this stuff and we'll play in a minute- I said, and smiled.
-Mm- he said, meaning yes I supposed.
I almost thought of not going back to him or say hi again while going down the stairs. I didn't need his pity, I could have just done what I was there for, socialising.
I left my bed sheet and bags in my room, then went back upstairs and looked for him.
He had short brown hair, a week old beard, a green squared shirt on top of a blue t-shirt. I pretended not to be very interested in playing with him as his attitude towards me wasn't very enthusiast and I didn't want to look so desperate for a game.
His laptop was still there, but he was sitting on a sofa near the kitchen in the smaller living room where all the sofas were.
I moved all the way to the kitchen to see how it looked like, waiting for reactions from him. When I passed by, he laughed, looking in my direction with another guy that seemed a friend of his, also looking at me. They were clearly making fun of me, I thought.

I looked inside the kitchen, bigger than the one in Hyde Park, but still small.
I made my move out of the kitchen, not willing to deal with that guy anymore, now just going to focus on the girls. I was off that day but I had to work the following afternoon for a short shift. I wanted to enjoy my day off, a different one from the usual day off of the latest months in my place in Warvick Avenue. I wasn't going to let any negative energy inside me, not that day at least.
I looked for a table where I could have sat down when he called me from my back.
-Hey- he said, coming closer to me.
He was tall, much taller than I thought, and he was holding a wooden chess board he had borrowed from the reception while I was in my room.
-Hey- I said. I was somehow reacting like he did with me. I had no idea why I was doing it, but I couldn't deny I was looking forward to playing with him.
He sat down and started setting his pieces on the board, and so did I.
-What's your name?- he asked, without question mark.
-Domenico-
-Are you Italian eh?-
-Yes-
-I'm Spanish-
-So what's your name?- I asked, this time in Spanish. He didn't reply, and kept moving the pieces like if I had said nothing. So annoying, I thought, he was acting rude to me.
He was clearly better than me. He could calculate better in general and at some point, I made my usual mistake that allowed his bishop to go all the way to the corner of my side of the board and win my rook.
It was going to be a humiliating game, but I didn't want to stop it then. I continued, and tried to counter attack. I played another silly move and this time he spoke.
-That's your worst option, you have a better one- he said, in Spanish.
One of my pawns was in a square from where I could have taken either his bishop or his knight. I chose the knight as I felt tremendously under pressure when an opponent's knight

was in my territory, with all the squares it controlled at the same time. I considered the knight the sneakiest piece.
The game went on for a bit more when I realised my position was very uncomfortable and my opponent was targeting a few weaknesses of my territory. Then, I resigned.
I craved another game, but I just wanted him to be the one to ask for it as I didn't want to look too needy and upset.
He suggested one more game. We swapped colours and started.
Meanwhile, his friend who was sitting with him on the sofa came over. He looked cool, a black leather jacket, a neat looking shaved face and short dark hair. He was hitting on a girl he saw before on her own at the table next to us. He was clearly a player. I noticed how he left the sofa to go straight to that girl with curly hair and introduce himself with a confidence I envied. He didn't blink, nor smiled or looked too serious. He just went and talk to her. I wasn't going to be the only player in that place, and even if I was, I apparently had some competition. Besides, I wasn't so fast, so cheeky and so well dressed like that guy.
He looked at me in a way that made me feel like he didn't like me. Maybe it was my style, not at all neat like his, I was not as tall as him and I felt I had too many holes in my cheap jacket pockets and on my shoes when he looked at me.
-Hi- he said, definitely less friendly and keen on getting to know me than he was with the pretty girl he was flirting with a minute ago.
-Hi, my name is Domenico, nice to meet you- I replied, trying to look as indifferent as him.
-Adrian, from Bologna- he told me in Italian. He spoke perfectly, but something in his accent was unsound to me.
-And I am Rey, from Valencia- the chess player finally introduced himself.
-Are you going to keep playing this boring game forever, Rey?- Adrian asked him.
-Shut up man, you don't understand anything- Rey replied.
I felt like I wanted to be friends with them. They were cool, one of them played better chess than me, and they seemed very confident, the way they talked and moved was so casual that I realised straight away I had something to learn from them. I could have been at their level soon, but I needed to

be with them and slowly get rid of my insecurities. I didn't have many, but I was still too shy and too careful sometimes. Rey went on to beat me again, then we got rid of the chess board and the two went back to the sofas.
Adrian invited me to hang out with them and have a glass of wine.
There was something that made all those people seem like a family in there.
I sat down on a black sofa just next to another one which was already taken by people who were too busy to pay attention to me. A short guy introduced himself and shook hands with me.
-Hi, my name is Giorgio, what's your name?
-Domenico- I replied. -Are you Italian?- I went on.
-Yes, I mean no, I'm Romanian, but grew up in Italy, I'm Adrian's cousin- he said, pointing his finger at him.
Now it all sounded clear, Adrian was Romanian, which explained his untraceable accent. Adrian didn't seem to like that comment and said something to his cousin in his language, which made him laugh.
Meanwhile, Rey was sitting very casually on his sofa, his legs on the small wooden table in front of him. A very attractive girl with beautiful brown hair was sitting next to him, looking at him with an expression I could not decode.
-You are so pretty- Rey told the girl next to him.
-Oh Rey, stop it- she said, not sure if she really meant it as she smiled and blushed in a matter of seconds.
-Hey, Domenico is Italian, we have another Italian here, like if they weren't enough- he suddenly said, and somebody looked at me.
Two Spanish guys shook hands with me, they were both dark haired, they told me their names and so did I, but I wasn't sure they were going to remember it a few minutes afterwards.
I liked Rey, he appeared careless of anything happening around him. He seemed to just be constantly lost in his thoughts, not responding to a question after he was asked one and being the only one with his legs near people's food and his arms wide open. He was sitting in the middle of the sofa, but he was so tall that with his arms he would reach

both edges of it. Eventually, he would leave his thoughts for a bit, ask a loud question to someone or make a comment about a girl passing by the hall and ignore anyone replying to whatever he had asked.
While I stared at him, two girls left the kitchen with two glasses of wine and sat down on the nearest sofa. They looked quite attractive and were busy talking to each other. They clearly wanted to be attractive as they were barely wearing any clothes.
In a second, Rey and Adrian jumped and looked at each other. No smile, they looked like they had just seen food after three days of starving. The girls were in their early twenties, very attractive, and I assumed not easy to get. My two new friends clearly didn't overthink this. In a matter of seconds, they made a move towards them, not planning anything or talking to each other. They introduced themselves and sat down in front of them, picking up the nearest wooden stools.
The girls were surprised. Probably, they had never experienced such approach by anyone. Rey and Adrian clearly couldn't care less about it, and sat down there like if they knew them already. They talked for a bit and I tried my best to hear what they were saying, how they approached and what made the girls laugh at anything they said.
I was shocked, and feeling miserable. I wished they were three, so that I would casually join them.
I had some obstacles to overtake if I wanted to get there. This was why I lost many chances back at the previous hostel, and so in bars and clubs.
I stood up and went to the supermarket for some food and when I returned, few minutes afterwards, the guys and the girls were gone.

That night was quiet, nothing was really happening.
I sat down at a table next to the vending machine when Rey came in the living room with another guy. He was also quite tall, short hair and dark skin. He was originally middle Eastern, I thought, but the way he dressed, talked and moved was very European.

The guys went past me and Rey said hi looking at me for just a second, then continued the conversation with his friend. The other guy smiled at me, but they were walking quick and I did not manage to smile back at him in time. I went to my room, downstairs, then right, then right again, bottom of the hall, last door on the left.
I went in and found two girls with an American accent, talking to each other and putting some make up on, getting ready to go out.
-Hi- I said.
-Hey!- they replied together, then smiled.
-You girls are American aren't you?- I asked, almost entirely sure I already knew the answer.
-Yes!- they replied, this time laughing.
The girls looked actually pretty good, one was blonde, and the other one brunette. The brunette one had a white tight top and was quite fit. The blonde one was also in good shape, and I noticed she wore a long white skirt with a slit.
-Any plans for tonight?- I asked, pretending to just wanting to know what they were doing out of curiosity.
-Yeah, I mean...- they looked at each other -we were going to go out but then these two guys asked us to have a few drinks before that and we thought... I mean, they were nice so...why not?- they giggled.
-Oh cool, enjoy your time then, I'll see you later I guess- and I left, pretending I was going to be doing something. I couldn't complain about timing this time as that was my first day in the hostel and the girls were there before me. I didn't know when they had arrived, and anyway, even if they were asked for drinks by someone, I didn't have much to blame it on my speed.
Unlucky, just unlucky, I thought when I was sitting in the living room upstairs and started drinking my can of beer. Next to my table, Rey and the Arab guy were setting the table up, talking to each other and seemingly excited, I didn't know about what, but I couldn't pay attention to them. I wondered if Rey wanted to challenge me at chess, but it wasn't the right moment I guessed.
I went to the toilet and decided to shave and maybe go to a bar. Besides, I needed some fresh air too.

On my way back, I saw the two American girls at the table with Rey and his friend, who was pouring drinks for the four of them.
I moved further away and tried to socialise with some random people by the other side of the common room, resigned.

The vibe at the hostel confirmed my feelings and cleared my doubts.
I wasn't ready to live in a house. I wasn't ready to live like a rat. Humans are complex animals, our skills and actions determine the beauty of our lives, and living like rats was a way of living designed for others, not for me. Western culture conceived happiness as the achievement of the highest amount of material goods. The more you have, the happier you are. This is the main message that media spread.
I thought about this while I was automatically walking towards the supermarket taking a right on Herbrand Street to the main street where the underground was.
They want me to believe in owning things as the way to feel good, so that I would invest all my lifetime trying to own more and more, spending more time and money, too busy with sticking to completing this plan to have a look around and focus on how to feel good for real.
Spending a period of time in a hostel does not match with their plan though. You cannot own things if you have nowhere to store them. The hostel was not an ideal place where to store things. You had a locker where you could put your most valuable things, but it was just big enough to contain both your laptop, rucksack and a bunch of books. You couldn't own a table, chairs or a big screen tv. Tables were in the common room, there were plenty of them and even if the hostel were to be fully booked, and it most of the time was, there was always space by design. You only lacked privacy.
But even there, I had more food stolen from Michele in three months than in Hyde Park hostel in six months. I knew for sure that when I would return home at least half of my food would be gone, and no one would tell me who the thief was.
I wanted to live around tourists because they always had

enough money to buy their own stuff and didn't need to steal it from others.

June 2015

I got back home after my weekend in Russell Square and decided to inform the guys about my departure. I obviously had to tell Marco about it too.
The gate that would lead me downstairs to the basement room where we were living appeared less attractive than ever.
I phoned Marco.
-Hi Marco, I am sorry to say this, but I have family problems and I have to leave London for a bit, you know, so I'm going back to Italy...-
Silence for a few seconds by his side, and finally he spoke.
-Are you sure about it? I won't argue with this, I hope your family is ok-
-Yeah, thanks for that, I appreciate it, and I'm sorry about such short notice...-
I planned to move to Russell Square at the end of my last paid month. I could sacrifice a few more weeks in there so not to lose any money. The wait and my depression would have had a less bitter taste knowing that things were going to improve soon. Everyday would have taken me closer to the moving day so I had almost no problems staying a bit longer.
I told Andrea and Michele as soon as I went back inside.
Andrea was disappointed, a sad look on his face. Michele was too busy in his own world and after acting sad for a few seconds, he went back to the room to play his favourite video game.
Andrea followed me to the kitchen. I was excited, I was in a good mood and couldn't be bothered talking to anyone, too lost in daydreaming about all the adventures that were likely to happen in the future.
-It will suck here without you, you are my favourite one- said Andrea, hitting a spot in my brain.
I looked back at him and felt actually sorry, so I thought about what could have been the best thing to say.

-I am sorry, but this is a necessary thing to do for my mental sanity, I am depressed, and no matter how much I like you and how great you are, I have to leave as I am not happy. Know that I am your friend and I always will be. I will visit you as much as possible and we'll have some good fun together- I said, being honest.
-Yeah, but you know... You are the best behaved in here and the one I can trust the most. Michele steals food all the time and I don't feel always sure that he will pay rent in time and he would have to ask me for money, and I'm afraid he won't pay me back because he's unreliable... Franco is crazy, I don't like him, I mean I don't have real reasons to be against him but he's not friendly and it feels like one day he'll kill us all...- he ended his rant with a nervous laugh, then looked at me in the eyes and continued.
-You are the only one that is mentally stable and regarding Claudio... well he is alright, but he comes back home at night and we are of a very different age and... he is alright but...- then he stopped.
There was no logical way I could deny anything of what he said so I turned silent and looked down to the floor.
-If I could take you with me, I would, but I can't force you to do it- I came up with this, not even knowing why. He laughed, thought about it for a minute, then replied. -Well maybe I would, you know I kind of miss the hostel too...-
We were escalating. My attempt of not hurting his feelings made me say something that I didn't expect him to try and do as well. He was so nice and was always keen on sacrificing himself for others. Young and good northern Italian raised in a village in central Lombardy, near the lakes and nature.
By his side, he was just overreacting. He said something that probably wasn't entirely true. There was nobody that could leave the hostel life without good memories that would force a smile on their faces after all. He probably did miss some of it, but definitely not as much as I did.
I wasn't going to put pressure on this though. I wanted him to be happy, and he was happier in the house. He was dating a red-haired Italian girl, friend of Michele, chilling and sleeping with the same girl all the time. That wasn't what I had designed for me at all.

We had dinner and went back to the room. Andrea kept remembering the good times at the hostel in Hyde Park, sounding fun to me. I would agree with him every other praising sentence about it and subtly trying to push him to come follow me. Maybe, if he had moved in there with me as well, I would have felt clean, in a way that my short-noticed departure wouldn't have been that much of a betrayal but more like a necessary thing to do.

June was flying past me. The pleasure of knowing that times were about to improve had the capacity of making time go faster.
By then, I had finally decided I wanted to become a waiter in the hope of making better money. I could see how many of my colleagues were making some decent tips. Some of them stated they would pay the monthly transportation expenses with tips, some others stated they would pay rent. Those were the people I disliked the most and I was sure they were lying.
I had worked with some good teams of runners and I sometimes enjoyed specific shifts with specific people so much that I considered the idea of staying a runner. The problem was that as soon as some of them became waiters, left the job or got fired, the teams had to change, and because it was a team job, I needed all the other three working with me to be cool people. If one of them was a toady one, we couldn't have enjoyed working according to our rules. The sneaky person would have talked to a manager out of fear that once it had been found out that one of us was rolling a joint, breaking a glass on purpose or even eating from the leftover of a customer's plate, a manager could have made a mass layoff and send everyone home and him, the innocent one, was going to be included. Many were the colleagues I had that proved to be sneaky people or just boring at work, while few of them just couldn't care less about the incredible income of the restaurant and decided that their work life had to have more dignity, and therefore established a connection with me. I was the hardest worker, but I also believed we were outrageously underpaid, and the only way to compensate the money we weren't given was to

take longer breaks, steal food or get vodka shots and wine hidden into paper cups. The chances that a new team of runners that would be happy to share alcohol and lack of interest in their personal growth at the expense of others were so slim that I realised I had to go my own way, become a waiter and let my mental health at work depend more on myself than on the attitude towards work of the others.

By the end of June, I was finally set to start working as a waiter. My training would have gone on for five days, three of them on morning shifts with Mirek and two of them with Pierre.
I was looking forward to starting, although I was way more excited by the idea of moving into the hostel in Russell Square.

July 2015

I carried my suitcases all the way down the same room I slept in on my first night. I was in room 10 now, the one in the basement.
I left my stuff on the floor and lay down in bed. The idea of taking a nap was appealing. Nothing could have stopped me from being socially happy now, and I felt like I deserved a nap. I didn't even want to go and talk to anyone in that moment, just be with myself, and think about how I managed to change my life, in my idea, for good.
I could have been stuck in a place I didn't like because it was cheaper, but I chose a place where I would have been socially happier. I could have continued doing my job because I was the longest time working runner and knew the job better than anyone else, but I chose to change that, hoping to make more money and relieve my back pain. I could have continued staying on the sofas with my former flatmates, smoke weed and never worry about anything, pleased by the fact that none of the people around me was doing better than me in life, but I chose to eliminate weed. I closed the curtains of the first and only bed I found out to be available, the second one of the three level bunk bed by the end of the room, and fell asleep.

The training as a waiter was going well, at least I thought so. Some of the managers were really happy to see me stepping up, they were the ones who always liked me in general. Some others didn't seem as happy, they thought I wasn't smiley enough to pretend that I cared about how my customers were doing for a whole shift, or that my patience wouldn't give me a long life on the floor. I couldn't argue with this point. All patience did up to that moment, was to allow my co-workers to let the steam off on me and my managers to exploit me more, adjusting all their future decisions about me and imposing them when they were normalised. All it takes to normalise something is the agreement of the parties, and I wasn't generally capable of saying no, which often threw me into some real bad deals at work.
Mirek sat me down on table 50.
-We are going to go through some plates here. We can order some from the kitchen and we'll analyse them together. What's inside, in what quantity and all that sort of stuff. You need to know about allergies and so on...-
-Can we order anything we want?-
-Yes- he said, hiding a smile. He was great, very professional too.
-Then order your favourite food and we'll go through that I told him.
-Fair enough, I won't challenge you- he seemed to have struggled a bit with his brain before answering.
I made sure that in our order there was a plate I always wanted to taste but never got the chance to. These two eggs covered with dark yellow sauce with paprika on top, leaning on two small loafs of bread, and some spinach on top of everything.
Mirek kept speaking but I stopped listening. I had finally started eating, although I realised I didn't want any of it any more after only one bite. I found it disgusting, which made my trainer laugh.
By 5 pm I was at home, my bike locked in front of the Great Ormond Street Hospital.
I noticed Rey and Adrian were there, sitting together on the sofa, surrounded by people, some of them I already saw

before. Their legs on the tables, lazy, talking passionately about something and laughing.
I sat by a central table and pulled out a book.
-Hey, are you girls German?- I asked two girls sitting on the table in front of me.
-Yes- said one of them, smiling.
-What's your name?-
-My name is Jess, and she is my little sister Alma- she added while hugging her.
She laughed, good sign. The plan was to focus on her and wait for her young sister to go to sleep before hitting on her.
-Do you girls like London?-
-Yeah, we arrived yesterday, and today we have walked so many miles, and now we're very tired- she said, and her sister asked for a translation.
-How old are you?- I asked with the nicest of tones in English, looking at her.
She replied in German to her sister so she could come back at me.
-My sister is just very shy, she actually knows the numbers in English, right?- she said now, looking at her and hoping that she would say something, but she just kept staring at me, laughing nervously.
Jess looked very German, blonde hair and tall, no makeup, or maybe just a little bit of it, so little that I couldn't spot it.
-You know what? We should rent up bicycles and have a ride around- I suggested all of a sudden after a few minutes of chatting, encouraged by the fact that Jess seemed very keen on talking to me.
-Yeah, if you think it's a good idea...- the two sisters sounded very excited, then went to their room to leave their stuff and get jackets.
I looked around to see if Rey was anywhere near, but I couldn't find him. I hoped he had been looking at me, smoothly flirting with Jess. I imagined him checking the whole thing out from the sofa and making comments to Adrian.
My view was ambitious though, as Adrian was talking to someone by the sofas and seemed to be doing just fine without checking me out, while Rey was just behind me, and

was calling me while I spaced out. It took me a few more seconds to realise he remembered my name.
-Dom, hey, what's up man? Wanna play a chess game?-
My heart pounded.
Why did I want the attention of that guy so much? Maybe, he just happened to represent anything I wanted in a friend at that moment.
He was handsome, flirty, friendly and loved chess. He lived a better life than I did, and this had to be the reason why I liked him. I thought he could help me.
Now, that was my chance to show him I had something better to do, that I was busy and I didn't depend on anyone to enjoy my time. Partially, this was also true.
-Yeah... actually let's play another time, right now I'm busy man...-
-Oh, you're working on a girl eh?- and laughed.
I winked and just smiled back.
-Alright, see you another time- he said, and left.
The two sisters came back, clearly excited.
We left the hostel and made a move to the right, passed Guilford Street, turned right and right again towards the rental bike platform. Each bike cost two pounds and could be used for a whole day, providing it was taken into a different platform within thirty minutes each time it was rented. I remember how once I forgot to make sure it was safely parked into a platform near Hyde Park and how scared I got when I found out it wasn't there anymore. Someone else had taken it, but then parked it somewhere else. I got charged about 12 pounds for that.
-Ok, so let's just have a ride around King's Cross, ok?-
They were very sweet, naïve as far as I could tell.
The two girls jumped on their bicycles, not before taking a picture of the whole situation.
At some point though, I realised they were looking pretty scared.
-You see, we never ride in Berlin, we grew up with public transports and never really used anything except buses and subway...- Jess said, embarrassed.

-It's fine, no one is judging you for this. It's not very common to be able to ride a bicycle, so that's fine- I came up with one of the most inaccurate statements I ever made.
For a few minutes, things seemed fine up to when we reached Euston Road.
-Right, I want you to cycle with me on the pavement, I don't really want you to cycle on the road- I said, quite seriously.
-Yeah, that's what we're doing...- I noticed they had already taken that decision before I suggested it.
The more Jess enjoyed it, the more chances I had that she would reward me at the end of the night, I thought.
Eventually, we made it to Camden through Eversholt Street and then Camden High Street, not without problems though. Alma risked her life twice, a car behind her honked at some point and the driver shouted something I couldn't hear properly.
We stopped for a moment to have some water, and then we all got back on the bicycles to get back home.
Rey was next to the entrance door of the common room, on his phone.
-This way- I told them, making sure we walked past him, so he could see me.
He looked at me, almost shocked. Maybe, he underestimated me.
We sat down at an empty table.
It turned out that the other friend of Rey, the middle eastern looking guy, was sitting there before us. He came back from the kitchen and saw us, then stopped for a second. I saw his stuff, a jacket and a bottle of orange juice on the table were there before.
-I'm really sorry, I didn't realise the table wasn't free- I said.
-No no, please, I'm happy to have you here with me- he said, very kindly.
-Thanks man- I said with a smile. That was my chance to finally introduce myself to him. I missed the right moment when, a few days before, he went to the kitchen and found me cooking, tired and stressed after a long day at work, not paying attention to anything else happening around me. He tried to make eye contact with me and I avoided it, for some reason.

I remembered how I spilled some tomato sauce outside of the pan and a swear word from my mother language came out of me.
-Italian?- he asked me, with a big smile, happy to find a way to start a conversation.
-Yes- I replied with no enthusiasm.
Then he gave up and left, still smiling.
But that right then, was the moment I was going to introduce myself to him and be nice, so I followed him to the kitchen.
-Hey, wanna come to the table and play with us? We're going to play a drinking game now-
-Oh well, I don't drink alcohol, but I'll definitely join you for a bit. I'm very tired, and definitely going to sleep soon-
-Oh alright, what's your name by the way?- I asked, getting to the point.
-Mina, yours?-
-Domenico- and we shook hands.
-What's your football team?- he asked me while we made a move towards our table.
-Juventus, yours?- I asked, trying to seem excited by the topic.
-Paris St. Germain- he replied, proud.
-So you're French?-
-Egyptian, but I grew up in Paris-
He had a sense of belonging to the team of the city where he grew up. Unlike in my case, his support for his team made some sense.
He was making an effort to stay up a little bit more. He was happy to get to know me. I suspected he was waiting for that for some time, and I was glad it finally happened.
-So, guys, take this paper- I said, then cut a paper out of my exercise book into four pieces and gave a piece to each one of the people at my table.
-We write down the name of a famous character from cinema, history, politics, whatever, we pass it to the person on our right, we stick the papers we've received to our forehead, then we ask questions to each one of us to find out who we have written on our forehead- I had seen this game being played in a film from a few years before.

Everyone looked excited, Mina looked just pleased to have a chance to do anything that could get our friendship started. It just wasn't the right moment though, the guy really needed to sleep.
We only had beer and wine at our table, meaning that no matter how many mistakes we did, not only didn't we manage to figure out who we had written on the papers on our foreheads, but neither we managed to get any drunk at all.
-Alright guys, I think I'm going to hit the bed now- Mina said at some point.
He was very polite and seemed just genuinely a good person. Not like me, faking interest in others just to try and get sexual satisfaction, although I liked to think of me as a genuine person too.
I never really had a sexual life before and my constant chase after it had become a real obsession.
I had to interrupt my thoughts when I realised that Alma and Mina were already gone.
Jess was looking at me, but I couldn't decode her face. She looked... sad? Disappointed?
I stood up and looked at her in the eyes.
-I think I'm going to bed- she said, sounding exhausted.
-Oh yeah sure, what room are you in?-
-10, you?-
-Same. I'm going to get one more small cup of wine and then I'll go to bed- I lied.
-Ok, see you- and she left.
I went to the kitchen, cleaned up the glasses we had and quickly went downstairs.
I opened the door and made a move inside the room, slowly, then pretended to look for something in my luggage on the floor.
She was there standing, now looking at me.
-Oh hey, you're here- I said, surprised to see her staring at me now.
-Yeah, I was going to go to the toilet again...-
She hadn't finished her sentence when I grabbed her by her waist and pushed her against the wall, all of this while trying to be as gentle as I could.

She then tried to get out of my arms, and I let her go. I wasn't going to go for it if she wasn't into that, but I needed to know if she was acting or not.
-No, it's not a good idea...- she said, unable to hide a smile. I was letting her go, but kept my arms in a position that would have made it easy for me to grab her back.
-I like you- came out of my mouth. She smiled again and made a move the way out, walking slowly. Way too slow. She stopped at some point and checked if I was looking at her. I didn't hesitate any longer. I grabbed her back and forced her to the wall. She was just acting.
A sound stopped us.
-Oh my God, it's my sister- she said.
-Hey?- the voice of her sister from the top bed by the bottom of the room.
-Hey, I'm here, I just went to the toilet!- I understood her language now.
-See you tomorrow- she whispered to me then.
I went into my bed and closed the curtain.

The weather was just getting better and better in London by mid-July. I was off the next morning and decided to have a walk in Russell Square Park. The idea of lying down the grass for a bit crossed my mind so I decided to give myself half hour of relax on my own.
Londoners looked better under the sun. Their attitude improved when the sunshine showed the sky under a lighter shade.
The two sisters came to the park. We talked a lot and sometimes looked into each other eyes without speaking, just laughing.
-So sad to go back home today, London is great- Jess said.
-We can keep in touch, I'll be happy to talk to you and we'll probably meet again- I said.
She smiled, her sister didn't understand a word probably. They left that day.

In the next days, I understood that Joseph, the old black man I spotted on my first visit in the hostel, was also a long-term stayer. He had apparently moved in there several years

before, and had taken almost an unquestioned possession of the second last table towards the windows, near enough to give him a good sight of the television.
I caught him always speaking to new people each time. He introduced himself by proudly saying he was African, and if the people he was chatting to didn't find an excuse to go away from him, he would just go on and talk for an unlimited amount of time about Ghana, and about all the politicians he could recall that were originally from the country of the people he was talking to. I had to notice, at least at first impact, that his knowledge about politics was impressive, way superior to anyone else I had ever spoken to. He could tell much more than me when it came to Italian politics, up to the smallest details. A knowledge you can only expect from someone that spent every day of their lives following the news, reading newspapers and travelling a lot.
Joseph revealed he was a highly located person in society back in his days in Ghana, and his father was a prominent member of the communist party that was very popular during the 60's.
I was just resting after a long talk with him one afternoon when I suddenly received a text from Andrea.
-Hey Dom, what are you up to? I haven't seen you in a while-
I was so lost into my new life at the hostel that I hadn't even talked to Andrea for quite a bit. I needed an excuse for that.
-Sorry, I have been so busy, you know I never text in general but I'm happy to see you one of these days?-
No reply for a bit. I texted again.
-Do you still work in that pizza place near Covent Garden? I can come around if you want-
No reply yet. He would usually text first but then not reply. I never understood those people.
I went back to the hostel and took a nap.

Few hours later, I woke up terrified. The light of the sun, made feeble by the window, entered the room and spread out a little bit everywhere. I was sweating. A nightmare. I looked around myself for a few, very confused seconds. What happened? Where am I? Am I still at the hostel?

I moved down the step and felt the ground underneath my feet. I had a quick walk around the room.
Yes, that was the hostel, Russell Square, London.
I sat down again, slowly calming down.
I had become so obsessed with the idea of leaving Italy and failed so many times out of my lack of organisational skills that being in London was still something I could not entirely believe. I hated dreaming to be still living in Italy.
I used to have negative thoughts every time things were going well in my life.
I was staring at the wall. The smell of food was pleasant. I had left room 10 for room 51 that day.
I checked my phone. For some reasons, I was always happy to wake up to a message, even just one.
-Come over my workplace today, there's lots of girls there, you'll be happy, and I may get you a discounted pizza- Andrea had texted back.
What a perfect message, I thought. I already couldn't wait for the moment to come. Those few hours before that were going to be long. A few chess games online, food and beers will entertain me and make time go faster. Positive thoughts shushed my negative ones for the day.
I had a shower and wore my usual white v-shirt under my not-that-elegant black blazer. I wasn't going to combine shirt and blazer, girls had to know since the very beginning that I wasn't going to be a normal man in a normal relationship consisting of me sitting at a table with them, clean clothes, clean tea cups, gossips and a stable routine while they were in control of my emotions and prevented me from sleeping with any other girls just until they had met someone better than me and left me with the excuse that I wasn't paying enough attention.
The fear of being the only committed person in the relationship left very few possible solutions. I could have started a relationship with a girl I didn't really love and cheat on her, or just start an open one.
I left my place quite well dressed anyway. Not too smart nor too shabby.
My shoes were too clean, I noticed while walking to my bike, parked near Queen Square.

I only had black trousers. I couldn't bother buying trousers of other colours. I needed black ones for my work, and black ones to go out. Why buy different ones if one colour was just good for all purposes? I was ready to party even right after work, I could have just changed my waiter shirt with any, while my shoes and trousers were just fine for everything.
I finally reached Andrea's workplace in Earlham Street. I locked my bike to the nearest post and looked towards Seven Dials Pillar in the middle of the roundabout.
People were sitting by the Pillar, eating burgers or noodles from small shops nearby. Other people walking out of the theatre, happy about what they had just watched, some others rushing somewhere. People outside pubs with their pints and cigarettes, lights from each one of the seven streets, cab drivers honking, constantly stressed by the thoughtless pedestrians, too happy to be paying attention.
I liked that place a lot. My mate Andrea and his co-worker from Sardinia made pizzas until 10 pm, then they would close the kitchen and the tables and chairs would be removed from the floor to give space for people to dance the current hits. Sometimes you would listen to some famous songs from the last decades, the ones that remained pleasant to the ears of people no matter the passage of time.
The cherry on the cake was the free entry feature of the place. You get your chance to check if there was any friendly girls downstairs without having to pay for that and, in case of bad luck, you could just leave and come back inside later on, or just go back home if the mood wasn't the best.
My phone rang.
It was Giorgio, my mate from my town, another person I had near me that I rarely looked for. I liked him a lot, but I didn't generally look for people. I only looked for girls, and for that I needed wingmen, and they could be any guy next to me in that moment that looked even slightly good enough to approach with me and increase both chances of success.
I wasn't going to call a friend of mine and ask him to come where I was. That was a common problem for people that wanted to meet up in London.
The chances that your friend happens to be near you in a giant and spread-out city like London were tiny. You also

needed your friend to be off or to have evening shift scheduled for the next day and, on top of that, you needed him to be in the mood.
Even then, your working-class friends are likely to be dead tired after a whole week of hard work and their greatest pleasure may consist of films and wine in their beds rather than in chasing after girls.
That was the main reason why I lived in a hostel. There was no comparison between the number of fun nights I would have collected and counted on my deathbed at some point and the number of fun nights a normal person would have had.
Giorgio came downstairs, visibly drunk.
-How many beers did you have?-
-Like ten or something, but I'll get more now-
-Chill man, I don't see the reason to cross the line-
-There is no line- he told me, confident.
He was trying to prove something to himself, maybe.
-Hey guys!- Andrea jumped on me and pushed Giorgio to get attention.
-Hey, look who finished work finally-
-Yeah, finally...- Andrea was clearly tired.
-Guys, let's drink- I suggested, and we moved to a table by the bottom of the floor.
-How was work Andrea?-
-It was fine, I really need this beer now though- he said, and had a sip from his bottle, then went on.
-This guy today, a damn stupid vegetarian came to order pizza with pepperoni and that's what he got, then he came and complain about it- and he laughed.
-Wait, what? Why would a vegetarian order pizza with pepperoni?- I wondered, truly curious about it.
-He didn't know, he ordered this pizza from the menu and didn't check the toppings properly, so I told him to talk to the manager, and so he did-
-I bet your manager reimbursed him the whole thing and apologised, then you had to bake another pizza for the guy- I said, almost entirely sure that that was what happened.

-Are you joking? That guy was an idiot, it was his own problem, that's what my manager told him- him and Giorgio couldn't stop laughing for at least two minutes.
When I heard the word manager, my brain would show me the first and only association it had made with that word. The manager to me was a guy in an ironed shirt or a woman in a dress being polite to the extreme. In fancy places, customers were always right, even when they were wrong. A customer in my restaurant could have enjoyed the dinner of his life, claimed he didn't, received apologies and leave without paying.
-Alright, I see those two by the counter, who's with me?- I suggested at some point.
Andrea was shy in the approaches. Giorgio wasn't.
-I'm your man this time Dom- Giorgio didn't wait a second. He was drunk though.
-Hi- I smiled while approaching a red-haired girl. Giorgio was supposed to get the other one. I checked if he had done so, and noticed he was talking to her too.
-Hi- said the red-haired one.
-What's your name?-
-Sophie, what's yours?-
-Dom, nice to meet you. You're very pretty Sophie, don't tell me you're here with your boyfriend though- I often came up with that poor line.
-No I'm not, me and my friend Hannah are in London just for a day, going back home tomorrow...-
-Oh I see, how do you like London?-
-London is cool! We're loving it, right Hannah?- she turned around to see if her friend was ok. She didn't seem to be developing any chemistry with Giorgio though.
Giorgio was drunk, and he had started caressing her arms in a weird way.
I looked at him for a second, trying to communicate him my thoughts. He was getting another beer now.
I looked for Andrea, but couldn't see him anywhere.
A minute later, I saw he was taking care of Giorgio, making sure he didn't mess things up in the place where he worked after all.
-Sorry, your friend isn't really my type- she cut it short.

She was hotter than her friend, with her brunette short hair, her dress and her naked shoulders. Besides, she was looking at me with dreamy eyes.
The two black bartenders were now looking at me, somehow annoyed. I wondered why, but I kept focusing on what was happening that night.
-Guys, can I ask you for three beers please?- I said, on fire, ignoring it wasn't my turn in the queue.
-Yeah sure, just a minute- one of them said with a stressed look on his face, then he went to talk to his colleague, both of them now looking at me, unhappy.
-Sorry guys, I didn't realise it wasn't my turn- I said. They couldn't hear me though. They kept looking at me, more stressed.
-Yeah man, one minute, can you wait?- They misunderstood. They thought I was trying to get their attention once again, but I was trying to apologise.
Yeah whatever, I don't need these people to be happy with me or not, I'm having a good time here, I thought, and focused on the two girls.
-Hey guys, how's it going?- a tall black guy just came from behind us.
I noticed he was alone and felt relieved. He could have kept one of the girls busy while I hit on the other. I did want the brunette more, but the red-haired would have done too.
-You're on fire tonight, aren't you?- he told me and laughed.
The less black guys in here, the more chances I have, I thought.
-My name is J, what's yours?- he shook hands with me.
-Call me D I guess-
He understood everything. He saw how the two travelling girls were up to fun and that we could have made up a last-minute team and make it happen.
He started focusing on the brunette, the most attractive one.
I figured he was aiming at her since the very beginning.
I was desperate, and she was clearly desperate too.
-Girls, wanna leave this place?- I suggested after a bit of small talk, having no idea how the plan would go on.

I didn't have a place for them to stay. I lived in a hostel, and the only downside of living in a hostel was that I couldn't bring my preys from outside of it.
-Yeah- said Sophie. Hannah was less drunk and less interested, I thought, although the black guy was so fun she couldn't stop laughing. Keep it going brother.
I looked around to say bye to Andrea and Giorgio, but they were nowhere to be found.
I'll text them late, I thought, and I left holding hands with my victim.
-Oh guys, by the way I'm sorry, but my place is not available... my flatmates got his parents sleeping there tonight so...- I made up in that moment.
-Yeah, we're staying in a hotel just in Bloomsbury- Sophie suggested.
Perfect, three minutes walk from the hostel.
-We booked a room for two though, I don't think we can let you guys in, the receptionist won't allow that- said Hannah.
-Maybe we should say good night- she went on.
My world was crumbling, I couldn't even speak.
-I'm sure we can sneak in- said J.
-Yeah, wouldn't be my first time- I said, confident from the outside.
-I don't know... it's not a good idea-
-Hannah, can I talk to you for a second?- Sophie took her friend a few metres away from us and talked. They seemed to be having a fight for a second. I looked at J. and he looked at me. I could tell he was feeling the same way I was. He was excited, scared, happy and panicky at the same time.
We didn't say a word. Then, the girls came back.
-Yeah, we can give it a try I guess, but we don't want to walk there...-
-Taxi!- I shouted straight away.
A black cab parked near us in a matter of seconds.
-Jump in guys, it's on me!- I said.
-Bloomsbury area please- I told the taxi driver.
-That's a lovely area- he replied, with a thick British accent.
-Yeah, you guys know everything in London don't you?- I asked him.

-Yeah, we have to pass a test to drive this beauties- the driver replied.
-I bet I could pass that test you know, I love London a lot and I've been cycling pretty much everywhere- I said.
-Oh I bet that's not enough- he replied and laughed.
-Thank you sir, have a good night- I said, drunk enough to leave tips even after the taximeter had hit 20 pounds in a ride that, I swore, took no more than five minutes to be completed. An outrage to my bank account, knowing that I had to give three to four hours of my hard work for five minutes of someone else's work. Covent Garden and Russell Square were very close.
-Ok, we'll go in first, our room number is 108, first floor- and they went in, without adding a single word.
-Do you think they left us like this?- I asked J.
-God knows... we have to give it a try anyway- he said.
-Let's go in together-
-Sure-
We got in. The receptionist was there. He looked sleepy though.
I put a polite smile on my face. He looked back at me, rude enough not to say hi, just nodded his head. I smiled. Saying hi would have been too suspicious, I thought.
We approached room 108. We could hear the girls speaking behind the door, excited.
We knocked.
Silence.
A few seconds passed, then Sophie opened the door.
-Come on in- she said.
-We're not going to have sex with you guys, but we can hang out here if you want- she added.
-Yeah sure, no problems- I lied, certain that they lied as well.
I sat in bed next to Sophie and put my arm behind her shoulders.
-You know, it's my time of the month tonight so we can't do it I'm afraid, but you're such lovely guy and I've had a great time with you, and you can sleep here next to me if you want, it's just... no sex, I'm sorry...-

She clearly had no idea how desperate I was. She didn't know me if she thought some blood would have stopped me.
Insane, I thought.
J was working on Hannah on the other bed. I wasn't sure he was going to be successful, Hannah was playing very hard to get.
-No...- Sophie said every time I tried to lift her skirt up. I hesitated, but then I saw her smiling. I kept touching her, applying more and more force.
-No...- she said again, still smiling and unzipping it for me.
Absurd, I thought, how girls took the matter of consent so seriously and yet literally played with it during the action.

August 2015

August in London is pleasant. You can walk in the streets in the morning with a t-shirt and shorts without worrying about the weather suddenly getting cold enough to force you to carry a jacket with you all the time, just in case. That happened in June and July but not in August. You get a few random quick showers every now and then, but it never gets cold. I preferred it to the Mediterranean August weather, which is unbearable and makes you sweat so much you would rather go somewhere and sit near a fan than staying outdoors. My skin was quite pale and it was easy to burn it under the sun.
When you live in England, sometimes you end up thinking you'll never see the sun again, sometimes you would forget about its existence. Then August comes, and you look up to the sky. It looks beautiful, lighter colour, less clouds, a friendly way for the day to start. More people walking in the streets, everyone looks better, girls wear their flower dresses and lie down in the parks. People act more like humans than like robots.
I was given morning shifts as a waiter now, although I preferred working in the evenings. Waitering in the evenings was just more fun, I didn't have to prepare coffees at all, I basically just had to run and put the orders through the computer, wait for the runners to carry the tray and leave the plates on the tables. Besides, my co-workers during the

evening shifts were the best ones, the ones with a good attitude at work.

Now that I was a waiter, I was looking forward to achieving two main goals. First: improve my life by coming back home with more energy and enjoy the nights out in the bars and meeting new people everyday. Second: prove the waiters who complained about everything that the only thing in that restaurant that had to be changed was their own attitude. Most jobs that are considered hard are actually not hard if your teammates give you a good time.

The waiters who complained about customers being rude were also the ones who disrespected the runners, constantly played the victim card with the managers, asking for different shifts all the time declaring no flexibility, threatening the managers everyday with "I'm leaving this job, I'm tired of this" no matter how many privileges they were given because of their attitude.

-Morning Dom- Mirek greeted me that morning.

-Morning- I said. I was late again.

-Now that you're a waiter and you're definitely not the most skilled one, I suggest you at least improve your punctuality- Mirek didn't seem happy, and that was a rare face from his side.

-Yes, you're right, sorry- I said, quickly placing the jam pots in the centre of the tables, menus in between them and salt and pepper by the other side so to keep the menus standing still.

-The labels have to face the entrance door Dom- he said.

The Polish waiters were looking at me, snorting, unhappy with me.

Some posh people would complain about not receiving a service in the timing they expected based on their lack of understanding of what it means to work in a busy kitchen in central London, not to mention their arrogance, and the fact that most of these people have never really worked a day of their lives. On the other hand, most posh people just looked posh but actually acted super nicely and humble to waiters. Personally, I knew I could ignore the rude comments of the few with a smile, feeling actually amused and careless of their reactions.

Few people liked me as a waiter. I was by far the hardest working and fastest runner in that place, I trained about at least ten different runners and achieved several top scores weekly targets that allowed my restaurant to end up being the one with the greatest income at the end of the month. They did these competitions on a monthly basis and the managers pushed us to achieve these goals. "The more we make, the more bonuses we get", they said.

The bonuses were only given to managers though, which meant that our only reason to work harder was to achieve such bonuses for them so that they could be happy about our work. We never really got a single penny when we crossed these targets.

My request for a daily 6 am to 4 pm shift was accepted and that was my new regular shift, which I got to like eventually. I wanted to spend my nights in the hostel rather than in the restaurant, cleaning stuff while everybody else was outside. I often thought about how great it would have been to live without having to work. I'd start my chase in the early morning and have the entire day to get at least one.

-Dom, you forgot to toast the bread for the gentleman at table 51, you know?-

-Oh sorry-

-It's ok, it's done now- said Marta, one of the Polish waitresses that always worked on the front of the restaurant in morning shifts. She was excellent and impeccable in her service. She also sounded rude but had an amazing attitude towards the others. She looked unfriendly but never got mad at anyone, even though she clearly was in the position of complaining. She worked faster and better than anyone, not a single fake smile, not a single unnecessary complaint, just constant swearing against the managers in her language. At the end of her shift, the expression on her face wouldn't change at all.

-Aren't you happy your shift is over now? Can I see your smile now?- I mocked her.

-I am happy, indeed- she said, and I didn't doubt it. I just couldn't see it.

-You forgot ketchup on table 33-

-I'll bring it now- my chance to prove my attitude was the right one. It made sense to organise the waiters to work in sections, but it didn't make sense to avoid helping out on busier sections and to complain when somebody covered your table. Some waiters and waitresses were able to complain even about that though.
Sometimes I would work on the 50's section but had someone waving at me from the 30's one. I always replied with a smile and told the customers I would have been there in a second. All customers would reply with a smile and appreciate it. It was the waiters who just missed to understand that. Waving made the place look friendlier, I liked it.
-Hey guys, how are you?- I would ask the hands waving customers.
-Good thanks, just the bill please, we're in a rush-
-Oh sure, I'll be super quick- I said, comprehensive, not because I wanted to feel like I was a better person, but just because there was nothing wrong with them being in a rush. They asked for it kindly anyway.
-Here is your bill, hope you enjoyed your food- I said with a smile while they inserted their card in the machine.
-It was amazing, thank you!- they replied, stood up and left in a rush. I quickly cleaned the table and meant to reset it when Emma approached me.
-Domenico, thank you for taking care of my table- she said, a furious look on her face.
-No worries- I said, smiling. My idea was that if I showed good attitude towards someone that had a bad attitude towards me, they might change for better. However, the truth was, as I found out after trying for months, that most of the times this just led to someone taking advantage of that and feeling entitled to treat me even worse.
Then there were two options. The first one was to fight back and play their game. The second one was to continue having a good attitude and hope that with the passage of time, the wall they had built out of their own insecurities will actually crumble apart and they'd improve their attitude. I struggled everyday to choose which idea I should have applied to my life to make it better, but unfortunately I always chose the second one.

In fact, it took less than a minute to find out that she wasn't actually grateful to me for helping her out.
-He just covered my table, why would he do that?- Emma was complaining to a manager, furious, not realising I was close enough to the counter to hear her.
-Well, maybe you need to work faster then!- the Greek manager told her, and shut her up, just like that.
Oh, such a pleasure, such a pleasure! I enjoyed that moment so hard I decided it was my moment to hit more. I checked my tables were all sorted, table 51 had paid and Przemek, my favourite runner, was cleaning it already. Well done, I'll give you a pound after this. Table 52, a couple was sitting there, holding hands and waiting for steaks to come. Steak knives were on the table, no mise en place needed. No one was sitting at table 53 and neither at table 54. Table 55, waiting for mains, no mise en place needed. Those two old ladies were showing gifts they bought for each other. Yes! I thought.
She complained about me with a manager that was by far the hardest working one. She used to dismiss any complaints made by anyone with a firm voice that no one could argue against. I knew that she liked my hard work and she wouldn't listen to her, but this could also be the moment to show her that the best we could do was to fire her.
I checked the tables on her section, the 30's, and they were a disaster. I didn't wait a second.
Giving someone a bill to pay wouldn't have been enough. I had to take orders, do the mise en place, maybe even serve them wine and ask them how they were doing. A full proper service at any of her tables while she was complaining about me being helpful had to have been a great move in the eyes of a proper manager.
-Hello, how are you?- I asked this old couple, never been happier to know how some strangers were doing.
-Yeah, we're ok and you?- one of them replied with a smile.
-I'm great thanks!- I replied, honest.
I was glad they asked for wine as well, so I could do more for them than just taking the orders. I had almost entirely forgotten about my tables, too busy caring about someone else's tables for the sake of destroying them.

I put the orders through and had a quick look at my section. It looked just fine.
I made my way to the wine shelves and picked mine.
-Dom, what are you doing?- my manager just asked me.
-Working- I said, trying to show I wasn't at all under pressure. What I was doing was my job. Helping on other tables was my job. We were supposed to be a team. Those people were poison, we had to send them home, for the greater good and for my greater good.
-I'll do that table now- the Greek manager interrupted my thoughts.
-Are you sure?-
-Yes- she said, annoyed. All I needed to do now was not mention Emma, pretend that I wasn't having any problems on the floor and I was more than happy to cover other sections when needed.
She took a bottle of red wine and made a move to the table I was serving.
Emma looked mad, behind the runners' station, letting the steam off with Lena, who worked as a runner and who had an identical attitude to her. I went by the runners' station and thanked them for their hard work. Emma was still speaking with Lena in their language, angry, now almost crying. I ignored all of this and went on to my duties. What on earth could have been going on in her head? In what way was she twisting reality so that her colleague would think she was right? "Dom just helped me at my table because he believes we are supposed to be a team. I tried to get him punished for this and the manager did not listen to me. It's so unfair!". This sounded crazy to me, but I concluded that she was just looking for support from another person that she knew to despise me a lot.
I hated Emma and Lena. Emma had this red, short hairstyle typical of those "woke" people who claim to be fighting social injustice whilst, in my opinion, they were just looking for self-promotion in society. I once heard her saying she was vegan for a couple of months and then came back to eating meat. This meant that the only reason why she became vegan in the first place was out of peer pressure. In fact, what person chooses to stop feeding the meat industry to

save animals, and then chooses to stop doing this a couple of months later? Besides, I often heard her saying words like sexist and homophobic to respond to any statements someone made that she disagreed with, even when they presented no rational reason to be judged like that. A typical toxic cunt.

Regarding Lena, she hated me since the very beginning, always acted anti-socially with me, but never told me the reason. She once said I was lazy and that made me very angry, I couldn't deny it. She also had short dark hair and was in a relationship with Salvatore. I genuinely had no idea about what he saw in her, but I guessed they were perfect for each other. He really could lift her mood up with his jokes at least. Anyway, I wished I could get rid of both of them.

Riding the way home at night was somehow pleasant as long as I could play music in my earphones. It was an excuse for me to be with myself, something I happened to be doing all the time anyway.

I jumped on my bike and cycled across Cliveden Place, Eaton Square, the Mall, Trafalgar Square and kept cycling through the Strand, then turned left on Kingsway until I could see Holborn station on my right side. Five more minutes the way north through Southampton Row until I got to Russell Square, parked my bike and rushed into the hostel in Guilford Street. My colleagues were taking much longer to get home where they would lie down in bed, same thoughts, same ideas, same nights, different films but same position of their laptops on their laps, same cup on their nightstands, same people in their chats, same partner, same sex all the time, providing they had any.

In my case, I had no idea what was going to happen, who I was going to meet, if I was going out or not, even what I would have had for food. In the hostel, you always had some tourists sharing their national courses with you, boasting about how good they were. An appreciation would have made them very happy.

One afternoon, I was in the common room, left my bag on the table and had a look around.

-Hey Dom!- someone just hugged me from behind.
It was Andrea.
-Hey!- Michele approached with a big smile and shook my hand.
-Guys, what...- and nothing else came out of my mouth.
-We decided to make a surprise for you- Michele said and smiled. Andrea was apparently very happy to see me.
-Well, this is just great...- it was weird, but certainly a good surprise.
-By the way Dom, we were cooking some pasta, wanna join?- Michele suggested, knowing the answer.
-Yeah sure, the usual pasta with more onion than sauce, right?-
They laughed and made a move to the kitchen.
-It's crazy you guys are here now. It's unreal- I said, unable to contain my excitement any longer.
-Yeah, but I thought about what you told me that day... I was just too bored there in Warvick Avenue, I needed to shake my nights like you do you know...- and laughed, looking at me.
There was always that naïve look on his face. Andrea was that guy that was so nice sometimes it could make me feel like I was evil even if I had done nothing wrong at all.
We talked a lot and I worked under his instructions, being terrible at cooking, and at some point, we were done.
-Ok, it's ready, I'm starving- he said.
We carried the hob and three plates to the living room and took a seat at the nearest table. Michele came right away.
-That guy crashed me. He only played with a knight and didn't allow me to take any initiative. I've never felt so bad at chess- he said.
-You were playing a chess game? Who with?- I asked, surprised.
-He just went to the kitchen, I saw him- Michele said, chewing with his mouth open.
I felt tempted by chasing after him and ask him for a game. I tasted a little bit of pasta and pretended I wasn't lost in my thoughts.
-Guys, I'm just going to go to the kitchen and get more salt- I said.

-Yeah go ahead- Michele said and the guys kept focusing on their food.
I had just reached the kitchen when I realised there was no way for me to know who the chess player was.
Luckily, this guy was the only person in the kitchen.
He had light brown, short hair and was wearing a black jacket, a bit of an untidy look, a bit chubby.
-Excuse me, are you the chess player?- I tried to get his attention while he was making pasta himself.
-Yeah- he replied, his voice was hoarse, as if talking cost him a big effort.
-Would you like to play a game with me when you're done with food?-
-Yeah sure, alright- he said whilst looking at the stove and adding to the tomato sauce way more cheese than I would have ever done myself.
-Alright, talk to you later then- I said, waiting for a reply.
He didn't reply. I stood next to the door for a few seconds, then I left and rushed to my table.
-Dom, the two bartenders weren't happy about you, they spoke the worst things when you left the other day- Andrea told me as soon as I got back to our table, and he sounded very serious.
-What? You mean the two black ones?-
-Yes, they said you didn't want to wait for your turn when you were being served. You were with the two girls from Liverpool-
-Oh, I see....- I was surprised.
-I don't think I did anything wrong Andrea, really- I continued, thoughtful.
-Do you reckon?-
-They didn't like that I was handling two girls at the same time I guess- I said, serious.
-No Dom, I don't think it's that at all. They said you weren't respectful even though they've given you so many free drinks all the time...-
-Look, I never asked for those free drinks, I've always wanted to pay anytime they were offering me stuff, also, I mean, I appreciate them being nice and so on, but I don't think I

acted disrespectfully. Tell them how about when I was waving my ten pounds note so I could pay them?-
-Dom, it's not about paying, they don't care, they've given away thousands of pounds worth of drinks in that place, they don't care at all, really, it's the way you acted...- Andrea was calmly explaining the story to me, but I was getting upset.
-Did you see how I acted?-
-No, I was outside taking care of Giorgio who was puking on the pavement just by the main entrance- Andrea still held a serious voice tone with me.
-Well, ok Andrea, thank you for letting me know. I don't really know what to say, except I have nothing to apologise- I cut it short.
-Looks like I'm going to have to find a new place to pick up girls then...- I said, then had another bit of pasta and continued -It's not the end of the world, I'm sure I'll find something, it's London after all-
-Yeah, I don't think they want to see you again down there- Andrea told me, causing my heart to pound with pain. That place was perfect for me, and I honestly didn't know any other one that could be compared to it.
-Do you wanna play?- the chess player appeared all of a sudden and was speaking to me now.
-Oh yeah, sure- I replied.
We were done with our food, Andrea took a cigarette and was ready to go outside for a quick smoke before cleaning the dishes.
-Don't worry about it guys, I'll take the stuff around me here and I'll clean as soon as I'm done playing, thanks for the dinner- I added.
-We'll see you later right?- Michele suggested.
-No, I'm going to sleep soon, I've got to wake up early tomorrow morning- Andrea replied before I could.
The guys left and I sat alone with the guy I had just met. The chess board was already on the table.
-What's your name?-
-Mark-
He never smiled until that point, but somehow he didn't look unfriendly. It was hard to decode.
-Where are you from?-

-South London-
-What are you doing in a hostel? I never really find English people in a hostel, especially if they are from London- I said, curious.
-Can't really stay at my place right now- he said. His voice claimed the end of that conversation.
-White or black?- I asked him, even though I was still curious.
-Up to you- he said, and grabbed the black pieces.
I moved my knight into the game. The idea was to rush my pieces to the centre of the board as soon as I could.
Things seemed to be going on smoothly. He always had a move to play back, fast, very fast actually. He had a reply for everything without taking his time at all. It seemed like he played by heart.
We had played about twelve to fifteen moves from the beginning of the game and my situation looked strange. I hadn't lost any material, not even a single pawn, but there was a problem. I didn't see any good moves, no captures, not even the possibility for my pieces to be placed into better squares. I slowly recognised he had complete domination over the board.
-I can take it- he said, pointing at one of my pieces. He figured what move I was planning to make and stopped me from doing that because it was going to be a blunder. I would have been happy to win something from him. In his case though, not only he didn't have to struggle to beat me, but he was even alerting me against my own mistakes.
-I resign- I said, and shook his hand.
-Good game, played well- he lied.
-Hey- Rey had just appeared out of the blue.
-Can I have a game with someone?- he said whilst sitting next to me.
-Yeah sure, you guys play, I'll watch-
They started their game. Rey moved fast, just as fast as Mark. It seemed like the two guys knew what they were doing.
The game between them went on for longer than it went between me and Mark. Rey's position didn't seem very bad after all.

I reckoned I would have liked to see Rey losing, because that would have meant that Mark was just out of our league. I looked at the board, trying to understand what was going on. The score in terms of material was equal, but the difference was that Mark's position of the pieces in the endgame was better.
The game was an easy win for Mark, who looked very confident. The same expression on his face since the very beginning of the game, always calm, in complete control of the situation.
-Mm... I resign- said Rey.
They had another game where Mark won again, this time faster than before, then Rey stood up and left. I took my chess board and put it back in my bag, then said bye to Mark, who looked at me for a second, with the same expression on his face, didn't reply, but just stayed on his bench, silent.

-I've met that guy, the chess player who beat Michele, he beat me and my friend Rey too, he is too good- I told Andrea the next afternoon in the kitchen, while we were making lunch.
-Didn't you know him already?- asked Andrea whilst cutting a brown onion into slices.
-Well, no?-
-He was staying at the hostel in Hyde Park, I remember him- he told me, but didn't even ring a bell.
-You must have met him on a night I wasn't there, I was probably working or something... well, obviously, I can't have met all the people you have met and vice versa-
-Well yeah that makes sense - he said, and smiled.
He wasn't angry any more about the night at his work place. Or maybe he just didn't want to think about it. I chose not to mention it, although I was still upset.
-Dom, can you cut those tomatoes for me?- Andrea brought me back to reality for a second.
The food was ready and we were taking it to the common room when a bald guy stood up from the sofa and followed us. We sat down and so did he, just next to me.
-Hi- he said, and smiled.
-Hi- I said back, waiting for him to go on.

-I saw a chess board on this table but I knew you were cooking so I waited- he smiled, then continued -You know I can't help asking for a game to anyone as soon as I see a chess board, it's stronger than me- he finished, giving me something like a justification of his request where it just wasn't needed.
-Yeah sure, would you like to eat with us?- I said, trying to force a smile that, for some reason, didn't appear on my face.
-No, I've just had food, but thank you very much- he said again, and moved back to the sofa.
I finished the food as fast as possible.
-Wanna come for a cigarette?- Andrea asked me.
-I don't smoke?- I replied to him, surprised he would ask me that.
-Oh yeah, I keep forgetting... but what about weed?-
-Well yes, every now and then, but probably not right now, it will make my day unproductive. Also I'd rather not to, maybe not in general- I said, getting a bit carried away.
-Wow- he replied, and laughed.
I stood up and wished Andrea a pleasant day at work, then looked for the bald guy. He was in his twenties, slightly chubby, and very friendly-looking.
-Hey, I'm going to quickly clean up my stuff in the kitchen, wanna set up the board and I'll be with you in a minute?- I asked him.
-I feel like I want to learn even more languages just because of the girls in this place- was his reply.
I stopped for a moment, then laughed. I didn't expect it. He looked a bit nerdy and polite, too nerdy and polite to be interested in girls.
I wondered what kind of guy he really was while I cleaned the plates.
I came back to the table and he had already set everything up.
-Ready?- he asked me, and smiled again.
-Yeah sure- and I played my first move.
A few moves into the game and I started feeling uncomfortable. I felt like there were too many threats going on. Also, my opponent started giggling.

That's rude, where are your manners now?
I pretended I had things under control and castled my king. He smiled.
-I can take your queen- he told me, and giggled again. I stayed silent for few seconds.
-Do you want to take your move back?- he said.
No, All I want is you to stop giggling to be honest.
-Well, I resign. I didn't play well- I said.
-No no, you absolutely did- he said, his face unable to hide how happy he was that he had beat me.
I felt like not playing with him anymore. He was superior to me, and not polite at all at the end of the day.
-Play one more?- he asked, happy like a child.
-Yes, let's play-
I lost again, and his giggling got a bit louder now.
-We should play again these days- I told him, unable to stay one more minute at his table.
-Sure, I'm leaving this hostel in a couple of weeks anyway- he added.
-What's your name?-
-Vittorio, add me on Facebook-

I found out Vittorio had uploaded a post on his Facebook profile after taking a picture of me turned by the other side. He had played blindfolded and beat me. I could see the board, he couldn't. He would just call his moves out loud while figuring out what his best move was by just trying to keep the position in his head. The effort seemed huge, but not only did he beat me, he also didn't make a single mistake. He never missed a move nor misunderstood the position. He saw better than I did, even though I was the one who was actually allowed to see the board.
Vittorio boasted about his blindfolded victory over me on his Facebook account, but at the same time praised me for being "a wonderful, sweet guy from Apulia".
Vittorio would usually try to get attention from others. If you didn't notice his qualities, he would find a way to tell you about them.
We were just playing a game once when one of the receptionists passed by us and he said something in Arabic to

him. The receptionist replied, surprised and pleased that a foreigner could know his language.
I didn't react to this. I knew exactly where he wanted to get at. He wanted me to say "Oh wow, you speak Arabic, that's like...unheard before".
I went on with my moves. He didn't last long before going back there so to gain appreciation from me.
-Yeah, I speak Arabic-
-I see... did you study it?-
-Yeah, well I actually speak half the number of languages that are spoken in this hostel- he said, pleased with his own words.
-How many?-
-Four- he said, then looked around, half smile on his face.
-I know six of them- I said. I couldn't wait any longer either.
-Oh, really?- he replied, surprised.
-Yes, definitely not as good as some years ago, but still- I felt like it was becoming a challenge now.
Mark came from kitchen. He was carrying a hob with a soup in it and a spoon on his left hand. He usually ate directly from the pan or the hob.
Unlike Vittorio, he wouldn't use any social media platforms and had an old-fashioned phone. He was introvert and would never talk about his life. We basically only knew his name.

There were random thefts back at the previous hostel where I was staying. In Hyde Park rooms were cheaper and so were the people.
Russell Square was different though. It was slightly more expensive and therefore there were way more tourists than long-term stayers, who had chosen that hostel for the lifestyle rather than for economic reasons.
I loved how I could leave any item on a table in the common room for an entire day and still find it there at the end of the day. The chess board would constantly be on a table, and Mark, Vittorio and I would have games anytime we happened to bump into each other.
Vittorio was attending university classes in Russell Square, I was working on morning shifts at the restaurant and Mark worked as a courier in food delivery.

-Guys, tell me something. Where do I go wrong... why are you always beating me at chess?- I once asked them. The guys thought about it for a few seconds, exchanging amused looks.
-Principles Dom, you're not following them. You're clearly just moving your pieces in the centre of the board waiting for tactics to appear, but you open wrong anyway- Mark explained.
-You need to know what you're doing, learn some opening theory, learn to put your pieces into their best possible squares- Vittorio continued.
-Where did you learn such principles?-
-I used to do chess at school- Mark replied.
-I used to go to a chess club and study from books- Vittorio said.
They had a chess education, unlike me. I never got the chance to play with anyone because nobody played in my town.
-Alright, I'm off to work, few more deliveries before going to bed- said Mark.
-Yeah, I'm already going to bed actually, going to wake up early tomorrow morning- said Vittorio, and shook our hands before leaving.
I had just finished with all the cleaning when I suddenly saw Rey standing next to me.
-Hey- he said.
Tall, so tall, his legs crossed and so were his arms. Just the laziest possible position one who could have while standing.
-Hey Rey, how are you?- I said. I was always glad to see him.
-I'm alright, just came from a good business night, 1k tonight- he said, without changing his facial expression.
-1k? You made it in one night?-
-Yeah- he said, still sounding sad.
-What do you do?- I asked, half of me definitely not going to believe whatever he replied, half of me genuinely curious.
-I fuck people for money- he said with the same voice tone. He sounded like it was something boring that he wasn't extremely lucky to do.
-I see...-

-Yeah, and tonight I saw someone and I was given this money, but I have to pay back some debts I have so I've already got rid of most of it-
-What kind of debts do you have?-
-I gambled, I bet a lot, wasted thousands of pounds in this way...- he said, some pain in his voice. The expression on his face was perfectly aligned with what he was saying.
-How much do you still owe? Do you owe to people or to some casinos or something...-
-People- he interrupted me.
-How much have you made with your job so far?-
-A lot- he said, and smiled.
-20k?-
-No- he laughed for about a minute, then looked very sad all of a sudden.
-At least 100k- he said.
-That's impressive, I want to do this too- I said, pretending to be joking. I couldn't fully believe him anyway.
-It's not easy, you know- he said.
He hadn't changed position at all since the beginning of the talk. Sometimes he would bite a tomato from a plastic box next to him, sometimes he would bite a bit of his bread baguette. He was so lazy that his way to have a sandwich was to give a few random bites to bread and tomato, just so to taste both of them, but without having to cut the baguette in half and the tomatoes into slices so they can fit inside of it. It made sense that he worked as an escort. The only work Rey could do had to involve something he had to do anyway. We left the kitchen and took a seat by the sofas area.
It was late night and the common room was almost entirely empty.
-I think we are compatible- he told me then, suddenly.
-What?-
-We are compatible- he said again.
-Ok man, if you say so...- I was acting cool. I didn't want him to think I was actually very happy to hear that.
-Ok I'm going to sleep- he said, and left, leaving some food on the kitchen counter.

September 2015

I landed back in London from my holidays in Greece, looking forward to seeing the hostel again, but most importantly, to see if Rey was still there.
He didn't seem to be very excited about me in general but, for some reason, I was.
I happened to be in a good team moment at work, although I was quite indifferent to my job itself. I enjoyed being a runner because it allowed me to space out a lot while I carried out all my repetitive duties that only required my arms and legs rather than my brain, but now that I was working as a waiter, this was no longer possible. I needed to focus at work so to avoid mistakes that would have been embarrassing.
Working as a waiter was lighter than working as a runner by the physical point of view, but harder by the mental one. Dropping a glass on a table would have cost a free dinner for the customers and a very poor figure.
I had to say though, that in Sloane Square you didn't really get sent home easily anyway. They forgave mistakes when it came to costs. If you wanted them to fire you, you had to drop and break an entire box of glasses everyday for a whole week at least. The restaurant made so much money and gave away so many free dinners that what counted the most for the managers was that the customers left the place smiling. Some of them would have written down a positive review and some of them, the well-known mystery diners, could have been there at any time during the month. Any positive feedback that were to reach the desk of the head office was their greatest interest.
For the waiters, the greatest interest was getting the tips, that also came from a lot of smiles and free stuff served by the end. Some of us, for instance, would prepare the bill beforehand, prepare the coffees ordered by the table and then leave the bill saying "coffees on the house", obviously without telling the managers.
On the other hand, the greatest interest of the runners was to leave soon enough to be able to take the tube the way home. Most people of the staff would take a much longer time to get home by bus than by tube and the longer you

spent to get home, the less you could sleep. This meant trouble as many of us were closing in the nights and restarting work in the morning, maybe even for another double shift.

By law we knew we all had the right to have eleven hours rest from one shift to another, but if it took you two hours to get home by bus at night and one more hour to get to work by tube the next day, you were left with only eight hours. We literally couldn't make it. Or maybe we could, but going straight to bed and forget everything else, from shower to laundry, from reading a few pages of a book or from attempting to writing one. The only way for us to live healthy was to give up any other activity for work.

Sometimes the restaurant would give you less than eight hours rest from a shift to another. Those who complained would get the rota changed for them. Those who didn't complain and acted agreeable would be exploited.

The logic of the agreeable person was simple. "If I show them maximum flexibility, eventually I will get the maximum reward".

Now, this simply didn't happen.

Pay rise in the workplace arrived when you repeatedly asked for it or, as in my case, when you threatened to leave.

Runners in our restaurant were the bottom of the pyramid. They were many, they held the greatest weight, got paid the least possible money and carried out the most number of duties.

I had no doubts about who were the best waiters to work with on the floor, Manu and Pierre.

Manu was the first to use the free coffees strategy to get tips.

-I bet you didn't put those coffees through the till- I commented with a smile once, during a busy evening.

-It's not my fault if they pay shit money here, I wouldn't be doing this otherwise- he quickly replied whilst approaching a table.

-We apologise for the delay in serving the food, so the coffees will be on the house- he said to a well-dressed man and his wife and daughter. They looked like a well-off posh family.

-Oh, thank you! Much appreciated- they replied. I checked when the food was put through his table and realised it definitely didn't get there later than expected. Eventually, when the customers were gone, I saw a 10 pounds note left on the table just for him. He put it in his pockets and winked at me. He was always able to make at least 50 pounds per day like that.

Runners didn't have any tips if not the ones from the waiters. All waiters had their strategies to get tips. In my case, I didn't have any. I didn't care at all.

At the end of the day, I rarely got tips as a matter of fact. People clearly rewarded different attitudes. They might have been aware of the fact that fake smiling waiters were just looking for money, but didn't really care about it, as long as somebody smiled to them.

The attitude of some waiters at work could have been very annoying sometimes. Sometimes, they just looked for an excuse to make you unhappy.

Filip was great at this. He was able to spot a little stain at the bottom of my apron and go tell the managers about it. He wasn't happy until he had got the attention of any of them and forced me to do something about it.

-You clearly don't care about the standards of the restaurant if you show up with a dirty apron- he would say, in a disapproving tone, loud enough to be heard by the nearest manager.

Manu and Marc would laugh whenever he would say something to me. They laughed both at the situation and at him.

-This guy is very unhappy- Manu would say in our language at the staff table, amused.

-Yeah, he just decided to make my life hard- I said, sometimes very annoyed with it.

-There's always going to be that one person that wants to piss you off Dom, you have to accept it- said Ciro, giggling.

-Not really, I mean, I used to think this too, but sometimes the team can be just perfect- I said, looking towards the ceiling.

-Really? In this place?- Ciro asked, genuinely surprised.

-Well yeah-

-He's joking- Manu said, then went back to his plate of spaghetti.
I thought about telling him that he was the proof of what I was saying, that if I could have, I would have chosen to work with him everyday.
I didn't say it though. Manu would have made fun of me. Him and Pierre were bantering with me all the time, we could have joked about anything, but I didn't want to give people too many things to mock me about and telling Manu that I wished to be always working with him would have made everyone's day.
-I enjoy working with Pierre a lot- I said.
-He doesn't care about you- Ciro took advantage to have a dig at me, sounding as evil as he could.
-Yeah, Ciro is right, he doesn't care about you, he probably doesn't enjoy working with you at all- Manu added, then the two looked at each other and giggled.
-Impossible, he can be as unprofessional as he wants to when I'm working with him since he knows that I won't speak, or complain, or kiss a manager's ass or something-
-He does it with everyone- Manu replied.
It was mostly true. Pierre was just cool.
He had fun at work. He purposely broke glasses every now and then just to amuse himself and the runners, he would sometimes leave plates onto tables calling them with different names, constantly mocked me when I was a runner, made jokes about the managers, even in their faces sometimes. He was also one of the most skilled waiters and, in my opinion, the fastest one.
He had a thick French accent that was so hard to understand, but very attractive somehow. Sometimes I heard him stating "if they don't promote me to manager, I'll quit this job", which made me think he had some ambitions, but at the same time he would give you many proofs to believe he had none.
-The waiter was rude and rushed. He served us fast, but he didn't smile once- Daniel once read a report out loud, trying his best not to burst out laughing until the very end of the line. It was a mystery diner report that he had taken from the notice board near the kitchen.

Some of us were sitting there while he read it. Me, Manu, Ilaria, Ciro and Pierre himself.
He wouldn't even blush. He waited for everyone to stop laughing and said -Next time I want the report to be much worse- with Ilaria dropping some tears out of laughing too hard.
-Do that, and it would be the last thing you do in this restaurant- the general manager had appeared just behind him.
-At least I hope you don't find it funny for real, you were probably joking I assume- he added, looking serious.
-Yeah sorry, I was joking- Pierre replied, a serious expression quickly showed up on his face, but went back to the amused one as soon as Daryl was gone.
Other waiters would have reacted in a very different way. I was pretty sure I would have reacted just like Pierre, publicly at least. Inside of me I could have felt some fears probably, especially if Daryl were to tell me off just like he did with him.
Emma would have driven mad. She would have made a big scene to Daniel and probably required the managers to act about it. She would have cried and complained until someone had punished Daniel. She was unable to banter.
Ilaria would have disliked it too, Ciro would have pretended to like it, but he would have plotted to do something at Daniel's back eventually. Manu would have enjoyed it too and would have had no resentment towards him, Marco, the Sardinian waiter, an excellent one to work with, would have laughed but then tried his best for something like this not to happen again.
The way people behave under a specific aspect of life would most of the times affect also other aspects of their life. This allowed me sometimes to predict people's political opinions, their favourite music genre or if they were into cars in case they were men or into babies if they were women.
I would sit on the staff table for half hour after finishing my food, too full and too tired to stand up, looking at the other tables and listening to their conversations.
My restaurant was in Sloane Square, mostly visited by upper class people, talking about a limited number of topics.

Between all the conversations and words I had purposely or accidentally heard from people, I don't remember my ears ever catching anything else besides finance, holidays, gossip, looks or plans for the future.
-What are you doing still here? Go home and take a shower, you stinky hobbit- Ciro passed by table 50 where I was sitting. I didn't reply.
-Well, listen, I'm going to need this table for some customers now- he came back a minute later, getting serious.
-I don't believe you- I replied, getting serious too.
-Then I'm going to have to speak to a manager- he said, actually serious. He liked to joke, but he didn't like it when you asked him to stop.

That evening, the living room was packed. Lots of young students from Holland, the usual school trip.
-One good thing about these students is that no one under the age of 16 is allowed in the hostel, so they're not too young. One bad thing about it is that it's still illegal- I heard Rey saying this to Adrian, who laughed.
The two were sitting on the dark sofa, looking lazy.
-Hi guys- I said, passing by.
-Hey- they replied, apparently not enthusiast to see me.
I went to the kitchen and just felt upset.
Why couldn't I be friends with them? Why didn't they feel the same about me?
I was walking back to my table, meaning to not even look at them when Adrian asked me how I was doing.
-Hey, I'm ok and you?- I said, trying to sound the least interested that I could.
-Good too, why don't you sit here with us?- he said, still not smiling.
I took my plate and my beer and then reached them by the sofas. Rey didn't seem to be willing to talk to me at all.
-How was your day?- Adrian asked me.
-Usual day at work, you?-
-I just finished my shift, I'm tired, I can't wait to be in bed, but this guy wouldn't let me- he said, pointing at Rey.
-Stop speaking Italian- he said, then returned to looking at a group of girls behind us.

-He has a passion for girls, doesn't he?- I said, paying attention that most of the words I had chosen to use were similar to the Spanish version of them.
-He's obsessed- Adrian said.
-Alright, I'm not staying here any longer, bearing these two bitching about me- he said in his language and stood up, then walked in the direction of the kitchen, but decided to just stop by the nearest sofa. He fell on it, his weight made the remote that was on the sofa jump and fall to the ground. He didn't really sit, it was more like he had let himself fall because he couldn't be bothered making all the moves that were necessary for one to sit down.
Adrian seemed to have read my mind.
-Why? Why are you laughing?- Rey asked, looking at us.
-Have you been working a lot today, Rey?- I asked him.
Rey just looked away, pleased that it wasn't the truth.
I was just done with my food when Adrian and some others of the group had decided to go to bed. It got late and I didn't even realise it.
I looked around and noticed that none of the students was left in the common room.
-Do you want to play some chess?- Rey suggested.
-Yes, sure-
We sat down at a central table.
-The one that wins two out of three games is the champion of the hostel- he said.
-Works for me- I replied, although I wanted to play way more than three games.
We set the clocks on an app on my phone. Five minutes for each player.
I needed to win at least one game. It was about my reputation, I wanted to be considered a chess player, one that people could challenge every now and then. Not the sparring one that I had become.
Mark and Vittorio were out of my league. I just couldn't beat them, I couldn't finish them off not even when they had made some stupid mistake and I was in a situation of clear advantage. I was, sometimes, scared of winning. Sometimes all they needed to do was stay calm and keep playing until I

gave up my own advantage because of my fear of playing a bad move which usually led to playing the worst one.
Rey was not impossible to beat though. He played less accurate moves than the other two and wouldn't often spot his best move whenever I realised I had made a mistake that could be punished. He was more experienced than me, but lazier in his thinking.
We played our first game, and I won it.
I looked at him and saw a disappointed look on his face. He didn't expect it.
-Reset your board, it's two out of three- he sounded a bit nervous to me.
Is he so upset for losing against me? Did he invite me to play just to feed his ego?
The second game started. Rey had sacrificed his bishop in the very beginning of the game taking a pawn next to my king, giving him a check. My king was forced to move but it wasn't a problem. Actually, his was a bad move, at least according to what Claudio told me every time I played it myself.
But the thing was, that I was not able to keep an advantage on until the end of the game. If I had spent enough time thinking, I could have found a check mate in three or four moves, but I needed that situation to arise. If I had an extra piece and all I needed to do was just go on and dominate my opponent with my material advantage, I would have almost certainly lost.
Eventually, I would have felt the pressure of an internal struggle going on. Losing a lost game was fine, but losing a won game was painful.
Painful because I knew that I lost it by myself, that it was totally my fault. My opponent played rubbish moves and gave me a win in my hands, but I played even worse and rejected the win to get a loss in exchange. It was the quintessence of being a loser.
I played fast and didn't make good use of my available time. Rey had a bit more time than me. He played much faster, but he slowed down a little bit as he saw that I was trying to consolidate my position and actually win that game. He needed to win that game or I would have won my first small

tournament of the hostel and he would have been the first one to lose it to me.

-Resign- I told him, trying to sound in complete control of my emotions. He needed to think that finishing him off for me would have been just a matter of time, that the win was inevitable. I exploited a real fact, an easy win, to make him believe that I could have achieved it just because the win was theoretically easy to get.

-Are you joking? I'm not going to resign, I can clearly see it's costing you a lot to finish me off- he said, calmly, while still focusing on the board as hard as he could.

He hit the weak spot. He understood I was struggling and complicating things by myself. My voice tone didn't trick him. I looked at my clock, just twenty seconds left. His clock had about one minute left. I had focused on trying to find check mate but eventually couldn't find it. Maybe, there just wasn't any real mate net, but at least I had cleaned up even more pieces away from him. I had now a huge advantage and he was just moving his king around the board. With few pawns left, I kept checking him with my major pieces and I saw him smiling. He kept escaping checks and just waited for me to run out of time. If that had happened, I would have lost the game even if I was one move away from check mate.

I wasn't going to win that game, but I decided that neither was him. I started collecting all his pieces while he kept moving his king right in the centre of the board. By the end, he only had his lonely king, but my clock had just got to zero.

We kept our eyes on the board after the end of the game. He laughed.

-I can't believe you didn't beat me- he said, amused.

-Shut up, you should have resigned long ago- I said, frustrated, which made him laugh even more.

We played again and this time I lost, which forced us to keep going.

-The one that wins three games is the champion of the hostel- Rey reminded.

-Yeah, whatever- I said, happy to keep playing more. Chess was highly addictive.

Eventually, Rey won all the games until he reached three wins and I was left at one win and a draw.
-If only I had won that game where you played complete rubbish, we wouldn't have had to go further- I said, all my disappointment came out for his amusement.
-Hey, do you see these two? Go talk to them- Rey pointed at the last table near the vending machines, half hour later.
I looked at my back and saw them.
I stood up right away and didn't waste a second to prove Rey that I was a potentially good wingman. I wouldn't have cared about their rejection at all in that case.
I approached their table.
-Hey, do you speak English?- my usual starting line. The reason why I asked it was that I always got a positive reply, which made girls want to reply more questions.
-Do you mind if I sit here?- I asked while taking a seat.
-Yeah sure- they replied, smiling.
-Americans? You kind of sound like you are- I asked.
-Oh, that's great, I love baseball- Rey showed up and sat next to me.
-Oh really? Well, we're not big fan of baseball, but that's cool- and they laughed.
-Me neither, I prefer football- I said, and they laughed even more. That was a good sign. There was nothing to laugh and yet they did.
-What are your names by the way?- I asked.
-I'm Hannah and she's my sister Olivia- the girl with the straight hair hugged her sister while she answered me.
-Are you girls going out? You know, we could show you around- Rey didn't waste a second.
-Oh well... it's a bit late now, don't you think?-
-No- Olivia interrupted her. The two looked at each other and communicated something. That was the moment to push.
-We'll just go for a walk and come back soon- I said. For some reason, Rey nodded his head yes.
-Actually, there is a bar I wanted to go to. It's called Pottails and it's in Soho- Olivia said.
-Oh ok, Soho is like ten minutes walk from here- I said.
-My app says twenty minutes- said Hannah.

-We know a shortcut- said Rey. I wondered if he was aware that her navigator would probably know what the shortest walk option was.
The two sisters didn't laugh this time, but simply looked at each other, until Hannah gave up.
-Ok, we're quickly going to grab our jackets from our rooms, shall we meet up at this table?- Olivia asked.
-Sure, we'll wait here-
Olivia looked at me again and smiled, then the two went downstairs.
Rey and I stood up and went back to our table, brought the chess board back to the reception, then went back into the common room and reached the same table.
-I think Olivia likes you, although I prefer Hannah-
-Good, so we both have our targets now- I said.
-I don't like Olivia- Rey put an expression on his face to remark his words.
The two sisters were looking at us by the door between the common room and the reception.
-Are you guys ok?- Olivia asked.
-Yeah... Oh, by the way, we've decided to go there by bicycle- I said.
-You're paying for that, aren't you?- Rey whispered in my ears.
We left the hostel and reached the bikes platform in front of Russell Square station.
-Let's take two bikes actually, you girls can sit and we'll ride you to Soho-
Obviously not because it was going to be fun or anything, but because otherwise I would have had to pay 8 pounds instead of 4.
Half hour later, we left the bikes at the platform in Carnaby Street and looked for the bar.
Few minutes walk between the streets of Soho, packed with people also because of the good weather, and we were in the bar. Olivia kept looking at me and smiled while we were going downstairs.
The place looked a little too fancy for me and Rey. He was wearing a shirt with red and black squares, blue jeans and

trainers, and I was wearing the same fake leather shabby jacket I used for every occasion.
When we approached the counter, Olivia already knew what to order.
-They can give you a tea pot full of vodka here, I saw it through the internet, we have a similar place back home in the US- she said.
We split the bill and moved towards the centre of the place. I noticed that the tables were moved to make space for a tiny dance floor. The music was not too loud, which was nice.
I started dancing with Olivia and Rey took Hannah with him. Olivia kept looking at me. Was it really worth trying? I suddenly felt nervous and got a faster heartbeat, just like anytime I was sober.
She kept smiling and getting closer and closer until she kissed me.
Smooth, a move I should have copied from her for future references. I didn't even realise that she was that close to me.
Rey looked somehow shy. I didn't see him making a move on Hannah, they were just dancing.
-Do you want another drink? I'm not sure I could drink more- Olivia said, then chuckled.
Definitely not, this place is expensive.
-We could go out for another ride, what do you think?- I suggested her.
-Yeah, why not- she went to grab her jacket from the table while her sister looked at her the whole time.
Hannah had a strange expression on her face.
Rey seemed careless, not looking for anything but just a good night out.
We decided to leave the place. The two sisters seemed to have enjoyed it after all.
-This place was alright. Also, we should play chess when we get back- Rey said.
Was he trying to stop me? He saw that I was doing well with Olivia and now he wanted me to go and play chess with him? Maybe yes, but I was very tempted to say yes anyway. Who said that something was going to happen anyway? I should have just stayed with him. I couldn't try and fail, I needed to

just give him the impression that girls were of secondary importance to me. In this way, no matter what had happened, I wouldn't have looked unsuccessful.
-I'll go get the board from reception- Rey said, a bit anxious as we got back to the common room.
Something must have happened between him and Hannah, I thought.
I joined the two sisters at the table in the common room.
-So you guys are going to play chess now?- Hannah asked me.
-Yeah, we really love it- I said.
-Come next to me- I told Olivia, who stood up and sat down on my left. Maybe, he was just shy that night. I saw Rey being a very confident man up to that moment, but that didn't mean he couldn't be shy for a night, or just insecure about her reaction, or maybe, he didn't even like her. Hard to be though, Hannah was really attractive.
Rey came back and sat in front of me. He saw my arm on Olivia's leg and just smiled, making no comments.
-You guys look good together- Hannah said, making Olivia laugh.
-Yeah thanks- I said, concentrating on the game. I knew I had chances to have sex, but I was mostly focusing on my chances to beat Rey at chess.
-I should check mate him soon- Rey said at some point, and he was right. My king had many pieces aiming at his direction.
-I've won though, see, my opponent wasn't careful enough about his king- I said while looking at Olivia.
I had no idea if it was going to work or not, but I could have started an attack at least.
I checked his king with my bishop, forcing him to make a move towards the centre.
-See? Now I can check him with my knight and force him to come even closer to my pieces- I explained to Olivia, who seemed to be doing her best to try to follow.
-And how are you forcing him to come closer to you?-
-I've just checked him. He can't leave his king there-
-Oh, I see, otherwise you can capture the king next move- Olivia observed.
Rey giggled.

-Well... no, you can't capture a king, but to be honest that's the reason why he can't leave his king there, so you got it-
-How do you win then?- Olivia seemed genuinely curious.
-See, you attack the opponent's king and if he has no squares to go to without getting taken next move, then that's when you win-
-So, it is about taking the king then-
-Well, your observation makes sense. The thing is that when a king has no squares to go to without getting taken, you just call it check mate, there's no need to continue playing-
-Oh, I see, but why can his king not go back?-
-His rook is attacking the rank behind my king- Rey said. He sounded annoyed for the explanation.
-Play- he told me. He had been waiting for my move and now he just wanted me to play.
I check mated him.
-That was fun- said Olivia, then got closer to me.
-How about you come to room 50 in a few minutes?- she whispered before I got the chance to accept Rey's offer to play again.

In the next days, I was able to say I had found a better routine. I was still not sleeping much, but I had made an adjustment.
I used to wake up at 5 am like each day and I was able to be at work by 6 am, I would finish my ten hours shift and rush back to the hostel so that I could go and take a nap, since staying awake didn't work.
Sometimes I would fall asleep on the sofa by the common room until the security guy picked on me.
-Hey, you can't sleep here- he would tell me. He always sounded harsh although I was able to spot kindness in his tone.
He was Arab, like most of the staff. Arab men always gave me the impression of being rude because of their accent, the way they generally spoke and their body language, but it was often just an impression.
I somehow still had it on the guy who kicked me out from Hyde Park hostel. I never managed to get my money back from the hostel website after my bookings got cancelled, and

now I couldn't look at another Arab man without spotting some physiological traits in common that would remind me of him, especially since they wore the same uniform. Even though receptionists at Russell Square seemed to be kinder, I still didn't want to attract the attention on me too often. I didn't want to become the guy that they had to pick all the time until getting rid of me would have become their best option to find some peace.

After the nap, I would go upstairs and see what was going on. Sometimes the hostel would be quite empty, no preys around and no one of the group was there. Then I would reconsider the idea of going back to sleep or just stay by the tables and wait for something to happen.

That evening, I woke up after a nap in room 10, then went upstairs to the common room. I was feeling well rested and in a very social mood, even more than usual.

I reached the common room and look towards my left. Rey and Adrian were sitting on the usual black sofa, apparently enjoying what seemed to be a cheerful evening with all the members of the group.

If the hostel in Hyde Park was smaller and you could have even ended up staying a whole night up without talking to anyone at all, the hostel in Russell Square was very different. There were way more people and the common room was almost three times as big, which forced me to readjust my strategies regarding the chase after girls. In fact, my smooth, decent and planned approach was having a hard time in the new hostel.

First of all, the presence of many people affected my chances negatively. Girls on their own were sitting at a table for a few minutes before somebody would sit there with them.

Secondly, those two were much faster than me at that.

-Hey, how are you?- a guy next to me was speaking. I was so lost in my thoughts that I didn't notice I was sitting in the middle of the main group of the hostel.

I looked around me and realised that Laurine, the attractive girl with the thick French accent was looking at me. Carlos, the Spanish guy I saw my first evening in that hostel was having a conversation with Mina, apparently about football.

The others were spread around the sofas, somebody just chatting, somebody slicing bread and making sandwiches for others, somebody pouring drinks into plastic cups.
The hostel seemed to have a stable group of people that, just like me, had decided to live there for a certain amount of time. I did want to be part of that group and I was already in a friendly, but still too polite relationship with some of them. I needed more though, and next to me there was a good chance.
-Hey, I'm ok and you?- I replied, getting rid of my book.
-Do you want to go out for a cigarette?- Andrei asked me.
-Oh, well, I don't smoke, but I'll follow you-
-Guys, wait a second, I'll follow you too- Laurine said.
We went outside and I found myself unable to start any sort of flirt with her not only because of the presence of someone else, but also because I was mostly caring about my social position in the hostel. I liked the people in there to the point that trying to be part of the same family was a priority.
-She's really hot- he told me when she went back inside.
-I agree-
-Come with me, round the corner, I want to smoke a joint, I hope you smoke those, at least- he didn't really put a question mark at the end of the sentence.
-Well, yeah, I guess I can make an exception when it comes to that stuff, I'll just have a few puffs- I said. A few puffs wouldn't have trashed me, I thought.
We entered the short alley that led to Queen Square and sat down.
-Do you know how many of these I smoke everyday?- he said, proud.
-No, how many?-
-I don't know, but many. It helps me cope with my work- he said, lighting it.
-What do you do?-
-I work in a pub in Soho, and you?- he asked me.
-A restaurant in Sloane Square, not too far from Victoria station-
-And how is the money?-
-It's rubbish. We work a lot and get the minimum wage, we just survive basically-

What I said was true, since we got paid the minimum wage, but I did try to make it look like I was very unhappy even though I wasn't. I wasn't just surviving. I couldn't really complain since working hard was natural to me and the money I made allowed me to travel and enjoy nights out in London without worrying too much.
-Oh, it's a shame, well, I'm making more than 2k per month at the pub-
-Oh, ok, you have to work a lot for that to happen- I said, trying to calculate how many hours I had to work per week to get that money.
-Yeah, I do work a lot, I mean, I'm always working, lots of double shifts, openings, closures...- he said, then passed me the joint.
-I make 10 pounds per hour. 10.50 per hour- he went on.
-Oh, I see, so definitely not the minimum wage-
-Oh, definitely not. You should quit your restaurant and come to work in my pub, we're cool people, the team is great and the pay is much better than in your place- he said.
-Oh, well, if that's how they pay you, I mean, your minimum wage is apparently almost 4 pounds higher per hour than ours- I said, passing him back the joint. I was already feeling less able to think, or to just make logical assumptions. He was getting paid 10.50 per hour. Was it actually 4 pounds more than me? How much was I making per hour? 7.25 per hour, as far as I knew.
Oh, that makes it 3 then, 3 pounds difference.
And 0.25 pence.
3.25... So why did I say 4 before?
-By the way, 3.25 less than you is what I make per hour- I said, slow.
I was high enough not to realise that he was still talking. I just wasn't listening.
-What did you say?- I asked him.
-Yeah, you heard me. In Italy I used to shag this woman. I used to work as a painter and I was doing some works at her place, when it all started, you know, clearly her husband wasn't able to make her happy, so I took his place, you know what I mean?-
I laughed, actually amused by that story.

-Wow, you must have been very lucky, I mean, I've never been in a situation like this, but what if the husband had come back anytime and saw you?-
-Oh, that actually happened- he said, then had a few puffs and looked back into my eyes.
-Really?- I asked him, trying my best not to sound sarcastic.
-He saw me, and recognised that I was just better than him, so he stayed in the room and watched me shagging his wife. He got to like it to the point that he kept inviting me to his place, sometimes we had dinner all together, you know-
-I see-
-Yeah!- he looked at me, as if raising his voice could have made his story more credible.
I suddenly felt very weak.
I made that mistake again. I smoked weed despite knowing how unable I was to bear it, and now I wasn't able to continue talking to him.
I didn't want to tell him that though. I was sure he would have understood, but I decided to resist, and maybe even try to tell him more about my past.
-Are you high? I can see that- he said, and laughed.
-Actually yes, are you?- I asked, hoping that he was feeling just the same so that we could have both go back to bed with a perfect excuse. No one was going to be the rude one.
-No, not at all, I'm used to this, I smoke so many of them each day, just like people smoke a pack of cigarettes-
-I'm holding a massive one, mate- a brilliant and unbeatable excuse had come to mind.
-Oh brother, go back inside, actually, let's go back inside together- he said.
-Yeah, I'll see you back in the common room- I told him.
-Yeah, see you later- he smiled and shook my hand.
I went back to my room downstairs right away.
Definitely a very different person to me, but friendly and polite, like everyone seemed to be in that hostel.

I woke up at 4 in the morning on my own, even though the alarm was set at 5.

Waking up without hearing the alarm meant only two possible things. Either I had woken up before the alarm rang, or I overslept.
Obviously, my first thought was the negative one. After few seconds of fear, much more overwhelming than it should have been, I would find my phone and press the button to light it up and show me the time. Except once, a few months before, I never overslept, making my work life cv impeccable, since I had never missed a day, not even calling in sick. That day was no exception, although I needed a few seconds to calm down after finding out that I woke up one hour before work.
Weed forced me to sleep, but I was feeling too energetic to fall asleep again, also because of the nap I had taken the previous afternoon.
I stood up, got dressed and went upstairs.
Rey was there, the only person in the whole common room.
-Hey, what are you doing still awake?- I asked him.
No reply.
I sat down in front of him and looked at him for a few seconds. He kept focusing on his laptop. Sometimes he could be so rude and would make me feel stupid, just ignoring me. Why couldn't he understand that I wanted to hang out full-time with him?
I stood up and decided to move to the sofa when he called me.
-Hey Dom, do you want to play chess?-
After the usual three games and negative outcome, few minutes were left before I had to leave to work. Me and Rey were now lying down on two sofas, in front of each other, looking into different directions, too lazy to do anything.
-How is work going these days, Rey?-
No reply again.
I stood up and decided to go to work already. A slower and safer cycle to work that I wished I could have everyday actually.
-We should go for a trip together, we are compatible- said Rey suddenly.
His voice hid some excitement, some real desire.

I was curious to know if he really meant it or if he was joking, but words left my mouth on their own.
-We should go to Sweden, there's a lot of blonde girls there- I proposed.
-Oh yeah, or maybe Amsterdam, what about Amsterdam?- he suggested back.
Both were places I had never been to before, although I really wanted to go to Sweden.
I remembered a Dutch man I once met in a pub in Woodstock Street during a football game we were watching. Just a normal, friendly conversation with the typical northern European man in a suit that spoke with a thick accent and a strong desire to tell you everything he knows about your country and your politicians.
-I was in Sweden last month, I'm married now but I'm telling you since you're young, there are many, many blonde girls there, you have to go to Sweden if you get the chance- he told me while he chewed his dinner.
I wondered if he knew that his words and voice would have remained inside my head since then.
-We can go to Amsterdam, there are cheap tickets- Rey brought me back to reality.
-No, Rey, look, Stockholm will actually be cheaper, see?- I showed him the screen of my phone, hoping to convince him.
-It's such a deal, besides, the dates are slightly different from the flight to Holland, and the dates of the flight to Stockholm are perfect for me since those days will be allowed by my managers- I lied.
-You can't go on these days?- Rey showed me the screen of his laptop.
-Well, it would be less comfortable for my managers so they might reject my request- I replied just to find out I couldn't really lie to him.
-Or maybe I could but it would be better for me to get these dates- I said, making sure that my words expressed my desire to go to Sweden without actually lying.
-Alright, let's book then- Rey agreed with Stockholm.

The trip was only one week away and my requested days off got accepted with no problems.

Getting to know that my trip with Rey was happening with no obstacles and that Lena had just handed her letter of resignation from work to the managers in the same day was great, great news.
-Look at you, all smiling tonight, who's this pretty boy?- said Marc, passing by.
-I saw that too- Daryl said loud from the coffee machine area.
I wasn't a toady person at all nor I cared about the approval of anyone on top of me in my work place, but my body reacted on its own. Everyone likes to feel appreciated after all.
Salvatore and Lena were sitting at the staff table. She showed some sadness, but also satisfaction on her face at the same time.
How could such nice and smart guy be in a relationship with such mean person who was clearly depressed? He was her saviour, the man who brought some joy into her life, the man she couldn't do without to survive.
Lena was a very traditional girl. Hard to get, she didn't wear make up nor I ever saw her with some more skin-exposing clothes. Instead, she would always wear a backpack and dark jeans.
She wasn't even attractive to be honest. Just annoying on lots of aspects.
I passed by their table.
-Hey, how are you?- Salvatore smiled at me.
-Good, very good- I gave him the biggest of smiles.
-Would you like some bread and butter?- I asked.
-No thanks, just bring me an espresso please, and hurry up- he bantered, then laughed.
His girl didn't smile at all, but actually looked at me with a face full of hate. Her eyes concentrated on mine. Her face became slightly red while her boyfriend didn't notice a thing.
I hope that shit staff risotto you are eating will somehow go down the wrong pipe. I know that liking or disliking people is something we have little control on and I don't blame it on you if you hated working with me, but one thing I would like to make clear with you. Disliking me was your problem and you weren't able to act superior to how your emotions

dictated, therefore you're a child. A child that made my life hard just because you felt like that, but you had no reason to. I should have reacted in many past occasions, but I never did because the price I would have had to pay was too high and you weren't worth it. Besides, I think there's at least one to five highly depressed people in every single workplace in London, the chances of meeting a person that is just like you are very high too, so I'd rather not react at all and let you go. These words I so longed to tell her echoed in my head only. My hands, connected to the vibe I was into, prepared Salvatore's coffee, put the cup on a small plate and the spoon on the side with a bit of extra noise.
-Is everything ok Dom?- Marc asked me, kindly.
-Are you trying to break the crockery? That's expensive, you know that?- he said, smiling.
-Sorry, I was just trying to do it fast- I said with a big fake smile on my face. I wanted Marc to be happy about me. He was by far the best manager we could have had.
I brought the coffee to the staff table and served Salvatore while I got ready to tell Lena what I thought about her. The same words that had been floating in my head for months.
I looked at her and smiled, just a smile.
I didn't tell her anything. For a moment I even thought of wishing her luck for the future, but I knew she wouldn't have replied to that.
I went back to work.

I kept wondering if Rey was looking forward to travelling with me just as I was.
Why did he ask me to travel with him if he seemed much more interested in spending time with the others of the group rather than me? Why did he say we were compatible if the only thing we did was playing chess every now and then? He barely talked to me.
I left my bike outside the hostel and slowly walked in. My shift ended earlier than usual that night. It was 10.30 pm and I was already back home, hoping not to find Rey in the common room.
The pleasant hubbub of the tourists, voices of people who were free from any negative thoughts was the perfect

welcoming sound. They might have had a few big or small problems back home, but not on holidays, especially because they were young.
Rey was sitting at the same table where I first met him, one of the central tables of the row by the other side of the common room.
Adrian, Mina and two girls were sitting there with him.
-Dom, Dom!- Rey waved his hand at me and shouted so loud that people from few other tables looked towards us.
-We're going to Sweden together, to get the blonde girls- Rey said, proud, with a smile ear to ear.
Everybody laughed.
-He won't stop saying it to everyone- Mina said. His beard looked very neat as usual when he stood up and shook my hand.
-We're going to have fun Dom, take a seat- he told me.
-Just finished work?- Mina asked as I sat down.
-Yeah- he noticed I was still wearing my waiter uniform underneath my broken jacket.
-So, why Sweden?- Adrian asked me and patted on my back.
-I've never been there so I thought it could be interesting, also I'm glad that Rey agreed on that-
-Liar!- Rey pointed at me and laughed.
-Join us for dinner?- Mina asked me.
They were already eating. A chopping board to support a big hob with almost no food left since all the rice had already been served. I saw one of the two girls was keen on taking the very last two spoons of rice, but stopped right when Mina asked me if I wanted some.
They clearly didn't have enough food for me since they weren't expecting me, but Mina's culture was speaking loud. I was pretty sure that he was the one that cooked and I knew that if I had said yes, he would have gone to the kitchen and just cooked some more rice for me, or maybe he would have just offered half of his plate.
-No thanks, I've already eaten- I said, with a tone that claimed no further invitation.
-Enjoy your dinner guys, I'll see you next time- I said. I felt like an intruder, even though three people at that table were

friends and the other two were basically the reason why I was there in the first place.
I headed to my room downstairs. I couldn't help smiling while I touched the handle of my door with my key card.

Rey was the kind of guy that didn't really show any passion in particular. He never engaged too passionately in a conversation, never wanted to go deep into details, never talked for too long and especially, never listened to what people said.
Sometimes I would approach him in the common room while he was playing chess on his laptop and asked him something, or maybe just said hi and he would give me no signal that he had heard me at all.
-It's ok, he does it all the time- Laurine smiled to me with a comprehensive expression on her face. She always sat by the corner of the black sofa, her brown wavy hair looked always shiny.
On top of it, Rey didn't seem to care too much about the rest of the group either.
As I noticed with the passage of time, the group wasn't perfectly united. We all shared something that bound us together, the fact that we were all there and were part of a family that we didn't really choose. The atmosphere was perfect and very friendly from the outside, but I suspected that it couldn't all be just perfect from the inside too.
I thought about this while I walked to the supermarket in front of the tube station and bumped into Adrian the following evening.
-Hey, where are you going?- he asked me.
-Supermarket, you?-
-I'll go with you- he said.
-How was last night?- I asked, not knowing what else to say.
-Good, it was alright, you?- he asked after having a puff of his cigarette.
-I just went to sleep actually. You need to thank Mina from me when you see him next, it was very kind of him to offer me food-
-I won't speak to him, I actually try to avoid him generally- he interrupted me, still looking straight in front of him.

-What do you mean?-
-I don't really like him, I mean, I've got nothing against him, but I just don't like him too much- he said.
-Why is that?-
He had another puff of his cigarette and seemed not to be keen on replying.
-Leave it, doesn't matter- I said.
He seemed not to have even heard me.
Mina was quite different from Adrian.
He liked football and was very sociable, but I didn't know if I could have classified him as one of the hunters of the hostel. He did start a lot of talks with girls, but his main quality was to get people together and just have a good time. He could unite people from three different tables in less than a minute and get all of us to move tables so to stick them together and have more space. Eventually, about twenty people who didn't know each other up to a minute before were now cast into an improvised big family dinner.
Food usually got replaced by drinking games by the end of the night, but I rarely saw Mina hitting on a girl, at least not in the obvious way. He was the fun guy just liked to chill.
Rey was loud and cheeky. He didn't seem to plan any chat at all. He would approach a girl anywhere, either by a table in the common room or even on the stairs. He would ask her where she was from, make comments about her nationality naming things or people that she certainly knew and most of the times just leave after making some compliments. Sometimes I saw girls pleased by the fact he had started talking to them and disappointed, or just very surprised by the fact he wouldn't carry on answering their question as they noticed him going to focus on another girl. Besides chess, he couldn't focus on anything else for more than a minute without getting bored of it.
I once sat at a table near the sofas when an attractive tall girl with brown hair and blue eyes sat in front of me. She looked so good that I couldn't say a word, and besides that, I was a planner type of guy, and it could have taken me up to five whole minutes before making a move.
-Dom, is the plug working over there?- Rey asked me in English from the table on the opposite row.

-Yeah, sure, come here- I said while he was already about to take a seat.
-Where are you from?- he asked the girl at my table whilst plugging his laptop.
-Holland- she replied, a bit surprised.
-You?- she now asked, then she slowly put her hands under her chin and started staring at him. Her eyes got suddenly bigger and a big smile appeared on her face. She seemed hypnotised by Rey.
He was the only one tall enough to make a move on her and hope to have a chance in that room and probably in the next square mile after all.
-Spain. What room are you in?- he asked, just like that.
-115, why? Are you in the same room?- she replied. She didn't seem bothered that he asked her that, but actually pleased. Was he going to get her? So easily? How could he get someone so attractive without any efforts?
-I wish- he said while he started a game of chess online.
-You wish- she said, still smiling and looking at him.
That was it, I just couldn't believe it. The difference between dreaming and getting was apparently just a matter of few words and a cheeky attitude. Why was I not the first to hit on her?
I felt jealous to the point of thinking about moving away from them.
Jealousy had taken control of my body, forcing it to stay there and see how the thing went. Key to my relief was Rey's failure. Any last-minute accident, any words a little bit too rude, anything that turned her off would have worked for me.
And then it happened for real. Rey had stopped talking to her and he was now focusing on his game.
I looked at her and noticed that she seemed to be waiting for something, like another question or any other jokes, but Rey just couldn't care less now. What happened? Why did he just stop?
-How is work lately?- I asked when the Dutch girl stood up with a serious expression on her face and left after being ignored.

-Not good at all. I'm actually broke, I need some money- he said, remote.
-How much do you need?-
-A lot- he said, now serious.
I didn't continue.
-I actually just need about 100 pounds to survive, I should have a business set for one of these days and it's a big one, I could make a lot of money out of it-
-I could give you 100 pounds if you want- I offered impulsively.
-Really?- he said, now changing expression on his face.
-That would be great, and I'll give you back as soon as the end of the week, I promise- he added.
-Alright, let me grab them from the cash machine then-
-Hey Dom!- he shouted after I stood up and made a move towards the reception.
-Yes?-
-I can't wait to go to Sweden with you-

The weekend arrived, and the two of us got to the airport exhausted, since Rey had insisted on spending the night awake and avoid the risk of failing to hear the alarm.
When we reached Stockholm's airport that early afternoon, I was negatively impressed with a seriously undercrowded view.
-This seems like a desert, I mean, where are all the people?- I said.
-It's the weekend, they're getting ready for the night- Rey replied. He often used optimistic replies to cut off any sort of superfluous conversation, although I had to say he wasn't looking any good at all.
-We're getting into town much quicker than it would take us in London- I noticed out loud, just to say something after an awkwardly silent half hour whilst we were in the bus on the way to the city centre. Anyway, Rey kept looking through the window with an absent expression on his face.
-Are you ok, Rey?-
He looked at me for a second or two, then spoke.
-I know I owe you money, I'll give you back today if this goes well, ok?- he replied, apparently pissed.

-It's fine Rey, easy- I said, pretending like I hadn't been thinking about that money at all up to that point and that I would have probably forgotten if he hadn't reminded me about it.
-So you're saying that you might meet someone for money here? Do you have like... contacts and customers everywhere in Europe or what?-
-A website with my profile on it- Rey said with a tone that claimed no reply without looking at me.
-I know it's private, but... can you tell me more?-
He looked at me and smiled. He then took his phone out of the pocket of his brown faux deer jacket and showed me the screen. A list of messages, some open and some not as I could spot from the little envelope symbols on the left. One message literally said "are you in Stockholm yet?", but that was all that I could see before he took his phone back and zipped it into his right pocket.
-What site was it?- I couldn't see it since he kept his thumb on the upper side of the screen, where the web address would usually appear.
-I can't tell you that or you'll look for me and it's about privacy. I select people very carefully before deciding if they can get to know this or not- he said.
-You're right- I agreed, but my crave to find out was becoming almost painful now.
-Do you know where to go now?- Rey asked me when we got to the Cityterminalen, the central station.
-15 minutes walk apparently- I said, looking at the phone navigator.
-Hmm- Rey snorted.
-Are you tired by the any chance? I might take a nap before going out tonight- I suggested, slightly scared that he would find it boring or just unexpected.
-Yeah, definitely, a nap is a good idea- Rey agreed with me, luckily.
There was literally no one around us and it was a Friday afternoon in the city centre. What was going on?
We kept walking straight, following the instruction of the navigator.
Rey had been silent for a bit when I looked at him.

Was he worried? Too tired? Were my thoughts too emotional? Did he regret travelling with me?
-Come on Rey, it's all going to be fine, we're going to have fun- I said impulsively.
-Why are you speaking nonsense?- he came all of a sudden, annoyed.
A second before he spoke, I saw him putting something into his left pocket, the one further away from my sight.
-Are we close to it?- Rey said, his voice seemed calmer now.
-It's here, we have to turn into this Luntmakargatan street-
We stopped in front of a small flesh-coloured building with a lot of small windows. Silence, all around us, and it was 5 pm.
-How much better does it look here compared to our hostel?- I said after the two of us were checked in, making Rey finally smile, although for only a second.
Our room was empty. Just the two of us would have been sleeping there that night maybe.
-Dom, listen, you take your nap and I'll be back here soon, ok?- Rey told me all of a sudden.
I turned around and looked at him as he was leaving the room in a rush.
-Wait, what?-
He stopped.
-I'll be back here in less than two hours- he said, looked into my eyes for a few seconds, then left.
I lay down. The bed sheet was softer than the one back home, I thought.

-Dom, Dom, wake up!- Rey shook my body gently, but enough to wake me up.
A few seconds of confusion, then I got up, still silent.
-It's late, it's like 9.30 pm-
-Oh, really? We have to rush then, we're still in time to go to a club- I said.
-Here is your money by the way- he said, then put 1200 Swedish krona under my pillow.
-I think that's what it was that I owed you, so now we're cool- he said. He looked much more relaxed now.
-Rey, did you fuck someone?-
-Yes, for 2000 krona-

If what he gave me was 100 pounds, then what he made was something slightly less than 200. Who paid that money for sex?
-Don't get me wrong Rey but... I mean, you're a very handsome man...-
-Rich people- he interrupted me.
-Yes, I get that, they're obviously rich, but can't they find anything cheaper than you? I'm sure there is...-
-Let's go downstairs and play chess- he suggested, cutting it off.
-Just a quick game, but then we shower and leave, ok?-
-Yeah sure- he said, although he didn't sound to mean it.
We found the common room and the kitchen in the basement of the hostel, parqueted floor everywhere, the two main colours being white and wooden brown made it look very cosy, and I was expecting it from Sweden.
-Dom, I'm too tired, do you mind staying here for the night?- Rey suggested, pretending to have just come up with that idea.
Something was off and I needed to find out what was going on with him. I saw him having a look at some papers he had in his pocket too many times, but he was always able to keep their content hidden. I also noticed that every time he looked at them, his mood experienced sharp changes.
-Can you show me your papers? What are they?- I asked.
-Nothing, let's play- he said.
After our usual best out of three games gave me the umpteenth negative outcome, I decided to agree on not going out. I was very tired too. I had slept no more than three hours in the last thirty-six ones and I didn't want to push him too much since he was probably even more tired. He didn't really have a nap that evening.

The next day we woke up in the early afternoon.
-Oh man, we messed up the holiday, I'm so sorry, I was the one supposed to wake you up, but I didn't hear the alarm- I was mumbling when we were going down the stairs.
-It's ok Dom, no worries-

I did promise Rey to wake him up at 10 am since his phone was off and we didn't have a suitable charger for Swedish plugs yet, but he didn't seem to care much anyway.
-Dom- Rey suddenly stopped right in front of the main entrance of the hostel.
-I need to sleep a little bit more- he said, then looked at me as if he was in pain.
-Oh, I see... are you sure you're ok?-
-Yeah, I am, I just need a nap. I promise we will go out tonight- he said, then just waited for me to say yes. His eyes showed me that there was no way to convince him otherwise.
-It's ok, I'll go have a look around, talk to you later- I said and left. He seemed very depressed when he turned his back to me.
Stockholm didn't seem to have anything more unique than any other places I had been to before. A typical northern European city with very old streets and buildings. The major streets felt like Paris, but with far less people and cars, whereas the internal streets looked like the ones in Barcelona, but with far less sunshine and litter.
It felt quiet, safe and clean, although not a place I could have lived in for more than a couple of months before getting depressed.
-Dom, where are you? I woke up, let's go out- Rey just texted me.
-I'm already out, do you want to meet me by the river?- I started texting him where exactly he could have found me since I had decided to take a break after a long walk when I saw he was texting too.
-No, come here. We'll get ready to go out together- he replied.
-Why would I come back? I'm already showered and everything-
-Cool, then come here so we can leave together- he texted back, as if he was the one that was trying to show the other a logical fallacy in his request.
By the time I reached the hostel though, I found out he wasn't ready at all.
-Well, don't you think you could have got ready by the time I came here?-

-Let's go to a bar and play chess there, what do you think?-
he ignored that.
The underground in Stockholm looked incredible.
It all looked wider and cleaner than London tube, from the halls to the trains. The ceiling of our stop was painted with mostly blue colour, which made me feel like being in a massive igloo with a view on the dark sky.
When we got to our destination, I saw that there were definitely more people than the total I had seen up to that moment, but it was still not to be compared to a London night out.
We looked around for a minute. A block of buildings with many small bars and clubs on the ground floor, some famous fast-food chains and small street food shops were lined up in front of us. They were all quite busy, but with no queues outside, no shouting, fighting nor drinking in the streets.
London was a very distant reality.
That night, Rey and I initially ended up in a bar for metal music lovers, then left and got to a club after picking up my Tinder date, a very pretty, Polish girl named Olga. Eventually though, when we figured that the club was too posh and that Olga was too shy, we decided to call it a night and walked home.
I wasn't sure that our weekend away made any sense since we mostly slept and visited nothing, but I was glad I got to spend time with Rey.

By the end of September, my relationship with Ilaria and Ciro had become so good that we would open up to each other more and more often, or at least from my side. Every word they said to me seemed to be orientated to my improvement at work, even though I was just hopeless as a waiter.
What allowed me to be able to take care of my section was simply the fact that I ignored the standard of the restaurant in general.
Anytime my managers were not looking at me was a good time to skip some unnecessary steps to serving the customers. I would often bring napkins on my hands rather than on a tray, cutlery on a plate with no folded napkin on it at all and I would skip asking customers if they were enjoying

their food or not with pleasure. They were eating food they personally picked, cooked by trained chefs after all.
I used this mental mechanism to feel better about myself sometimes. The truth was that I wasn't good enough to follow all the standards without going really bad on the timings so that my only way to go to work everyday and feel like a valid member of the team was to accomplish all of my duties without having to get help from others. If the priorities of the restaurant were the money and the positive reviews of the customers alongside the productivity of those who worked there, my priority was to finish my job in time to go home and get some rest.

I didn't usually realise when specific times I was living were good before they were gone, but those ones were so good that I would even realise they were. Right then, I could feel the disappointment for its end before it all ended.
Me and Rey were now back at the hostel, closer than ever before. Mina and Adrian noticed it and congratulated with me about it. They were both impressed by the fact that Rey was hanging out with someone, basically.
-He was always sitting on the sofa, just waiting for girls to pass by or sticking to his laptop but now... I don't know, with you he's different... what have you done to him?- Mina commented to me once.
Adrian also told me he had similar thoughts about it, and I couldn't help feeling pleased.
In the next days, Rey and I would hang out every time we had a chance to, although I was working a lot, which reduced the amount of leisure time available.
More often than not, I would come back home too tired to actually wait for Rey to come and meet me. If he wasn't by the usual sofa, waiting for him for more than five minutes without doing anything to keep me awake meant that I was going to easily fall asleep on the sofa.
Mina and Adrian were always kind to me and nudged me awake anytime I had my head on the table.

On one of my days off, Rey introduced me to Arlena, a girl from Nicaragua he had met in his room. She shook my hand

and smiled to me, but I found myself not being able to smile back immediately.
She looked very south American, slightly shorter than me and a bit chubby, as I noticed when she sat down in front of me and took off her jacket.
-I would love a game of chess- she said, pretty excited about it.
-Yeah sure- I said, suddenly hypnotised by her buxom silhouette. Her coat made her look much thicker than she really was. Her body wasn't very skinny, but just full-figured. She probably realised I was staring at the shape of her breast, well visible because of her tight black jumper and said nothing about it. Rey was chuckling though, he had noticed that.
-We should go out tonight, Arlena wants to dance- Rey said. I was definitely not in the mood, so I preferred not to answer.
-Where are you from Arlena?- I asked.
-I'm from Madrid- she said.
-And where are you from?- I asked to a red-haired girl on the table next to ours.
-Me?- she almost jumped out of surprise.
-I'm from France- she continued, a very shy voice while she blushed. She looked very attractive, with straight, long, dark red hair and a very pale skin colour. She was wearing black leather trousers and a probably fake fur, making her look like a fancy girl.
-Do you want to join us?-
-Yeah, join us- Arlena looked at her and gave her a big smile. She stood up nervously and slowly walked to our table with a cyder in her hand.
-Oh well, I don't know- she initially muttered, but then got convinced by Arlena, who loudly stated she had to be one of us.
-Alright, we'll wait for you here then- said Rey, looking happy whilst the girls went to their rooms to get ready.
-Dom, tonight is going to be great- he told me, overexcited, whilst I was still trying to figure out what my best move over the board could have been.

-And oh, by the way, I already did my job with Arlena this afternoon, I brought a mattress from my room to the laundry room- Rey continued then.
I totally didn't expect that. I felt suddenly jealous as it happens anytime I knew of someone getting laid with a random girl, although it also depended on her look.
-We need to buy alcohol, our key to success tonight- Rey added, getting up.
-Look at you, standing now, are you even going to go to the supermarket and buy stuff by yourself?- I mocked him. He was so lazy I once heard him asking a young girl who was passing by to go and buy stuff for him from the supermarket in exchange of one pound commission. Besides the shock in hearing that from Mina and Adrian sitting at his table and me having food on the table next to him, we found out that the girl didn't speak English good enough to understand or to reply. When she kindly asked Rey to repeat what he said, Mina recognised her French accent and explained to her that what that guy said didn't matter in their language.
-No, I'm giving you money, you can go buy vodka and I'll wait for you here- he said.
-I'm not doing it-
-You won't have to pay for it, I'm paying the full price-
-Alright, then wait for me here- I caught my chance.
I found the three of them and some other people gathered outside the entrance of the hostel.
In the group there were also two German girls, one with big glasses and very long, dark curly hair and one chubby one with blonde hair and a very German face.
-I'm slightly tipsy, if I do or say anything that you may not like, I want you to tell me- I told Alice, the French one, as we were on our way to Camden.
-It's ok, I don't think you're dangerous- she said with a smile, making me wonder how not dangerous my face truly looked like.
-You guys want to smoke weed?- a black guy showed up and asked us as we reached Inverness Street, right in front of Camden Town station.
-No mate, thank you- I said.

-Alright guys, let's go into this bar here- I pointed at the first place with music right in front of me.
-What's in your pocket?- I asked Rey, careless of who was around us for a moment.
-Nothing- he replied quickly while putting some small papers back in his pocket.
-Ok guys, let's go in, I want to dance!- Arlena was literally dancing in the streets now, unlike the two German girls, who appeared actually quite reserved. In that moment, I realised that I hadn't ask their names yet.
-Dom?- Alice whispered in my ears.
-Yes?-
-I want to smoke some weed, do you mind getting some for me? I can pay for that- Alice was holding a 20 pounds note in her right hand and seemed very keen on her plan.
-Oh yeah, sure- I said, definitely keen on helping her on that, but not on smoking weed. It would have ruined my night and I would have had to go home and sleep, I was sure of that.
I told the others that Alice and I were going to be away for few minutes, and then I led her round the nearest corner.
-Here- I said to her, trying to get her to be as far as possible from the eyes of the passers-by from crowded Camden High Street.
We sat on a step and I started rolling a joint, doing something I didn't like for a good cause though.
-So, do you really live in the hostel?-
-Yeah, it's a cool place, do you like it?- I said while I finished it off.
-Well yeah, I like it of course, but there's no way I could sacrifice my privacy to that point, I need my space- she said, as if I wasn't able to understand that.
-Yes, well, that's a downside of it, but the thing is, that's the only downside of it- I said, while I lit the joint.
-Here you go, it's weed from the streets, it doesn't taste any good- I said, passing her the joint.
-Yes it does, I like it actually- she said, glad, and started smoking as if she was in a competition.
-You're smoking so fast, are you even enjoying it?- I asked.
-Oh, I'm sorry, there you go- she tried to give it back to me.

-I didn't mean that, I was just wondering why you're smoking it so fast, I don't really want it to be honest-
-Don't you? Are you kidding? I love weed, in France I smoke everyday- she said, sounding nostalgic.
She was in France yesterday, how hard was it not to smoke for one day?
-Damn, I've almost burnt my lips- I said, when I tried to light it and the flame almost reached my face.
-Oh, that would be too bad for me then- she said.
My legs petrified as my brain processed that. I looked at her just to double check she was really that hot just to find out she was staring back at me.
-Dom? Are you coming in or what? Hurry up man- Rey sent me a few texts before I actually felt my phone vibrating.
-What took you so long?- Rey asked me when we were in the bar. A relatively small place, but with a lot of people, and the music wasn't too bad. Popular hits with some sort of reggae time signature, a strange mix, but not unpleasant.
-Are you going to tell me what's upsetting you? You keep changing your mood from happy to sad in a matter of minutes- I asked him.
-Nothing, I just don't have much money now- he said.
-And? Wait, why did you pay for the vodka and the other drinks?- I asked him.
-You're not being very friendly now- he said.
I realised that the girls were all dancing, Arlena and the curly German girl were very close to each other. Was I going to allow that to happen? No, Arlena had to choose me over a girl, I had to at least try.
I hadn't flirted at all with her, nor I cared to pay any sort of attention since I was just focusing on Alice the whole time, but Rey told me Arlena was easy and I could have achieved something with her, maybe without letting Alice know, then focus on her the next day. As far as I knew, Arlena was up for it that night and Alice was going to be much harder to get.
I got close to Arlena's ear.
-I like your body a lot- I came up with those words for some reason.
-Yeah ok- she said, then pushed me away with her arm and kept dancing.

I wondered if Rey was looking at me while I hit on her and I hoped he wasn't laughing about such quick rejection.
I found him sitting on the sofa, his usual place.
-Do you want to go home? This place sucks- I suggested him.
-Yeah, let's go- he pleased my wish straight away.

October 2015

In the first week of October, Claudio called me to tell me he was coming to live in the hostel for a while since Marco decided not to renew his deal.
-Wait, why? Didn't you live there for like four years or something?- I asked him, surprised.
-Yes, but I went on holiday for two weeks and when I came back, he told me that my room was taken- he replied with an anxious voice.
-Wow... Listen, come to the hostel just for a few weeks and meanwhile I'll help you find a new place to stay- I lied. I was just going to wait for him to enjoy the hostel for a few nights until he would have decided to stay permanently.
Regarding Rey, he wasn't the same anymore after the night out in Camden.
-What happened to him?- I once asked Laurine when I saw him in the kitchen with his arms crossed and a very depressed look on his face.
-I don't know, nobody knows, and to be honest, we were all expecting you to give us some news- she told me.
I filled a small hob with water and was turning the stove on when he finally spoke.
-Dom?- he asked, timidly.
I looked at him to show him I was listening, but I still didn't say a word.
-I'm leaving the hostel. I may not come back- he said, sounding truly sad.
-Rey, what happened?- I asked him as he was leaving the kitchen. The unexpected news was about to hit me, but I couldn't really believe it yet.
-Things aren't good, I need money- he said and then moved towards the sofas area.

-Is that it? Is it the only problem?- I shouted from the kitchen, then waited a few seconds, hoping that he will come back, accept money from me, as much as he wanted to, then just chill and pay me back in the future. Who cared about it anyway?
-Rey!- few people looked at me when I left the kitchen and shouted his name.
The water had just started boiling when I realised I wasn't hungry anymore.
-Hey Domenico- a sweet female voice called my name behind me right when I was putting the hob back into the cupboard.
-Hey Arlena-
-Have you seen Rey?- she asked me.
-Yeah, he just left- I told her, not willing to continue that conversation at all.
-Are you ok Domenico?- her voice sounded so sweet that I couldn't help replying.
-Not really, I mean, Rey told me he's leaving the hostel, and he was acting weird lately-
-Yes, I know, he's a bit depressed, but you are his best friend, so I thought you might have the power to cheer him up- she said.
-Did he tell you that?- I asked her, trying to sound amused instead of flattered.
-Yes, he always talks about you, literally all the time and to everyone- she said.
-Then why is he leaving? He says he needs money, fine, I can give him some- I sounded desperate now.
-Well, don't give him money, I already gave him some myself, but he hasn't given it back to me yet- she said.
-I gave him money once and he gave it back to me sooner than I thought he would do- I said as if it could change anything.
She shrugged her shoulders, then smiled and left.
I saw him again very few times around, but he was just as moody as in the last weeks. I tried texting him, but he ignored all of my messages.

Claudio checked in into the hostel later that week, and after just a couple of days, things started going the way I planned.

-When are you going to start looking for a place?- I asked him casually during a chess game we were playing.
-Mm... I don't really mind staying here a little longer to be honest...- he replied slowly while he thought about his move. I knew it was going to happen.
-Hello, can I have a game with you?- Rey appeared suddenly and sat down next to me, facing Claudio.
-You're joking right?- I asked him, serious.
-What?- he asked without looking at me.
-Listen, we're playing a rematch after this, and probably a few others afterwards- I said, challenging him.
Rey stayed there for a minute, looking very annoyed at my words, then he stood up and left.
-Who was he?- Claudio asked me.
-Rey, the guy I mentioned to you back when we were living together, the Spanish guy-
-A bit weird, wasn't he?- he noticed.
Rey came back and sat next to me again.
-Can you give me 100 pounds? I'll give it all back to you as soon as possible- he said quick.
-If you tell me what's going on then yes- I replied.
-I'm moving to Arlena's new place and staying there will save me some money- he said.
-Right- I thought about it for a minute, then I decided to give him the money and waited for his reaction.
-Thanks- he said, and left again.
Rey left the hostel with Arlena the next day, but he promised to keep in touch.

Claudio worked night shifts for McDonalds in King's Cross area, and seeing him regularly was becoming much harder than during his previous days at the hostel when he was still on paid holidays.
One night of mid-October, Claudio was off and texted me to go meet him at the hostel while I was out with my bicycle.
I found him sitting at one of the tables by the giant mirror.
-Hey, I finally see you again- I greeted him dropping my jacket on the bench next to a girl who was sitting at the same table.

-Oh, hi Clelia, I didn't realise you were here- Claudio had just noticed her.
-Hi Claudio- she replied.
-Oh, I didn't realise you were Italian- I said, looking at her. She had long brown wavy hair with light tips. Her look was casual, not at all fancy.
-It's ok, my name is Clelia, and yours?- she said all in one breath, making Claudio laugh.
-Domenico-
-Do you live here or are you on vacation?- she asked me.
-I live here, I work in a restaurant- I replied, trying to focus on my game with Claudio, still unbeaten by me.
I looked at her with the tail of my eyes and saw that she was looking at me with a sweet expression on her face. She looked weird, somehow just polite, or maybe even charmed? Whatever, the smell of tobacco from her was very unattractive.
-What about you?- I had to ask, just to be polite.
-I need to find a job as soon as possible before I run out of money- she spoke very fast again, taking no moment to breathe.
-Oh I see, well, I could ask my managers if they're interested, we might probably need someone, I mean, we always do- I said.
-Oh, that would be amazing!- she sounded very excited. She looked more relaxed after that bit of our chat.

I realised I was really looking forward to helping that girl while I was cycling to work the next morning. She wasn't my type at all, but she looked fun and confident and something inside of me wanted to reward her for that.
I texted her right at the beginning of my shift after Matteusz confirmed to me that we were desperate for more staff.
-Hi, can you come to Sloane Square? You can have a trial shift today. Just take a black t-shirt, trousers and shoes with you-
-How is she by the way? Is she any good? Any experience?- Matteusz just remembered to ask me.
-Yeah, she's good- I lied before he could change his mind, although I suspected he wouldn't have cared much anyway

when I noticed he went back at flirting with the two Polish waitresses right in the middle of the floor.
-So who's this girl?- Alice asked me. Of course, Alice wanted to know.
-No one, just a girl I met at the hostel, she's looking for a job so I thought I could help her- I said, not sure she would buy it, but I was being honest.
Clelia showed up a couple of hours later, introduced herself to Matteusz just like she did with me the previous night and started her trial shift as a runner.
In less than half an hour, everybody gave me positive feedback about her. They all liked how confidently she spoke and especially, how she acted.
By the end of her four hours shift, she forcefully took my place on the drop off a few times, denied doing it when I asked her about that, learnt everyone's names in the kitchen, told a few jokes and showed no sign of shyness or submission to the managers.
If they hire her, it won't take long before she becomes the new head runner, I thought. Her skinny legs and her small waist lied about her strength.
-Didn't you say you were a waiter last night?- she asked me.
-Yes, I am- I told her, -But the thing is that we're experiencing staff shortage lately, so they put me here since I'm still the best and most experienced runner- I explained her, honest.
-Or maybe you're just full of shit- she snickered, making few people around us laugh.
-You're kidding, right?- I asked her, appreciating the banter though.
-Nah, I'm kidding, I know you're not lying, maybe they put you back here because you're not good enough, that would make more sense- she said.
Alice liked her immediately, and so did many others.
-This girl is cool, eh? I mean she's fun to work with, I guess?- Matteusz asked me the next day.
-Yeah, I think so- I replied while I prepared two glasses of red for an old couple in my section.

-Alright man, I just texted her to tell her she's hired, so now you can be happy and put a wider smile on that face- he said, then patted me on my back.
-Good- I replied, fairly pleased. She was fun, and we needed less drama in that place after all.
Clelia texted me after leaving the restaurant.
-Thanks for saving my life. If it wasn't for you, I'd be still crying out of anxiety and fear right now- a bit dramatic, but pleasant to read.

Not getting to see Rey around anymore was hard. Claudio's shifts forced us to see each other once a week, Adrian worked very long shifts and came home too tired to think of going out. He would rather just hang out by the sofas sometimes, but not look for anything more than just a glass of wine before sleep. Besides that, me and him weren't really as close as I was with Rey. Adrian was more adult, whilst Rey was much more extrovert and keen on unexpected plans and impulsive choices. Rey didn't care about working at all, especially if compared to Mina, which I could also rarely meet because he worked on very early shifts. He was always the first one to get up and call it a night before heading to his room, followed by the group's loud disappointment.
Carlos was a ghost too. He worked for Pret in front of Russell Square station and came home always after midnight, knackered just like everyone else.
Just like that it happened, that from a perfect September, the hostel gradually lost some degrees of fun. The departure of some and the intensification of work shifts of some others, forced most of us to prioritise the progress of our careers, whilst abandoning the previous priority, chilling and enjoying each other's company. We were there temporarily, we all were, except for me.
I was there right for that reason. I thought we could all have worked on our careers whilst also taking care of our social life. If I could, why couldn't the others too? The only answer to this question was that, no matter how hard they tried, they were just too tired. In my case in fact, I was very tired after work too, but social life was to me so important, that I

even sacrificed precious hours of sleep just to be in the common room with people.
In fact, when Mina proposed me to go watch a football game on the following Wednesday, I felt like that was going to be the best thing happening to me for the whole of October.

Something that kept me entertained though, was seeing Clelia at work.
She had a few arguments with people both from the runners area and the kitchen, ending up with her making rude jokes about them and just laughing, then telling them off and leaving everybody shocked.
-Fucking retard- she blurted out while sitting at table 50 in front of me at the end of my shift.
-Who are you talking about?-
-Everyone. We need a revolution in this place and I'll tell you who we need to get rid of to make this place work- she said.
-This risotto sucks- she added after tasting a bit of her food.
-Well, it's food for stuff so they don't really care...-
-We work for them, meaning that we should get better food!- she said now, louder.
I didn't know how to react. In my first weeks in the restaurant, I acted always submissive, or if not submissive, at least I made sure I had a pleasing attitude, but that was part of my insecurity mixed with my hard working ideals anyway. I thought it was great that someone could gain confidence and make claims showing teeth on her first days at work already, but I thought that maybe many people wouldn't have liked it for that and that it might have compromised her job even.
-Clelia, can you calm down?- Matteusz asked her.
-She's right though, the area is a disaster today- Marc noticed while he carried a tray of glasses away. Clelia kept loudly chewing her risotto.
-Domenico, can you make me a coffee, please?- she then asked me.
-Sure- I said, trying to figure out what kind of person was sitting in front of me. She was skilled and learned fast, not to mention her bossy manners.
Well, do I care about it? I'm a waiter after all, I thought while I asked Ilaria to make a coffee. I wasn't the best at it.

Clelia was becoming popular in the hostel as well. I saw her smoking a cigarette with Adrian when I came back home late after a closure shift and a few people inside the hostel also told me they had met her and that talking to her was sometimes exhausting. She had way too much energy and always something to comment about.

When she added me to her friends on Facebook, I noticed that me and her already had a few contacts from the hostel in common. Could it be that she was looking for alternative options? Maybe looking for another job?

That was my idea when I moved to London after all, to take any job that would have given me some stability while I looked for another one at the same time, then quit my unwanted job for the one I wanted.

That was me though, and my pace was much slower than hers. I planned to work in Sloane Square for no more than a couple of months, but I had been there for over a year already. It took me eight months to become head runner and two more to become a waiter, while it took her about a week to become respected by most, to get better staff food, to learn all the places of our tools in the restaurant and even to make some claims about her preferred shifts. Never would I ever have spoken and acted like that at the beginning of my work for any company, although she was, as many around us noticed, very similar to me, or at least to my current me, the only difference being how long we bore uncomfortable and unacceptable situations at work before changing our attitudes from being submissive to being bossy.

Actually, I struggle to remember a single moment where she acted agreeable, I thought while I was parking my bike in front of the hostel.

About a week after I had met her, Clelia told me she was looking for a place to move into. Unlike Claudio, she had no intention of staying in the hostel any longer.

-Oh my God, I need my space! How can you live here? I mean, one year? Seriously? I can't wait to have my own room and just lie down in bed...- she said with dreamy eyes looking at the ceiling once.

One night, I took a seat at the table near the tv and I started texting with Rey. I had suggested him to meet up for a night out, but he still hadn't replied.
He wasn't ignoring me though. Every now and then he would remind me that he hadn't forgotten about the money he owed me and that as soon as he got some new job done, he would have paid me back and all would have gone "back to normal", as he added at the end of every message.
The sound coming from the television and the voices of an Asian couple on the table next to mine were very relaxing. It was then that Clelia spotted me from the sofa, headed towards me and sat at my table without asking.
-Are you hungry?- she asked me. -I've got some more in the kitchen-
-What is it?- I asked, trying to look inside the bowl where she was eating from.
-It's all vegetarian, in case it's not ok for you-
-Well, I'm actually vegetarian so that will do- I didn't mind some food to be fair.
-Fine, then wait here- she ran to the kitchen and came back with another bowl for me.
She looked at me for a second and then looked away, simpering, then looked at me again. She was acting as if she was happy, or even excited to be there with me.
-It's all very good Clelia, this is such relief compared to the food of the restaurant- I said while standing up trying to take the plates to the kitchen.
-I'm glad you liked it- she said, then quickly stood up and blocked my arm.
-I'm taking this stuff to the kitchen- she said, firmly.
-You cooked it so I should probably...-
-No- she looked at me, serious, then she smiled when she saw I was confused. I didn't know how serious she was being. -You found me a job, so I owe you- she said, her voice much softer now.
-You owe me nothing, I'm glad to help- and she let me go.
I went out and rolled myself a joint. How did I end up smoking weed again? I turned the corner from Guilford Street, entered Herbrand Street and sat down on my usual step into the small alley before Bernard street.

Michele was back in Italy, Andrea had found his own place in Forest Gate, and Rey was so broke he had to crash at Arlena's.
It was weird. I decided to live in hostels so that I would never have to be alone, but I was feeling very alone.

By the end of the week, Clelia had to leave our fully booked hostel just to move to another one in Earl's court as she still hadn't found a room to move into.
She would often send me short and confusing messages, sometimes very sweet, sometimes very rude.
-Hey, I may move into this new place soon, so thanks again for being so kind to me, but I'm glad I'm leaving the hostel, or I'll end up becoming like you- she texted me while I was high one night and -I'm running now and I can't believe I'm saying this, but I could move into a room with you if you like!- I received when I was preparing coffees on a quiet Sunday evening shift.
I couldn't deal with such an emotional attitude. It was all wasted energy for me, so I would usually just reply with -It's cool, I'm glad to help- or -I'm not moving into a room with you nor with anybody else, but thanks for the offer-
I couldn't deny I started to fancy her though. It probably wouldn't have happened if it wasn't for her personality though. Her mood swings, her messages at night, the way she shouted back at anyone who challenged her at work made of her an entertaining subject.
I didn't find her dumb, and I knew by a few random conversations we had at the staff table that we were connected on some aspects such as cinema and music.
-Why are you staring at me? Wanna fight?- she once asked me at the end of our closing shift.
I didn't reply. I was staring at her nose, then at her dark eyes and her lips. Nothing of her was particularly attractive for me, but I still felt weird.
I started missing her at the hostel, thinking about her and checking the rotas on my phone just to see when we were scheduled to work together next, feeling a hit of excitement whenever I found out that we were either opening or closing together, which meant more time to take it easy during the

shifts to just talk and listen to her thick Sicilian accent bantering with me.
People noticed this and started gossiping.

-You've got to hit on her before somebody else does. Remember, she's fresh meat and there's lots of horny men in here- Alice told me once.
She is always dramatic, but this time she might be right. Why do I feel anxious about it though? I don't even fancy her. Or do I?
-What the hell is wrong with you right now?- Clelia asked when she passed through the runners area and saw me pensive. I didn't usually reply because I knew it bothered her and it was part of our bantering.
-You look cute today- she said touching my arm gently. I looked at her once again and tried to solve my internal debate. Why did I like her even though I wasn't attracted to her?
It was by the end of that shift that I realised my eyes were lying to me. Too tired and stressed because of the recurring double shifts I was working, I didn't pay enough attention to notice that she was actually very pretty. My taste was wrong at first, but now it started seeing right. That had to be the only answer to my question.

Alice's words echoed in my head a few times each day for the following days. Was I going to let somebody else get her instead of me? After I was the one that met her, got her a job and introduced her to everyone in there?
No, I couldn't let this happen. Maybe I didn't really like her too much, but I was no Santa. I found her first, and I was going to make a move on her before any others could. If she were to reject me, that would have been just fine, but at least I would have tried and failed rather than waited and missed out.
My problem was though, that I didn't want to invest the amount of time and attention Italian girls usually required for something to start.
As a consequence, after much thinking, I concluded that I wasn't going to act on it since I wasn't really attracted to her

after all, although I couldn't deny that it was hard not to think about her when she kept sending me messages, most of them rude enough to always put a smile on my face and get me to reply.

Clelia kept improving at work as far as I could see, but I was slowly getting fed up with her sudden mood swings. I started thinking that her apparent confidence and bossy manners might have been just a way to seek attention rather than a work-style ideal.
Everything of her attracted me, but the more I tried to keep a distance from her, the nicer she acted. The more I wanted to help her when she asked for help, the more she rudely rejected it. The more I tried to avoid answering her texts, the lovelier were the words she wrote until the point I couldn't help feeling something and typing a reply. In a matter of days, she became a constant thought in my head. The thought of her accompanied me alongside with all other normal and random daily thoughts. The need of knowing where she was and what she was doing kept popping up and I found myself dealing with that.
The next day, I concluded I had to ask her out at the end of her shift. Maybe we could have walked to Earl's court that night, I could have taken her to her hostel and find out where it was.
By the time I locked my bike in Sloane Square, I had thought of at least five different scenarios and ways to ask her out together with positive and negative responses. Her shift was going to end one hour after mine that night, meaning I could have just waited, maybe had some food and a beer and then go for it.
Crazy, how hard it was to make a move on her, especially knowing that in other situations and with other girls, it was sometimes the easiest thing in the world.
Clelia was right there at the entrance when I entered.
-Hey- I greeted.
No reply.
My legs, heavy when I saw her, became suddenly much lighter and my heartbeat had gone back to a normal pace

when I left my backpack in the upper shelf of the runners' area.
This is it, I can't deal with this, I have no patience for highly emotional people in my life, especially people who are rude. I tied my apron tight and quickly tried to make my hair look less messy than usual while looking at the mirror and approaching my till in time for the start of my 5 pm shift.
-You're late- Daryl appeared behind me.
He was right, I was one minute late.
-My apologies, I have no excuses, I overslept-
-I appreciate that you're saying that, just try to be more on time from now on- he said, firm.
-Sure-
-And iron your shirt, you've been told a few times already- he said while turning his back to me. His white perfectly ironed shirt tucked in his trousers didn't make me want to look anywhere close to it, but it was the rule of the restaurant, which proved he was right twice in the same conversation.
My shift didn't start well, and Clelia wouldn't talk to me again. This time though, I wasn't going to care about it. Every time I had service coming to my table, I would also hope it wasn't her carrying the big tray and fortunately, most of the times, she wasn't. Every time I cleared tables and brought plates and cutlery to the drop off area, I would also hope that she was on the floor in that moment, maybe taking care of the requests of the managers or just carrying the big tray around until I found out she volunteered to be at the drop off area just like I did when I was a runner.
Most of the times I would just ignore her and pretend she wasn't there, but I was also trying to show I wasn't pissed or anything. I wanted her to understand that my patience for her games was over and that she had to speak her intentions clear to me at some point.
Over the course of the shift, I noticed with the tail of my eyes that she looked at me a few times and eventually tried harder and harder for some eye contact, but I played even harder and won that round when she brought the big tray for service at table 62.
I smiled at her, took the plates to the table and thanked her.

-Domenico- she said very timidly, lowering her voice down, -I know you must hate me right now, but you have to know that I have a crush on you- she said while looking down to the ground, then ran back to the runners' area and left me stunned right there for a few seconds, processing what just happened.
Can this be it? Did she finally say it? Is this the reason of her emotional swing and unbearable moody behaviour that seems to be reserved only for me?
I couldn't wait one more second. I followed her to the drop off area and saw her throwing dirty cutlery and crockery in the dirty green boxes, ready to put them all into the biggest box and take everything down to the kitchen porter at the same time, a strategy I had taught her which no other runners wanted to follow since it broke several restaurant's standards and that, if caught by the wrong manager, could have got you fired.
-I have a crush on you too- I told her, serious, then quickly moved away back to the floor after noticing she simpered.
-You guys look so sweet- Ilaria told me in my ears one hour later while I was cutting a bread baguette.
-What do you mean?- I asked, knowing exactly what she meant, but just waiting for her to feed my hopes.
-She clearly likes you- she said with a big smile. She loved gossiping, like most members the staff.
-What makes you say that?- I asked, begging for her to say more or to even give me some more reasons to believe that, maybe something I hadn't seen before, or some words she might have told her in private, or that she heard her saying.
-A girl can always tell- she blinked at me.
Clelia's words kept echoing in my head until the end of my shift, giving me some hard time focusing on work.
It had to be my night, I thought just before Matteusz came to talk to me.
-Dom, I'm going to need you to stay until closure today- he said while writing stuff on the paper schedule.
-What? I'm not going to, I'm busy otherwise. You can't force me to- I muttered instinctively, panicking.
-I know, I know, but I need you mate- he went on saying and turned his back at me heading to the runners area. This is

annoying, oh, so annoying! But wait, isn't Clelia leaving pretty much at the same time then? I could close as fast as I could and maybe ask her to wait for me at the staff table, but how do I tell her...
-Oh really? That's great, I couldn't wait to go home to be honest, being here today feels even worse than usual- I heard Clelia saying loud while I passed by the runners area.
-What happened?- I asked her.
No reply again. Suddenly, she looked as if she was mad at me.
I was busy, very busy on the floor and I had lots of customers to take care of. I needed to send mains away at table 61, put a steak knife on 63, bill for 64... or was it the other way round? I went back to the floor, racking my brain about it. Was it a lie? Did she say she liked me just to know if I felt like that and now she was turning me down?
That was the only explanation that made sense. My heart was beating faster now and the feeling of disappointment confused me and made my pace slower in the next minutes.
-Finally!- I heard her saying while she took her backpack from the shelf next to mine. She was going home earlier, that's what Matteusz told her before. She was happy to leave before me after lying about her feelings.
I went back to my section, not meaning to work any fast-paced anymore. I didn't have to after all.
Clelia was standing by the bread section, already signed off the register, looking at me. She grinned when she noticed how confused I looked. She turned away and sauntered out of the restaurant, her wide grin still on her face while I became aware that none of my visions were going to become true and that she was just enjoying torturing me.

By the end of October, the Rangers were scheduled a staff meeting in Tonteria, the posh night club next door. We would have used their dance floor as a meeting space to discuss what changes we needed to apply to improve the way we were organised and our service in general. Some of our last reports from mystery diners weren't very good, reason why many of us believed that was some sort of emergency meeting.

That was also going to be the first time in about a week I was going to see Clelia.
My two days off and hers never matched that week, plus I got three morning shifts finishing at 4 pm while she had evening ones.
Clelia kept pulling on a grin on her face every time I tried to make eye contact with her and deliberately ignored me.
Besides that, I had a feeling that she was somehow happier to see any members of the restaurant except me, seeing that she greeted them with hugs and words such as "I missed you" even when she worked with them the previous night.
When the day of the meeting arrived, I felt almost entirely careless of Clelia. Somehow, my stress reduced a lot, probably because I realised it wasn't worth it.
My impression was proved right when we gathered down to Tonteria's dance floor for the meeting and Clelia's grin disappeared from her face when she noticed I didn't pay any attention to her moves, but just focused on talking to Manu.
-This place is packed with lots of good quality pussy at night- said Manu when the meeting was over and me, him and Jacob, the Polish waiter, went to the staff room to get changed.
-You're going to need to build your body if you want some of that Dom- added Jacob, making Manu chuckle.
-It's fine man, I don't have any problems getting it to be honest- I replied.
-I don't doubt it, but we're talking about the quality here, not the quantity- Jacob replied, and Manu laughed.
Then, Jacob left, and finally I was left alone with Manu, which gave me the chance to finally let out something that I needed help with.
-I don't know what's going on, I thought she liked me- I confessed to Manu before he could leave. He stopped, understood I was being serious, then spoke.
-It's because of the way you are, you're just the friend guy-
-The friend guy?- I hated him for saying that, but it wasn't the first time I heard that.
-Yes, you are the type of guy girls want to be friend with. You are sweet and all of that stuff- he said to me while he

hanged his sunglasses over the last bottom of his shirt and praised his figure into the mirror.
-What should I do?- I asked him.
-You have to ignore her- he said as if it was extremely obvious.
-Could you tell me how that could possibly help?-
-That's how it works. You are young and you don't know this but I'm telling you, and remember, this is how it works. If you act mysterious, just like me for example, they'll like you. You have to be a challenge for them, not an easy fish to catch. Be natural and careless, don't even think of thinking about them and especially, reject any proposal of going out together, that's actually the best thing you can do- he said whilst fixing his hair, loving himself into that mirror.
-What? I mean, I think I can kind of understand the whole ignoring and challenging thing but... how is rejecting her ever going to work?- I asked. -And anyway, we're not planning to see each other since she keeps ignoring me if you really want to know-
-That's why you want her- he said.
I got silent, not knowing how to reply.
Then he spoke again, this time with a warmer tone.
-Now listen, I'm older than you and I like you Dom- he said while he looked at me in the eyes.
-You text her that you want to meet up and talk with her one of these days and then, just before the day comes, you say you're busy and you can't meet up, giving no clues on when the next time could be-
-That's absurd- I looked into his eyes. He didn't seem to be lying, and besides that, Manu often gave me good advice in the past.
Right in that moment, Clelia's text appeared on my screen.
-It was good to see you laughing today...- I stared at it for a minute, then I texted back.
-Meet me tomorrow after work. I need to talk to you- I replied, making sure Manu spotted how strict my words looked.

As scheduled, the following afternoon I texted her again, cancelling our meeting.

I had no idea how that was going to help me with my goal, but in case of failure, that would have at least taught her a lesson on how to treat other people with respect.
Her reply came straight away.
-Sure, I hope you're ok...- with a smiley face.
Weird. That was the first time she sounded... submissive?
I felt somehow powerful when I left work and headed back to Russell Square.
The next day Clelia and I were in the same shift. She greeted me timidly and stroked her hand on my arm while she asked me how I was doing. I decided to carry on with Manu's strategy and acted careless, recognising her existence, but showing no interest in involving it with mine.
-Hey Clelia, good thanks- I said with a smile, then kept acting busy even if the floor was half empty.
With the passage of hours, she got more and more frustrated with everyone and more submissive with me. I literally heard her telling off each one of her teammates that evening from the floor. Her luck was that everyone in the runners area was Italian that day so that her words wouldn't have caused her many problems in case somebody were to hear them from the tables.
-Hey Dom, I'm actually scared that you may tell me off even before I get the chance to- she told me at some point, laughing nervously afterwards.
By the end of the shift, she had kissed me on my cheeks twice while I left plates and cutlery by the drop off area and asked me to stay with her after closure.
I couldn't hold it any longer. Being the bad guy was not my thing, it just wasn't part of me. Besides that, it was only supposed to last a few days so to get things straight where they had to be. If she needed a proof that I was a man, I gave it to her, but how could I get her to like me if all I did was pretending that she didn't even exist?
When every customer was gone and all chairs were on the tables, I found her sitting at table 50 with Marcelo and Tom.
-Dom, come here, we're having some red- Tom invited me over.
I sat down, finally concluded that it was time to treat Clelia like a human being.

Marcelo was definitely one of the nicest people at work. He flattered me all the time with random compliments about how hard working I was. He appreciated me a lot and according to what he said to me once, he always voted for me when the restaurant organised a small poll for runner of the week, but I really needed him to go now. The same went for Tom, but he was the manager and he had the keys to close the restaurant after all.
When we all got up, I told Clelia to follow me outside.
She caressed my arm and followed me in silence.
We stood next to the entrance, chatting and bantering until our colleagues were gone, and then I kissed her.

November 2015

Finally, it was done. It was all just an act. She wanted me since the very beginning, but who cared anyway? She acted and played hard to get because she wanted to see how far I could go, how long I could bear her sudden bad mood attacks before giving up trying to get her and it all made sense after all.
I left my bike in Sloane Square, usual place, ready to start my evening shift. I even stopped the music playing in my earphones. I was excited, nervous, all because she was going to be there too. Just for a few hours though, her shift was going to end at 9 pm, but it was better than nothing.
-Hi- I said with a smile to both Ciro and her who were chatting by the entrance.
Ciro replied, but Clelia didn't.
With the passage of time, I found out that she had begun weird with me again. She would pull an angry face anytime I looked at her, but cheered and made jokes with other runners anytime I passed through their area.
As the hours passed, she had said no words at all to me, but before the end of her shift, I decided to complain on her face.
-We kissed. I mean, we kissed, what happened now?- I said, unable to hide how frustrated I was about her mood swings.
-Listen, leave me alone, ok?- she said, looking mad at me and rushing away, although I could swear I saw a grin on her face

while she took her jacket from the hanger and hugged Ciro on her way out of the restaurant.

Back at the hostel, Claudio was giving me a hard time at chess. I thought I would have been able to beat him at least once or twice, but now I was afraid that he was going to leave the hostel undefeated.
He told me he enjoyed the hostel, but he was also looking for a room at the same time.
-I'm not in a rush to leave, but to be honest I'd rather live far from work and spend a couple of hours in the tube than having to wake up to check out and change rooms all the time- he once told me.
Staying in the same room forever was Joseph's privilege. He was the only one that never had to check out and in.
It was when Claudio was gone for his usual night shift that I realised he had put some ideas in my head.
Was it really that good to be there? Wouldn't a room be a more comfortable place after all? How could me and Clelia be able to sleep next to each other if I still lived there?
Clelia... I had completely forgotten that she wouldn't even look at me. She was just playing with me, she enjoyed being in control of whatever was happening between me and her. I did nothing wrong to deserve being treated like that though. Was it a message I didn't reply to? Was I rude to her sometimes? Should I have sent her a message the night after the kiss?
I wasn't supposed to know though. Questioning myself gave me no answers, but all I knew was that my story with her was going nowhere. It was over before it even started. She had had a second thought probably.
-I would like to move in with you if you like- just like that, a text message appeared on the screen on my phone.
It was Clelia.
Clelia? Unbelievable, both the fact that she texted me and especially the content of her message.
-You have to make up your mind. You can't behave like a crazy child and now ask me to move in with you. Besides, I'm happy in the hostel- I texted her back.

If she didn't want me anymore, it would have been fine, but at least she had to know that I wasn't relying on her mood changes when it came to my life decisions. She didn't care about me at all and now she wanted to move in with me? She probably just needs somebody to make a phone call because her English isn't good enough. She once told me she wasn't confident to make phone calls in England yet. Now she'll have to deal with that on her own. Who cared if she didn't like her hostel? Who cared about her needs?
Maybe my tough reply would have kept her away from me. Maybe Manu was right again, he was older and more experienced, but his theory on how to treat girls was just unacceptable for me.
-I'm sorry about last days... I would love to see you tonight- her name appeared on my phone again.
Unbelievable. I had to look at her message for a few seconds before jumping to a conclusion. Why did she act nice only after I treated her with less care? What game was it that she was playing?
-You are right in everything. It took me just a little bit of toughness to get her to be sweet to me. I owe you, thanks a lot- I texted Manu right then.
He did help me. A great feeling was now spreading all over my body. Right in my head and in my heart I could feel a peak of pleasure, related entirely to the story between me and Clelia and how things had changed in the last minutes. She was sweet to me now and waiting for my reply. I was the one that didn't care and she the one that cared and that made me feel good, not for her suffering, but rather for the absence of mine.
But what I knew in that moment was that she was waiting for my reply, that she was thinking about me and that the sooner I replied, the sooner her longing would have been over and so would my pleasure.
Look at what I have to do when I deal with them, I thought while I went outside. My usual joint before going to sleep would have helped me worry less about everything and also fantasized harder about her finding a shelter between my arms where she could have crouched safe and happy.

-Sure, see you tomorrow- I couldn't help making her wait any longer. She gave me such feeling, and the least I could do for her was to treat her like she deserved for doing that. Of course I was going to see her.

Our date was set for 8 pm in front of Earl's Court tube station.
She looked casual, a denim jacket, backpack and her hair on a ponytail. How was I going to act once I saw her? We hadn't been talking for about a week since after the kiss and she had no idea of how I lived my last days in the hostel just before receiving her message.
I concluded that she didn't have to find out about anything related to my feelings and that I should have just acted natural.
-Hey Clelia- I said to her with half a smile.
-How are you?- she asked me, quite loud.
-Don't be loud, there's people around us- she laughed.
-You're an idiot- she said while she hit my arm with her finger, as if it could sting it.
-Let's stop here, I love Franco Manca-
-What? How much is this going to be? I'm quite short on money you know- she said.
-Franco Manca is the best place in London for a pizza. Not only probably the cheapest one, but also the tastiest by far-
-How do you know?-
-I've been here longer, I know things- she laughed again. My way of judging things wasn't to be praised though. I was the kind of person that never went for anything new as soon as he found something that was good enough to settle. If all people in the history of the world had been exactly like me, we could have built a very well-functioning society based on hard work and honest trades, except for the fact we would have never explored a single mile away from a land that we thought was good enough for us.
We sat at a table for six with other two people on the other side.
-Hello- I greeted them, not happy that they were there to spoil our intimacy, but happy I could give her a proof that I wasn't picky.

-That's weird, people sitting at our own table- she whispered to me.
-This is London, not Sicily, so stop being narrow-minded- she kept laughing at my jokes and I loved it.
-So why are you vegetarian by the way? Is it for some crazy health reasons?- I asked her.
-No, I just once saw a pig I used to know being killed-
-You saw it?-
-Well no, I mean, I knew that pig and he was a good pig and then they tried to make me eat it and that was it- she said, all in one breath and with a tone that claimed the end of that conversation.
-Fair enough, and by the way do you have a boyfriend now? Just to make things clear, you never know- I said in a jokey tone, even though a part of me was taking it very seriously.
-Idiot, I wouldn't be wasting my time here with you if I had some entertainment already- she said, nodding her head no, catching my sarcasm.
-Entertainment?-
-Well yeah-
-I'm not your entertainer, I'm actually quite pissed off about your attitude in general-
-Oh shut up, you like me, don't you?- I could feel her lack of confidence in that moment. Manu would have used that moment in his favour, he would have kept her longing, or at least not given her a clear answer, but Manu was wrong. I did recognise his skills, but he was the one that chose a life without love just because he couldn't bother bearing girls. He made the easy choice, but I wasn't him and I was no longer going to follow his instructions. I accepted the deal all men need to accept if they wanted to feel the way I was feeling. Clelia had suffered an entire day waiting for me to confirm her that I was still into her. Oh, if only she knew!
-I like you, but I also need to make sure you like me too because sometimes it doesn't seem like it- I said.
-Of course I like you, you're probably better in bed than my ex I guess-
-What? How can you tell?-
-I'm not saying it, but his dick was small, so I dumped him right away, that loser- she said while chewing loud.

-Well, I don't think I have that problem- I said, visualising mine and comparing it to a supposedly average size.
-So, what's your goal? Would you like a boyfriend? In general, I mean- I asked her, trying to be casual after leaving the pizzeria.
-Not at all, I don't want any men stuck in my way- she said.
-Wow, wait, tell me once again, why did I come meet you tonight?- she laughed, then she answered the question.
-Just so you can fuck me and then leave me alone, that's why- she looked at me and laughed again.
I stopped for a second.
That statement slowly lit a bulb in my head, helping me to get a picture of the story, to understand her more and more. Clelia was a girl who got disappointed about some guys that probably treated her in the same way Manu suggested me to do up to that point. Somebody in her past was rude and acted in the manipulative way she was acting with me now. Eventually, she got tired of not being loved the way she was loving him and found a way out of that situation. She subconsciously decided that all men were a danger to her self-esteem and that she first had to test the guy, his capacity of bearing her mood changes and yet still care about her. If she needed to know that I was different from her exes, I would have accepted the challenge and win it easily. The reason why she wanted to be alone was obvious. She preferred being on her own and enjoy some random sex rather than allowing someone to chain her into a monogamist relationship where she has feelings for him and he uses them to bend her down to his will. Of course she lied, even if she didn't even know she did. She was going to be mine, I was going to prove her that I was no asshole.
-Are you ok?- she asked me.
I had been visibly off the clouds for about a minute. We were right in front of Earl's Court station again. I hoped I didn't move my lips during my intense thinking.
-Yeah sure, follow me- we turned left on Barkston Gardens and kept walking for a minute. Now I just needed to find a place where we could be alone, far from others.
-Let's break into this park, it should be easy- I proposed when we got to Courtfield Gardens.

-Are you mad?- she sounded excited and showed no hesitation to follow me.
The park was beautiful, just like so many others in London. The sight might have not been perfect because of the dark, but I could see how tidy it was. Dying trees left their leaves on the ground, all on the grass and none on the small street-like paths with benches located in random places.
-I wondered if they planted the trees on strategic places so that leaves won't touch the paths-
-What about the wind, you idiot?- she told me, still excited. I loved the way we bantered.
We sat down on a bench in the middle of the park, the nearest one to a pretty Victorian style, pale-coloured small gazebo by the other end of the park. I couldn't take my eyes off of her.
-So, you've been wondering if I was ever going to talk to you again, haven't you?- she mocked me.
-No I wasn't- I lied.
-Silly you- she jumped on my lap.
I found out I wasn't going to get that lucky that night after the fifth time she pulled my hands away from her nipples.
-Don't get too excited. I know how you're feeling, but it's not happening-
-Fine- I resigned at some point.
We spent some more time talking about our lives and where we were heading. She told me she didn't want to be in London for more than a couple of months, that she was moving to Edinburgh soon because London was too big and she couldn't feed her soul and feel free in such urban jungle. She told me how her mother was the most important person in her life and that her father was a piece of shit who liked to bully people and got a criminal record for punching someone in a gym just because he was sitting in his favourite spot in the dressing room.
-Where are you staying? I'll take you home- I said.
-We're close, I think it's like two streets forward on the left-
-How are you finding it?-
-Hostels are fun but I need a place. I might be moving into Marco's place, he said there's a room available there-

Marco, my colleague. When did he ask Clelia for her phone number? When did they talk about it? How does he know?
-Marco? I didn't know you guys were in touch outside work-
-I knew you would react like that- she said, struggling not to laugh.
-It's not funny. It's going to be hard to keep you away from men that will try to get you in this city-
-You can't stop them and you shouldn't try to. It's either you trust me or not- she said, firmly.
-Now sit down here- she added while pointing down the pavement near some parked scooters and a bin in Trebovir Road.
-You can't own me- she went on.
-That's not what I meant. I never would like to nor I possibly could anyway- I said, honest.
-Then why do you worry?-
-Everyone is hitting on you at work-
-I don't care about those losers, so now shut up-
Someone smiled while they saw us lying down between the pavement and the street.
-I'm in love with you- came out of my mouth all of a sudden.
-What?- she said, a smile on her face got wider and wider while I stared at her.
Did she actually not get that? We were speaking our language after all.
I repeated it, making her smile become a laugh. She didn't reply, but at least seemed flattered.
We talked a little bit more, then we kissed good night.

After that night, things seemed to be more stable between me and her.
We didn't act anyway obvious at work, but people around us started realising it and asking questions.
-You don't have to worry about me anyway. Clelia is a very different person than I am- Marco told me at some point during a quiet shift.
-Why do you think I worry? Are you kidding? Take it easy, and anyway, there's nothing between me and her-

-Oh come on, everyone knows, it's so obvious- he laughed, then he went back to the runners area to pick up some new wine glasses for his section.
-Oh Dom, Dom, Dom, what are we going to do with you?- Ilaria came from my back and took a blue cloth to go wipe some of her tables.
-What? What have I done?- I replied, taking the joke.
-I'm not happy with you Dom- she said, clearly not joking. She sprayed some sanitising product on her table and went on.
-Look at her, the way she hugs everyone and the way she treats you, not to mention the way she gets closer and closer to Salvatore. I am afraid that you might not see any of this, but you must pay attention to me: you need to cut it all off, and as soon as possible, or it will be too late- she said.
-What?- she still looked very serious.
What was she talking about? Things between me and Clelia had just started to be good and now she was telling me to cut it all off? Was she just jealous because we were in love and she was breaking up with her boyfriend, as she admitted herself few days before?
Strange though. Ilaria was nice to me, always, since when she became a waitress at least, because she used to be just mean when we were working as runners together.
-Look- she pointed towards the kitchen area, visible from table 50 where I was sitting, folding napkins.
Salvatore was leaning on the wall and Clelia seemed to be very close to him while she listened to what he was saying. She seemed charmed by whatever he was saying...
Ilaria laughed, not amused, but rather satisfied as if she managed to prove the point she was trying to make. But she couldn't be right, not at such early stage of my relationship with Clelia.
-This is why science fails to understand that, although the answer is...- I heard Salvatore saying to her while I went down the stairs to get to the staff room to get some more napkins.
Was Ilaria right? Was there something between them? I was feeling pretty stressed now... How was I supposed to go back to work like that?

I was just about to leave the staff room when the sound of their voices approaching stopped me.
-Hey!- Clelia said, surprised to see me there.
-Hey- I replied, my voice so feeble I wasn't even sure she heard me.
Salvatore smiled at me.
-Hey, how are you?- he said, louder than necessary.
-Good- a big smile on my face too, just not to look upset.

In the next couple of days, Clelia kept texting me to go back to her place and "make her happy", calling me a fool, a loser or a faggot anytime I found an excuse not to.
It wasn't because I wasn't keen on that obviously, but I had to make her understand that rude girls were a turn off for me, that I would rather sleep alone than with them.
-So, when are you guys going to be an official couple?- Ilaria asked her at some point during a busy shift.
-I'm trying hard, but this guy isn't into me enough- Clelia replied while carrying the box of water bottles downstairs.
That was a lie. She wanted sex and she wanted to dump me as soon as possible, but what if she was saying the truth? She had the power to make me feel good for entire shifts at work, and who was I to say no to that feeling anyway?
-Do you have a bit of weed?- she once asked me after closure.
-Not today, I'm sorry, I don't usually take it on me when I come to work. It's at home if you want to come by- I suggested while I caressed her wavy hair.
-Where, the hostel? Are you kidding?-
-If you come, I'll pay you a taxi to get you home-
-That's not the point, I mean, we can't be together at your place cause it's a damn hostel-
-What? There's a lovely step outside there where we could smoke-
-No Dom, I'm not coming. You can just come to mine, actually, yeah, come to mine- she tried once again.
-Not today- I had to resist, although it was getting harder now, and the fact that she was sitting on my lap didn't help.

By the second half of November, Clelia's general attitude improved both towards work and me.
She kept hugging everyone as usual when she started her shift, but unlike ever before that, she started not only recognising my existence, but also giving me the best hug.
I never believed that an eight or a ten hours shift could last so little and it could be so pleasant. The angry comments from the kitchen for each little mistake we could make with the timings or with the orders didn't affect my mood at all and neither did the way managers put me on the work rota or the absurd requests they made.
It all became easier basically, and the fact that Clelia kept saying she felt something for me meant that I should have no longer waited to go to her place.
-I don't have a booking in the hostel tonight- I made up at the end of our shift.
-Does that mean you're coming to mine?- she sounded very excited all of a sudden.
-Fine, but just because I need it for tonight- I joked, struggling to step up to her pace while she led me to the tube station.
-Where are we going?-
-Stockwell, that's where I live- she said, fast and all in one breath.
-Are you ok?-
-Oh my God, will you shut up? Thank God you're coming to mine tonight, so I will finally find out if you're worth something- she laughed at her own words.
-I'm still in time to leave, you know- I said while we changed train in Victoria.
-No you won't!- she said taking my cap and hiding it into her bag.
-No! That's my father's, give it back to me-
-I'll give it back to you when the time comes- she smiled.
How could I even find her unattractive when I first met her?
-Dealing with you is exhausting- I told her when we left Stockwell tube station.
-Tell that to all my exes, many of them found out I was a bitch when it was too late-
-Why are you saying such bad thing about yourself?-

-Because I'm a bitch- she said while she let me in her flat.

December 2015

A few issues got stuck in my head and became more and more important when December arrived.
How was I going to make my relationship work if I didn't have my own place? Was I going to go to her place every single time we wanted to be together? Did it really make sense to stay in the hostel?
None of the guys from the hostel seemed to be particularly active by the social point of view, they were all working crazy long shifts and Rey was gone anyway. Besides that, I couldn't focus on picking up girls since I was in love with Clelia who, by the way, kept pushing for me to move out of my home.
-How are we going to make this work if you live with other people in the same room?- she once asked me at the restaurant.
-How am I going to make it work with you if you spend more time with Salvatore than with me?- her eyes opened up twice as much when these words escaped my mouth, impulsively.
-You're kidding, right?- she asked, serious.
-Yeah, I'm sorry. I just... noticed that you guys talk all the time and the way you listen to him and treat him in general is... just so much better than the way you act with me- I took a break for a second, unable to look into her eyes, then I went on. -I'm slightly ashamed for bringing this up to be honest-
She stared into my eyes for more than ten seconds before speaking.
-Don't worry about him. I love talking to him, but it's nothing more than that- she said, a very warm voice tone.
-I know I don't have to worry- I smiled at her.
What was I even thinking? I shouldn't have brought that up, that made me look so needy! I was scolding myself while leaving the restaurant at the end of my shift when I remembered that I hadn't got to work with my bicycle that day, as I found my tyres pinched that very morning. God if I didn't hate the tube so much... I thought while moving

towards the rent-a-bike platform right behind my restaurant, although I had to suddenly stop.
Clelia and Salvatore were outside together, wearing jackets on top of their work uniforms. He was sitting on one of the bikes and she was listening to something he was saying. He seemed to have captivated her attention now to the point she almost fell on top of him, their legs were literally crossed with one another, but without direct touch...
What was going on? What was Salvatore doing with a cigarette? Didn't he always say how bad smoking was and how proud he was that he never started smoking?
I ran to the tube station, I couldn't be seen without them thinking I was spying on them.

Within the first week of December, I was going through an internal conflict that forced me to spend a couple of hours per day in deep thinking.
Why did she talk much more to him than to me? Why did we never go out together, but always ended up at her place? Why wasn't she texting me at all, while she even told me that her and Salvatore would text with each other up to late night?
My suspicions seemed to be well-founded or at least not unjustified. They kept popping up in my head in several moments of the day, while another part of me kept reminding me that she was indeed an attention seeker and that I was not doing much to give her enough, not to mention that Salvatore was in a committed relationship with a girlfriend that would often come visit him at the restaurant, and that he was an interesting person after all.
I wasn't scared of Salvatore taking Clelia away from me anyway. However, he was paying a lot of attention to her.
-Hey, wanna hang out today?- I texted Clelia one afternoon.
-Why don't you go to hell?- she replied.
Again, that unpleasant feeling of something getting stuck in my throat any time I felt like things between us weren't going well. Why was she always rude?
-I'm going to Green Park this afternoon for a smoke if you want to join- I texted back.

-Actually, why don't you come to mine? It's only a few stops away from Green Park and you'd be doing something useful with your life-
-No. Have a nice day- I texted, earning some abstract Manu's approval.
-Hey? I was kidding!- she said when I picked up her call.
-Why don't you come to mine and then we could go to the park together?-
I can't see anything wrong with this request, I thought while leaving Stockwell tube station and walking past the Stockwell War Memorial and turning left to take the steps up to her flat facing Clapham Road.
I went up the stairs, reached the third floor and then knocked on the door of flat 86.
-Hey Dom- Marco opened the door for me and let me in for a coffee. Their kitchen was slightly messy and a bunch of dirty plates came to my attention.
-Hi there- Clelia came into the kitchen and greeted me with a kiss.
Her hair was straighter than usual and smelled like flowers. She wanted me to get there so she could score, I knew this before of course.
Anyway, my goal was to have a cup of tea with her and take her to the park for a walk, then we would have just talked and got to know more about each other. I wasn't going to let Salvatore become more intimate with her than I was.
-Clelia, where's my cap?-
-In my room, come and take it-
-It's not happening though, I just really want the cap, it's my father's-
-I told you, it's in my room, come and I'll give it to you-
I resigned.
Her room wasn't too bad, a big window, a desk to work on, read, study in peace...
What the hell was I still doing in the hostel?
-I'm going to get my own place, and I'm doing it mostly for you- I said.
-You should- she said while she took her trousers off.
-What are you doing? I said it's not happening, and also, where's my cap?-

-Your cap is in my wardrobe, take it-
I didn't hesitate to take it and put it in my bag.
-Salvatore gave me this book- she pointed at the book I saw on the desk, which worked for me as a perfect excuse to open it.
"To Clelia, a smart, sensitive and amazing person I have been lucky to have met". Salvatore bought her a book and wrote this down for her.
-What game is he playing?- I blurted out.
-I said don't worry-
-You keep saying that, but I also see how you guys are getting closer and closer-
-Enough!- she said. -You have to trust me, you are the one I sleep with, he's just a person I like to talk to, alright?-
-Right, I'm sorry- I said, feeling embarrassed.
-Anyway, I'm not in the mood to go to the park, you just ruined it. Now make me happy please- she was naked before I even realised it.

My cap!
I figured out I had forgotten it at her place the previous night right when I saw Clelia entering the restaurant the following day.
Weird though, I was pretty sure I put it in my backpack...
-Did you hear the news? Pierre and Laura are leaving this month- Ilaria said sadly while she left some dirty plates in the drop off area.
-To where?-
-They're leaving London, maybe they're going to Italy together- she shrugged her shoulders.
They met in the restaurant and now they were leaving to somewhere cheaper or closer to home, probably with a better job for both of them.
That news was a surprise, I was going to miss Pierre a lot, and Laura too.
-I received an offer to work as a teacher in Italy and Pierre will learn the language, he's already learning it actually- Laura explained to me at the staff table before the beginning of her shift.

-This coffee is for you my love- Pierre said in Italian, still keeping a very thick French accent that amused everyone at the table.
-Your life is about to change forever Pierre- I said, but he couldn't get it.
-Alright Clelia, I'm going home, have a good day at work...- I tried to tell her before she started her shift, but she stood up looking furious and didn't say a single word.
My relationship with her was confusing me, taking a lot of my time and energy, and on top of that, I thought it was making me depressed.
I thought about Pierre and Laura just like the ideal situation I wanted to be in, but Clelia was unable to offer me that. Did it make sense that I kept pushing for something I wanted to see happening if the other person had completely different goals?

-Dom? Dom? Can you hear me?- a girl had just called me from a number I didn't have in my contacts, sounding pretty desperate in her tone.
-Yes, yes, I can hear you- slowly realising that the person on the other side was Arlena.
-Could you please come to meet Rey one of these days? He is so depressed that he wouldn't even get up from his bed, I don't know what to do about it- she sounded in panic.
-He says you're his best friend and he misses you- she went on.
Rey... how could I neglect him so much? If only I hadn't been busy day and night thinking about Clelia and dealing with my fear to lose her... I should have paid more attention to him, but I literally forgot about him.
-Sure, I could come tomorrow, ok?-
-That's great, and by the way Dom, would you be interested in moving in with us? It would cost you less than 300 pounds per month and the location is great- she started describing her place just like an estate agent would do, but I wasn't paying attention to her words anymore. She was wasting her time with me because I needed to move in for Clelia. If things between me and her weren't taking off properly it was also because I was still living in the hostel and moving in with

Rey and Arlena wouldn't have helped the privacy issue as they shared a studio flat apparently. Also true though, was that Clelia wasn't talking to me again for no reason at all.

Clelia hadn't spoken to me for about three days in a row when I was on my way to Holland Park tube station, where Arlena was waiting for me.
-Rey misses you a lot- she said, leading me to her place, just one street across Holland Park Avenue, closer to the park itself.
Rey seemed to be sleeping tucked in by a pair of duvets.
-Rey, wake up, come on, it's 2 pm!- I said loud, but nicely.
They were staying in a basement of a great looking building in what had to be one of the most expensive streets of London.
-How can you afford this?- I asked Arlena.
-Private landlord, he made a good deal for us- she said from the kitchen.
Her curvy body would have caused a reaction from me, but I couldn't stop thinking about Clelia. Maybe, if Rey didn't wake up at all, I could have just left and go visit her. If sex was what she wanted, I would have given it to her and the first thing I would have done once I left their place was to look for a room for me and maybe just take the first one available, I had some money in my savings account after all...
-Did you see what Rey did here on the table?- Arlena came back from the kitchen with two bowls of pasta and tomato sauce she had heated up for me.
Rey had drawn a chess board on the table, using a pencil to colour up the dark squares.
-Oh, how cute- I said, feeling like a father reading the first real sentence written by his child.
-Hey Dom- Rey finally got up.
-How are you man? Do you want to move in with us?- he said without waiting for me to answer his first question.
-I'll think about it, I'm not sure yet- I said, having no intentions to agree on that plan. Their place wasn't too bad neither in size nor in the company I would have got, but that would have made me lose Clelia for sure, especially since things between us weren't good at all.

-Why don't you come here with me in bed for a minute? Don't worry about the table, I'll clean it later tonight- Arlena asked me after I was done with my food, about half hour later. Rey had given me a few chess games, then he was gone to sleep.
-Look, I'm going to have to leave in a minute-
-It's ok Domenico- she took my jacket off. Her breast was about twice as big as Clelia's, and yet I kept thinking about her, visualising myself running away from that place and moving into a room just so I could call her and tell her we could finally be a couple, but my thoughts got interrupted when I noticed that Arlena was touching me.
-I don't think it's a good idea- I told her nervous, trying to take her hands off of me.
-I know Dom, I know...- she was now going harder on me until it became almost hard to reject her. Did I really have to be tough to a woman?
Her hands were now on my belt, forcefully removing it while her lips were on my neck. I couldn't help it any longer, I had to do what I had to do.
If our story is already over then I'm doing the right thing. If the story will be over later, than this won't be a chance I missed out on. If our story will continue until the end of our days, then that's her fault for abusing me emotionally and anyway, I thought while Arlena moaned hard under me, this didn't mean anything.

Clelia waited for the end of our morning shift to face me the following day.
-You're such pussy- she said with an angry expression on her face, then smiled and tried to hug me.
-I'm tired of this, I can't do this anymore. I'm exhausted, and I don't think this is going anywhere- I blurted out when we were sitting in Sloane Square.
-Fine, as long as you're happy- she said, seemingly indifferent to my words. My throat got clogged again and my heartbeat rate faster.
-If you could know how I feel when you treat me like this, you wouldn't- I stopped talking when I saw she was struggling to hold a grin from appearing on her face and also because I didn't want to expose myself too much.

-All I'm trying to say is that I don't think this is very healthy for me if there is no stability and you keep acting like that- I said.
-Fine, goodbye- she stood up and left.
I couldn't believe it. Just like that? What did I do? Why did I say those things to her?
-Clelia!- I shouted, a few people turned their head to me in crowded Sloane Square tube station except her. I tried to grab her arm, but she rushed and successfully got inside the gates.
Another night of self-torture was ahead of me. There was no way I could apparently fix my story with her, I messed it up and it was all my fault, I shouldn't have exposed my feelings that much.
Best thing to do now was to just chill, not think too much about it and eventually, she'll have missed me. As soon as I went home, I deleted all my research for single rooms from my saved pages in my laptop and went to sleep.

-Stop looking like that, put a damn smile on your face- Ciro grumbled to me the next morning while taking a tray with new wine glasses for his section.
-Leave me alone Ciro-
-She'll realise you're sad because of her, you've been like this for few days in a row and it's time for you to understand what kind of person she is- he said in one breath.
-What do you suggest I do then?- I followed him to his section.
-Look around yourself better- he said.
Clelia and Salvatore were tight in a hug, right between the kitchen and the runners area, their faces very close to each other.
-What game are you playing?- I asked Salvatore when she went to the staff room to get more salt for the glass machine.
Salvatore showed to be surprised at first, but quickly changed the look on his face.
-We're just friends, we talk a lot, that's true but... I'm glad you make her happy, we talk about you most of the time- he said, a confident smile followed.

-What do you guys talk about the most?- I tried to keep sounding firm in my position even though he just made me feel good by saying that.
-She's very interested in spirituality and I help her out with this-
-Why don't you tell me something I don't know then?- I challenged him.
I found anything related to spirituality just nonsense, but how much did I really know about it?
-Come with me- he led the way to the back of the restaurant, then he finally began talking.
-I talk to her about karma, I tell her how it works, and I also just pay attention to her in general, especially her emotions, another thing you don't do, but that you should do- he said, still sounding very confident.
-What's karma?- I asked.
He smirked for a good ten seconds before he actually spoke.
-It's not something I'm going to explain to you now, it's more of a path of life you need to go through so that your eyes can open-
-Do you think you could give me an idea now?- I didn't want to sound rude or biased although I couldn't deny I was.
-Ok, let me break it down for you. In simple words, it's about cause and effect and the relationship between them. Every action has a repercussion that will affect you directly in life and it's something beyond your control- he said and paused, analysing my reaction. I stood still.
-Go on-
-Well, basically the idea is that what happens to you has been caused by your actions. If you do good actions in life, good events will return to you and if you do bad actions, bad events will return to you no matter what, but there's more to that- he continued, maybe after spotting the shocked expression I probably had on my face.
Was this what was hypnotising her in those days and weeks? Was this that was capturing so much attention from her and made her want to discuss up to late night? I couldn't believe it, there had to be more to that.
-Please go on, I mean, I'm very interested now, it's so fascinating- I said, trying to seem honest.

-Well, I'm afraid we'll have to go back to work now, the kitchen will get very busy soon, but if it's not too busy later on, we might come here for another talk- he said.
I pretended to be truly interested in what he had to say, but what I really wanted to know was how to be attractive to Clelia. How could any mentally sane person ever believe in this?
-Where were you?- Clelia asked me when she saw me coming back to work with Salvatore.
-Just chatting a bit- I answered. Wait, was she speaking to me again now?
-So, did you find a room for yourself or are you still in that place? I mean, how are we going to fuck if you're still there?- she asked. Her face showed disappointment and negative criticism with no trace of smile or sarcasm.
-Why don't you go fuck yourself, will you?- I replied. The excitement that spread all over my body when I realised she was talking to me again didn't manage to win this time. This time I was going to fight her manners.
She laughed.
-You're silly- she gently touched my arm and hugged me tight before I could reject her.
-I'm tired of you being overemotional- she told me.
-What? Are you kidding? I hope you're kidding- I blurted out, shocked.
-Can you stop arguing? We're getting busy on the floor- Marc came into the runners area and dropped a tray of dirty cutlery and plates randomly picked up from some of my tables.
-If this is making you neglect your work then maybe I'll have to put you on different shifts so that you don't work together anymore- Marc looked between me and Clelia and went back on the floor, angry.
I turned around to look at her. It was all my fault. It was me that neglected my section because I was obsessed with her. She was sneering now.
-Who are you laughing at?- I asked her.
-Idiot- she kept laughing, enjoying I got scolded by the manager that liked me the most.

This relationship is exhausting, and is it even a relationship? She has complete control over my actions and my feelings. I'm feeling trapped, I wonder if she even thinks about me during the day like I do.
I thought about these questions all the time, as if they were set on a loop in torture mode.
-It's so easy to control you- she once said with a grin when she saw me in a rush cleaning all my tables and getting them ready for dinner rush. She knew I couldn't reply.
But why was she enjoying this? What kind of person would enjoy giving another person problems? Especially their partner?
But I'm not, I'm not her partner. Ilaria is right, I need to get out of this relationship before I lose my brain with it. Clelia's drop off area was clean and ready for dinner while my section wasn't, and if I wanted to be honest with myself, I couldn't blame it on her more than I had to blame it on myself.
At the end of my shift, a glass of wine was truly deserved. I did handle my section well, I worked fast and without distractions. I ignored Clelia the whole time and focused on my work. Matteusz told me I improved a lot and Marc was now smiling at me again.
The less I cared about her, the faster and better I worked, the more I smiled to her when she carried the big tray to my section, the more frustrated she became with herself and the sweeter she acted with me.
As I predicted, she came to me while I was sitting on my own.
-I would like to talk to you if you wait for me- she told me.
Oh, no, now I'm going to go home, I won't let you ruin my mood, I thought.
-Sure- came out my mouth.
Well, I'm still in control of the situation. This is how I need to act with her, I just need to keep it going like this.
-I'm sorry, sometimes I'm unbearable- her arms gently embracing my body.
-You know I'm in love with you, you know I can bear all sort of problems that there could possibly be, but not if they are caused by you, and for no reason at all- I said.

-There is a reason... it's because you are very important to me- she said with the sweetest of tones.
We were outside of the restaurant. Sloane Square looked even more beautiful from behind her back.
-I want to be in a relationship, it's been a while really and, to be honest, I have no reason to live in a hostel since when I met you, but you need to tell me what your goal with me is-
-I'll have to know you better before I make such choice... come to my place tonight and we'll talk, we just need to get to know each other better- she held my hand and kept her head on my chest for another minute.
-I'm moving to my new place by the end of the week. It was going to be a surprise- I lied to her.
-Oh my God! That's great! Oh, you're finally stepping up! Soon you'll be a normal human being I guess-

People were surprised to hear I was leaving the hostel, both at home and at work. Mina and Adrian wished me luck and made me promise to find some time to see each other every now and then. The receptionists seemed to be sad to see me go as well as Joseph.
-Why are you leaving?- he asked me with his usual loud voice, sometimes hard to understand because of his accent.
-I think I may be able to focus more on my ambitions when I'll be alone in my room- I lied. My only ambitions before involved getting laid with a lot of girls, but it was all cancelled now that I had found love.
-I wish you all the best- Joseph said sadly.
-Thank you Joseph, the same for you-

My appointment with a guy who spoke with a German accent on the phone was set for noon at his place in Holmside Court, few minutes walk from Clapham South tube station. I took the first room that was good enough in terms of price and distance from her place after working on one of the fastest research of home ever made, since it all happened in the same day.
That area was going to be further away from work and from central London where I liked to be, but the transport connection wasn't too bad after all.

A tall blond guy who revealed to me to be Austrian led me to flat 27 on the top floor of this white block of flats where I was moving into.
-Nice to meet you, Mark- a blond guy in his forties with an English accent shook my hand. He was fit and had very short hair, didn't look like a red flag for potential future flatmate. The living room wasn't too bad. It had two sofas and a wooden table for four, direct access to a massive balcony from two different sides, allowing a view on the park and on the roofs of the other buildings.
-I like it- I said.
-Good that you like it- said Mark. -Only thing, since I live here too, no smoking will be allowed at any time in the building, I hope that works for you?-
-Yeah sure, I don't smoke- somehow true. I hated tobacco to be honest.
-So tell me, why are you leaving me this room?- I asked the Austrian guy.
-Well, I have to leave London for work reason- he said, sounding untrue.
Was there anything wrong? I sat on the sofa, thinking.
-Let me be honest with you- Mark spotted the expression on my face. -We have a flatmate here, a French woman who is a bit crazy. She's not going to be a problem for you since she travels most of the time so you might not even see her at all anyway-
-What's with this woman?- I asked.
-She doesn't have great social skills, let's just say that- he said in a serious tone.
-That won't be a problem- I said. I couldn't care that much about her. Besides, I was glad that there was a woman there after all.
I sent pictures of my room to Clelia right away. A big bed took about half of the available space of the whole room, which left just a little space for the wardrobe and a tiny desk near the window.
So exciting, I thought while I undid my suitcase for the first time in over a year. Some of my clothes kept showing a cross-like fold even after I had hanged them in the wardrobe. I left my shoes in the corner and my laptop on the desk. I

could have worked on my idea to write a book later that night.

-That looks great!- Clelia replied to me that evening, referring to the pictures of the room I had sent her.
-You should come over for dinner, what do you think?
-I work until closure tonight, but I could come afterwards?-
I didn't know what to reply, but I knew what she wanted. I wondered if all people in relationship stare at their screen, working out a reply. I wondered how they all did this.
All I knew was that she was just coming for sex.
Fine, I guess I'll have this joint downstairs and I'll think about what to tell her.
What is it? The alarm? How is it possible?
Clelia's name was on my screen. She was calling me.
-Clelia?-
-Finally you picked up the phone! How are you my sweet marshmallow?- she asked.
-I'm good, but what's the time?- so sweet she called me like that, if only it wasn't 2 am.
-I just finished work, do you want me to come over? Send me your address-
-Clelia, it's late and I don't think I'm able to entertain you today, I'm feeling a bit depressed to be honest-
It had been going on for a few days, but I hadn't told her anything just not to upset her. I wasn't in my best mood and I just wanted to see her when I could make her laugh or feel good in general.
The day before leaving the hostel, I had closed myself behind the curtains of my bed and felt sad as never before, but I didn't know what it could have been about.
-Just give me your address, come on!- she told me, still with a gentle tone.
Clelia was coming over, she had called me five times, forcing me to wake up. She really wanted to see me.
It didn't take her long. I had just left the shower that I received a message saying that she was downstairs.
-Hey marshmallow- she greeted me with a kiss when I met her downstairs.
-Hey you, so good to see you-

-I can't wait to see your place- she told me through the stairs.
-I'm really tired, so you don't mind if I keep sleeping, right?-
-Sure, I just came here to see you- she said.
-I just had a lovely conversation with Salvatore before coming here- she told me after tucking me into the blankets and lay down by my back.
-He's just so smart, he knows a lot about life and makes me feel...-
-Lost? Confused? Of course, he only speaks bullshit- I said.
-What? Are you serious?-
-He says a lot of things that aren't real, they're just impossible to prove because they're wrong, but they sound beautiful and the way he talks makes him appear as he is the holder of all the truths, but it's just a lot of bullshit. You have to be careful to him- I blurted out.
Did I go too far? I definitely shouldn't have warned her to be careful to him. Salvatore wasn't a threat for her, but he definitely was for my relationship.
-Strange... you're not the first one to tell me that. Also Marco told me to be careful to him...- she sounded pensive.
-Exactly, guess why!- I said, having no idea why Marco would warn her about him.
She got silent.
-I would say that I love you too, but it's just that I don't say such thing, you know- she surprised me all of a sudden.
-Well, it's ok Clelia, I feel that you feel that though- I said, slowly.
-I do- she said, finally somehow responding to when I told her some time before.
-Although, I have to say I feel very unsatisfied right now- she said, slowly, then rubbed her body and hand through my naked leg.
-No Clelia, not tonight, I'm too tired, good night- I said, honestly too tired for it.

The next day, coming home from work felt better than ever. My awareness that Clelia felt just like I did was pure happiness to me. There was no greater pleasure in life for

sure, I thought while I left Clapham South station and walked through Nightingale Lane.
-Hi Dom- Mark greeted me when I went in. -You're lucky to have Clelia, she made some improvements to your room- he said with a smile.
-What?- I looked inside my room and found out it did look different, but how?
-What did she do?- I asked more to myself than to him.
-She did some shopping and then she asked me to help her out- he did hear me, but now I could see.
A brand new blue duvet with two new pillows were on my bed, replacing the white shabby looking blanket and single pillow that were there the previous night and a small useful container with some of my dirty clothes inside was under the desk. She must really be in love, I thought.

By the end of December, my story with Clelia became more and more stable. She reduced her emotional acts and started treating me as I deserved. She wouldn't stop speaking to me all of a sudden for no reason, she wouldn't insult me in front of everyone, she replied my messages right away, asked me questions about other girls that posted comments on my Facebook posts, admitted thinking about me more often than she wanted to and once she even waited outside the entrance of my flat until 6 am to find me coming home drunk after a night out at the casino with two friends who came to visit me from Italy.
These acts did nothing more than confirming that Manu was wrong and that some girls just required a bit more work to trust you and it made perfect sense to me. She made my life an emotional hell, but now she was giving it all back to me. However, this still didn't change the fact that we only met for sex. There was never a time that she accepted my proposal of meeting somewhere and just talk and if she did, she made sure it happened near her area so that she would invite me over.
Rejecting her was hard and she knew it. I didn't have a great sentimental life up to that very moment and she was the very first person that told me to have feelings for me in person after all. She would laugh any time I told her how she

was the first real love story of my life and always made me notice how lame it all was since she was a few years younger than me and had many stories, of which all of them ended by her out of boredom.
-Soon I'll get bored of you- she told me.
-Impossible, I am very good in bed-
-You used to be, but now I'm getting bored, I don't feel the same because you spoiled me with your hard manners, so now I just need to get another man- she told me, sounding serious.

-What's your plan for Christmas?- I once asked her.
-What? I don't care about Christmas-
-Well, me neither, but there won't be any transport available that day and we're both working, so I thought you could stay at my place? It hasn't seen you at all, you know, and it misses you- I tried to sound jokey, but subtly revealed something I was thinking and that kept worrying me inside my head. It was as if my mouth penetrated my brain, took the most uncomfortable hidden thought I had in those days, and vocalised it on its own.
In fact, Clelia hadn't come to my flat at all after the first night I moved in there.
-I don't know... I might just stay here and sleep in the rooms upstairs, the hotel is offering rooms for restaurant staff so that's a good chance to avoid spending money- she said, not sounding entirely honest on her goal.
What money was she talking about? The taxi was on me and it wouldn't have been a problem at all. Besides that, didn't she want to sleep with me, especially after more than a week without sex?
-I can't recognise you, you should be craving sex and I'm offering it to you- I said, smiling.
-Look, I've already promised Salvatore to meet him, ok? And don't try to control me or to tell me what to do. I do whatever the fuck I want- she said in a strange tone.
Salvatore was behind us, busy with sweets by the microwave table in the kitchen.
Did he hear us? He was particularly slow in moving his hands...

I saw him following Clelia downstairs as soon as she ran down, having a break, but I couldn't follow them because of my busy section.
The feeling that I thought to be gone forever had returned. I went on to work with my throat clogged up just like it did every time I felt I lost her in past occasions.
Ilaria was right, I had to break up with her before she destroyed me. I wasn't good in relationship, I had to go back to the hostel and make it up for Rey, maybe give him all my money if that was what he needed.
-Tom? I have to quit this job, I'm sorry- Tom appeared shocked to hear that.
-Are you sure?- he replied nervous after a few seconds.
-Yes, what's the minimum notice I have to give?-
-I don't know, you're going to have to ask Daryl about it- it seemed like he just didn't want to help me out at all.
I met Daryl right when my shift ended.
-Daryl, I would like to leave this job, I'm sorry about that, but when is the soonest I could do it?-
-Is it because of Clelia?- he caught me by surprise. Tom told him already.
-I know you guys are in a relationship- he saw us near the tube station a few times when we closed together.
-I just need to leave- I said, trying not to sound too harsh.
-I can transfer you if you want. It would be a shame for the company to lose a hard worker like you- he said.
-Oh well- I didn't think about that at all.
-Actually yeah, I would appreciate it a lot, if that doesn't cost you too much trouble- I said timidly.
-No worries at all. Does Leicester Square work fine for you?-
-Yes- I said, grateful.
-Alright, I'll see what I can do for the quickest transfer- Daryl smiled and left.
I left from the back of the restaurant. I didn't want to be seen by anyone. Cycling home would have been the best option to let the steam off, but home wasn't the hostel any more...
Can I cycle home to Clapham South? Yes, but there are no rent-a-bike platforms there.

Why was I in such situation? Clelia and Salvatore were outside, still talking, their bodies were very close to each other this time. I resisted the desire to knock him out and just went all the way back. Any emotional response would have given more power to that woman and I couldn't allow it. I had to listen to Manu in the first place and not doubt him at all.
The weather was already dark in the afternoon. The Christmas lights in Sloane Square looked very different to me while I crossed it the way to the tube. I just wanted to be home as soon as possible and do something to keep me entertained and not think about it.

The next morning Daryl told me I could have started working in the other branch right from the week after Christmas.
-We will miss you here Dom- Monika told me on my last shift.
-Yeah, I wish you all the best- Marta added afterwards.
It feels weird to leave this place, I thought while stepping outside of the restaurant.
-Why are you leaving?- Clelia was outside, Salvatore sitting on the nearest bench. I hated everything of him in that moment, from his long curly hair to the smallest detail of his sneaky face. I wanted to tell him to stop looking at the opposite side and look at my face, to stop acting like a friend while he built his relationship with her slowly, time by time pretending that it was just friendship, intoxicating her with theories that no thinking human with some understanding of how the world works would have ever bought, but which happened to work perfectly on a highly irrational person who lived on drama and attention from others. He was perfect for her, but I wasn't. He realised it and he went for her, I couldn't blame it on him too much, except for the fact that he acted like a friend and even texted me once to tell me to pay more attention to her and that we looked great together. None of these words came out of me for real though.
-I just need to work closer to home and I'm honestly tired of this place- I told her, my last attempt of trying to sound in normal conditions.
-I see... still up for the Nutcracker?- I had completely forgotten about it.

-Oh yeah, sure, I can't wait to see it- I told her, still acting normal. I could have exploded any time later on in the day, just not in front of her.
I had bought tickets for the ballet, for a visit to Harry Potter studios and for a trip to her place in Sicily for both of us, all in one morning spending more than 300 pounds.
-Alright, talk soon- she kissed me.

She kissed me right in front of him... great! And she also reminded me that we were going to go to the Nutcracker together.
Maybe it wasn't all lost after all, maybe it was all in my head. It all felt different when I left the tube and walked home. She still wanted me, and not him. He was just the guy who taught her stuff she was interested in, while I was the one she wanted on an intimate level. My legs moved faster than usual when I walked up the stairs and got to my flat.
Mark had invited some guests over, but no sign of the French woman, her room was still locked with a small padlock from the outside.
I do feel much better tonight, but is it worth it?
My mood depends entirely on her mood swings and it was only my fault to have fallen into that trap. Now I have to make a plan, talk to her more often, maybe tell her everyday some fun fact I can google, or just tell her things I know, but if she is into spirituality, I have no way to get her to like me. What can I do?

The day after Christmas, I woke up to a message from Alice, the French girl from the Camden night out.
-Hey sweetie! So... tomorrow I'm landing in London, are we still set for me staying at your place for a few nights? I'll move out as soon as I get a place for me, but I was just double checking- a few smiley faces with kisses after her words paralysed me.
I did text Alice once telling her that by the time she would have come to London I would have already left the hostel and she would have stayed at mine, but I was drunk when I did.

Alice was pretty hot. Was I going to tell her I had a girlfriend or whatever that was?
The day of her arrival, I picked her up from Clapham South station and helped her with her suitcase.
-How have you been? Did you like London to the point of coming back here stable? Or did you like me that much?- I asked her, a bit unsure about how she would have taken it. I didn't want to show her any flirting intentions since she was going to be in my place and I didn't want her to feel uncomfortable. I wanted to play fair after all.
-I have a girlfriend anyway, so you don't have to worry- I said, regretting it as soon as I noticed that she blushed at my previous joke and she got weirdly surprised at my last words.
-Really? I didn't know that- she said. Should I tell her I was kidding? Maybe it's not too late, I can just say that and I may still have a chance, but she kissed me in front of Salvatore, maybe to remind him that I was her man...
-Well yeah, but she's cool with you staying at my place, actually, you two could meet up and become friends I guess- I could feel that she had become uncomfortable for real now.
Alice stayed for a couple of nights and then left. She said she found a room in Shadwell and that she could move in one day before the end of the year, promising to spend New Year's Eve with me, Clelia and Andrea.

January 2016

The night of the Nutcracker ballet, Clelia and I agreed on meeting up in Leicester Square. From there, we would have reached the Coliseum theatre in St. Martin's Lane.
-I never see you dressed like this, and by the way, there is no dress code-
-Well, I wanted to dress nicely tonight- she replied with a big smile. She was wearing a fancy black dress with trousers on the bottom, but she looked a bit clumsy in it.
When the show began, the curtains opened slowly. A house, a fence and a small alley with two men standing still on it showed up while the musicians played the ouverture. It was hard to hold my excitement and Clelia seemed amused by

how deeply I focused into trying to follow the music step by step.
On the other hand, she wasn't focusing at all.
I noticed it since the beginning of the first act, but with the passage of the minutes, the expression on her face became more and more bored. On top of that, she kept checking her phone and texting, sometimes smiling and then quickly putting her phone back into her small black purse.
I really wanted to check on her, but I didn't want to look suspicious. My chance came when she yawned for the fifth time.
I spotted Salvatore's name on the top of her screen, a message with a kiss and a little heart next to it when she quickly turned off the whole screen, preventing me to see more, all happening in a second. I pretended I wasn't looking.
-Are you ok? Tired? We could go home earlier if you like- I said, getting more and more nervous.
-No, I'm ok, don't worry- she replied, rushed and nervous before zipping up her purse fast and taking it to the other side, further away from me, as if I could take her phone from it.
We didn't talk for the whole second act. A feeling of disappointment was gradually overwhelming me, and at some point, I could no longer follow nor enjoy the music.
The message came from him, maybe I still have no reason to actually get upset. She smiles every time and texts him even when she is with me though.
No, I shouldn't be proud, I should be open minded, I have no right to suffocate her with my jealousy.
I shouldn't be insecure about our story, but I can't see how that can be possible, after all what you have done to develop insecurity inside of me every single day.
-Can you tell me what's going on?- she asked me for the third time, visibly frustrated after not receiving replies yet.
I couldn't tell her I was ok, she had to know I wasn't, and at the end of the ballet, I stood up and left on my own.
I couldn't do this. I hated myself for reacting like that, I wished I wasn't doing it and yet I was doing it. I was acting weak, hysterical, and that was partially due to my

inexperience in relationships and partially to the fact that my date had made sure I felt like that.
Clelia managed to eventually stop me by the tube.
-Is this how you treat me? Does it seem right to you?- she asked me, loud.
-What? You're texting with that son of a bitch even when you are with me? Couldn't you wait for when we say good night?-
-You have no right to tell me this. I expected more from you, but now I realise you are very narrow-minded. If you can't accept me having a male friend...-
-You can have as many friends as you want, but he's not one!- we were getting louder and someone started looking at us.
-I told you I want to be free- Clelia was scolding me, and I felt miserable. I was feeling miserable everyday.
-Free...- as if I was chaining her somewhere. I couldn't reply fast enough though. I was still standing in the same place when I saw her disappear in the overcrowded tube entrance.

Well done for taking my Nutcracker night like that.
I'm not going to be so selfless to blame it on myself today. Don't come on a date with me and spend time on your phone with someone else, and I'm not narrow-minded, I couldn't possibly be defined like that.
But maybe, he really is just a friend...
No, she wouldn't hide her phone like that and by the way, the message had a heart on it. Friends don't send that stuff, or actually they do a lot, it's just me, I wouldn't send a heart not even to her, maybe that's all my fault, maybe I should have sent her some hearts.
I did what I had to, I didn't send her hearts through messages, but I told her that and she never even replied.
Time was passing, but I just couldn't fall asleep. I kept looking at her Whatsapp page just to see when she was online last and did the same thing with Salvatore's. Every time they were online together my heartbeat got faster, every time he was online and she wasn't, I pictured him sending her a message and waiting for her to see it. He was online way more often than her in general since he had a girlfriend already.

3.01 am and they're both online, maybe talking about me...
Clelia must be telling him how silly I acted and he's telling
her that she should talk to me and explain maybe...
-Clelia, I'm sorry about today, I acted jealous and I shouldn't
have. You're the one I love and I can't imagine not spending
my life doing my best to make you happy- I texted her.
If she had any doubts about how I felt for her or felt like she
lacked attention from me, there were not going be any
excuses now.
Five minutes later, her reply arrived.
-Dom, I'm sorry but we can only be friends from now on- I
stared at the message for a few minutes, shocked.
This didn't add up with any of my conclusions.
There has to be a mistake, this message doesn't really say
what it says.

So, this story is over, just like that, and it's all my fault.
I poured half pint of milk into a big bowl, filled it with
cereals in the kitchen and took it to my room. The flat was
empty and silent even in the morning.
I decided to use an hour of my time running in Clapham
Common before getting ready to go to work.
The park was wide and plain, not many pathways and a
couple of small ponds as I could see while I ran from the
corner in front of Clapham South station to the one near
Clapham Common. I wasn't looking forward to my first day of
work, but I had to do this.
My new workplace was near Leicester Square tube station.
Very crowded at pretty much every time of the day, I found
the restaurant dangerously punctual for my first day there.
-Domenico, right? I'm Frank- a guy in his thirties with a dark
blue shirt and a thick French accent greeted me by the
entrance.
-Nice to meet you- I smiled, feeling I hadn't done that in
ages.
-So you'll work as a runner for a week before we set you up as
a waiter, were you aware of this?-
-Yeah sure- Not a clue actually.
I got changed in the staff room downstairs, much smaller
than the one in Sloane Square and got ready to go upstairs

where the kitchen was, ready to get more instructions from other runners.
-Hi, nice to meet you, Ilaria- a brunette, a bit short Italian girl with olive skin introduced herself to me in the kitchen.
-Hi, Dom-
-I've heard you were a waiter. Why on earth did you decide to step back and work as a runner once again?- she said smiling.
-Well, it's just for a week actually- she made me smile for real, at least just for a couple of seconds.
-Fair enough, I hope they'll make me waitress soon-
-Is it too hard to be a runner?- I thought about how much I truly enjoyed it back in Sloane Square.
-Not too hard, but waiters get much more than us here, especially with all these tourists-
We started folding napkins over napkins and just kept talking for a bit while the chefs stood with crossed arms or just insulted each other with swear words from languages nobody spoke, but with meanings everyone knew about.
Time was slower than usual. If only it could get busier...
-You can't check your phone here in the kitchen, I mean, it's fine to me of course and today seems to be fine to everyone, but when the head chef comes back from holidays, which is tomorrow, then trust me, you won't be able to use it once without regretting it-
-Yeah sorry, just checking an important email- I replied.
Clelia and Salvatore were online.
A relatively quiet day of work ended eventually. I had to run a few times up and down the stairs, asking Ilaria to stay upstairs and take care of polishing cutlery and folding napkins all the time. She asked me if I was ok and why I would ever choose to be the only one in charge of running up and down the stairs.
-I love keeping myself busy, it's like doing gym here at work- partially true after all, but going up and down the stairs allowed me to check my phone more often than I could in the kitchen, even if I got no results from that.
I left the restaurant after 1 am and started walking north through Charing Cross Road only to then remember I didn't live in Russell Square anymore. I stood still for a minute,

unable to express how I was feeling. It was going to be a much longer route to Clapham South.

With the passage of the days, I became more and more sensitive towards what really happened. I was feeling numb at first, but now I was feeling the aftereffects.
I lost Clelia, and this time it wasn't one of her usual manipulative actions. She clearly stated that it was over and I was feeling less and less keen on doing anything, but thinking about it. The thought of her interrupted any others more often than I wanted to and it was all going from bad to worse.
Am I not supposed to improve? I though while waiting in the queue in the supermarket near the petrol station. My consumption of food increased a lot and so did the one of alcohol and weed. After three days, the pain I was feeling reached a point I couldn't even imagine possible.
Shame on me, how can I feel so bad when so many people have real problems? What about the Harry Potter studios experience? Aren't you looking forward to that? I stared at the screen of my phone while I rolled a joint by the step underneath my place.
The day of our visit to the studios that we so intensely craved to see together is tomorrow and all you do tonight is posting a picture on Facebook with Salvatore and the other guys from the kitchen?
I miss you, but you don't miss me and this doesn't match with the things you said to me. Every night I get high on weed, smoking more than I can bear just to make sure I fall asleep and wake up very late, right in time, and sometimes even late for my evening shift at work.
Work? In Leicester Square?
That's not even supposed to be my work. I used to work in Sloane Square and I used to like it. I did hate it for a long time, but eventually it all got better.
And what is this place? I hate this flat, it's silent, every time of the day is silent and it freaks me out to hear steps of people walking through the stairs at night. I was supposed to be in the hostel now, with Rey and my other friends.

All has changed, negatively, and it's all my fault. I wasn't good enough for her, I wasn't smart enough. Someone who knew more than me had come round for her and educated her under things I didn't know. She found her source of knowledge from him rather than from me. He built a reputation with her while I wasted my time being nice and down-to-earth.

Karma... What is it that I needed to know to take your heart? Why did I spend my life believing into science if I could have gone further and learn what was really behind it? Of course you chose him, he knows the truth they don't tell us, and you figured you'd be happier with someone better than me.

Karma... between the many results I encountered online, there seemed to be one leading meaning that all of them agreed on. The "law that brings back the results of all thoughts, words and actions to the person who produced them".

Unbelievable, it's just unbelievable...

I stared at my screen for a minute before having the courage to go on with that. I couldn't look at the surface, I had to go deep, but how could I choose to go deep if the key meaning was itself pure nonsense and just a lie for gullible, naïve people?

The video I was watching went on, and with a satisfied smile and voice, the man in there said that "just like a boomerang, all people that harmed others will be hit back".

I had to stop it there.

How? How could you fall into this? This is...

I looked at the dark cloudy sky for a minute, too impressed to go on. Then, I tried to keep going.

I mean, lots of horrible things happen to good people everywhere and every time, how blind did you have to be to believe in this? Wasn't it clear, that to believe into this, all it took was just the choice to do so? This is a faith, it doesn't give you any proofs!

One more minute, just one more minute...

"Bad actions get stored into people's genes and soul and get recorded in the sky. Then, when the time comes, the sky itself will take care of the redistribution".

I couldn't handle it any longer.

-What about Anne Frank? How do you explain that, you twat?- I said out loud, right in the middle in the night, sitting alone on the step. A young girl that was passing by in that moment literally crossed the road, scared, rushing away from me.

I went to work with the waiter uniform in my backpack for the first time after two weeks I was working in my new restaurant. The managers said that it just wasn't busy enough for me to jump on the floor and so just cut a few hours for everyone and asked me if I was ok working one more week as a runner.
I couldn't care less obviously, since I was still a bit nervous about the floor in general, but also looking forward to dealing with more tourists rather than just local Chelsea people.
Most people were very nice and friendly with me.
-I've been to Sloane Square once, it was a nightmare, very busy- the Mexican manager told me.
-I've been there too on a cover about last year, I'm so happy not to work there- a waiter added.
Ilaria was entertaining me during work. She kept offering to smoke weed with her at the end of the shift, and we talked about a lot of different things. She told me about her love for Sardinia, the place where she came from.
-I noticed all people from Sardinia are very proud about it, I mean, at least between all Sardinians I've met so far- I told her once.
-It's the best place in the world- she said. -Best nature and best people. If you have a friend from Sardinia, trust my word, he'd never act behind your back, but will always be on your side no matter what-
-I believe you- I said, not keen on giving her one pretty convincing proof that at least in one specific case, she was dead wrong.
-So what happened with your girlfriend?-
-She wasn't my girlfriend, but yeah whatever, she just called it off, not sure why-
-It happens to everyone- she said, gentle.
We were smoking in Trafalgar Square that night. I wished we could have just kept going for longer. It was when I was

alone that I thought about her the most intensely, but the pain was much relieved when I was with people, and especially when I reached a certain level of highness.
Weed had the power to make me miss her more, to make me think about my parents and to make me more and more aware of death and how inevitable it was. I hated it, but I kept going because the more I smoked, the sooner I reached a peak of unawareness. At that point, I was so high and stupid I couldn't even find the way home, and that was the mental state I was getting to every single night so not to be physically able to think about her.
The usual weekly 20 pounds I spent for weed became 40, and with an agreement with my dealer, I got to spend 50 to get more than what I could have got with 60.
On the other hand, my shape was getting better and better. Slowly, I found out I could run faster, longer and getting less and less sweaty and tired every single time.
I started waking up at noon everyday so that I could run around the park and do more exercise for my back, my shoulders and my arms.
I drank about a full pint of milk half hour before going down for sport, a lot more cereals and fruit than ever before and almost half kilogram of pasta before going to work, where I would have got some staff food as well. The more I did sport, the more I ate, but the more I was alone, the more I thought about her, the more I needed to get stoned or drunk to bear the pain.

By the second half of January, my finances recorded I was about one 1k below the line of 3k I promised myself to never break.
It's fine, 2k is still more than most of my former colleagues in Sloane Square confessed me to having.
Talking about Sloane Square... Ciro was calling me.
-Hey puppy, how are you?-
-Don't call me like that-
-We're having a staff party on the 25th, are you coming? I'd love to see you-
-Well...- Clelia might have been there. -Sure, I guess, why not?-

Ciro was able to say the meanest things to me and really give me on my nerves, but he thought about me and did a lot of small, good things for me over time that made me feel grateful and got me to like him, pretty much like Clelia did with me.

The thought of that night improved my mood a bit. I had spent more than two weeks in pain and things were slowly getting better. I still felt upset from day to night, but the pain had stabilised slightly below the usual line.

I started to feel like doing things. Reading was impossible, I spaced out a lot while reading and spacing out meant being sad.

What I needed was mostly physical, finding a way to get my body busy so that the brain couldn't think. Or maybe going out for a walk... my mood wasn't the best to go out of course, but I needed some rolling papers and it was too late to get some at the supermarket.

I decided to run to the closest open late off licence, about one mile away from me.

Crazy, I had been living in my new flat for about a month, but never gone out except for my physical activities in the park. I didn't even know what was by the other side of Clapham South tube station and I found out it was much louder than my side. I kept running because that was the only way to think less, but I had to slow down at some point. Clapham Common looked very different from Clapham South. It took about ten minutes run to see a completely different world, a world I had forgotten about.

People everywhere, queuing up to get into clubs and filling up bars, younger ones mixing drinks with plastic cups while sitting by the grass, girls, many girls, so close to my place and I didn't even know it.

I sat on a step next to the tube station, where young people were still coming off from a lot.

Only a few months ago, that was normality. I used to hang out with Rey and meet new people everyday. I was confident and cheeky, but now I had lost it all. I had a job I didn't want, lived in a place I didn't like, lost one third of the money I had, and got to bear the endless pain of a breakup.

I kept smoking my joint, sitting alone, surrounded by countless people looking for fun and potentially looking forward to meeting me, but there was no way I could have found the strength to go and talk to them and even if that were to happen, I wouldn't have lasted long before they felt negative energy coming from me and let me go.
The weather isn't that bad, maybe because I've been running. One joint here, maybe someone will notice me. This looks great, it's full of life. None of these people feels like me today, they're all happier, probably.
-Arlena, do you want to come to my place tomorrow evening?- I texted Arlena on my way back home. The sight of people being alive and happy helped me more than what time had done in weeks. If time wasn't going to help me, then I would have taken the lead. All I needed was that feeling, no matter how short it was, I just needed to multiply the number of times I felt just as good as I was near all those people. I would have even bought a camping tent and moved there if necessary.

Surprisingly, I woke up to Arlena's positive reply. She was coming over that evening.
Yes, something positive is happening later, now I just have to wait for it. I have to set deadlines and meet them, that feels good, I thought while tidying up the room and opening the windows. I need to have something good scheduled each day and the wait for it will help reduce the pain.
-All the way from Holland Park?- I asked her that night, when she arrived with her bicycle.
-Hey Dom!- she hugged me, her buxom body pressed against mine, oh, I hope she's come for the reason I meant.
-How are you? You disappeared Dom- she said.
-Yeah, I haven't been in the best mood actually- she ignored that. -Are you hungry?- I continued.
-I'm not very hungry Dom, all I want is to lie down next to you-
-Well, if that's what you want...-
-Rey keeps talking about you, when are you guys going to meet up again? He wants to see you, not just text you- she told me when we were in bed.

-Oh Arlena, actually, do you think I could move in with you guys?- I asked her, hopeful.
-It might be too late now because I might have to leave London for a bit, I think my mother is sick, but she doesn't want to tell me-
-Oh, sorry to hear that- another real problem that made me feel ashamed of feeling sad.
-Besides, Rey owes me about 500 pounds and it doesn't seem like he will be able to give them back to me anytime soon-
-What the hell? That's a lot of money-
-He keeps betting. I keep finding betting papers in his pockets, he told me he quit, but he never really does. He owes money to other people too-
So, that's what those papers were about, that's why he kept hiding them from me.
-I see.. I gave him money once and it's fine if he won't return it, but I won't give him any more though, in case he asks-
-Exactly- she said, getting closer and closer to me.
Your body feels warm, so warm and so good, but you're the wrong girl. You look more attractive than her in every aspect of your body, but you're not her. Someone else was supposed to be here, someone else is who I really want.

The night of the staff party, I sat on a bench by the crossroad where Great Marlborough Street and Carnaby street meet. Ciro was supposed to be there soon, and I wanted to enter the club with someone. The idea of going there on my own wasn't very appealing since I was the one who left all of them just a couple of weeks before.
We went into a club in Ganton Street, the dance floor was downstairs. The sound of loud music brought me back to some of my very first London pub crawls nights out with tourists from the hostel in Hyde Park, about a year before, but it seemed much more than that then.
Everybody was there except her. Clelia had a natural despise for people and for anything social that didn't focus the attention on her. Salvatore was there, talking to Simona, pouring her a drink.
Simona was an Italian girl who had started working for Cote in November. Her and I had some real chemistry, although I

never made a move on her since she was Italian, had a boyfriend, and happened to be there when my story with Clelia was developing.
Oh, Lena is here too... Maybe I should just go and tell her what's happening between her boyfriend and Clelia, I would love to destroy them, maybe give some pain to both, how great would that be?
-Dom, good to see you man- Alex hugged me from my back. -I miss you there in Sloane Square- he added.
Alex, or Sasha, was a half German half Russian young guy who started working as a runner in early December.
-Oh, I miss you too man, and I miss everyone else actually. I wish I could go back in time- I said sadly.
One by one, runners, waiters and managers came over to say hi to me, still standing by the counter, waiting for a beer that might have taken some time before coming to me. Many between them confessed to missing me and that the runners area was the dirtiest it had ever been.
-You're a shit waiter, but we need you back, as a runner though- the sous-chef told me. I knew he was going to be there, he was a player and in those nights things could happen. Not to me though, I wasn't successful in such situations.
-Dom, come with me, I have to tell you something- Alice whispered in my ears at some point.
-Hey Alice, I honestly don't care if it's about Clelia, so you can spare it- I said, serious, but with a joking face. I knew they were going out all the time and seeing Alice always caused me some anxiety. She would have made her name eventually, she liked her a lot even though Clelia didn't care about her at all.
We moved towards the toilet, so that no one could hear us. Please tell me something I'd like to hear Alice, I feel miserable.
-Are you joking? You can't do this here!- the usual club toilet guy came out and shouted at us.
-Oh, yeah sorry, trust me, it's not what it looks like- I said, a bit nervous now.

I wasn't going to make a move on Alice and neither was she. We were both tipsy and walked into the male toilets without realising it.
-Now you have to leave!- he kept shouting and got very close to me.
-You're joking man, you must be! I've paid to get in here you know-
-I don't care, get out of here!- he pushed me towards the way out without much effort, then he made sure his two colleagues upstairs knew about me and left me in their hands.
-Dom, what happened?- Simona was there. At least Salvatore had left her alone. She wouldn't have gone with him anyway.
-They kicked me out. They thought I was taking Alice to the toilet with me-
-Oh, what a shame- she smiled.
-Are you ok anyway?- I asked her in a sweet tone, feeling something.
-Just a bit drunk actually, and you are so handsome Dom, I've always wanted to tell you- she said, her voice sounded very tender, as if she wasn't herself.
-Thanks, I have to say I've always found you beautiful too- I said.
We were outside the club. Her brown hair were straightened more than usual just for the night. Her pretty big brown eyes that made me turn my head towards her a few times at work. Oh, if only Clelia could see me right now.
-So, are we going to go to a toilet? Somewhere? I don't know...- she looked down the ground, smiling.
-My place?- I suggested, impulsively.
She nodded her head yes, still smiling, clearly drunk.
-Follow me to the tube then, it won't take long- I hoped that the Northern line still worked and that Salvatore had made sure that Simona and I were leaving everyone to go and have sex. He might have taken Clelia away from me, but Simona was genuinely very attractive, even though I knew I was going to wake up still sad the following day.

February 2016

Cote in Leicester Square was a better place to work in than in Sloane Square by far.

My parents used to tell me that annoying people were going to be present everywhere in my life's path, and that the best way to deal with them was to have a good attitude and remain humble, hardworking and honest.

They might have been right on the fact that it's truly hard to find a workplace or a household where nobody decides to be annoying and take advantage of you, but they never mentioned that the reason why said annoying people behaved annoyingly was due to the fact you were humble, hardworking and honest.

I found myself at times walking somewhere and feeling some pleasure by filling my head with negative thoughts that increased my hate towards a certain thing, or in my case, a person. Up to that point nothing had ever happened outside of my head and I was pretty sure that nothing was ever going to, but I couldn't deny how often I would run in the park whilst gathering all the lies I had been told, both by Clelia and Salvatore and replaying them in an endless loop that increased my desire of revenge every time a logically righteous conclusion had been drawn out of each loop.

I need to make sure that I don't hate anyone if that's not justified. I need to make sure I'm right, I thought while every clue of the story seemed to be leading to a unanimous verdict.

Most of my thoughts started with an "if", continued with a "which means that" and ended with the start of the following thought, either the exact same or a different one that aimed at proving my innocence to the eyes of logic and the deliberateness of the evil act committed by the defendant. Then the hate reached a peak when my body trembled and I found myself running faster and losing too much energy, and finally, I would go home.

-Mark?- he was in the kitchen, and this was the moment to speak.

-Hi, Domenico. Oh, by the way, I forgot to ask you, about paying your rent this month...-

-Yeah, about that... Look, I'm tired of this situation. I haven't been able to talk to my parents at all nor to watch a film or anything because we don't have wi-fi here and my phone never gets service in that room. Now, I know that it's not your fault, but I was told that there was going to be wi-fi here and I was never given the password. Yes, the French one has it and she hid it from you, but that's your fight and not mine. I'm disappointed and I'm not paying the full rent. Actually, I may pay you the whole rent, but I'm leaving on the second week of this month- I said.
I wouldn't have been able to say this if I hadn't been madly angry with everything. Oh, what a relief, shouting it all out!
-I'm sorry Mark, it's not about you, you're a very good flatmate, I'm really sorry about this- I added, calmer now, but unable to look at his face.
-It's ok Domenico, I understand. It's not the first time that crazy woman spoils the atmosphere in this house- he said, pensive.
Right then, a door slammed open, and someone rushed towards us.
-What did you say? What did you say?- a black woman with a blue dress shouted while approaching us. After more than a month I had been living next to her room, I finally met her.
-I'm saying that you're an insane person and all other flatmates are leaving this place because of you, including the new guy- Mark tried to remain calm, but his voice was raised now.
-I'm not crazy! You're such a piece of shit, and if you say that once again, I will kill you- she was out of her mind now. I wondered if the neighbours could hear us.
-Ah, go to hell, I'm not listening to this- Mark stayed in control of his emotions and headed to his room.
-No, you are not going anywhere- she shouted and came back from the kitchen wielding the biggest knife we had, now trembling nervously, holding it at the height of his chest.
-What are you doing?!- I shouted at her, unsure if shouting was the best option. She seemed totally out of control.
-Don't you dare...- Mark looked at her with a killer face, but didn't move at all.

-You should put that away. You don't need it- I said, very slow after ten seconds of silence where we all looked at the knife, but nobody dared moving a finger.
-You can give it to me if you want- I suggested her, but got no reply.
-Domenico, whatever happens, you are a witness of this and I want you to take action, ok?- Mark said, eyes still on the knife. The woman was struggling to breathe now.
-Sooner or later- she panted -I will kill you- she said, then headed back to her room.
-Did you hear that? In case, you witness, right?- Mark asked me again, serious.
-Of course Mark- I assured him.
That was fun, I thought while lying down in bed. It totally distracted me, at least it made me feel alive... I wish something like this could happen everyday until I leave. How could I forget what my resolution was about? I have to do stuff to feel better, or at least not to feel dead inside. Today was the day I gave a sudden notice to Mark and therefore the landlord, tomorrow will be the day I quit my job and ask Simona to come round again.

Simona agreed on seeing me back in Clapham South area for a coffee, which translated into the language of adults, meant sex. She said we couldn't meet up in her area because she lived with her boyfriend, which was perfect not only because I didn't have to go anywhere to get laid, but also because I could try to do with her the exact same things I did with Clelia. Basically, an idea I had to try and think less about Clelia was to delete her uniqueness by redoing all what I did with her with someone else. If I had walked hand in hand with Simona from the cafe to my place, Simona would have been the last person that had done that very thing with me, and Clelia would have become one from a more distant past, consequently harder to remember.
Simona wasn't going to walk hand in hand with me though, she wasn't the type.
She was sitting in front of me in the cafe. I didn't drink coffee, so I ordered a hot chocolate. I thought it was

supposed to improve my mood or give me some energy boost, but nothing happened.
You couldn't see the sky in February, just a massive, endless cloud that covered the whole surface of every possible corner you might try to look at.
-You're looking prettier than usual today- she smiled, then the expression on her face went back to what seemed to be pure agony.
Does she just want to go straight to the point? She came all the way here probably expecting something more.
There are a few things I would like to ask, but I don't know how bad they might sound, and I just want you to know I have no intention to complicate things between us, both because you are already taken and because I am dead inside.
-How's work?- she asked, as if speaking cost her some real efforts.
-Pretty good, but I gave my notice today actually. My last day will be on Sunday, and also the day I'm moving back to the hostel-
-You really like the hostel, I remember you talking about it a few times when I started working in Sloane Square- she was smiling now. -What's so special about it?-
-Oh well, let's just say you get laid a lot- she laughed.
-Does a handsome man like you need to live in a hostel to get laid?-
-Yes, because I always want a different girl, you know- I smiled, knowing to be reporting a past opinion of mine that she might have not believed since she knew I had quit my job because of one girl and moved away from the hostel for the same reason.
-I liked it with you the other night. I hope your boyfriend doesn't catch you though-
-Don't worry about it, it's all safe. He doesn't suspect a thing- she said, slowly and as if she was tasting her own words. She was someone else's Clelia. Does every man have a Clelia?
-You're not the first one I have sex with outside of my relationship with him. I have had many more, but he still doesn't suspect a thing, he just loves me too much anyway, and I love him too, he's my one and only man, but I need to have sex with others, I would get too bored otherwise- she said.

My brain processed her words very slowly now.
-But it wasn't like this at the beginning- she continued.
-When I was about 20 years old, I was madly in love with a guy back in my hometown, but I found out he had cheated on me with a girl that used to be my best friend and I just couldn't believe it. They just told me that at a party and I was so in love with him- she said, still slowly.
-That day I also found out he had cheated on me with about twenty girls and some of them were there at my party-
-He basically slept with all the girls of your town or what? You can't be too many up there between the mountains- I said, trying to defuse the conversation.
-A very small town yeah, so you can imagine, all young people just have sex with each other all the time- she said, dreamily.
I thought it was the exact opposite, but I'd rather keep this for myself.
-Wanna go to my place?- I asked at some point.
-Yeah sure- she said and stood up straight away.
-It sucks- I let out of my mouth while we walked past the pond to get to the pavement in Nightingale Lane.
-Oh Dom, you're such a handsome guy, you can get much better stuff than that girl- she said in a cuddly voice.
Don't say that, I know that there is better stuff, your face and body look better than hers, but I want her!

Two days before the end of my staying in Holmside Court, my mood had improved a little.
It started taking about half hour or one full hour before I felt any pain at all in the mornings. Most of the times I would wake up just fine and feel absolutely nothing during my breakfast until I got ready, either for sport or for work. Keeping busy every single second had become important to preserve my mental sanity.
I didn't know why it hurt so much, why I thought about it so much and especially, when it would stop hurting, but one thing I knew for sure. Anytime I was busy, that pain, no matter how intensely I was feeling it, would literally cease its presence, but for that, I needed an activity that required my constant attention.

Online chess was great for that, although the other side of the coin was that it also had the power of making me angry. I was a very poor player, my rating barely crossed over the line of the 1000 points and considering that any respectable player's rating had to be over 1600 points and be consistent about it, it all just made me feel frustrated. Whenever I reached my targeted rating, I just started losing a lot, sometimes crushed by someone who played better than me, sometimes by someone who played worse but didn't resign and eventually won either thanks to the clock or to my horrible endgame management.
-Clelia, I need to talk to you- I sent her a text before I could reason and make the right choice.
Countless amount of time I had spent thinking to text her, typing and deleting, writing at times long paragraphs and keeping them saved but then deleting them three days afterwards. I tried to combine some sort of sweetness, desire and coolness into a message but then, whenever I read it out loud, it just sounded needy.
I sent her that message right when I was finally doing a bit better, but why? I don't want her to know I'm thinking about her! What can I do now?
-Yes sure...- she replied.
Is she ok? I thought she was going to ignore me.
-I'll come tonight after work- was this too hard?
-Ok, I'd like to go to sleep by 1 am though...-
-I'll be before that, and it'll be a minute-

That night, I ran to Leicester Square tube station before it closed. My shift ended at midnight, but I wanted to be sure not to miss the last train.
It will be pointless, wrong and maybe just hurtful to see her, why am I even going there? I need Manu and Marco to tell me to man up, I know they would, but I can't text them now to ask them to text that back to me, can I?
I am a joke. I hope no man finds out about this, I hope they don't know what's happening in my head right now. Desperate for a gentle touch of a girl that came suddenly into my life and left the same way. I chose to ignore the theory of how to deal with girls as it was explained by older men, Manu, and

the history of the world because I thought that the type of love I would have got was going to be the real one, the one without barriers, that didn't require me thinking about any strategy on how to keep it working but just was.
Stockwell. Shall I leave? Shall I go home? Yes, I'm going home, oh, she's going to text me back and look for me if I just don't show up, I'm still in time.
Why show up at her place? I'm not feeling any cold even though my jacket is in my backpack.
-Hi- Clelia opened the door of her flat when I knocked. I remembered you more attractive.
-Hi- I said, trying to look and sound just fine. You have no idea how much emotional pain you have caused me in the last weeks and how I wish I had never met you at all, but maybe, it's not your fault.
-Come on in- she said, her voice was gentle.
-How have you been?- she asked me when we were in her room.
-All good, usual life. I'm enjoying my job, but I'm leaving it by the end of the week- I said.
-Oh, why?- she sounded very sweet, no sign of her usual aggressive and mean words.
-I want to come back to my usual life in the hostel, I'm not very happy right now, I don't like living in a room and the flat is always empty- I said, sure that my voice sounded just plain.
-I'm sorry to hear that you're not enjoying living in that room, but maybe you're not ready for that- she said, slowly.
-You should show me some stuff about art. I know you like it a lot and I tend to ignore it- I said.
She showed me a few paintings from the internet. Her knowledge and passion for visual art was clear. Salvatore tried to talk me into this some months before I met her and I dismissed it. Kindly, of course, but I couldn't care less about paintings. You are just perfect for him, you were made for each other, but I've been doing it well with you in bed and I know that's what you've always wanted. If only you wanted to do it now, I would consider all those days in pain worth it.
-It's very late and I'm so tired- she stood up and still spoke gently at some point.

-Clelia, I have invested a lot of my time, energy and even money for our story. You did nothing to stop it while it was happening, but you stopped it later on. You're not seeing me anymore, I wonder what happened- I stood up as well. I couldn't have left without asking her the question that I asked myself every second in the last three weeks.
-Well... I need my space Domenico. I have just restarted drawing- she stopped for a second to show me a butterfly that she had drawn on her paper book.
-Clelia, this is not true. This is not the reason at least. I don't understand how my presence in your life would stop you from drawing or from doing anything else. I never spent that much time with you anyway since we met about once or twice a week. I wouldn't want to own you in any possible way, but I hate to be lied to, I don't deserve it- my voice remained calm until the end.
Saying that was a massive relief, I could feel my body getting lighter.
Clelia got silent for half minute, then spoke.
-See, when I moved to London, I was overwhelmed by so many different emotions, fears and insecurities, and you... you were the person that allowed me to make it without driving mad. I needed you then, but now I don't need you anymore- she didn't look at me at all while she said this.
Why didn't you tell me then? Why did you waste my time?
-I understand- I said.
-Domenico- she stopped me when I had just left her flat, silent.
-I love you- she hugged me, then closed the door.
It's not the love I want from you. I can feel my heart breaking now, but I know this can only improve from now on. Few more days of work, and then I'm taking some time off from everything.

I got home at about 2 am and found Mark still awake.
-Hey Domenico, how are you?- he asked me, polite.
-All good, Clelia broke up with me, so yeah, not the best mood actually- I didn't want to say it to him. We weren't friends and he was an experienced man. Why did I have to humiliate myself in front of him too?

-It happens, but now don't call her again- he said. Does he know?
-The best thing to do now is not to show her that you're thinking about her or it will turn her off forever- he told me. Nice of him to tell me the same thing that all guys say all the time. He doesn't know that I had already messed that plan up already.
-Thanks, I'll make sure to do that- I said, trying to go to bed.
-Domenico, it has been nice meeting you. I wish you all the best for the future- he said, and we shook hands.

That Sunday morning the walk in Nightingale Lane to the tube stop didn't feel so bad. Apart from the heavy suitcases I was taking back to Russell Square, I was excited about the full-time social distraction that the hostel was going to offer me, not to mention that I was finally unemployed and didn't have to return to Cote any more.
However, the best news I received came from Rey.
-Dom, I'm making some booking in Russell Square hostel, will you be there? Book there man, come on, we should be together, we will be back Dom- the usual multitude of texts sent by Rey to only ask one question.
Time flew on the tube. Maybe I could just leave the suitcases in my room and go for lunch somewhere, to have a treat. When will Rey be there too?
Finally, Guilford Street, once again.
I walked in slowly, carrying my suitcases up the few steps between me and the entrance, as if the pace I was going at could confirm my brain that it was happening for real, just in case.
Room 10, the usual one, the cheapest one down the basement.
Not much had changed. Joseph was still there. He didn't see me, his eyes were on the television.
Not too many people were there, just a quiet afternoon, the way I liked the afternoons best.
I sat by the sofas, right in front of a very pretty, blonde girl with blue eyes, probably slightly younger than me. I saw her since the moment I got in, but I couldn't be bothered thinking to start a conversation.

The blonde girl smiled at me. A bald heavy-set man was sitting next to her, his arm comfortably leaning all over the upper side of the sofa, covering almost all of it. He looked like one of those American actors that play the tough police officer or fighter in films.
-Hi man- he gave me a big smile and spoke loud, as if he was really happy to see me.
-Hi- I said, polite. I don't know if we will be friends.
-What's your name?- he asked, very friendly. Smiling back would have cost me an effort, but he deserved it.
-Dom, you?-
-My name is Adam, she is Alessia, from Italy and Joao, from Portugal- he pointed at the pretty girl and at a guy with curly hair and blue eyes that just sat down with them.
-Nice to meet you guys- I said.
The guy called Joao didn't seem very enthusiast and just lifted his eyes to cross with mine for a second, then went back at shaking the bag of tea out of his cup before throwing it in the nearest bin.
Adam told me he came from Egypt. He had a thick accent that made it almost hard to understand.
Joao kept looking everywhere apart from my direction, apparently not really interested in getting to know me. I wonder if broken-hearted people look like it and he was good at recognising it.
I looked into the big mirror by the wall. I was happy to be there, but I wasn't feeling any healed.

Rey got to the hostel the next day.
He looked completely different from the last time I saw him. Besides the very first time he did something like hugging me, he also seemed very happy.
-How have you been my brother?- he asked me, radiant.
-Well, not too good, I'm still going through a massive breakup...-
-Let's take a seat here, let's play a game of chess. I missed kicking your ass- he didn't seem to have heard a single word of what I said.
-I missed the hostel- he said while setting up his side of the chess board -except when there's a school trip- he continued.

A large group of students had just entered the hostel and gathered around in the living room while their teacher gave them some instructions out loud in a northern European language.
-We are back Dom- Rey looked the happiest man alive.
-What makes you so happy Rey?- I asked him, curious.
-It's just good to be here with you, and I can't wait to see Adrian and Mina actually- he said.
-Hi guys- a young guy with short, dark brown hair had just approached us. A friend of his was just behind him, blond, with pale skin and blue eyes and quite tall, just like the other one.
-Hi- Rey replied.
-Could I ask for a challenge to one of you? I'd love to play- he said.
-Yeah sure- I said, -at the end of this game my friend will challenge you-
He smiled and moved a few metres away from us, leant on a table and crossed his arms, looking at us, his friend still speaking to him.
-He looks very nerdy, I think he might be a very good player- Rey felt just the same as me, probably due to the squared glasses that this guy had and also by how keen he seemed on a challenge.
-He's literally staring at us- Rey whispered again, chuckling.
-Would you like to take a seat, guys?- I asked them.
The two of them sat at our table.
-My name is Stian, from Norway, what about you guys?-
After a friendly introduction, Rey and I challenged Stian at turns. He had a superior technique at chess and dominated me for the whole game until the moment he blundered a rook, which allowed me to transform a miserable game into a lucky win, making me quite satisfied about it.
-The only other Norwegian people I know are the world champion of chess and Breivik, but you might not know the last one because you're a bit too young- I said. Maybe my vodka and coke was already kicking in.
-Magnus Carlsen is arrogant, and his jaws make him look like a Pitbull. Regarding Breivik, well, they just keep saying his

name on the news at any convenient chance, which is getting annoying to be honest- Stian replied.
We were sitting all together in the sofas area after playing about ten games. Rey was sitting comfortably on the sofa, talking with two girls from the same group of Norwegians.
-I cannot flirt with you because you are not 18 yet, but I'm ready to wait one more year if necessary- Rey was making those two girls with blonde braids laugh a lot and they just couldn't stop looking at him from the opposite sofa. I was having a conversation with Stian and a few other guys about how the Norwegian state worked with pleasure.
That night, with the alcohol, the new people I just met, my first chess win in a long time and some debates about politics had cast me into a mood that a few months before was just my normality.
For most of the time in fact, I focused right on what we were all talking about without pretending.
In the same night, we met Vetle, a guy who surprised me with his philosophical questions taken out of his school book, and Fran, a very attractive blonde girl that was there within the same group, who showed me how to improve my drawing skills.
-Dom? We should go to Norway- Rey suggested me later that night. -You need to get another holiday from work or something. We have to travel again!-
I looked at him for a minute.
Shall I tell him that maybe we should do next month? Oh, I'm actually unemployed now...
-Next week? But not Norway, this time it will be Amsterdam- I said, smiling and hoping to be doing much better for the following week.

It was going to be my first time in Holland. Rey had never visited it before neither since his very first travel abroad was to London, right when he moved to the UK by the end of 2014.
We found a cheap flight for the end of the following week and grabbed our chance. I would have looked for work as soon as I was back in London, or maybe, I could have asked

to be readmitted at Sloane Square... They all wanted me back there after all.
If Clelia were to leave the job herself or die, I would have continued my life in my beloved Cote and pretend that I had just gone for a long holiday before coming back to work, like a celebrity.
I have to contact Daryl, or actually, Tom. Tom has always been super nice to me and to everyone in general, he'll say yes, but how do I tell him?
-Rey, I should go back to work in Sloane Square, I want to, I think- I once told him.
-Dom, that's pathetic, is this the value you give to yourself?-
-Rey, we've talked about it already. Just because you don't work it doesn't mean other people shouldn't work either. Not everyone has a penis like yours or charges the same hourly fee-
-I wasn't speaking about that. All I'm saying is that you think like a poor person, so you'll always be poor and it's not a good life- he said, confident.
-Poor? I'd like to remind you that you still owe me 100 pounds- I said, getting a bit frustrated now.
-That's not the point. I can make 200 pounds in one hour. You have to work two long shifts at work to make what I make per hour-
-I told you, I can't do your job. It's not my fault- I interrupted him, losing my patience. How hard was it for him to understand?
-This is also why your laptop is a piece of garbage and you always buy cheap clothes, that you don't even care about-
-Mate...- I stopped. I wanted to say so many things at the same time that eventually I couldn't pick a single one.
-You owe me 100 pounds, rich man- I said, cold, then left. He left unsatisfied too, I'm not sure why.
Idiot. People overstep the boundaries anytime you let them.
Rey was near the sofas later that night. The hostel was quite full, the buzz of the people mixed with the sound of the tv, the cutlery that touched the plates, the wine cork getting removed by two girls who refused any help and eventually succeeded, followed by a celebrating clap and whistle by some other friends were my absolute favourite sound.

A few weeks ago, an unbearable silence forced my thoughts to float inside my head and gave me not a single moment of peace in a flat I didn't like with a psychopath and a man who was rarely there. Now, the hostel, where everyone was happy and carefree except me.
-So now we're not talking or what?- I gave up on that. I couldn't have a fight with Rey as well.
Rey ignored me, too keen on showing some papers to a bald man in his forties with a tracksuit.
I sat on another sofa, further away from him. Why, if I'm a rational person, why do I love spending time with highly unstable people?

Few days before the travel, I could say I was already getting closer to Adam and Alessia.
Adam was a construction engineer that worked in Saudi Arabia and then moved to London both for work and to enjoy a social life that he was seemingly very keen on getting. He would always be the first one to approach people and tell them to join the rest of the group for food and drinks. You could hear his loud laugh from the distance and often see him with his arms on other people's shoulders while telling them sweet things, all of this while being very respectful and decent.
Alessia and I were talking a lot. She played the guitar and worked as a waitress in a restaurant in Oxford before moving to London. We became friends in no time and I felt like I could tell her how I was truly feeling those days.
-I wouldn't have said it, you look just ok most of the times when you are with us, but to be honest, I kind of see it sometimes, I just didn't know- she told me.
Overall, things were getting a bit better, or at least, better than they were.

We had to catch another early flight and for that, we decided once again to stay up the whole night.
Rey and I spent too much time between the chairs of the waiting areas in the airport when we realised that our flight was doing last calls already.

We landed in Amsterdam and then took a bus to the city centre. Our hostel was in Leidsekruisstraat, a very central street in the middle of one of the many concentric small islands in between the many canals that characterised the city.
-My father likes to call it the Venice of the North- I said.
-How far is it? I need to rest- Rey ignored that.
-Stop complaining, we've just arrived, but yeah, I agree with taking a nap before going out-
The hostel had a very narrow entrance with stairs that allowed only one person at a time to go upstairs to the reception.
-It's all thinner than in Russell Square- I noticed a tiny living room with three wooden tables with a vase in the middle of each of them and a small sofa by the window, next to a vending machine.
-We should get some vodka before going out- I said while we got into our room with eight beds, all empty but one where a man was sleeping.
-Yeah, you go and get it, I'll give you money afterwards- Rey said, then looked at me and went on -I might have to go for a business, you know, one of mine-
-Oh no, no! Is this going to be like in Sweden?- I asked him, slowly starting to feel angry.
-No, I promise, I'll be back for party tonight, and it's not for sure that I'm doing it anyway-

We woke up in the evening and had our first shots in our room. A young couple, German girl and middle Eastern guy, were undoing their suitcases, and an Asian man was napping by the other side of the room.
We finally decided to get going.
-Hi, do you speak English?- I asked a girl who was sitting by the tables in the small living room while me and Rey were going downstairs, tipsy already.
-Oh, hi- she replied, very timidly.
-What's your name?-
-Lottie- she sounded almost scared.

Her blue eyes, very pale skin and her dark red fringe with hair that barely touched her shoulder made her look very pretty to me. Was I being too aggressive though?
-What's your plan for the night?- Rey asked her. We were literally leaning on the table, and the receptionist was looking at us.
-I don't know, I think I'll watch a movie- she said.
-You're in Amsterdam, why not going out?-
-Oh well, I'm flying back to Australia tomorrow and I've only got five euros left- she looked embarrassed. Me and Rey laughed.
-Come with us, drinks are on us- I said.
She hesitated for a few seconds, then spoke.
-Fine- she smiled, and followed us downstairs.
The streets of our area were all quite small, typical for an old European city after all. The bricked buildings looked all beautiful with dark red or brown prevailing colours which somehow made everything else look more reddish.
We walked a few minutes and reached the main square of the area, then took a seat on a table outside a bar.
-They'll give us ten shots for ten euros, not too bad- I noticed.
Lottie was finally getting a bit more talkative, but the fact that she was sitting in a good posture and not laughing much made me think she was just too nice.
-Let's do twenty shots then, just to start- Rey said, eyes constantly on his phone. He hadn't spoken almost at all up to that moment.
-Are you checking your bets?- I asked in Spanish.
-No, but I have to go now, you know why- he stood up and left without even say bye to Lottie.
-Where is he going?- Lottie was surprised.
-Don't worry, he'll come back one of these days- I said.
-Still up for twenty shots?- I asked her, tipsy enough not to care and to pay more.
-If you want- she said, shrugging her shoulders, pretending she was going to be ok even without drinking and that she was glad even for the mere company.

Rey, you're an idiot, last time I'm travelling with you. You left me alone with her, and she's finishing all the shots on her own, damn it if she likes to drink, I thought.
I rushed to drink as much as I could, pushed by the idea that I didn't want her to brag with her friends in Australia about how she ripped off a naïve dude that paid all her drinks before going back to the hostel on her own.
-How is your European trip going? Best place so far?- I asked her. Drinking so fast and so much was something she could handle, but I couldn't. I needed water.
-I wouldn't know about my favourite place, but definitely my favourite experience was in Belgium. I met a couchsurfer that hosted me and showed me around for two days and it was incredible. I think I got a crush on him while he took me for a ride around his town, and the nature was...- she was excited by the memory of it. That was her peak moment of her trip and it made sense. It would have been everyone's peak.
-So you liked the guy, eh?- usually I would feel a bit jealous to find out that the girl in front of me had a crush on someone else because that meant no chance for me, but I felt nothing right then.
I guess I'm not ready to move on from my story yet. Well Lottie, it's good to share drinks with you tonight, you're good company I must say.
-Yes actually, but the best thing is that nothing happened- she said, now blushing.
-Oh yeah, I agree with you, yeah, it's all much better when it doesn't happen, right?- I said, the alcohol had kicked in well.
-Yes, because then it sticks in your head and you try to figure out all sort of ways in which it could have happened- she was getting excited and drunk, possibly.
-I feel you. By the way, let's go for a joint, shall we?-
She was way more talkative and excited now. I noticed she was about as tall as me before we sat down on a bench.
After a few puffs she was looking a bit confused, sometimes looking at me as if she was very happy to see me, sometimes focusing somewhere else.
-Are you ok?-

-Yeah, I'm just happy- she said. She looked more and more attractive to me.
-Let's go to a bar, let's dance- I stood up at some point, and she followed me without hesitating again.
-Rey!- I saw Rey literally walking towards us in the crowded Leidseplein square.
-Hey Dom, sorry, my phone went off and I was just going to the hostel- he said, not surprised we had bumped into each other.
-Come with us, bar- I said, now feeling high.
Eventually we got to a bar, got more drinks, Rey and Lottie along, the man still being weird, slightly passive but still more extrovert than the average person, the woman acting completely different from the moment we had met her, she was out of control on the dance floor.
After singing along a Spanish song together at the karaoke, we decided to head back home. Rey was tired, Lottie and I were wasted.
Lottie looked fit. Her black top highlighted her curves, her naked belly and the alcohol were teasing me hard by the end of the night. Rey seemed not to care too much, he had probably just had an orgasm with a customer anyway, and now I wanted Lottie.
We looked at each other for a few seconds, smiled as if we wanted to say something, but then went on to say good night and got into our own rooms.
-Dom, she liked you, you didn't realise it- Rey told me as he was getting undressed, ready for bed.
-Do you think so?-
I felt that way too, I had to say. She had given me her Facebook right before, and trying wouldn't have cost anything after all, I thought.
-I'm not going to sleep now- a text came from her right in that moment.
-Meet me downstairs- I texted back, overexcited.
I found her outside, leaning against the wall of the hostel. The zip of her jacket was wide open despite the cold, and I wasn't going to miss that universal signal.

She stared at me as I got closer to her and kissed her without saying a word, then she nodded her head yes when I told her to come to my room upstairs.
All beds in my room were now taken, but everyone except Rey seemed to be sleeping.
Rey looked at me while I got Lottie naked in my bed, none of us caring about the missing curtains.
Lottie was enjoying it, and so was I, along with Rey, who was looking at me from his bed, smiling, now getting naked as well. Who would have cared if anyone had waken up?
-You know, I think my friend wants some too- I whispered to her ear at some point. Rey had literally stood up and climbed into our bed silent, surprising Lottie on her face.
-Alright then, I'm going to fuck your friend too- she said, totally cool with that.
Yes please, I'm drunk and exhausted.
-What the hell is going on here?- the night shift receptionist had just entered the room and turned the lights on, the orange badge hanging on his uniform.
The German girl was standing, amused, everybody else slowly opening their eyes remaining in bed though.
-You cannot do this here, so go back to your room, now!- he said, strict.
Lottie was still naked on top of Rey and I had already jumped back on my bed.
She got dressed, silent but still smiling. I might have not finished, but her messy hair was a sign of victory for me.

The next day, during our check out, the receptionist apologised for interrupting our fun the previous night.
-Oh, if I knew you were Italian, I would have let you go on with it- he said, smiling and seemingly sorry. He spoke Italian and said he had lived in the north of Italy for many years.
-Don't worry, I understand, you were doing your job- I replied. Cunt.
We spent a quieter day and another night at a club, but the mood wasn't the same as the previous night. When a great night happens, the following one always lets down.

-You know what Dom, it's time for me to work too. A part-time job at least, just to fix my mindset a bit. Some regularity will help me not to spend so much money and not to gamble in general- Rey said pensive on the plane back to London.
-You're right, I'll make a good cv for you when we get back-
-I don't need that man, I'll get like ten interviews booked by tomorrow, trust me-
That afternoon, I planned to write an email to Tom to try and get back in Sloane Square as soon as I landed in London.
I was sitting next to Alessia in the hostel and devoured a full 12 chocolate bars pack from the supermarket, which had become a daily thing by then.
-Hello Tom, as I have mentioned already at the staff party, I would love to work for you again. Leaving was my mistake and I am sorry about that. I am aware I was not great as a waiter and to be honest I would love to work as a runner myself, and I am sure to be a potentially great member of the restaurant since I know it and remember all very well. I am available for all sort of shifts. Thank you very much for considering this Tom, and please let me know what you think-
It's sent. It's sent, so no more embarrassment. This feels better now, I just hope that if he feels like declining, he won't tell everyone else.
-You're doing everything wrong, you shouldn't go back there, they exploit you. That's not a good job Dom, you don't understand life at all- Rey spoke while he loudly crunched his crisps on his favourite sofa.
-Rey, we've already had this conversation-
-The way you let them treat you is what you think you deserve. If you want to be treated like that for the minimum wage then do it, but don't complain if you live like a slave-
-I like my life Rey-
-So why were you complaining about your laptop the other day? You said it's not good anymore, buy a new one then- he said, getting on my nerves.
-You see? You're not answering that, you can't afford a new laptop- Rey saw me silent and kept going.

-Rey, if your bank account situation were to depend on the contribution to society you have given so far in your life, you'd have starved to death long ago- I said, getting passionate now.
Rey laughed, and then left.
-He keeps asking me for money, this idiot, then says I'm a slave- I commented to Alessia.
-Calm down Dom- she said gently.
Tom replied to my email the same night, saying that he would have let me know as soon as he could, and that it was probably going to be a yes.
Good news, except for the fact I had checked my bank account for the first time since when I moved to Clapham and found out I had less than 100 pounds left and no job at that moment.

March 2016

My first shift back in Cote Sloane Square was scheduled for the end of the first week of March. Tom left a note in his last email regarding Clelia, specifying that any conflictual behaviour between me and her would have put me in the losing side of the debate automatically, and that I had to reply to him confirming I had understood this.
Clelia was a hard worker and also well organised. I knew that there were not going to be fights nor drama, since she didn't want me any more anyway.
Entering the restaurant felt weird.
I passed by my former co-workers, most of them still there and received some very warm welcome back hugs alongside some cold looks from people that didn't like me and, of course, mocking looks of those that saw me as a man with no control over my choices, a child basically.
-Are you back as a runner or as a waiter?- Tiago asked me from the kitchen.
-Runner-
-Yes!- some from the kitchen jumped out of joy and laughs, mostly mocking though.

-Oh shut up guys- I laughed back. The only one that didn't laugh was Salvatore, who kept his eyes in the opposite direction, avoiding me.

Work restarted normally. I was indeed still the best runner and in no time, all waiters that gave me some bad looks started saying they were glad I was back. Somebody literally hugged me during work and Daniel let me notice how the day I was back was also the first time in ages that he could find all wine glasses ready to be put on his tables.
The downside of being back to work there was that I had to see Clelia. Tom put me and her working on different shifts for the entire rota with two different days off for each of us so that we would have been able to bump into each other only three days a week in total, and only at the end of her shifts, which were also the beginning of mine ones.
Great, Tom is doing the right thing. I won't have to work with her, I'll keep my job safe and everything will go back to normal.
Clelia appeared on table 50, eating staff food. An invisible hand clicked a button inside my head that commanded the speed of my heartbeat to double up immediately, which made the rest of my body petrify. I rushed towards the bread section and threw a bunch of freshly baked baguettes into the oven. Wasn't she off today? What is she doing here? Salvatore just sat down next to her after finishing his shift, meaning that she was there for him.
Salvatore is with Lena though. He kept telling me about the importance of loyalty, healthy relationships and faith in Christianity so many times... He was just teaching her about the things he knew that she craved to know and that was it.

With the passage of days, it was clear that Clelia was not interested in me at all, I understood it from the fact that she was polite and respectful.
She didn't spite me, not even in the same friendly way she did with everyone else and even if I was aware of the fact that she was an incredible actress, I also knew there was nothing inside of her for me any longer. Slowly, I realised that nothing mattered. I didn't want to work. I didn't want to

do anything, I went back for her, I thought a million things, but the reason why I went back was because I still hoped to get her, and now all I had was a long shift until closure, then a long cycle home.
You used me for sex and I hate that I lost my dignity, but it can't be entirely my fault if I have been led to believe into what you told me.
You owe me a phone, two phones actually.
You're using mine, you broke yours because you're stupid and I gave you mine. Then you found out it wasn't working well so I gave you another one, but you didn't give it back to me when you decided to call it over. So, our story was over, but my phones and my cap were not?
I was trembling out of rage.
The thread of my thoughts had gone through the usual analysis of why it all happened to the fact that she was evil and needed to give me back whatever was mine, and this wasn't about my ego more than it was about justice.
If she didn't need me anymore, then why did she still need to use my phone? And the cap my father gave me...
At the end of the shift, I cycled home faster than I ever did before, drunk by the pleasure of getting a chance to interact with her and be bossy at the same time, which she liked anyway.
-Clelia, hi, I would like to tell you that I believe it's time for me to get my phones back and also my father's cap. I am in need for those phones since mine broke and a friend needs one. We hadn't been in touch obviously in the last times, but let's settle this though. Please let me know if I can visit you tomorrow before the beginning of your evening shift, since I need my phone as soon as possible. Thank you-
Not even a bossy word. It wouldn't have been me otherwise.
-Hi Dom, yes sure, come tomorrow, it'll be ready for you- she said.

I didn't miss not being able to sleep at night, not even a bit, I though while sitting on the tube to Stockwell. This is going to be my last travel to her place at least.
I fell asleep at dawn and then set an alarm just for this and I was almost late. No way I could wait for another day to go

by. I needed to take my phones and my cap from her as soon as I possibly could. I rushed towards her place, entered the building through the stairs up to the third floor, her floor, getting closer to her flat. I knocked at her door and crossed my arms.

I am still in time to smile and act polite, one more chance for her to give me back my stuff and leave it all in a civil way. As soon as I get money enough to pay for two more bookings in my hostel, I'll go look for another job and never see her again.

She opened the door.

-Hi- she said and smiled.

-I'm giving you back the one which has the wi-fi that works- she said.

She got two phones from me and now she was returning me just one of them. She highlighted that she was giving me the one with wi-fi working to convince me she was being generous, although I perfectly knew it was the one with the faulty keyboard.

She was keeping the better phone with her, and yet still tried to appear kind. A true professional victim. A devil.

-What's wrong? Are you ok?- she pretended to be worried or confused whilst looking at my stern face. I had been silent the whole time.

Really? You don't know what's wrong? Can't you just shut up and be a good citizen? No, I'm not going to show any weakness.

-It's none of your fucking business. Give me my stuff now- I said, my body almost shaking out of repulse for her.

She went back to her room, then came back and handed me my cap and the other phone, then she slammed the door and left, heading to work.

I was walking slower than her, quite satisfied about the final outcome.

That was the end of every hope, but it was also the dawn of a new me.

Or maybe, if I reach her, she will understand...

I ran fast and then reached her down the stairs.

-You owe me another phone- I told her.

-Well, yeah, but then I'd be left without phone at all- she said, confident that she could have got away with that.
-I'll just give it back to you soon- she was walking fast, rushing away from me, but I followed her.
-I hate you! I hate you!- I shouted at her after stopping her from the strings of her backpack.
She was getting scared, then looked at me for a second and tried to walk even faster when I let her go.
-I realised it- she said.
-I ended up in that place because of you! It was you! I didn't want that, you dragged me into this story and then you disappeared!- she kept ignoring me and walking faster.
I couldn't help it anymore.
I blocked her from her backpack again and pushed her towards the wall of the nearest building.
She was very scared now, and opposed to that with all her strength.
-You know what?- she said as I let her go again. She took her earring off, took off her sim card and gave me my phone back. I destroyed every chance I might have had, but at least I got everything back.
-Die in hell you dirty slut- I said, full of resentment and hate.
-Poor you- she said, and then I lost sight of her.

I hope you got scared, I hope I made you feel uncomfortable and that you will think it twice before playing with a man's brain for your own profit in the future. You're the only woman that made me do this. I didn't want to pull your backpack, but I was tired of being ignored, you were walking away from me with my phone, my belonging, you're a thief, you also stole a half bag of weed from me the day you slept at my place, you think I don't know it?
No, you didn't ignore me, you told me to go away from your life in two occasions.
Am I wrong? No, I'm not, I recovered my belongings from you because you were keeping them, they're mine, not yours. You're a thief and deserve no respect.
I reached the hostel with some sort of feeling of power. I hadn't felt like that in a while. The fact that she might have been intimidated by me kind of brought my mental state

back to when I texted her rudely under suggestions of Manu and she consequently acted submissive. Manu... he was so healthy when compared to me.

-So, you need a picture with your face, a good one, the second picture has to have your friends in it, then a picture with your body, and then one with a dog, also important. Those are the four pictures you need to have on your Tinder- he once told me when we were on our Uber the way to a football game we were playing with the kitchen guys in Battersea. His voice sounded far from me. Manu invested no effort in getting girls and yet he got many of them all the time. I had invested everything in one of them, and now I was bankrupted.

Well, enough thinking about this now. It's time to do something productive on my laptop, maybe a chess game first, or maybe...

I turned on the phones she gave back to me, scrolled down on her online profiles, but found nothing interesting nor incriminating. Why wouldn't they just make it public, sparing me a lot of time?

Salvatore and Lena might still be together while he works on Clelia. Maybe I can text Lena, I should be able to find her on Facebook.

I was sitting in the sofas area in the hostel. My laptop on the table next to me, a cable connecting one of her phones to it, and an application downloaded by the internet that should have allowed me to see deleted messages. I couldn't believe what I was doing, how deep I had touched rock bottom, but if only I could have had a proof that I was right...

-Lena, hi, I hope you are well. I know that we hated each other at work, well, actually I didn't hate you, but I would like to tell you something. I don't have a proof that I can give you, but to make it short, I think your boyfriend is cheating on you. Clelia, the girl I brought to work in Sloane Square just before you quit has been hanging out with him a lot and I did see them talking at night time and leaving together after work many times. I am not telling you this to try and spoil your relationship, you would probably wonder that because it's me, but I promise you that this is because no

matter what the feelings we have for each other, I thought you had to know-
She read the message straight away.
-Can I speak now?- she said, adding a smiley face.
-Oh yes sure, I'm sorry I took too long to explain that-
-Don't worry, I understand. I know all of this. He left my flat about a week ago-
-Oh, I'm sorry, I hope you're ok now- I texted, surprised whilst still processing everything.
So that was it, the proof I needed. It was all true. Everything that man told me was proven a lie, or at least a temporary idea he truly believed in that changed when he met Clelia, who not only conquered my heart with her cunning ways, but also his one to the point of destroying his relationship. Of course Clelia couldn't care less about the fact that he had a girlfriend already. If she wanted to sleep with him, she would have done it at any cost, getting rid of any obstacle that was on her way, even if she was going to sleep with him just once. Her personal pleasure accepted no challenges from basic moral obstacles.
-I'm better now, lost a lot of weight though, going to gym regularly- she added. Strange, I also dove deep on body exercise after the breakup.
-Yes, I'm much better than before actually- I cut it short.
-Are you sure? It doesn't look like it- she said. The first time ever she spoke nicely to me.

Rey and I were now looking forward to going back on the clubbing scene.
-Dom, I'm horny man, we need to go out tonight- Rey said, as if he was in forced sexual abstinence.
-I feel you man- I said, honestly. I had almost forgotten about that thing.
That night we went to the Tiger club, a nightclub with mostly danceable contemporary hits.
The club had three floors, my favourite one with music from the 80's on the underground level with a retro squared dance floor with tiles that changed colours all the time. It was perfect for our goal and for the girls we wanted to chase. Some of the girls who went to that club were looking for the

best possible men, some of them were just looking for fun, but the average look level and dress code was the right one. We weren't going for high class, but not even for hippies. At some point in the night, I lost Rey and the vodka I had drunk was kicking in real hard that if I had kept dancing, I might have ended up vomiting.
I stopped for a second by a sofa on the first floor and noticed a group of posh girls, dancing next to each other, but not too close, clear signal that they were all available. I made a move fast and walked in between them to have a better look at them.
As it usually happens with fancy dressed girls, they looked at me with disgust on their faces which was supposed to mean "don't even think about it", but I had no time for that and approached the one that looked more friendly, giving her my hand. She took it and I slowly led her arm to my waist, pushing her further away from her judgemental friends who were now staring at us from the distance.
-What's your name?-
-Jemma-
-Jemma, you're very tall- she laughed. She looked pretty good now that I actually focused on her face.
-What do you do?- she asked me straight away.
-I... I manage a street food business, Italian food basically, here in London... you?-
-I'm an occupational therapist-
-Cool, so you're not only hot, but also smart- I had no idea what that meant but I just made her laugh again. A decent, posh laugh that stopped when she realised I was going to kiss her.
Time to find Rey, where are you? You're supposed to be the tallest one in here. Man, I've got headache, I need water and some sleep.
I stood by the entrance, still trying to spot him when I noticed a brunette young girl that was grimacing behind me, moving her head just like I was.
-What's your problem?- I asked her, tough.
-Back off man- she said, her male friends were approaching me now.

I pushed her away with the palm of my hand opened up on her face when one of the guys pushed me hard.
That was exactly what I was looking for. I wasn't going to keep that. I pushed back, blinded by rage, jumping on him with the desire to harm him as much as I could when another one of his friends pulled my t-shirt from my back, tearing half of it away until we all got stopped by a couple of security guys. In a matter of seconds, I got kicked out with Rey appearing just then on my side.
-Let's leave Dom, this place is shit- Rey would say this anytime he didn't get a girl.
-Well, yeah, we're already outside-
We walked back to Russell Square together.

-Hey Jemma, how are you? It's the guy from yesterday- I texted Jemma the next day from a small step in front of a vacant building where I used to sit on after work, sometimes just to be alone with my thoughts.
I didn't think Jemma was going to reply after all. Most of the times I got numbers from clubs I didn't get a text back, no matter how passionate the kissing and groping on the dance floor was.
-Hi, I'm good and you?- Jemma replied a few minutes later. No smiley face, although she asked something back, which had to be a good signal. At least I had to try.
-Good, good thanks... what are you doing on Tuesday evening? Wanna meet up?- Tuesday was my only day off that week.
-I'm not sure I'm free on Tuesday- she replied.
I have a feeling she doesn't remember my name or that I didn't even tell her.
What next? She hasn't really suggested another day where she could potentially be free.
-Did you save my number with Domenico or with Italian Stallion? Those are the only two names I accept- I texted her.
-Thanks for reminding me your name actually, but to be fair I saved it as hot Italian guy- I was pleased to read.
I looked at the screen for a minute and then went offline. I didn't want to text right away, but neither could I just stop trying.

-Do your best to be free on Tuesday, I'm taking you to dinner in a French restaurant- I said.
-I'll let you know- she said.

She texted me about one hour later, saying that she was looking forward to the dinner with me.
Shame I had just tried to get some cash from the cash machine to find out I had about 40 pounds left in total.
I had to call Rey and claim my money back. This time he was going to hear from me. How was it that he always had money to gamble, but never to give it back to me? I needed it, it was mine and it was very disrespectful that he made me wait so much.
-Rey? I need my money back- I said firmly on the phone.
-Hey Dom, yes, I'll give it to you now, just finally getting up from my bed, catch you in the common room-
A minute later, Rey actually came back to me and handed me a couple of hundred pounds in cash.
-Oh, really? Are you sure? I mean, thanks Rey- I put the money back in my pocket. I would have only used a bit of it to make a short booking and keep the rest for the dinner. I didn't have big plans about my dinner with a girl I didn't even know, but I gave her my word and I had to keep faith to it.

The night of the dinner arrived, and Jemma confirmed that we would meet up in front of Sloane Square station. We were going to eat at Cote, which happened to be a good restaurant, kind of French and also cheap since I was a staff member, but she didn't have to know that.
I parked my BMX in Cliveden Place, just a minute walk from the tube but somewhere where she couldn't see it. I dressed as good as I could even though I had no fancy clothes at all in my suitcase. Black tight jeans, black full brogue I bought second hand in Italy many years before and rarely used, a white v-shirt and my black blazer. Never felt so overdressed before.
Jemma was standing inside the station. She was taller than I remembered, but luckily not wearing heels. She wore a long light brown trench coat that probably cost her twice as much as all that I was wearing put together.

She was way out of my league. I wished I was home playing chess with Rey and hitting on affordable girls. Shall I leave? Pretend I had an accident?
-Hi- I said, polite.
-Hi- she said, looking somehow tired.
She looked stunning. Rey was wrong, he kept saying she was fat after I told him I couldn't remember almost anything that night because I was too drunk. Maybe he was just wrong or messing with me.
-This way- I took her to Cote.
Clelia wasn't there that night and hopefully Marco was going to be my waiter. She didn't know I worked there, but I was going to make sure he didn't spit it out.
We sat down on table 53, lady on the sofa and man on the chair. Jemma's hair was dark blonde, straight on top with curled ends, her black dress showed her shoulders and neck, leaving me a lot to imagine and forcing me to make an effort to take my eyes off of the rip on her dress in her breast area. She was a hottie, one of those girls one can see in porn films. I should have got into Jemma's panties that night instead of being kicked out of the club. I had no chance now that Jemma was sober on a dinner with me, I thought.
-Jemma, I want you to take this dinner easy. I'm a very sociable person, so I like to meet new people all the time, get them to dinner, talk in general, you know this kind of stuff- what the hell was I saying?
Jemma waited a couple of minutes for me to pour water in her glass, but then did it on her own.
-So what about your job?- I asked after we had ordered.
-Basically, I am an occupational therapist-
-Yes, I remember that, but tell me more about the things you do at work- I was curious to know.
-Well, I help people with nervous system diseases to deal with life-
She is successful, and God knows how much money she makes. Oh, this story is definitely going nowhere. It's cool though, I won't see you again after tonight.
-That is so good, so helpful to society. You make me feel useless-

-Why? You sell food to people, that is helpful- she said, still serious. I was feeling more nervous now.
-Nothing that can be compared to what you do-
-Thanks. Tell me more about your job?- her big blue eyes under her deleted and then carefully drawn thin eyebrows focused on me. She looked like a celebrity.
-Well, so, I have a kiosk and I sell typical Italian products such as cheese, wine and so on- I pictured how a typical Italian food kiosk would look like in my head whilst describing it to her.
-Oh, I see, where?-
-It depends, we move according to the days and times, you know it all changes and I like my job for this reason. Always new people, new areas and so on- I kept going.
My goat cheese salad tasted good, and I liked it that she finished her glass of wine in two big sips.
-Careful Jemma, if you drink more you're going to find me attractive- I made her laugh right in a moment she was chewing, which caused her to almost spit her bite. She covered her mouth with her hand and swallowed it before laughing. A cute laugh.
She was very classy, good looking, she had great posture and apologised for needing to go to the toilet. No idea how I ended up there with her, but I thought she should never know I lived in a hostel.
-So yeah, I'm going to Italy for six weeks, two of my best friends are getting married there and we're taking the chance to drive around the country- she told me when we got the dessert.
The bottle of wine was finished. She had drunk almost two thirds of it and I did make her laugh a few times, but she was very well-mannered so I couldn't really know how it was going.
-My friend was asking me not to go on this date and stay with her. She's lonely after her boyfriend broke up with her- Jemma commented at some point, replying to a text from a friend.
I introduced the dinner by calling myself a sociable person who does these things all the time, and she said it was a date.

-Wow, I didn't know there were relationships in these days that are ended by the man- I replied.
-What?-
-Nothing. My best friend keeps checking on me though, I might have to send him a quick reply if you don't mind- I said.
I was texting Rey that I would have come back home soon when I noticed that she was looking at me, confused. Wasn't I supposed to text back?
-Sorry, he's my best friend- I added. Rey had just sent me a bunch of sexually explicit pictures from the internet and asked me if I wanted to share her with him.
By the end of the date, Jemma was acting much more relaxed and was opening up more and more to me. She confessed me to loving to drink and bragged about the fact that Australians were much better drinkers than Italians and that we were weak, and after two double vodkas she was ready to go home.
-Right, I'll take you to the bus stop that will take you home. Battersea is close to here, it won't take long-
We crossed Sloane Square. I did manage to get her tipsy and to keep the fact that I was working full-time as a runner in that place a secret, but I was still sober.
-Thanks for the dinner- I said, even though I paid for it.
-Thank you actually, oh, I'm sorry I should have said it first- she said, smiling and staring into my eyes.
-No worries- I said when we reached the bus stop. I was still intimidated by her look to try and kiss her again, but I concluded that I had to do it. I wasn't going to let her go without some of her tongue, especially since the dinner was on me.
I was cycling back home when I found a message from her.
-What have you done to me, Italian boy? Thanks for a great night- she texted me when she got home. She kissed good and my blazer still smelled like flowers.

It didn't take long for the evening shifts to spoil my sleeping pattern. I was spending a lot of time in the sofas area at night, enjoying seeing people falling asleep on the tables and dropping their beer cans on the floor.

I decided to let go of Jemma, concluding it was going to be a waste of time. Jemma belonged to a different class, moved, spoke and earned much better than me.

Everything between me and Jemma started with a lie anyway. At some point I was going to have to show her my business for real and that was not going to happen, although I had some hopes it could.

Me and Andrea had been planning to start a similar type of business for months. We would often sit on long phone calls, discussing all the details of a plan that seemed perfect, but advanced very slowly. All we had got up to that moment was an appointment with a banker to discuss a loan that was dismissed straight away since I couldn't provide him of a valid proof of address.

The bunch of visits I paid to his place where we spent time designing, drawing and calculating stuff that made us feel good usually ended lost in the smoke of weed that just made us want to eat and sleep. We would conclude that our meeting was somewhat productive and that weed and relax were truly deserved.

However, Jemma texted me back any time she appeared online and always asked me a question each time I tried to just send a definitive message. If I asked her a question she would text me back, no abbreviations, perfectly spoken English and only cute smiley faces every now and then. If I didn't ask her anything but just wrote her a message where I stated that I was going to sleep because work was too hard, she would make a comment on that and ask more questions to which I would reply nicely, without trying to be witty or funny.

I wanted to get rid of her, but I couldn't just dismiss her or ghost her without risking to upsetting her and I wasn't the kind of person that could do this without feeling guilty about it.

All I needed was her to dislike me somehow, but I paid for her dinner and that was clearly something she appreciated. I also couldn't tell her I lied about owning a business because that could have made her feel stupid.

-Wanna play a game?-

It was the middle of the night and a guy just approached me at my table. Rey was watching the tv sitting lazy on the sofa, the chess board we used a few hours before was still open and the pieces thrown a little bit everywhere.
His messy hair was dark blond at its roots, but it seemed like he had bleached all over his head and messed up a bit, or maybe his hair was just like that. His skin was pretty tanned and he had a bit of hair under his chin as if he had shaved a week before. He wore a scruffy sweatshirt with hoodie laces that came down unequally.
Nothing in his look showed that he cared about it at all, but he was overall a naturally very attractive guy.
Rey came and took a seat just in time to see me lose my first game. After that, we played two more in which I was both times successful.
-Do you smoke weed?- I asked him.
-Yes, I love it actually- he smiled back at me.
-I was in Mexico for four months with my girlfriend, then she went back to Vienna and I'm here for about a week, then back home- he was telling me after the games. His German accent mixed with the fast way he spoke English was fascinating.
-The thing I like mostly about weed is that it helps me learn. I can sit on my laptop and just learn the whole night-
-How? Every time I smoke it makes me depressed and gives me the worst thoughts... it also makes me stupid and I can't focus on anything- I told him.
-Then why do you smoke?-
-Good question, Alex-
We sat in Queen Square, a tiny, cosy square about one minute walk from the hostel and got silent for a minute.
-Were you swiping girls on Tinder?- I asked him. He told me he had a girlfriend, but I also saw his screen with the tail of my eye during a break from a chess game and the other.
-Yeah, it's working pretty well, you?- he said.
-Well, yeah, I'm there too, but I never open it- half lie. I did open it every now and then, although much less than I used to when I first downloaded it after my arrival in the UK.
-Didn't you say you had a girlfriend?-

-Yes, but I cheat- he said as if that was the most normal thing of the world.
-Nice, I do that too and I think it's a clever thing to do. I mean, I like to keep backup plans so that when they break up with me, at least I know I didn't miss any chance-
-Exactly- he agreed with a smile, sounding like I had spoken his mind out loud.
-Got any dates for this week?-
-An Asian girl tomorrow-
-Cool, let me know how it goes- I feel like I had spoken too much.
We went back in. I was too high to keep making conversation and I didn't want to make a bad impression on him.

It turned out that Alex's sleeping pattern was just as messed up as mine and Rey's. Bumping into each other was unavoidable and it happened every night.
Rey liked him too, which was surprising, since Rey couldn't handle a conversation for more than five minutes with any non-female beings without leaving to lie down somewhere else, away from the difficulty of talking and having to listen to people.
Alex dropped his education when he was in high school to study economics and finance on his own, went on to become a trader and collected vinyl for a hobby, bragging about a huge number of rare ones at his place that he sold for higher price on the internet and on a shop he planned to open soon in Vienna. It didn't take long to realise I felt always very keen to see him. I even bought extra weed just so he had a reason to hang out with me and refused to take money from him when he suggested to split.
-I'm not surprised that you like him. That guy is just like you. I mean, he's friendly and everything, but he doesn't take care of himself at all. His clothes are torn and his shoes are dirty. Also, I don't think he washes his clothes- Rey told me once.
-And what's wrong with that?-
-What do you mean what's wrong? You have to take care of yourself and you never do it Dom. You only take showers before going hunting girls or clubbing, but if you could avoid it, you would-

-I never avoid washing my body Rey-
-I once saw you going into the toilet downstairs with a towel around your waist just to wash your armpits by the sink-
-I was in a rush probably, and anyway, I don't care about what you say-
-Dirty people, you're perfect for each other, he could be your new best friend then-
-Great Rey. I'm going to the supermarket. Bye-
On my way back to the hostel, Rey was chatting to two girls in their early twenties.
-He's Dom, my best friend- he stood up and said loud so that I could hear him and follow him to their table.
-Hi girls- I said.
-Hi- they replied, looking...disappointed?
-They're from Australia, just like Lottie- Rey said and looked at me.
-Who's Lottie?- one of the two girls asked, curious. We both burst out laughing for a full minute before we could stop.
-What are your names?- I asked.
-Emily, and she's Monica-
Emily had long blonde and frizzy hair closed into a bun and a slightly plump, attractive body.
Monica had dark brown straight hair and looked a little bit more corpulent than her friend. Both of them were standing behind the bench as if they were too excited to sit down.
The two girls told us they were studying in Scotland with three other girls in their dorm and that they all decided to visit London for few days.
After a bit of talking, the girls said they were going to meet up with their friends and take a nap, but Rey insisted on making them promise that we would meet again later on in the evening to play drinking games and they accepted, visibly excited.

That night, Rey and I got the usual big bottle of vodka with a bunch of Red Bulls and brought it into the hostel.
-Rey, I'm telling you, they're not coming man. This is not happening so let's just go to a club or something-
-Can you stop it? I got them on Facebook, they said they'll be here soon-

-I don't know, they didn't seem too into me to be honest- I told him what I thought.
-You'll be alright, actually, we'll be alright. Vodka and chess is our strategy and it works, you know that. Chess to make them think we're smart, alcohol to make them want us- Rey highlighted something I also thought a few times but never said.
-Hey guys- Emily and Monica just showed up with a few more girls, sounding pleased to see us.
Their two friends were also Australians, two petite ones from different backgrounds. One was a white girl with brown hair and a white soft cardigan and the other was originally Indian, dressed a bit less than her friend.
After introducing each other we decided to play a drinking game that could have helped us achieve something that night.
Emily sat next to me while Monica went further away and sat next to Rey. She clearly fancied him.
Emily was pretty attractive, but I didn't like a few glances that she gave me every now and then and it seemed like it was going nowhere. The white girl was very decent and seemed to take my jokes too hard, so I started focusing on the Indian girl, who was actually the most attractive in there and also the friendliest one, but she was also sitting far from me.
Meanwhile, as it always happened with drinking games, the main topic turned to sex, which put me and Rey in trouble and let the girls around us go slightly dry for a bit until the Indian one decided to change the trend of the game by playing a trick to get the girls to finally drink.
-I've never been given oral sex by a man- she said, obviously playing it reverse, assuming that such thing never happened to us so that she could drink, but me and Rey drank again.
-Oh my God! I can't believe it!- the Indian girl opened her mouth wide, shocked while Emily stared at me now and came closer.
-Are you for real?- she asked me in my ear.
-That's how I am, I'm too open minded for this world, I know- I said, hoping it would work.

-I see- Emily seemed very interested in me now, the way she looked at me had completely changed in a matter of seconds. Rey was flirting with Monica by the other side of the table, his hand was on her leg.
-Time for club everyone- I announced slamming my hand on the table when the vodka began to kick in.
-By the way, I've never... I've never had sex with an Italian guy- she said into my ear when everybody was standing up and the noise would cover her words.
We went out with all the girls from our table, although Emily and Monica had already told us that at some point we had to leave on our own.
We started walking through Southampton Row, heading to Leicester Square area giving a show in the streets.
The two girls were really into something, possibly because of the alcohol they had.
As we reached the Verve, I figured I had to find a solution to that problem. Where and how? I kept groping Emily hard, checking what places of her body she wouldn't allow my hand to touch but found none, she let me everywhere.
-Rey, we have to take them to a hotel, we can't do this in the hostel, we'll get caught and kicked out- I said in his ear.
-Guys, what are you talking about?- Emily asked, suspicious. No more time to play decent.
-Let's go to a hotel, the four of us and fuck tonight- I spoke clear, taking a massive weight off my stomach.
Rey looked anxious about me saying it like that, but changed his expression when he realised the girls were very excited at the idea.
Emily came closer to my ear right away.
-Ok, but our friends can't know. They're very judgemental and we want to keep this a secret. They're not our friends really-
-Right, I'll call a cab and as soon as one stops, you run and jump, they won't even realise it- the girls didn't hesitate to agree.
-It's here, come on in- Rey had already done the job.
-Oh my God guys, if this really happens, this London trip would be the best trip ever- Emily sounded overexcited.

-Dom, I can't find anything online here, it's all fully booked, everywhere, except... here- Rey showed me the Imperial hotel in Russell Square, literally in front of the hostel, but the price was 140 pounds for a double bedroom that night. What were we going to do? Drop the plan? Tell the girls it was all cancelled? No way, not after all that excitement.
-Right, Emily, you come with me to the reception and we act like a couple. I'll pay for the room and we get in there, then we text them and tell them which room we're in- I pointed at Rey and Monica.
Fifteen minutes later, we were entering the reception of the Imperial hotel. A four stars hotel with a very silent, massive lounge room with fancy red carpeted floor and sofas. A few elegant glass tables and a golden coloured trolley to carry people's suitcases.
-Good evening, do you have a room for us two tonight?- I asked.
-Good evening to you sir. Yes we do- the man on reception spoke to me in a completely different way than the ones in Hyde Park hostel, and the only reason for that was based on the price we were going to pay.
-Which one is the cheapest one?-
-We have one for 140 pounds on the third floor, sir-
-That's a deal, thanks- I painfully paid with my card.
-Room 301, enjoy your night- he said and gave us a servile smile.
-Monica? Monica, you have to enter the building, turn left and take the lift to the third floor. It's room 301- Emily told Monica on the phone as soon as we were in the room.
We looked into each other's eyes. Emily looked a bit under pressure.
We had to wait. Rey's phone was dead and Monica wasn't replying to the texts Emily was sending. Wait...

-Dom, this is something we are going to remember for a long time- Rey said while taking a seat in the huge breakfast room of the hotel the next morning.
-So, this is how rich people have breakfast- I looked around. There were tables filled with hot food everywhere. All sort of cooked eggs, sausages, spinach, mushrooms were on the

nearest tables, toasted slices of bread with other pastries on the table next to it and a lot of different fruits on the table further away.
-This is how our lives are going to be soon Dom, this is our future- Rey repeated while eating his second fried eggs and bacon plate in a row.
-I am closing my restaurant tonight. I'll be cycling home dirty and exhausted later tonight- I commented resentful.
-That's your fault Dom- said Rey, confident in his words.
-Yeah, sure-

April 2016

In the first week of April, a young girl I had known for a few years contacted me to tell me that she was moving to London.
We were in touch for Russian-English language exchange from a website called Sharedtalk, where I spent countless days and nights during my late teen and early twenties.
After years of practice, I became quite strong with languages and reached some level of fluency in a few of them, something that many people looked up to me for, Rey being the one that praised me the most.
Darina looked much younger and more naïve than I would have said from her pictures. I had never video called with her and I was surprised to see her in real life.
She was six years younger than me, but almost as tall.
The shyest smile I ever received welcomed me, alongside a very formal hug.
-Finally nice to meet you Darina- I said. She laughed, sounding like a child. She barely looked 16.
-How was your flight?- I asked her when we sat in the bus.
She took her dark green bag off and left it on the floor between her legs, her big suitcase under my sight.
-Pretty well, I'm glad to be here- she said, laughing again, and speaking very slowly.
We reached the hostel where I had booked her to make sure she was safe. She looked so young that I was quickly developing some older brother type of feelings.

-Make sure you don't listen to anyone that tries to stop you in the streets. Keep your money, if you have cash, somewhere in bed with you, never take it off your body. When I came to London, I used to keep my money always in my pockets and sleep with my trousers on. Well, actually, I still do it- I realised while I gave her advice in the kitchen of the hostel. It was late night, and Darina opened a small purse attached to a necklace, took a couple of hundreds of pounds for the booking I made and gave them to me. She had probably around 600 there, all in cash.
-You need to put this money in a bank account as soon as possible. Also, it's not very clever to open this purse up just like that in the middle of a crowded hostel- I said, now worrying.
Darina didn't seem to care much. Ukrainian, with her currency, how could she even have all that money? She certainly didn't come from a wealthy family neither.

The next day, I took her to an interview in Pret a Manger recruitment centre, instructing her on what to say and what not to say so that she would be hired. I failed that interview myself, so I knew how things worked perfectly.
-Make sure you tell them you have no plans on leaving England, it's what matters the most- I told her more than once whilst reaching Victoria.
-I am definitely not going to ever leave England. I'm here to stay- she said, looking very determined.
-I am going to become a uni professor and teach English language. I studied so hard for this and that is the only future I see myself being in- she said, dreamy but firm.
I decided not to tell her that I didn't think she had any chance of succeeding in this. Not because of her skills or anything, but just because she wasn't English. What were the chances that they would hire her to do that job, if they could have hired someone native?
I didn't say anything about it, but just kept conversing with her.
-How was it?- I asked her when she came out of it.
-It seems it all went good. They said they'll let me know- she said, seemingly not very worried.

-Good- I said, glad.

April brought a new zest for life inside of me.
Rey and I had spent a weekend in Krakow by the end of the first week of April, and I loved every moment of it. We had booked the tickets only few days before and even though we didn't have much money at all, we managed to have a good quality time, also considering that Poland was very cheap.
I felt as if I was completely recovered from the breakup, although having to see Clelia and sometimes even work with her had the power to spoil my mood and the way I coped with work.
I looked at Salvatore, leaning by the kitchen counter eating an apple, as if the truth were to be written on his forehead. Maybe he got kicked out by Lena for some other reason. Maybe he's just her friend.
-Tell me something- I asked him.
He looked at me, confused.
-Well, only faith could make you understand. Science will always be behind and will never be able to explain a lot of things, but for that you will have to go on your own path- he wanted to cut it.
He still acted as if he really knew some dark secrets of life that most people were unaware of.
-For instance?-
-For instance, science cannot prove colour. According to science, there are no colours, but we can see them though- he said, pointing his second finger up like a teacher explaining something to very young children and sneering, confident he had caught me by surprise.
Is this even true? Damn, I'm not prepared here.
-What are you guys talking about?- Clelia asked us.
-Nothing- we said at the same time.
-Clelia?- Tom had just appeared in the runners area.
-Can you leave work earlier today? It's just so quiet and-
-Yes please- she said before he even finished.
At the end of her shift, Clelia took off her apron and went to sit at table 50, waiting for Salvatore who was now coming up from the staff room, dressed to go home as well. He had also

asked to leave earlier and since it was a quiet day, Tiago saw no problems in letting him.
At least I broke Lena's heart. If karma is real, the unjust way she treated me at work and the bad things she told the managers about me even though I was working so hard turned the other way round and hurt her back, causing her way more emotional damage than she caused me by stressing me at work. Just like the guy in the video said, like a boomerang.
-Dom?- Marcelo passed by the runners area and gave me a sign to follow him, interrupting my thoughts.
We reached table 25 where an old couple was sitting.
-The gentleman is a chess grandmaster here and I wanted to introduce you to him-
-Oh, hello- I said, surprised.
-Raymond Keene, nice to meet you- he said with a posh British accent. He was a pretty big man with thick white hair in his late sixties, sitting with his wife who smiled when I approached to shake his hand.
-Could you solve this tactic for me?- I pulled out my phone and showed him a puzzle I had been stuck on for the last two days.
-Bishop goes to f6- he said without thinking a single second. How did he see all the possible moves and chose the very best one? Is this some sort of joke? Maybe a typical pattern he must have recognised, but it wasn't a simple one, there were so many pieces on the board and there was no check involved.
-Why?- I had to ask.
-Because then this takes this and then you take this- he showed me with his finger.
I dragged the pieces just the way he said and he was right. He solved a problem I was stuck on for two days in a matter of time that I didn't even consider to be a full second.

-Domenico?- Tom came back in the runners area later that night. -I have to talk to you for a second, come downstairs- he said.
He looked at me in the eyes, serious, making sure that no one was around us.

-I have reasons to believe that you are drinking at work-
What? How did he find out? Well, everyone does anyway.
-Tom, I'm sorry, I don't think I understand-
-I have reasons to believe that you are drinking at work- he repeated, slower. I was hoping he would change his words a little when I asked him to repeat, but it didn't happen.
-Tom, no. I promise you, I don't. What makes you think that?-
-You've been caught on camera and a few staff beers were found empty in the fridge where you often go to drink-
My heart was pounding hard.
-I go to the fridge to do my restock, Tom, you know that- it was true, but I also did drink a lot at work.
-We're investigating further. Meanwhile, I'll have to ask you to go home and then wait for an email. Consider yourself on stand-by from work. Don't look for a new job for the next five days-
-Are you joking?- I was getting upset.
-You're sending me home and telling me not to look for another job? What if you don't send me that email? You know, I have almost nothing left in my bank account-
-This is not my problem, I'm sorry- Tom said, strict.

The first person I gave this news to was Rey, who didn't look anything more than happy to hear it.
-Your life can only improve now- he said, eyes stuck on his chess game on his laptop.
-Oh, that's terrible, what will I do without you?- Alessia commented, not sounding completely sorry to hear that if not indifferent. She had just started working at Cote after I had introduced her to Matteusz about two weeks before.
I couldn't tell my parents, they would have freaked out. I needed to ask someone, I needed to get some safety, find a job right away.
Four months before I was so safe and now I was walking on thin ice as never before.

Tom sent me an email the next morning telling me to show up in Sloane Square and discuss my situation with Daryl at noon.

I left my laptop with many open job application windows and cycled to the restaurant, my longest cycle to work. They were going to fire me, why would they call me in otherwise?
-Take a seat Domenico- Jonathan pointed at table 61. It was the first time I saw him sorry. He would make jokes all the time and compliments to me, he really liked me. I smiled at him anyway.
Daryl was helping some new waiters to set the back side of the restaurant ready for the busy lunchtime. He came to the table two minutes afterwards with a dead serious face and sat down quickly.
-Hello Domenico, we're going to quickly go through a conversation. Jonathan will be recording. You got your pen?- Daryl pointed at Jonathan who just sat down next to me with a blank paper and a black pen, and Jonathan silently agreed. I hope Jonathan can help me. I can't believe this is ending like this.
-Domenico, you've been caught on cameras drinking alcohol during your shifts-
-I haven't- I stopped him, feeling annoyed.
-We have seen you going back and forth from the fridge several times during your shift and empty bottles of beer were found- he spoke, imposing his voice on mine.
-Daryl, if you are going to fire me, just say it so that we don't waste time. There's no point for me to hope in vain-
-We have to do this Domenico- he said, referring to some legal procedures.
-If you're going to fire me then we'll skip this and I'll just say I quit so we say goodbye and that's it- I said, trying not to sound harsh.
-I'm telling you, you're going to be dismissed, but you have the right to talk-
-Well, I'm being fired without proofs, you don't have proofs so that's just unjust- I stopped him again, getting emotional. -I work hard here and I train people, you saw some empty bottles of beers and you're using them against me having no actual proofs-
-Why were you going to the fridge so often?- he asked.
-Restock-

-Don't lie to me, you don't need to restock six times per shift, you only need to do it once- he said, looking firm into my eyes.
Wow, I drank six beers in a shift that evening.
-It's like a way to take a very small break of about a minute-
-Do you know you're not allowed this?- he found a new thing he could use against me, this time having a proof.
-Alright Daryl- I stood up.
-Domenico...- Jonathan sounded truly sorry.
-It has been a pleasure to work here. Have a good day- I shook his hand and slowly walked away from the main entrance.
The rays of the sun entered through the glass door and shone on the parqueted floor. A good day, but definitely not hot.
I unlocked the padlock from my bicycle.
There was nothing to worry. I just needed to find work as soon as possible. This was a positive event. I won't see her anymore.
I looked back at the main entrance of Cote before leaving the square. Lots of memories of all kinds. My first London job and I messed up all by myself.

-Rey, I'm in trouble, I need a job as soon as possible- I saw him sitting at a table near the sofas area with two other people I had never seen before.
-Hey Dom, meet Victoria from Argentina- Rey introduced me to a young brunette girl with dark skin and a very innocent face. She was probably in her early twenties or maybe nineteen even.
-Hi- I said, totally not interested in talking to south American girls. She replied with a smile but then put her eyes on Rey again who was playing chess against a blond guy with long hair tied up.
-Hi, chess player?- I asked.
-Hi, no, I'm a chemist, just hiding here, nice to meet you- he shook my hand.
-He's got a very interesting story- said Rey.
-Well, not very interesting actually. I've got secret agents looking for me after I developed a drug that cures from diseases they don't want people to be healed from-

-I see, so you're hiding here in the hostel where they can't catch you-
-Exactly- he said, eyes on the board.
-Dom, we need to change our lives. I can't stay in London any longer, I'm suffering here man, it's depressing and we're not progressing-
-I've heard this before Rey. Now, here's the thing. I've only got 150 pounds left in my bank account and no job yet nor bookings made in here- I said, describing a very unhappy situation, but for some reason not feeling too worried. The half full hostel had the power to ease up my worries. For some reason, everything felt always somehow just good in there.
-You think like a poor, you'll never be rich- he said, trying to be annoying.
-Alright, I'm not going to reply this time-
-Let's go on a trip Dom, we deserve it. Life has no right to be so hard, let's go somewhere-
-Are you joking? I told you, I have no money and no job-
-We'll make money there. You can try and do some of my business too, it won't harm you to try. I'm inviting you, you'll be my accountant, managing my money and preventing me from gambling. I want to try my luck in other cities of Europe, too many people in London know me and I need new customers, besides I don't want to travel alone anymore-
-Rey...- I started. -Rey, you know how much it would cost you to support another person around Europe right? Hostels, food and so on-
-We have to try. Nothing happens if we sit and do nothing, and nothing happens if you work hard for the minimum wage anyway. Your goal of staying here and find another employment just to get exploited again is not going to take you anywhere. Come with me- he said, sounding more and more excited when he saw he was convincing me.
This idea is absurd, especially considering the money I have. This is pure nonsense, but I feel I'd go anywhere with you. We stared into each other's eyes for a minute, then I went on my phone until I found a ridiculously cheap offer.
-Going to Berlin by bus only costs 9 pounds, can you believe it?-

-Book it- Rey exclaimed, visibly excited.
-You'll have to take care of me, I'm reminding you-
-And you of me-
Victoria was still sitting next to him, closer now and the blond guy next to me, his eyes appeared scared whilst looking at the window by the bottom of the common room.

Only two days after being dismissed by Cote, I found myself going to Victoria coach station with Rey once again. Rey's initial excitement got slowly replaced by hesitation, and his words began to hide some fears behind the confidence of the moment the idea came out.
-We'll come back to London soon. We'll be alright, just a few days in Berlin. You only need one business of about 200 pounds if this is what you really charge per hour and we'll survive- I said.
We left London heading to Dover in the late evening. Our bus entered a massive tunnel that connected Dover to Pas-de-Calais in France in the middle of the night. Except for that stop, we were never forced to get out of the bus again, which left our sleep uninterrupted until we reached Germany.
The trip could have been worse.

Our hostel was a ten floors building with a proper pub underneath of it in the very centre of Berlin, just in front of Rosa-Luxemburg-Straße. We had about 20 per cent discount over food and some drinks whenever we wanted, but it was still expensive even after that as I calculated. If Rey were to abandon me for any reason, I would have been homeless with no chance of going back to London and retrieve the stuff I left in a room in Russell Square or maybe even to get a flight to Italy. Rey's situation was worse considering the debts he had, but better at the same time since he could make good money anywhere.
How did we end up like this?
The hostel where we were wasn't the cheapest, but it was the only one where we could sleep three days in a row. All other hostels were full to the point that just to save a couple

of euros per day we would have been forced to move everyday.
-I'll cook pasta and tomato sauce- I said after checking in at the reception and getting our key.
-I don't even have to nap or anything so I'll go straight to the supermarket- I added.
Rey was silent, but apparently less worried than before. Finally, we got into our room and after my shopping, Rey and I agreed to nap, but before that, I decided to check my profile on the new website, the one that Rey had convinced me to start using a few days before.
-We've got to set you up online, let's see if you could do some work. There will be lots of gay men here that you could work with. They might pay you for a lot of easy services that you'll be able to carry out with no efforts, trust me- he told me.
-Alright, about this, I did think about it and I guess I could try if it costs me nothing-
-It doesn't, it's free, I told you already-
Rey then created a profile for me on a platform for gay escorts, uploaded some pictures of my face and body and gave me a nickname.
-I'll charge less than you, at least I'll increase my chances-
-No- Rey interrupted me. -This is a horrible strategy. If you charge less, people will think your value will be related to your price, you lose respect and demand. You need to be intriguing, people have to wonder why you cost good money and desire you-
-This might work with you because you already have a lot of reviews maybe, but not with me. Why would they choose me over you? You have more experience and your dick is huge-
-That's not the point. You see, what you don't understand is that all people want different things. There are people that prefer me and people that prefer you. Some people will want you because you're hairier than me, or because they have some Italian fetish or something. No business can work if it charges less than others and your body, you, are a living business right now-
He did convince me, I thought whilst scrolling a few messages I had already received on the website. It was good that I was reading this behind the curtains of my bed.

I was indeed willing to settle for less and if somebody had made me an offer that didn't match with Rey's standards, it would have probably matched with mine. Rey wasn't going to be upset if he hadn't known after all.
One of the requests I had was to go to the toilet and show my penis hard on a video call. In exchange of it, a guy would have chosen if I was going to be suitable for having sex with his wife in front of him. The idea sounded absurd if it wasn't for the fact I knew many people liked this. It was one of their kinks and who was I to judge?
I came back from the toilet after about half hour, nothing stopping me from getting some rest now.
I'm not worried too much. We might finish everything we have, but it's ok. Spending time with you is something I would buy if I had to pay for anyway.

-Dom, wake up man, come on- Rey opened the curtains of my bed. The light was on in the room and I could hear some voices around me. I got up and found out Rey had just met and gathered a group of people that was going to go out. Two Mexican guys with typical look shook hands with me, both too friendly not to reply with the same attitude, a fit guy on his late thirties with very long blond hair from Argentina introduced himself to me too and so did a girl of around my age who just came back into the room, but was apparently one of us already.
Her name was Kelly and she was American, had straight brunette hair that reached the top of her shoulders and an incredibly pretty face that captured my attention immediately. Her skin was smooth and made her look even younger than she was. She wore a long, striped jumper that was tight enough to show a very attractive body, but yet didn't look like a provocative girl at all. She looked rather sweet and smart, also because, as I realised afterwards, she spoke even better Spanish than I did and all out of her personal study of the language, which showed skills definitely over the average since she was American.
Please, I don't want to think this, I don't want to care. Who's going to get her tonight? I need to hit first, Rey and the others won't wait long at all.

We walked all the way to a big club drinking from a bottle of liquor that Rey and I bought on an open late shop. Berlin was famous for its nightlife and this time I was actually going to have a proper night out with friend, since I didn't manage to do that the first time I visited.
-Dom, I like this place, and I like Kelly too, she's so beautiful- Rey told me in my ears when we were inside the club, still almost completely empty. Unlike Londoners, people started partying in the late night everywhere else in Europe.
-Yeah Rey, look, I'm not interested, but I suggested her to follow me in the smoking area before and smoke some weed and she agreed so you may hit on her, we'll go together- I said, taking a chance to show Rey I was leaving her to him simply out of goodwill.
It was when I said that that I realised that the little weed I had smoked before entering the club, mixed with the massive amount of alcohol I drank whilst getting there was about to make me feel sick.
It wasn't happening already, but I knew something was wrong with me, and that my brain was communicating I had trespassed the line.
After spending half hour in constant struggle between myself trying to let my good feeling state prevail over the one that wanted to drop down the floor and wake up the next day clean from that mess, I finally invited Kelly for a quick smoke outside. If I had left my joint and she had got high, Rey might have had some chances. The two of them followed me outside when the others were ordering drinks.
Kelly, I love the way you're looking while I roll this joint. I have no idea what you're up to, but I might be jealous of Rey if he gets you. If I were in a normal state, I'd go for it with no doubts.
-Rey, man, I have to go home, I'll see you tomorrow for breakfast- I said suddenly, with the two of them looking at me, worried.

The next morning, Rey woke me up again.
-Dom, you're going to be late for breakfast, there's a lot of stuff in there and we may just steal a lot of food to save money- Rey said, excited.

-Good idea- I said, realising to be hangover.
We sat at a table by the main entrance, far from the reception and the kitchen, eating as much as we could and packing as many loaves of bread and cheese as we could too.
-I hope we don't get caught and that we might have enough food for the whole day- I said.
-Any news from our website?- Rey asked me, fixing his eggs on a slice of bread and opening his mouth trying to finish it all in one bite.
-This guy wants to meet up, but he wants me to have a video call with him where he can see my body first, then he said he'll give me his wife-
-Don't do that. It's not true. They did it to me too, it's just a bunch of horny gay dudes that will masturbate while telling you what to do with your body on their screen-
-What? I mean, it doesn't surprise me but... it seemed very real though-
-They even took pictures of cash and sent them to me in the past. Just don't do it, you don't need this-
-Well, I did already. Yesterday in the afternoon. I did go to the toilet and gave them a show for about five minutes and now they're not replying any more. I felt too ashamed to tell you then-
-Don't be ashamed. There's a lot of bad people in this business-
-What happened yesterday by the way?- I changed topic.
-Nothing, I took you home Dom, you vomited just outside the club. The other guys stayed and one of the Mexicans kissed Kelly, I saw him. Son of a bitch- Rey wanted her too, just like all of us apparently.
-Sorry Rey-
-It's ok, I thought you were going to die, you were really wasted. That's what happens when you smoke that stuff- Rey always avoided both tobacco and weed and often scolded me for that.
-It's just because I mixed it with alcohol anyway, but yeah, you're right-
Eventually, Kelly joined us for breakfast. We finally had a chance to talk properly and exchange contacts. We wished her a pleasant continuation of her trip.

Within the next two days, our situation didn't give any sign of progress.
Rey had received a request for service in a place by the outskirts of Berlin.
I accompanied him to a place that seemed almost countryside and looked nothing like the city centre. We walked together a bit more than a kilometre away from the underground stop where we were suggested to stop by and reached a big house inside a massive black gate. The night was cold and the sound of dogs barking somewhere near was freaking me out.
-Rey, I don't think I should wait for you outside, it doesn't feel safe at all. It doesn't feel like we're in Germany here-
-Yes, go home Dom- Rey was entering the gate after messaging the man that contacted him through the platform.
-I'll stay awake until you let me know you're on your way back- I said. Rey went in.

-I'm not happy about yesterday. That place, and that guy- he said when we sat in one of the tables in the ground floor.
-What happened?-
-I don't want to talk about it. It's just... he was under drugs and he spoke very rude to me. His English wasn't very good either... I didn't like the place, I don't want to go there anymore, he even made a fuss to pay me eventually- Rey sounded very stressed. I had never seen him like that before.
-Alright Rey, don't think about it, it's done and you won't see him again- I asked nothing more. -As soon as my money will be over, I'll start taking count of whatever you happen to spend for me and eventually I'll pay you back with the passage of time- I continued.
-Let's go rest upstairs- he ignored that.

That night, we found out we had to leave the hostel because they had no availability the following day, which gave us no choice but to book another one.
Our new hostel was in Kreuzberg area, southern side of Berlin.

We got off at Kottbusser Tor underground station and headed to our destination. The hostel was based in the middle of a square, surrounded by lots of small pubs, bars and fast-food shops, some of them clearly exotic. Lights were turning on pretty much everywhere as the sky was getting darker.
-Rey, I've got another message. A guy just wants to meet up, he's bottom he said, I'm going to have to do this with him alone, but it's 200 pounds and that could change everything and give us a few more days of survival-
-Let me see- Rey looked at my message and typed some stuff on his own.
Eventually he said that the guy was probably real and that it was worth a try.
He gave me a pill to swallow with an energy drink and told me he would wait for me in the common room.

This is it, I'm going for it, I hope my connection won't fail before getting there, these things usually happen to me. I hope it will all work, also, it would be great to have a protector or someone checking on me in case the guy is a psycho. Well, that's why Rey took a note of this guy's address after all.
The underground travel felt alright. I didn't like that feeling initially, but I guessed that travelling for about twenty stops or whatever they were meant I was not going back.
I needed that money and if it had failed then fine, I'll have left.
I've been walking for so long, this guy lives so far away and he's not even picking up my call... Well, I guess I'll just go? What choice do I have? Yes, I'll have to go back, back to London, I'll find a job and live like a normal person.
Lost into my thoughts, I didn't realise I had finally arrived at the guy's place. A normal black door in the middle of thousands of other doors and houses that looked all the same. My battery was going to die soon and it was cold.
A buzz, then the door was open.
Ok Dom, confidence. Just close your eyes and imagine a girl. If he doesn't pay me, it won't matter because it will be over, and the fact that it will be over will compensate for everything.

Right, let's do it.
I knocked at the door and a man in his late fifties showed up, bald, quite short and with a grumpy look on his face.
-Hello-
-It's 100 euros- he barked, and looked at me as if a contradicting opinion on that was going to be responded with another bark.
-What? It's 200 actually- I said, hoping that he would slam the door on my face so I could leave completely innocent and tell Rey how keen I was on actually doing it, but how it didn't happen out of my customer's choice.
-100- he said again, in German this time.
-Ok, 100 euros, cash first though- I said, thinking about the video call I had with a guy that could have easily been him.
-Ok, no condom, no condom- he said and stepped aside to let me in, his face was less grumpy now, but still unpleasant to see.
-Don't worry about that, I've got condoms on me- I said, heading in with my heart pounding surprisingly less hard.
-No, no condom!- he insisted, sounding harsh.
-I can do it for 100, but it has to be with condom. No argues on that-
-Ok then, goodbye- he said and closed the door slowly, looking down the floor, maybe waiting for me to change my mind, but I was already flying down the stairs on my way to the underground station.
The sooner I left that scruffy dark neighbourhood, the better.

Rey was waiting for me on the sofa next to a massive window that led to a terrace and a smoking area of our new hostel.
-How did it go Dom?-
-It didn't, the guy claimed sex with no protection, so I left-
-You did the right thing. Damn dirty scummy people...- Rey commented disgusted while he moved sideways to give me space.
-Let's play a tournament Dom, I've found out you can get to challenge people of much higher rating if you play in a tournament. I've been doing this while you were away- he said.

-Rey, we're really short on money. With the money you made the other day and what I have left in my own pockets, we will literally touch zero in less than a week at best. At best Rey- I said, trying to be serious.
-The tournament is about to begin Dom- he replied, avoiding the topic.
His attitude towards the struggles of life was superior to most people. His secret was simple though. He didn't have a good problem-solving mindset to help him with that. All he did was simply pretending that nothing bad was happening. He could be in a completely chilled state even in a situation of life or death, and he was right.

The next day, positively impacted by Rey's mindset, I decided to go and check out a free historical tour of Berlin which I didn't manage to see the first time I had visited it.
It started from the Brandenburg Gate and it was all supposed to be in English. Rey declined my suggestion to join me for that and just decided to keep sleeping a bit more.
I got to my destination by late morning and joined a group of about thirty people that were also waiting to attend the tour. I recognised some British and American accents somewhere. The weather in Berlin was warmer than in London and walking to the Gate forced me to take off my jacket. Eventually, a man with ginger hair and beard in his thirties showed up and took place in front of the group, introducing himself with the name of Rob.
-Hi everyone- he shouted, -Any Australians here? Get your beers down because we're about to begin the tour- he continued when a few people had raised their arms.
Rob gave some insight on the Brandenburg Gate, built by King Frederick William II at the end of some troubled times caused by a revolution that was going on in Batavian territory. Definitely different than what I thought its origin could have been. I was expecting something related to a victory in a war or something more glorious than that, but the king probably just built it because they had nothing better to do back then.
-If you look at your right, you can see the Bundestag, the German parliament basically- the guide went on talking

about the history of the parliament and describing a special new feature of it.

-See, the dome on top of the building has always been there but it is only after the end of World War II that people are allowed to go up and walk inside the dome with the possibility to look down on the chamber of political debates. The goal is that people should always be able to see what you're doing and what you're talking about- he said, dropping the fun tone for a second and giving me goose bumps.

Rob kept giving a lot of information on history, but I knew most of what he was saying. He talked about the night of the long knives and how aggressively the Nazis were doing propaganda in Germany in the late 1920's.

After walking south for a few minutes, we stopped in front of a massive square where countless rectangular smoothly shaped stones stood, all aligned with one another but of slightly different sizes.

-This- he said, -is a memorial to the murdered Jews in this continent- he moved sideways so that we could all look better.

I don't remember seeing anything like this ever before. This is very... silent, so in the middle of the very lively Berlin centre, but distant from everything else. The tight paths that separated all stones from each other were straight and connected all sides of the square, but they were too long for me to see the other side of it.

-Who can tell me why these stones, or I should say coffins all look the same?- Rob asked.

-All Jews were deprived of their identities and not considered humans- I said, feeling a bit nervous since everyone looked at me when I raised my hand.

-Exactly. They were not even considered humans- he liked my words.

Moving away from the memorial felt good and relieving. Being in the middle of that maze walking on my own at some point was upsetting. It was outdoors, but very dark right in the middle of a sunny day.

The tour was pleasant, the guide was excellent and his knowledge mixed with fun facts kept people entertained, especially me.

I texted Rey and told him I would have been back in few hours during a break we took in a cafe in Friedrichstraße and then went back on, with Rob explaining how one of the major telephone companies in the current world once offered the Nazis some pieces of technology that helped them to create gas chambers and how one of the world most renowned stylist designed the first SS uniforms.
The more the guide spoke, the more I liked him. His jokes were recurring and it seemed like everybody else was enjoying them too.
-So, this is checkpoint Charlie- he pointed at the famous site I was looking forward to receive some explanation about. Who was the man in the portrait? And most importantly, who was Charlie?
-There's no need to ask me who won the Cold War. I think this shows it quite clearly- Rob pointed at a McDonald that literally stood in front of the checkpoint, one of the most famous of all the official borders between West and East Berlin.
-I'll tell you about that big portrait of the US soldier in a minute- he said at some point.
I bet it was someone who got shot while trying to bring forbidden information to the other side, giving his life for an ideal.
-...and the portrait has been there since then- I heard him when my thoughts were gone.
I was complaining some pain on the plant of my feet when we finally stopped again, apparently where Hitler's bunker once lied. People looked at the ground and moved their feet just to look better, as if the fact that they knew with certainty that Hitler was there could have been a chance to feel something. A monster, but still a celebrity.
-Just a parking area, that's what it is right now, but this is where some of the top leaders of the party spent the last minutes of their lives before the Soviets reached this city and ended the war-
At least this deprived current supporters of the party from the possibility to transform it into a worship site, I remember reading about this many years ago.

Eventually, the tour ended in front of a big and beautiful flesh-coloured building, enriched by long capitals and statues on top of it with a facade that covered the whole west side of the square where we all sat down for a moment.
-This is the end of the tour, and by the way, this place wasn't chosen randomly- he said sneering.
-This is where the Nazis burnt about 25.000 books in their attempt of erasing anything not German that existed before their rise to power. The university that stands behind you is one of the best universities in Germany, where many brilliant students that became some of world's pioneers of all sorts of subjects were produced and hopefully will continue to be produced. I mean, let's be honest, Berlin is dirty, poor and ugly, but it would be a shame to let the dark years we have discussed overshadow the amazing history of this city and its country. We all hope that education, which is the solution to all problems, will empower us to stop anyone that will try to burn books in the future, if it ever were to happen again.
We all applauded the tour, which was touching. The guide was excellent, and I promised myself I was going to write a very positive review about him as soon as possible.
-Thank you, this is all I can give you, I really have no more- I said, giving him ten euros and massively reducing my chances of survival.
I had to do it though. Everybody else was giving him cash and they definitely couldn't have enjoyed it as much as I did.

That was good, oh, that was so good. I feel like this day is changing my life, nothing will ever be the same now, I thought while standing in the busy train on the way to Kreuzberg.
I haven't paid for the ticket again, but that's their fault. Don't they know that people will take their chances to save money? There are no gates that separate people from entering the underground trains freely and that's absurd. One more stop and I'm home, although I can't deny I'm scared.
-Ticket anzeigen!- a man exclaimed out loud all of a sudden. The doors closed at the second last station and two men standing one wagon away from each other had just pulled out

a ticket check machine that they were hiding underneath their t-shirts.
Oh no, one stop from home. This can't happen.
Slowly, every passenger was showing tickets, somebody was slow in taking it out from their purse, maybe slow enough to help me, I had to leave at next stop, I really did, and I couldn't pay for the fine anyway. My heart was racing, and my legs felt heavier than usual.

-This place is a shithole. People in this city are poor, nobody wants to pay the full fare, Berliners are rats, nothing to compare to London- the first thing that Rey told me when he saw me coming back to the hostel.
-We've got lot of rats in there too- I said.
-We have to leave Dom, this trip has failed. We shouldn't stay here any longer, let's leave tomorrow- he said, stood up angry and sat down again.
-I just got fined. I had to pay a fine of 60 euros for not paying the underground ticket- I told him.
-Don't worry, I paid with my own money, which means I've got about 10 pounds left since I haven't used any of your money so far-
-Yeah, don't worry, by the way... can you check about tickets to Amsterdam?-
-Rey, look, I don't think it's the case to try more, let's go back to London, we'll figure something out-
-I have a contact. A man I already know from last time. He's a fat man that pays well just to give me some oral and hopefully I'll be able to see him more than once. Maybe two or three times in a row, which means we could leave Amsterdam with more than 400 euros for sure and be more than safe when we go back to Russell Square. I need you to come with me Dom-
I was perplexed, although also inspired. If the voice of rationality was giving me many reasons why that idea had to be declined, my attachment to Rey and the way I felt with him was suggesting me that, in times of misery, fun was a top priority.
-Are you sure? I mean, this is going to cost you money because from now on I'm relying entirely on you... so don't you think it's best if we separate here? Maybe you could give

me some money to survive before I get a new job- I asked, my voice feeble, hoping that he will not even consider what I was saying but just stick to the plan.
-Come with me. We'll be fine. Remember, together we are amazing, but alone we are shit-
-Flattery- I commented. -There are pretty cheap tickets to Amsterdam, we can get there for about 10 euros even, which makes me wonder, why did we use airplanes for such long time?-
-Because they're much better, that's why, you rat- Rey said, then went back to his laptop.

I considered Berlin a valuable place to spend a period of time, maybe even a relatively long one. I liked the German language and the average young Berliner's mindset, which I thought could have made a good connection with mine, but that was my second time there and my experience wasn't great again. The first time, I just saw my football team losing a final game of Champion's League, and this time, apart from the tour I attended, everything else went not the way I planned or hoped for. I got humiliated on a Skype call, fined by tickets inspectors, spent a day hangover after a night out that didn't even start, made no money at all but rather just wasted it, got mentally stressed and worried half the time, with my only entertainment being Rey.
The two of us reached Berlin main bus station, queued up and showed our tickets to Amsterdam to the driver when our turns came.
The other tourists who were there didn't look at all like the way we did. I recognised foreign accents, happy talks, people who clearly washed their faces and had clean clothes in their bags, folded and ready to use in their nights out in Europe. Rey and I hadn't slept properly in days, our clothes were getting sticky due to the hot weather, our faces didn't look any happy. We looked at the others and felt frustrated because, typically, we were going to be the ones to start a conversation and grab some phone numbers or just organise a night out, probably telling them we knew Amsterdam well or something like that, but right then, we didn't have any strength nor physical possibility to do so. I couldn't smell

myself badly, but I decided not to risk and just stayed away from people. Rey probably felt the same, I saw his face shining when he spotted some attractive girls in the queue, but he also seemed resigned.
-First thing first, I'm going to wash my clothes when we get there. I hope there will be a laundry machine in the hostel. We could use the same one we visited last time, what do you think Dom?- Rey seemed to be doing just fine. He had no idea about how I was feeling, at least sometimes.
Sometimes I felt like it was all normal and I had my usual 2k in my bank account and a few weeks of hostel bookings already paid, sometimes the awareness of the situation hit me hard and forced me to go back to reality. Why was he more immune than me to what was happening to us?
This trip was different than the one that got us to Berlin from London.
I just really wanted to sleep but I couldn't. The bus company was the same, but the seats were somehow less comfortable this time. The jumper I pulled out from my backpack and that I wanted to use as a pillow stank and Rey complained about it, forcing me to put it back in my backpack. Rey couldn't sleep either, but he didn't seem to be worried at all.

We arrived in Amsterdam in the late evening. Even there the weather wasn't that bad when compared to London. Holland wasn't a hot country, but at least the four seasons existed and they meant something.
We wore our jackets and walked in the same streets we recognised from last time, heading to the hostel we already knew which, by luck, was also one of the few with some vacancies.
-Rey, you know what would be great? We should just go out in one of those free entry bars, I mean, we have no money, at least let's get some love- I said, serious. Rey laughed.
-I hope everything will be ok tomorrow- he said with a serious tone.
-By the way, from now on we will have to pay for everything, every transport, bus or whatever- I added.
-No, we just have to be careful- he said as if it was an obvious thing to think.

-What do you mean? You can't just be careful that somebody won't show up on the train checking tickets. It's not up to you or anything-
-If you will be careful it won't happen- he repeated, annoyed. We checked in in our hostel, got to our room on the second floor and then went straight to bed, finally trying to get some sleep.

-Dom, wake up, wake up!- Rey looked very stressed and his voice sounded anxious the next morning.
-We are late, we are late!- he shouted, forcing me to get up and run down the streets, not sure yet of what was happening.
In a couple of minutes, we were outside the hostel, with Rey who was still trying to wear his backpack properly whilst running.
We ran towards Leidseplein to get the tram with Rey scolding me for the fact I didn't wake up the first time he called me. I felt guilty because the businesses he had to carry out were key to our survival. Without them, we were dead.
-Oh no- Rey stopped all of a sudden, his face worried like that was a surprise to me.
-The business is cancelled because I told my customer my arrival time and he just texted me, he said it's too late- he said, in pain.
We were standing in the square, packed with normal people doing normal things all around us.
After half minute spent in feeling responsible about it, I already began feeling numb to that.
The smell of waffles and chocolate from several shops around us, the people chatting careless, the restaurants, chefs smoking outside, people taking pictures, old couples walking close to us, some men in suits and a bunch of young people sitting on the benches of the squares, all contributed to make me feel safe. What seriously bad thing could possibly happen when so many people were around us? Worst case scenario, we were going to take something from them and pay them back in the future. I could have asked their contacts and make them a transfer eventually.

-Rey, I'm sorry, but why did you need me so badly anyway? Couldn't you just go on your own this time?- I tried to rationalise. Over time, I realised that my brain was taking the habit of escaping my personal responsibilities and think more like Rey.
-Why do you think I take these pills? To fuck my body up?- he shouted, still not looking at me.
-Man, look, come on, we'll get other chances, I'm receiving messages myself you know- I said, but he snorted. He knew I didn't have real chances probably.
-That's not the point Dom, you have to be punctual and professional with customers or they won't call you back- he said, much more upset now.
-Let's go back to the hostel and stay online. We'll get messages- I said, trying to push the mood up. We walked back to the hostel.
We sat in the living room right when the staff was already closing the breakfast area, although they were very kind and let us take some food first.
-I've got plenty of messages Rey, one of these people will probably want to see me- I said, only making Rey look even more annoyed than before. He didn't want to hear a word and kept scrolling on his phone. His inbox had way more messages than mine.
There was a tv broadcasting some American cartoons that I liked, which gave me a minute of mental rest from all the worrying and phone checking. I was sitting on the wooden bench, recalling my teens when I used to learn English by watching the exact same shows.
It was weird though. My worrying state, in the past a proper connotation of myself, was leaving me alone more often than I thought it would. I used to get slightly anxious and paranoid anytime things weren't under full control of mine, but now it seemed as if my default system had changed, and anxiety had become just an annoying little problem, well justified in such moment anyway.
-Let's go, we're going to the fat man- Rey said all of a sudden, then stood up and headed towards the way out, rushed.

We got back to the main square, jumped in a tram and sat away from each other, keeping an eye on different doors, ready to leave and run as soon as someone suspicious were to step in.
Within the following twenty minutes, the further away we got from the city centre, the less were the people in the tram, meaning that the chances to escape in case someone were to check tickets for real were even smaller.
-How far are we from there?- I asked Rey.
-We're almost there, just two stops left-
-Can we just leave now? We'll walk there, it'll be just one stop away- I tried.
-Don't be ridiculous Dom, we've been sitting here so far, nothing is going to happen- Rey said, still checking his phone.
-Rey, these things usually happen when you are one stop away from the destination- I said, but he ignored me again.
-We can't be late Dom! Don't you understand that the fat man is the most important person in our lives right now?- he said, sounding annoyed at me for even suggesting that.
Finally, we reached our stop.
All around us, fancy looking buildings and cars showed a good area of Amsterdam, giving me the feeling that the main difference between Amsterdam and Berlin was that one was, or at least looked, much richer and cleaner than the other.
-You wait here downstairs Dom, ok?- Rey told me before entering the building. I was glad to see his tone towards me was almost back to normal.
I sat down on the pavement down the building next door. That place looked lovely. What was I even doing still in London? Maybe I just loved London too much, there were too many reasons to be there, and Amsterdam wouldn't have been the same.
No more than fifteen minutes were gone when I heard Rey's voice again.
-Dom, Dom- Rey shouted from the distance right when I had found a perfect spot to sit down the nearest possible to the water of a canal.
-What happened?- I asked, not sure on how to take his premature return.

-The guy just came, literally just a few minutes, he was giving me oral and that was it- he said, radiant.
-Are you entitled to leave once they finish? Even after such short time?-
-Yeah, that's the whole point. He really likes me- he said whilst putting a bunch of notes into my hands to store for him.
-Right, Rey, I'm taking count of all the money I am costing you from now on and as soon as things are back to normal, I'll pay you back- I said, but Rey wasn't even listening.
We were safe, at least for a day or two, and that gave us both a feeling of euphoria for the following ten minutes, when for the first time we talked to each other about things we talked about in normal times.
For a little bit, we were fine, but it didn't last much. In fact, Rey was still in huge debts, and I was accumulating more of it. The difference was that for me, paying off debts required working, whereas for Rey it required quick sexual performances he was quite experienced at and that paid more than twenty times as much per hour than my work did. Our short-lived joy was, as I concluded, only given by the awareness that for a few more nights, we weren't going to lack any food.

Within the next days, our hopes began to slowly fade once again.
The fat man, who previously said he was going to need Rey several times and was the primary reason why we went to Holland, suddenly declared he was going to be busy with work and that he couldn't see Rey before about a week. Meanwhile, all men that texted me were just trying to either get to see my body naked or just get me to say dirty things so that they could masturbate or just fulfil their twisted kinks. Some of them would start a conversation by saying they were interested, but then asked me how hard I wanted to punish them or how good I was feeling thinking about owning them.
-Some of these people are just lonely, I can't blame it on them, but most of the others are just rats- Rey liked to use that word to describe people that tried to get free services.

Rey and I had lost track of any sort of regularity. We often found ourselves asking what the day was, our sleeping pattern was messed up and we happened to sometimes nap just so not to think about what was going on. The money we had from the fat man, less than 200 euros, served us to pay for two beds in the hostel and food for three days. Even then, consuming mostly slices of bread and cheese each day to fill us up with the least amount of money still had an impact on our situation, especially because we were receiving no calls.
-I thought you were the king in this business, that you had a profitable net of clients or something- I once couldn't help saying. Rey was no fraud, but he had always spoken very highly of himself in his business.
-Calm down man- he replied, his eyes on his chess game online.

By our fifth day in Amsterdam, we were down to about 40 euros in total for both of us and we had no hostel booked. To face that situation, we developed our only possible plan. We were going to book the cheapest hostel for one person and then get the two of us to sleep in the same bed, all whilst paying attention not to get caught by receptionists.
Eventually, I also had to realise that things from my side weren't going to improve because it seemed impossible to get work for me.
Rey had a long list of positive feedback and paid for a subscription that put him on top of the research, unlike me, God knows how far I was from a decent place in the rankings. According to Rey, the more rats contacted me, the harder I was to be found by serious and decent people who scrolled the list from the top and contacted the first man that inspired them enough to close the deal.
It was the rats that had already contacted everyone and probably got blocked by most users who eventually found me and tried to waste my time in exchange of pleasure, if they really were capable of feeling any.
By the late afternoon, Rey and I were officially successful in our plan, which worked fine also due to the massive size of

the busy hostel we were booked in, too busy for them to stop people asking them for key card at the entrance.
We were finally in bed, now enjoying the comfort of the mattress and clean pillowcases, much higher in quality than the previous hostel, when things seemed to get slightly better, with Rey stating he had just received a work offer for the night.
The illusion though, only lasted half hour, as the client apparently cancelled.

We had been in Amsterdam for exactly one week, and now had almost nothing left.
-Rey, we can't stay here any longer. We're homeless, like, actual homeless right now. Let's go back to London, let's be homeless there, at least somebody knows us. I think I could try and ask someone for some money and make a booking at the hostel- I said, still somehow resistant to the awareness of how bad things were, just trying to use the rational side of my brain for that statement before returning to not care much.
-Yes, we have to leave, but going to London doesn't make sense, I can't work there, there's nothing left for me. Let's go to Paris, a friend contacted me last night and he said he wants to meet me-
-Who? What?- I couldn't believe what he was saying.
-A friend, I told you-
-What about the place to stay?-
-It's just one night, then I'll meet him the next day. He's trustworthy, I've known him for a while- said Rey, confident.
-Book the tickets, we'll go there by bus, it has to be cheap, I'm sure of that- he said, as if saying he was sure of something he had no proofs of could increase the chances of what he wanted to happen for real. I was already looking for the cheapest option anyway.
I silently took care of the operation, booking the cheapest tickets available and a room in a flat for a night only for both of us in the city centre, ruthlessly killing my bank account once for all.
I looked at my friend, still silent.

It was absurd, because the less we had, the more we were travelling, and now we were on our way to Paris.

By the second half of April, Rey and I got to Paris.
Our room was located in Rue de Turbigo, near Etienne Marcel metro station. We had finally reached the city centre and knocked at the door of the flat we were going to sleep in when we met the landlord, a bald and short man in his sixties that came downstairs, acting rude as soon as he realised we didn't speak French.
-Ok, let me try again, excuse me, we are the people that booked a room here for tonight, through the internet- I said in French, slow and probably not without mistakes.
The man calmed down a bit and tried to put a smile on his face that was still red after shouting whatever he shouted just a minute before.
-I'll give you the keys- I understood this from his reply, still not even a word of English.
-Wait a second. You have to apologise- Rey said in English, looking at him with a threatening face.
-Rey, are you stupid or what? Shut up, he may understand you- I said.
-I don't care. I won't let this guy talk to us like that- Rey was getting out of control.
-We don't even know what he said, and also, I told you he's going to take our key- I tried to calm Rey down, but he had already pushed my arm away, now staring at this man's eyes who, expectedly, started shouting again and telling us to leave the place before he ended it with the police.
Right then, the two of us were in the street outside the building, and the guy had just closed the door behind us with strength.
-And now what?- I snapped, unable to handle it any more. All the frustration and the things I had to bear up to that moment, from the cold in the streets to the uncertainties about getting basic stuff for survival, from the hurting feet and consumed shoes to the sense of nausea I had after eating the same thing every single day for over a week by then. Everything was about to make me explode now.

-Why? Why do you have to be so proud? Even in such situation?-
-We don't need that guy, we are ok, just the two of us Dom, we don't need anyone else- Rey flattered me every time he did something wrong.
-You fool, where are we going to sleep tonight? I haven't slept on the bus and I'll collapse soon. I've been outraging my own body for too long without proper rest-
-We'll be alright Dom- Rey seemed to handle it, a confident sneer on his face.
-Right, look, everything, everywhere is... fully booked, or too expensive, way too expensive- I noticed whilst scrolling even the cheapest hostels on my phone.
-We won't find anywhere for both of us for less than 98 euros at least according to my results- I kept scrolling down on my phone for more, but still getting nothing better.
Rey and I had been standing next to the metro station for a couple of very long minutes when he finally spoke.
-My friend just said he could help us. He has a place for us to stay tonight, Boulevard Saint Martin, we have to go there. He owes me a bit of money, so he will make it up like that for tonight. It's walking distance by the way- Rey gave me the first good news in what seemed to be a very long time.

When we got to our destination, the sun was set, and the dark sky, together with a lovely temperature allowed me a moment of mental rest whilst looking up.
I had previously been in Paris with my parents, but it was all different now. Not the city, but rather my state. Back in the days, my dad took me, my mother and my sister to restaurants at every lunch and dinner time, and I spent my time both talking to them and spacing out, immersed in the beauty of the place around me. I loved the way Paris looked, and I remembered how I used to wish to be there on my own once and just explore.
Our flat was located on the top floor of a wide building with a central courtyard and lots of other flats on about eight floors that closed up the squared perimeter.
When we were up, a black guy with dreads welcomed us and showed us the place, which was lovely, small and cosy with a sofa and a small bed up to a mezzanine.

Right before the guy left, I remembered, maybe because of his look, that I still had some weed on me from London, stuck into a small pocket of my backpack and forgotten about due to the recent events.
The guy obviously accepted and kindly invited me to the roof of the building, accessible from a window of his flat.
We sat on the blue tiles and just smoked together whilst looking at the sky and making conversation.

In the early afternoon of the next day, Rey's friend knocked at our door.
He was a man in his late thirties with dark and short brown hair, fully shaved and well postured, as if he was one of those financial people that you usually saw wearing a suit.
-Hello, nice to meet you, my name is Fred- he said in a very well pronounced English.
-Dom, nice to meet you too-
Fred sat down on the sofa and began chatting mostly with Rey and discussing stuff I was ignoring, right until I was called.
-You're doing it too? Really?- Fred was asking me.
-Sorry what?-
-I didn't know you were in the business too, Rey told me, and since he says he might potentially meet someone later, I guess...- he looked at me and bit his lips.
-Oh, I see... Well, I haven't really done anything so far, so you might want to consider...-
-I'll pay you 150 pounds to have sex here now. I guess Rey could wait outside, right?- Rey nodded his head yes.
-Oh, yeah, sure- I said.
Damn it, I was getting used to the idea I was never going to have to do this and I would just pay Rey back with normal work.
-Ok, as I was saying, I'm not well experienced just so you know, so you're still in time to change your mind in case- I said and smiled to him, hoping he would choose to decline the offer.
-Don't worry about it- Fred was already getting naked, panting for happiness. I was his fresh meat and I was going to disappoint him.

Rey passed me his pill, then left for a walk outside. Then, I was moving to the shower when Fred stopped me.
-No, please don't, don't enter the shower. I love men's natural smell- he said with a pervert look on his face, although still looking decent to me due to his presentation.
Fine then, this man is clean and shaved everywhere, so at least it's not a bad start.

Half hour later, my first job was to be considered successful. I couldn't even focus on what Fred was telling Rey while we walked to the nearest cash machine to withdraw money for me.
It wasn't really the end of the world. I knew I wouldn't be able to make it for a living with this job, but at least I had recovered some expenses.
Straight after Fred was gone, I met a great improvement in my mood, especially after calculating that the money I made in that half hour was enough to already repay Rey for the money he had to spend for me in hostels and food.
-Rey, right now we're even. I literally owe you nothing right now- I said, happy, handing him the money that Fred gave me.
Later that night though, we were brought to connect with the reality of things once again.
-Dom, we can't stay in that place any longer, we're going to a new place tomorrow- Rey said. He was texting with the actual landlord when he told me that.
We started searching for a flat where we could have been on our own and work in case we were lucky, and eventually found the closest one available online to be also one of the cheapest ones.

Our new place was based in Rue Tiquetonne, walking distance from where we slept up to the previous two nights. The way Paris looked, its streets, its buildings and the unique type of architecture made it look beautiful at every corner.
-I don't know if stealing in a supermarket in another country would cost some extra trouble- I was reflecting out loud with Rey walking next to me.

-I don't think they will arrest me and keep me here until I found a job and pay them back before being able to leave, but I guess you just develop a debt with France and that you can't come back without paying them back- I realised I didn't make much sense when Rey ignored that.

Hanging out with Rey was strange. He was constantly arranging meetings giving a top priority to work and a secondary priority to sex with girls or trans. He took his eyes off his screen only when he played chess with me or when we were in a club and actual girls were around us.

For the rest of the time, he was either checking messages on the escort website or on Tinder. His sexual appetite was much greater than mine and that made him the best wingman. He was always up for having sex with anything that had reached legal age for consent.

I couldn't imagine how he would feel if he were to be alone for a minute, but I assumed he would spend his time planning the next meeting. As extroverts, the two of us enjoyed a better life than introverts, but miserably suffered whenever we faced loneliness, even if for a couple of hours.

-I've just been into a flat nearby, owned by a trans and, oh, it was stunning, so beautiful, but of course it is, she charges 3k per night- he said after reappearing that late afternoon.

-3k? Who the hell pays that money to have sex with a trans if you can pay less for a woman?-

-What do you mean by that? A trans woman is a woman- Rey had changed his relaxed tone with an accusing one now.

-Well no, don't get me wrong here, that works for me, but why if a man is straight and wants to get a sex service with a woman, why wouldn't he go for traditional ones? There is much more competition and prices are cheaper. You can get a very fit one for less than 1k in London, for the whole night, I mean-

-Having sex with a trans is a different thing and you can't know it until it happens to you-

-How is it different? If it even was better, and I guess it could really be, seeing the fares they apply, I still think I would go for a cheaper girl-

His face still looked a bit annoyed. I had to say something.

-I would love to do it, but I can't afford it. How much did this one charge you?-
-Nothing, they just enjoy it, I never pay for sex with trans-
-How come?-
-They like me, they want me, you know I'm huge-
Rey was lying down on the bed of our flat, the window open in a pretty warm afternoon.
The sound of people passing by underneath our building was pleasant, but I would have chosen to stay in the previous flat.
-Dom, I have to tell you something. My businesses are cancelled. Both of them- Rey raised his voice suddenly at some point, very stressed.
I stood silent, the pan with tomato sauce in it still in my hands. My brain was probably communicating to me that the only way to rationalise that moment was to stop doing anything else I was doing.
-We're ruined, this is bad, this is bad- Rey was now very nervous, worse than how I had ever seen him.
-Ok, we have to leave, let's go back to London, maybe I can ask Fred to meet me there, or some cash advance or something- he was saying.
-What about the people that you already know? Those who contacted you?- I asked, impatient.
-They cancelled!- Rey shouted, but then calmed down right away, or at least so it looked.
-Right, all tickets to London are expensive. At least 30 pounds each- I said, scrolling my phone looking for more information.
We both got silent for a couple of long minutes, and then I went back to the escort platform, as if logging out and in again could show messages that I had missed, constantly loading the page and hoping for one business, only one that would have taken us back to London at least.
-Rey, Rey, I've got a message. It's...- I kept reading. It was long and written with some poor English, probably translated by google.
-What?-

-It's absurd, the guy wants to pay me 600 euros to celebrate his birthday today, he wants sex, and dinner is on him afterwards-
-Wow, 600 euros- Rey seemed shocked as I expected, but not very happy. Was he jealous?
-We might be even able to get something different than bread and cheese or pasta with tomato sauce, or maybe, from now on we could even pay for the food we get-

Rey seemed sad when I left for Porte de la Chapelle, where my appointment with this man was set for that very evening. The station was far from the centre, and I didn't know how the guy looked like because the pictures he had on his profile were blurred or just bad quality.
He seemed to be bald but not old. I felt like I wasn't going to do anything with an old man, or maybe I could have tried, but it would have definitely failed quickly.
I started to think that he wouldn't show up and getting somehow happy about it when somebody waved his hand at me and gave me a big smile from an approaching distance. He was a man in his late forties, bald and with some little dark beard, about my same height.
I guess it could have been worse, but I definitely prefer Fred.
-Hello- I said, acting friendly. -Do you speak English?-
-Hi, a little bit, a little bit- he said with a thick French accent.
He told me we would have taken his car and reached his place, friendly, gaining my trust for the moment up to when I got into the car.
It took him no time to switch the language of conversation to only French allowed mode.
He started driving and we went further north.
Why couldn't he just give me his address? I would have got there by metro, he didn't have to bother and take me there by car, but I guessed it was his birthday and he wanted to be extra nice or something.
After about half hour, we were travelling on big roads, out of the living and busy Paris. I couldn't wait any longer and our pleasant conversation had to turn into another direction, but I also had to be careful not to turn him off.

-Where are you taking me exactly?-
-Saint Denis, I live there, see? That's the Stade de France, do you like it?- he said, excited, then laughed.
Ok, here I am, this might have been a big mistake. I need to get some information and send it to Rey, I hope my phone won't die anytime soon.
He's taking me far from everything. I wish this trip had never started. It was just desperate at first, but at least not dangerous. If I had felt in danger before I was wrong, we were never in danger, no one really starves to death in Europe, and everything would have eventually come back to normal.
Why did I feel in danger? Why did I feel like I needed to do something that my situation didn't require?
-He's taking me to Saint Denis, we're far from Paris- I sent this message to Rey making sure I didn't sound pathetic or scared.
His answer came straight away.
-You'll be alright Dom- he knew we needed the money, but he didn't know how I was feeling. On the other hand, he met lots of people in this business, so he was less concerned...
-Don't worry, you're safe! It's my birthday!- he said, very loud and excited.
He tried to cheer me up. Maybe he even knew how I was feeling, maybe my feelings were painted on my face. If only he didn't look like one of those maniacs in American films.
We reached a small town, pretty, very French looking and also, I assumed with pleasure, quite well off with all probabilities. Big family houses with gates, garages and some very expensive cars parked outside showed it was an area for people of a certain income. At least he wasn't poor. Maybe this is just what it's supposed to be and I'm overthinking.
He stopped the car in front of his home and let me in. There was no sign of the address and I couldn't take a picture since my phone was off.
I guessed right. He was well off. He had a living room, two bedrooms and two toilets. The apartment was clean and tidy, but I wouldn't have swapped it for my hostel in Russell Square for no reason in the world. Maybe yes, if it was more

central, but only at the conditions of throwing parties on a daily basis.

The first thing he did in his bedroom was to turn on his monitor and play some straight porn, then he bent down and gave me a condom. All I needed to imagine now was to be doing it with the woman in the video and that would have been it.

-By the way, just so you know, I have to ask you to see the money first, you know, out of previous experience-

-Really? Really? On my birthday? Are you a slut or what?- he thundered, catching me by surprise.

Well, yes.

-No, but...-

-It's my birthday, I want to feel like you're my boyfriend. I'm lonely, don't you understand it? I'll give you the money after the dinner as I wrote you. Now do your job- he said, very angry now.

Ok, calm down, he seems honest, he is lonely indeed.

He's not even masturbating, I thought. If he's expecting me to finish off with him then he has to know this is simply the most impossible thing. I wonder if gay men could finish off when they were passive just like that. How long does this have to go on?

He called himself satisfied after about half hour bent below me, then he let me shower and then, sooner than I thought, we were back in his car.

It wasn't even that late and we were already heading back to Paris. The worst part seemed to be gone, and the guy seemed happy.

Dinner now, oh yes, I need some food, some proper food. You know what? You have been nice to me even though you were rude, but that's because you're French and maybe I'm biased. Maybe I just want to say something that feeds an opinion I previously had but who cares, I'll make you a discount if you pay for dinner.

Finally, I recognised the place where he picked me up next to Porte de la Chapelle, which made me feel completely tranquil. If he hadn't murdered me in the middle of nowhere, he wasn't going to be able to do it in Paris.

-Here we are- he said, unnaturally excited at some point.

-So, get off here and I'll just park my car, ok?- he said nicely.
-Sure- I left and stood on the pavement.
I was texting Rey whilst keeping an eye on the guy, who was now moving his car forward, then backwards, slowly fitting it in between two cars, then moving it again towards the street as to remake the manoeuvre, and then left at full throttle.
I looked at that for a couple of seconds, confused. Why was he doing that?
Slowly, I began to understand, or, I already understood it and I was struggling to rationalise.
-You lied to me, you lied to me- he called me and shouted through his phone a minute later. -You said 21 cm and it wasn't, you liar!- he couldn't stop laughing. A maniacal, victorious laugh of someone who had just got the revenge of his life.
-Well, first of all, I know it's not 21 but it's 20, it's a fact, and secondly, just come back here. Give me the money, just 150 euros and then leave- I said.
He kept laughing, then played some loud music in his car for a minute with me listening to it, hoping that he would come back and talk to me, saying it was all a joke or something. Then, he actually did turn the volume down again.
-You lied to me- he said again.
-Come back here motherfucker!- I thundered, desperate, although already resigning, aware that there was no way that he would come back, but still not able to close the call until he did it himself.
Rey told me that I should have always taken money first, but I didn't. He warned me about the evil of some customers. At least, I hoped, he wasn't going to make fun of me.
I arrived home to find out that the bald guy had deleted his account and that there was no way for me to report him to the community.
Failure, no money left and an annoying feeling on my body that felt just dirty. Rey didn't make fun of me, but acted sorry, maybe relieved somehow, but I understood that.
-We have to go back to London, and play with Raymond Keene- I said, chess being the only thought that could make me happy in that moment.
-Who?-

-Raymond Keene, chess grandmaster. I met him in Sloane Square and took his email contact before they fired me. He's been in touch with me during these days and I've organised a simultaneous game against him in a pub in King's Road. He's just confirmed it, it's on the 27th- I told him after reading the last email that he sent me.
-How are we going to go back?-
-Bus, on my way back in the metro I checked for tickets and there are some cheap offers, they're still on. Can I please book them? We could leave tomorrow. I want to leave, I want to go back to work, Rey- I said, exhausted.
-Yes, let's go- he said, resigned as well.

Another person I had been in touch with was Jemma. There wasn't much texting between me and her though. Maybe she did realise that we had literally nothing in common, but she was also the first one to add a question mark at the end of almost each message, encouraging the conversation to continue.
We were so nice with each other, not even a swear word or anything fun. If she didn't look the way she looked there was going to be no way I would have kept talking to her.
Jemma was taller than me, smelled and dressed better than me. She added me on Facebook and a few minutes of scrolling her page were enough to confirm that me and her were incompatible. She looked good on every picture, held a glass of wine of champagne, posed in them with other girls who were also hot and curved their bodies the same way she did in picnics. She posted stuff about her job and cuddly pictures hugging dogs.
My profile had political rants against capitalism, controversial opinions in general and I appeared clearly drunk in all pictures, most of them at the hostel, called "home" in the captions.
I did lie to her telling her that I owned a business and that was dishonest, but at the same time I couldn't reveal her the truth. I didn't really hope to get laid, but she was going to be back in London in less than two weeks and she said she hadn't slept with anyone all that time in Italy.

I had to be honest, I didn't want her to think high of me and get disappointed when she found out I lied, and it seemed like the only thing left to do to remain honest was to not try any harder with her.
My conclusion was that I was not going to hit on her, and if she had hit on me and we ended up in bed, I will have considered her courting successful and acted nice until she lost interest in me.
Or maybe, I'll start a business and get rich so that we could get married, I couldn't deny that the vision of me actually being with her was glorious.

On the morning of the 27th of April, Rey and I arrived in Porte Maillot.
The previous night I managed to get in touch with Giuseppe, my very first friend in life, who had been living in Paris for an internship for a couple of months. We went to a pub and then visited the Eiffel Tower together once again, talked a lot about our past and our future, and then promised to see each other again as soon as the chance would have come available.
By that moment, I was feeling exhausted, drained out of every physical and mental energy, although somehow far from being any depressed or even disappointed.
The truth behind it, I assumed, had to be bound to how the brain was designed.
I was broke, but I had the company of someone I could trust my life to, I ate the same food everyday, but was never deprived of any for too long, I got humiliated by a sexual abuser, but I was alive, I made no economic profit at all, but I had a long holiday.
I was spacing out, trying to explain to me why I wasn't feeling the way I was supposed to, and concluded that my views about happiness were wrongfully tainted by the logic that a specific course of events was meant to define my mental state, whilst such was actually determined by an internal mechanism of its own that had little to do with the outside world, but rather had a lot to do with the personal perception of reality. We were in a very harsh state to the eyes of society, but not to ourselves, at least looking at our own faces. Rey and I were chuckling and not at all upset as

we found out when we began commenting the trip now that it had turned to its end.

In fact, it took nothing for both of us to go back in normal mode, and Rey proved it immediately.

-Let's sit down next to some girls- said Rey before realising that the bus was completely empty, or almost. There were just two young girls sitting on the very back of the bus.

-Let's go there- I suggested him. We walked casually between the seats pretending that we were just picking the most comfortable places and sat down a couple of seats away from them.

They were young, probably in their early twenties, both had a pretty pale skin and blue eyes. One of them was blonde and the other one had dark brown hair.

By the couple of hours it took for us to reach the Channel, the blonde girl had probably realised I gave her a few interested looks and I found out she was staring at me now, suspicious.

What could I do now? I should have given her the impression of the player and now I just looked like a creep.

-Hi, excuse me, can I ask you for a favour?- I said, sitting in front of her. -Can you wake me up when we get to the border?-

-Oh, ok- the blonde one said, timidly. She had two long tufts of hair on the side of her face and the rest of it tied into a bun. Her look was somehow sad, or confused, or maybe just indifferent. She looked at me as if she was resigned over something she couldn't cope with.

-Where are you girls from by the way?-

-Germany, you?- the blonde girl said kindly, but still without any sign of a smile from her red lips.

-I'm Italian, my best friend here is Spanish, but we live in London-

We went on to find out that their names were Lisa and Sara. They didn't look nor sound very friendly, but they were answering every question we were asking after all, which meant we had to stay awake and get that going.

Rey sat next to Sara, which was good. I didn't mind the blonde one in fact.

I felt like I just really wanted to ask for her phone number, but eventually I decided not to because she looked too innocent and nice, which didn't make me want to flirt with her just in case she developed feelings for me and I was forced to break her heart.
I shook their hands when we got out of the bus and said it was nice meeting them.
-Do you want to exchange contacts?- Lisa asked me.
-Oh, yeah sure, why not?- I replied, pretending I hadn't thought about it at all in the last couple of hours.

Once we got to Victoria, Rey and I jumped on bus 38, heading to Russell Square.
Sixteen days in three different countries lived under stress, fear and poverty, but at the same time I felt like it had made me happy. Maybe it wasn't too bad spending the last sixteen days in the least safe situation I had ever been in before. After all, that was the reason why I chose to live in a hostel. I learnt that the best feeling was given by the pleasure of the unpredictable, and no matter how bad things were going, the fact that there was no positive expectations about our trip made it look better than it actually was.
-What a trip just ended. I can't believe it- I said, more to myself than to Rey, who now burst out laughing, followed by me.
People could travel for fun, for work, for an adventure, or to just take a break. Our travel though, matched with none of such reasons. Even people who go on adventures still made sure to have the money for that, so what was ours?
Meanwhile, Lisa had texted me.
-Hey boy? Let me know if you are free these days since we could meet up-

The next day, our appointment with Raymond Keene was confirmed and set at 4 pm at the Chelsea Potter pub in King's Road.
I had created a group on Facebook with Rey, Mark, Vittorio and Claudio who all agreed on being part of the event.
We found Vittorio enjoying fish and chips with a fizzy drink and ordering a chocolate slice with custard cream on the

side, Mark sitting next to him and Mr. Keene and his wife by the opposite side of the same table, way too overdressed for us. After a bit of chess talk, boards setting up and handshakes, Keene explained us the rules of the day.
-I will play against all of you at the same time, which means I get the privilege to play white on all boards. I will play a move and then you think about yours. As soon as I get back to you, I assume you've had enough time to think and play your move, then I'll play straight away and go to the next board-
Rey sat on my left, Mark and Vittorio on my right.
Keene opened with pawn to d4 on every board.
There I was, facing a grandmaster. His rating was more than 1000 points higher than mine, meaning I had absolutely no chance to win, but I wanted to lose with dignity. I didn't want to get crushed, I wanted him to think hard to beat me. After about ten minutes though, my position was pathetic and my pieces were cramped. I needed to attack, that was all I could think of doing. The other option was to live longer and suffer more.
Unsurprisingly, I was the first one to get checkmated.
Vittorio and Mark resigned a couple of minutes afterwards and regarding Rey...
Was Rey winning? His position looked very comfortable, his pieces got space and he had a strong attack on his opponent's king going on. If he played it well, he could have actually won...
-I think we could call this game over- Keene told Rey just then.
-Yeah, I was going to resign soon anyway- said Rey, smiling, pointing out for me how his queen was going to be trapped soon.
After the second game was played and again lost by each of us, the grandmaster rewarded Claudio, the latecomer, with an autographed chess book for playing the best game of all, and we understood that the old couple was calling the afternoon with us over.

Lisa texted me several times that night. She said that Sara wanted to rest the next day, but that she still wanted to visit

London. I asked her if she was up for a bicycle ride and she agreed.

The next afternoon I picked Lisa up from Notting Hill tube station, near to where she was staying, a flat rented for a few days by an old lady that needed somebody to cook and clean for her.

We cycled through Regent's Park and ended up in Primrose Hill, where we set a small picnic with some apples and chocolate I had in my bag.

Lisa was very pretty, that kind of beauty with no malice that I really liked, but that also intimidated me sometimes. No matter how often she smiled and how actively she talked and gave me the impression she was enjoying my company, Lisa looked constantly sad, as if something really bad happened sometimes in her past and a part of her had died forever. I didn't dare asking her or even letting her notice I felt like that though.

She accepted my chocolate and smiled. She was beautiful in her denim jacket and long colourful scarf wrapped everywhere around her neck as if it was her mother that had dressed her up for school on a winter day.

-See, the music you listen to is important. You shouldn't listen to sad music, never. Your brain will get used to such frequency and will not train to activate other parts of it that will push your productivity and contribute to make you happy. You should change, even by force, the music you usually listen to- I told her at some point, remembering my breakup.

-Yeah- she cut it short, apparently bored by what I was saying.

-Are you cold?- she asked me after my third sneeze.

-Yes, it's cold- I complained.

-No it's not- she laughed. Never heard such sweet sound like her laugh.

I tried to take my eyes off of her a few times, but every time I did, I found out she was still looking at me until eventually I had to face it.

She put her leg on top of mine as to encourage me to go forward. This was happening very fast, although we had been talking a lot...

The next day Lisa, Sara and a guy called Bernardo that was staying in the same building with them came along to the hostel and we made pasta.
The way Lisa moved and talked produced in me a desire for sweetness, at times I even thought of hugging her, but I decided to play it cool.
She was curvy, dressed casual, and clearly had no care for fashionable looks, typical of German girls. I found it very entertaining to see her jumping around the kitchen and asking me how she could have helped me.
When the visitors time was gone, Latif told us we had to leave and we headed to the pub in Herbrand Street.
Oh, if only I drank coffee. I feel so sleepy, it happens any time I'm in London.
I couldn't even focus on what she was saying. She was beautiful, and I had the impression that it wasn't just me staring into someone's eyes, magnetised. Her two friends were noticing it too and were smiling, pointing at us.
We called it a night when Lisa was done drawing rockets on a paper back and front, which then I took back to the hostel with me and put in my own paper book.

The next night Alex contacted me, asking me about our night out that we planned a while before and that I casually confirmed, thinking that it would probably not happen.
-Hey Alex, I met two German girls, we're going out tonight, wanna join us?- I texted him back, hoping he would agree with that. Our goal was to go and get girls after all.
Alex agreed and the four of us met by Notting Hill tube station that night.
The main problem though was that it was Sunday and the chances for partying on such day in such neighbourhood were none.
I couldn't deny that I already knew it, but what else was I supposed to do? If I had gone out with Alex, we might have got no results anyway and Lisa was going to leave the following day. If I had declined Alex's meeting after postponing for so long it might have affected our friendship and the possibility for future meetings. I liked him, he was

always nice to me and also younger, another reason why I didn't want to look unreliable. Anyway, I had just made the introductions when I realised that the night was going to be a failure if nothing had happened.
We walked over some random streets and even checked for something on google, but found nothing that we could have done when I stopped and realised I brought these people in the wrong area and if I wanted them to like me, something had to happen.
-Guys, let's go to Piccadilly, there's probably some pubs open there- I said.
-Hey guys, are you looking for party?- a voice behind me just said.
Three men in their late twenties who had just left the supermarket with a few plastic bags approached us.
-Sorry guys, no mean to scare you, I just wanted to know if you're up for a house party, it's a boring Sunday you know- the man had slightly long hair and was wearing a shirt and shorts. His friends looked pretty well dressed too and my first impression that they were homeless slowly faded. A party in a house of complete strangers would have been just perfect for me, but I felt responsible of whatever happened to the two young girls after all.
I decided to decline, but politely, just as politely as that man had spoken to me.
-Ok- said Lisa. Alex and Sara seemed to agree as well. The only one who was worrying was actually me.
We walked down Holland Park Avenue and turned right into some tight silent alleys, perfect place for an assault. Where did I take you, Lisa?
The main guy let us in his house and a dog barked when we got in. Nobody that owns a dog could be a bad person, I thought.
False alarm, I thought while we were offered to sit down in the top floor of a beautiful house. A table with a bar counter and lots of spirits with leather sofas for guests and a chimney on the bottom of the room welcomed us. The guys treated us nicely and kept offering us all sort of stuff, including weed which I noticed Lisa truly enjoyed.

-So yeah, I do trading and play poker while my girlfriend owns a business. She designs fashion stuff and things like that- I absently heard the guy briefly explaining his story to Alex.
-I love this place because the glass ceiling makes me feel like we're on a boat when it rains- the guy said, cuddling his cat on his personal sofa.
A boat? Wouldn't you be uncovered then? Hold on, are people on a ship safe from the rain? Why was it taking me so long to find out?
Oh no, I'm high again. I've officially missed my last chance to get you, Lisa.
I sat on my corner, high and sleepy, painfully trying to stay awake when I asked Lisa how she was feeling about that situation and if she wanted to go to sleep. Damn weed.
-No, I'm ok- she said, looking at me tenderly.
-Wanna have a tour around the house?- I asked her. We went downstairs until we reached the basement where there were a lot of mannequins, cartoon silhouettes and all sort of equipment that that guy's girlfriend used for her business. That couple was young and yet wealthy. I imagined his girlfriend to be a fit blonde chick that made a lot of money. Lisa was looking at me, her sad and innocent look didn't drive my instinct, but I had to follow Manu's advice and do what I was supposed to do which, in his opinion, applied in every case.
-Hit on all girls, make no distinction. The sweet ones are just as bad as the bad ones- I heard his voice in my head and imagined a grin on his face.

Lisa and Sara had to be in Victoria coach station to take their bus to Paris in the afternoon and when Lisa told me that Sara wanted to give as much rest as she could to her legs after she sprained her ankle few days before, I took the chance to get to see Lisa again that morning and show her Kyoto Gardens in Holland Park.
The previous night, I took Lisa to have a pizza with me in Franco Manca in Earl's Court. We talked a lot again, and she even told me some fairy tales.

That afternoon though, I was counting down the hours that I could have spent with her and felt saddened for her imminent departure.
Sara met us in Victoria and I prepared for a goodbye.
-It will be hard to stop thinking about you, so I won't hit on other girls for the moment- came out of my mind on my last hug with Lisa, who retreated a little.
-No, we can do whatever we want- she said, somewhere between serious and tender.
-Oh, ok, I understand- I said, and then she was gone.

May 2016

The days spent with Lisa were the death blow to my bank account.
I didn't know how much exactly I had, but the last time I checked I had about 60 pounds left and I found out I wasn't very curious to know then. The heartbeat frequency I perceived anytime I opened my online banking app was at least something I could have spared to myself.
To respond to my applications were three employers. Two restaurants were interested in seeing me for a chat and for a trial shift to be planned afterwards. On the other hand, Starbucks asked me to let them know in case I wanted to go for a trial shift straight away.
I didn't hesitate to reply to them. I never worked in a cafe before, but I was ready to lie and say I had. My cv supported me in saying I worked for six months in a cafe in Italy, long enough to be a good candidate for the job, short enough to have an excuse to be awful at it.
My interview with Starbucks was set right on the day Jemma was landing back in London.
I did want to see her and at this point I had to also hit on her even if I was feeling fear to win. The idea of me actually having my way on a type of girl I never even bothered hitting on in the past constantly put me under pressure. Sometimes I thought that the best thing would be to just tell her I was dating someone or anything to get her away from me because my fear was to get close to it, feel to be one step away from victory and then lose it on the last moment.

Millionaires that lose all their money commit more suicides than homeless that never had any after all.
-I'm having very busy days actually so we might have to meet up next weekend, how about that?- I texted her, hoping that she will get bored to wait in the meantime and get someone else. A babe of her level could get a man in no time in London.

My trial shift in Holborn Starbucks was scheduled to be three hours long, after which I would have asked for a response immediately.
My manager was a blonde woman in her late twenties from Scotland who said she would sit downstairs while the assistant manager, a guy from Algeria, would take care of me.
I was placed in front of the coffee machine and just told what to do. I paid attention not to do things my own way even when I felt like it and just acted as confident as I could, activating my brain as much as I could so not to forget a single thing they explained to me, just in case they asked me to do it again.
It seemed it was going to be fun, seeing that the queue started from literally outside the shop.
The guys were busy nonstop in there, it was Holborn and lots of people from nearby offices rushed to get a coffee during their breaks before going back to work.
-Our manager cares mostly about standards rather than speed, although she also wants you to be as fast as you can, which makes it hard. It's ups and downs here, remember- another assistant manager that had just arrived for the beginning of his shift told me.
Breaking the ice for iced drinks, breaking cartoons and taking them to the bin room, taking bottles of syrups from the office and bringing them upstairs were some of the duties I was going to be carrying out in case I got the job.
The good news I received when I sat down with my manager was that they liked me and that I was hired. The bad news was that they told me they paid monthly and made no cash advance.

On the weekend, Jemma asked me what my plans were. She was really looking forward to meeting me again and even couldn't wait for the following weekend as I suggested her.
-Just in case you happen to be free, me and my friends will be in a bar in Piccadilly area tonight- she said.
I needed money real badly. I did previously decline a few offers from people that got to know about mine and Rey's troubled situation, but I had to put my pride aside now. I needed money for bookings in the hostel and for food. We couldn't keep paying for half of the food and steal the other half of it, trying to put stuff in our bag and rush away from the shops, especially after I got caught once and forgiven by the employee who took the stuff back and decided to let me go, making me feel even worse about myself.
-Mina, I'm sorry, this is going to sound... I don't know. Well, ok, look, you offered to help me with money and I said no, but I'm in real trouble right now and you know you can trust me 100 per cent-
-How much do you need?- Mina interrupted me and stood up.
-Well, 80 pounds will do to survive I guess... Thanks a lot man, you're great- I said, embarrassed and grateful when he quickly made a move to the cash machine. Meanwhile, I also texted Andrea and Claudio who transferred me 100 pounds each.

The weather in London was improving a lot, now finally warm enough to give a chance to girls to show off their flower dresses and to everyone else to go and sit on the nearest piece of grass for some wine and food.
Rey didn't wait much to notice the chance and suggested me to go to Russell Square.
-Rey, you know what? If you can lend me some money, we could go party tonight, there's Jemma and three other chicks she's taking-
-Yeah, let's do it, I'll pay for the drinks before we get there- said Rey, looking forward to it.
He was gambling again, and now enjoying one of those moments where he was up on the balance.
So that was it, I accepted Jemma's invitation.

I was wasting her time and I was sorry about it, but it was her that was asking for me all the time. All I did was flirting with her in a club and take her to dinner. I never mentioned feelings or anything, I never illuded her of something. I knew she was looking for something serious with someone at her level, but what was wrong if I was the middle guy? The guy she could entertain with before her prince arrived? None of us could have possibly got hurt, and besides, I had been texting her for too long not to try and get my reward back. I promised her I would take three other guys with me, but I didn't reply when she asked me if they were decent. My friends were very good-looking, but they certainly weren't going to behave.

That night Rey, Adam, Ignacio and I left the hostel and walked through Shaftesbury Avenue, heading to Great Mindwill Street where Jemma and her friends were.
Ignacio was the new receptionist at the hostel, a guy from Argentina. He had a bushy, well-kept beard and dark long hair pulled backwards. He had Italian origins and was about my height, which would have helped me not to be highlighted as the smallest guy that evening.
Walking in their company made me less nervous, especially since I had the wildest members of the crew with me.
The bar Jemma chose for the party said it all about them. Fancy, everything was fancy, from the men in suits and the women in high heels to the sofas, the lights and the lame music for horny and overemotional people.
-Hi, they're with us- Jemma came out and told the security guys who didn't want to let us in because Adam and Ignacio weren't dressed fancy enough.
-Hi Jemma, good to see you, how are you?- I asked her, attracted, but also slightly uncomfortable at the same time.
-Hi, so good to see you too- she said, looking for a hug she didn't get.
The dance floor downstairs was just as boring as the bar upstairs. Lots of decent looking people with glasses of wine and prosecco that sat near each other, someone standing, many taking pictures.

-I need to get a few pints, just to warm things up- Adam said and patted on my back, reminding of how good our side of the world was.
-I'm afraid you won't find any here mate- I said.
Maybe, if Jemma gets a man tonight, we could all just leave to somewhere better and just be boys.
Rey took no time to start flirting with one of Jemma's friends, a pretty, petite blonde girl from Poland, whilst Ignacio got pretty chatty with the other two ones who were laughing at his jokes.
-Right Jemma, wanna go to the Tiger place?- I suggested her at some point.
-Do you? Don't you like it here?-
-No, it's not fun. Come on, let's go- I said, acting a bit rude as I was slowly feeling less interested in her. How could I date someone that liked that kind of environment?
-Yeah, sure, let's go- she said, sounding worried.
Half hour later, I managed to get the whole group to a dance floor, which at least was going to be more entertaining and less posh than the bar we were in.
Jemma was being nice in every aspect with me, even though I wasn't really caring. I didn't know why, but I just couldn't help hoping that that night could have just been me and the guys.
Jemma's friends were all occupational therapists just like her and worked in different hospitals. Jemma was clearly very selective of her friends and of the man she dated. I felt like it made more sense now that the very first thing she asked me was about my job.
If only she knew that I was in debt with multiple friends and had just got hired at Starbucks, she not only would have dumped me right there, but also felt embarrassed in front of her friends.
I couldn't flirt with her like I did with everybody else, because it made me feel guilty. The problem was though, that the less I cared, the more intrigued she was. She had no idea she could have got a much, much better deal than me.
I looked at her, gorgeous in her long skirt and the black top. Maybe, if I had done something sweet for her right then, she would have left me, maybe.

She was very close to me now. I knew that Rey was looking at me, which I didn't mind.
-Are you still in the hostel?- she asked into my ear when we were dancing.
-Yeah, I had to leave my room, had a fight with the landlord, I'm still looking for a new place- I lied.
She thought about it for a few seconds before responding.
-I'm not sleeping in a hostel tonight- she said, making no sense.
-Then you'll have to sleep at your place- I said, feeling my stomach going upside down all of a sudden.
-Are you not coming with me?- she asked, surprised.
I couldn't believe it. This was really happening. It couldn't be.
-Yeah- I said, not acting any longer and leading her outside hand in hand, rushed.
I called a taxi just to make an impression on her, regretting it right after she told me I should have got an Uber because it was much cheaper.
We got to Battersea and walked to her flat at the bottom of a big square with buildings surrounding a neat looking garden, then walked through the wooden steps to her door.
I wasn't going to believe it was happening until it happened for real. I had a feeling that my stomach was jumping up and down, making me unable to relax.
Jemma led me to her bedroom, whilst I slowly became more and more aware that I was going to score, and that even if I didn't, my friends didn't have to know.
They saw me leaving with a girl who was far above the average, and that was enough for me to secure my place in the hall of fame of our family. Nothing else mattered more, and in worst case scenario, I could have just finished things by myself to cover the disappointment.
But that wasn't going to be necessary, I realised when Jemma took off her top without waiting for me. Maybe, she knew I wasn't sure about it, or maybe she was just very into me, especially after all the things I didn't do for her.
So, this is it, the peak of my sexual life. This is the best I'm ever going to get. In the future, I would have certainly got better deals in terms of compatibility, income comparison and sentimental situation, but this was a different story.

I need to enjoy every moment of this, I thought when her golden hair waved and hid behind her back, her naked body in front of me right now. Apparently, all it took to get a girl that was far beyond my possibilities was my perseverance in lying about my status.

The next day I went back to the hostel and found out the guys enjoyed the previous night a lot.
-I'm sorry guys, I don't usually do this, I mean, I only left because it was late and...-
-No need to explain anything man, I understand perfectly. You had a good night, eh?- Adam gave me his usual big smile.
Rey told me he was going to go on a date with the Polish friend of Jemma and there was no sign of Ignacio anywhere yet.
That afternoon, a tall guy with dark curly hair approached me at the table near the sofas area and asked me for a chess game. I gave him one when Rey was chilling with his phone and beat him without too many problems.
After the game, the guy asked me a few questions about some of the moves he played that were clearly wrong and I started explaining my thoughts with pleasure, but there was something in his face, in his accent or in his good manners that I gradually disliked more and more until I just left for a nap. Some people I just disliked by instinct.

That night I found Rey sitting on the usual black sofa.
-Are you going to do something with your life sometimes?- I asked him.
-My life is much better than yours- he said, sounding very confident.
-Do you think the red-haired girl is too young?- I asked him, pointing at a girl by the sofa in front of ours sitting next to another girl, seemingly very young too who was keen on drawing something on a piece of paper.
The red-haired girl was now looking into our direction, but not into our eyes. She seemed completely absent-minded for a while.
-Hi girls- I said and they both looked at us, surprised.
-They look a bit out of their minds- said Rey in Spanish.

-Where are you from?-
-Germany, you?- they smiled, which meant we had to go on. The red-haired girl's name was Victoria, she was 18 and was in London for the weekend with her friend, also called Victoria and also 18.
The other Victoria had dark brown hair tied in a long braid and participated to the conversation we were having politely, but never responding to any attempts of Rey to turn the talk into some more fun stuff. I didn't even think of hitting on her at all in the moment I realised she was drawing what seemed to be a monk in a long brown tunic and an aura on top of his head.
After trying several topics, the only one that finally got the red Victoria interested was politics, which she stated to love. If Rey got turned off by that, it was the opposite for me. I invited Victoria outside with me for a joint and she accepted with no hesitation.
-I believe in monarchy- she said while we crossed the street to reach the small dark alley that led to Queen Square.
-I believe in socialism- I said, hoping that she would feel glad that I was sharing my real opinion. By making a controversial statement, I wanted her to think I had been learning about politics enough to develop my own opinion and that the opinions of the others didn't matter because mine had passed all the tests.
-I don't believe in that. I like the idea though, especially regarding equality, but I believe in a hierarchy. You cannot build a society without a hierarchy, we are not all the same and some of us, the smartest ones, will have to make sure the society works fine-
-Well, a socialist society is also governed, the power never really goes to the proletariat anyway if you think about it- I said, making her laugh.
Rey approached us in the middle of the conversation, asking for a bit of my joint.
-Do you have a boyfriend?- he asked her suddenly. He knew nothing about politics.
-Oh well, this is going to sound weird but I only lost my virginity last month- she said. -I grew up in a very religious family and I was forced to a Christian education, so I never

really had the chance until...- she stopped for a second, then restarted.
-I just couldn't resist any longer and I had sex with a guy last month and I realised that everything they told me while I was growing up was wrong, really everything- she looked very pensive, somehow embarrassed or maybe even in pain.
Rey asked her more and more questions about sex to which she answered promptly, stating that all she wanted to do in life was to go through every sort of sexual situation. That girl went through frustrating teens and now she felt like exploding.
Rey looked into my eyes, but I was too slow to respond.
At some point, Victoria stood up and asked for a hug to both of us. How to proceed now?
With my surprise, Rey called himself tired and said he was off to bed, which abruptly slowed the pace of my heartbeat.
-Good night- she said. He replied by waving his hand.
Victoria sat down again and asked me for a bit of weed.
-Only if you've had it before- I said.
-I'm the queen of the world, I have full decisional power over everything, so you owe me that joint if I say so- she said with a smile.
I kissed her. Her arms held mine tight and she moved her tongue fast, so fast that I didn't doubt a word of what she said before about her desires.
-So, do you wanna have sex?- she asked me as soon as I pulled off from the kiss to smoke more.
-Yes-
-We can't go to my room though, my friend will see us-
-The toilet then-
She thought about it for a very, very long minute.
-Ok- she said.
We went past the reception. The night shift receptionists seemed distracted, definitely not focusing on the cameras. Rey was still on the sofa, lost into his phone.
-Go to the third toilet, the middle one just in front of room 12 and I'll come there in a minute, so we don't look suspicious in case they're looking at the cameras- I said and she agreed silent.

I went to the kitchen, had a glass of water I didn't feel any need to because of my excitement, and then headed to the toilet, slowly.
I opened the door and entered.
She had already pulled her trousers down and was staring at me with a voluptuous look.
-I don't have any condoms- I said.
-You won't need any-
Glorious, thank you.
Knock knock.
The sound of someone knocking the door about a minute later gave me almost a heart attack.
I gave her a sign to be silent. Maybe it was just a random guest looking for a vacant toilet.
Knock knock.
-Can you come out please?- the voice of one of the Arab receptionists froze my body from head to toe.
Victoria looked at me, scared, paralysed just like me.
Then, we slowly walked out of the toilet, the receptionist looking at us, disgusted.
-Follow me upstairs and take your key cards please- he said.
Victoria and I followed him in silence.
Is this it? Is this the end of my staying in Russell Square? I can't believe it, it can't be, I couldn't bear this pain.
-Domenico, you know the rules. You know you are not allowed to do this in the hostel- his colleague told me back upstairs.
Every word he said hurt me. Only ten minutes before my criminal record was clean and now it was all ruined.
-I'm really sorry but yes, I know you can't do this in the room because of respect for people- I said something they probably wanted to hear, -I just thought that I could do this in the toilet since we're not really showing anything to anyone- I continued.
-That's not the point- he smiled, but I interrupted him before he took my word away and kicked me out impulsively.
-I'm sorry, I promise I won't do anything like this again. I love it here and I can't imagine living anywhere else. I beg you to give me another chance- I said, looking at him firmly.

His colleague behind me snorted. He was the one that caught us and he was probably expecting less hesitation from the man behind the reception.
He thought about it for a few more seconds.
-Alright, go back to your room, I hope this never happens again. If it does, you'll get out of here- he said.
-Of course, thank you very much- I said, grateful.
I headed back to the common room to tell Rey what just happened. I even wanted to ask Victoria if she wanted to follow me outside, but I found out she was already gone.

Two days later, I went shopping with Rey after a long chess session, and on our return, we found a double pack of the chocolate bar we used to buy everyday next to our laptops on a table in the common room. The pack was wrapped by a paper that said my name with capital letters written with different colours.
-What is this?- I said, surprised.
-I think I know who sent you this- said Rey, laughing.
-Who? I hope it's not a man- I said, looking around me suspicious.
-I know who sent it to you. It's someone who really likes you- Rosa the cleaner appeared from behind me.
-Hey Rosa, tell me then, who is it?- I asked her pretending it wasn't really important because if she had seen how curious I was, she might have chosen not to speak, just to see me squirm.
-You'll have to find out- her and Rey couldn't stop laughing and looking at me, doing exactly what I feared.
I unwrapped the paper. It said "you are very hot man" in capital letters inside.
-Right, you guys are useless, I'm going for a nap- I left them still laughing.
On my return, Rey was keen on talking to a pretty petite brunette and a bunch of other friends of her at the table on the bottom of the common room.
-Here comes my best friend- said Rey loud, welcoming me to the table.
Rey was sitting next to what seemed to be the cutest one. There were two girls with dark blonde hair in front of me, a

blonde guy with a nerdy face and a very attractive girl with dark hair, long by one side and shaved by the other side, which took about half of her sex appeal away from her.
We spent hours chatting and by the evening some of them left to bed. It was pretty common for some Americans in London to be jet lagged, go to sleep in the afternoon and wake up to watch tv in the middle of the night until breakfast came.
Meanwhile, Mina, Victoria and a bald guy in his late thirties from Canada joined the table, with the Canadian who started explaining the rules of the drinking game he wanted to play.
-I'll give four cards to each one of you that you'll keep covered, then I'll put spoons in the middle of the table making sure that there's one less compared to the number of cards. Next step, you look at your cards and start passing them to each other clockwise and as soon as you have four of a kind in your hand, grab a spoon and everyone else needs to rush and do the same. The one that is left without spoon to grab will have to drink- he concluded, happy for the attention.
Within a couple of hours, after drinking and talking about all sort of stuff, I noticed that the girl Rey was working on was very friendly, but also weird. Sometimes she seemed very absent-minded. I made a few flirty jokes literally with everyone, noticing that the very hot one bantered with pleasure, but nothing was really going to happen. I received a few signals from the girl with dark blonde hair sitting near Rey though.
-I should add you on Facebook so we can keep updated in case we all go out next days- I said to her, to which she agreed timidly.
Later on in the night, most were gone to sleep, but me and Rey were still awake.
Rey was resigned about the girl he was hitting on and just told me he saw her like a friend now, while the girl I was now focusing my attention on, called Molly, was still sitting on the same bench, giving me a simper look.
-Molly, I know it's late and you may probably want to go to sleep but just so you know I'm heading to Camden area for a

pint now. I usually go there on my own when I don't work the next morning- I lied.
-Yeah, sure, let me go grab my jacket- she replied, then rushed to her room and came back, ready to go out.
We headed to Camden through Eversholt Street and chatted while also trying to spot some open late off-licences that could sell us alcohol under the counter, but I knew that the ones that we were walking past didn't do this. I checked with them several times before, but still acted as if I didn't know it.
-Seems like we're not going to get any alcohol tonight, it's just too late- I said.
-And what? It doesn't really matter, does it?- she asked, gently, maybe having no idea I needed it for her much more than for me.
We reached the Camden Head later on, but they didn't let us in as we were too late and the place was going to shut soon.
-Well Molly, I'm sorry, I haven't been able to give you a night pint, so we walked so far for nothing- I guess we can just finish what's left of my vodka, it's in my backpack- I told her.
-I actually really like it like this. I'm having a good time- she said, looking firmly into my eyes with a smile on her face. The lipstick she quickly pressed on her lips before going out and the way she looked at me claimed no other conclusion. We stayed together for few minutes until I suggested her to go to her room in the hostel.

By the second half of May the hostel was getting very busy. Rey and I were spending every moment together and were meeting plenty of new people everyday. Jemma and Lisa kept texting me on a daily basis, although the person I was definitely most keen on replying was Lisa, the only one I actually had real conversations with. With Jemma I was very reductive, I gave no possibility for a conversation to start. On the other hand, Lisa was great. We talked about everything, from science to politics, from music to history, even fairy tales sometimes. Anytime I received a message and saw it came from Lisa I replied straight away, but when it came from Jemma, I replied after hours.

The story between me and Lisa would have been just perfect, we were connected on many levels, but it was impossible because she was in Paris and I was broke, whereas the story between me and Jemma could have never happened, even though we lived in the same city.
Oh, if only I could swap them, I thought, but the only thing that made sense then was to be in touch with both at the same time. Sometimes I would send a message, then copy and paste it so I could send it to the other one, being happy anytime Lisa replied and almost indifferent when Jemma did.

At work, my manager Jo said she was very satisfied and happy that she hired me, which seemed to be also the opinion of most others.
The job wasn't too bad and the shifts were more acceptable by the human point of view than they were in Cote.
I didn't have to run anywhere in Starbucks, I just had to stand by the coffee machine and be as fast as I could, but at least my legs were spared the work.
I enjoyed greeting the customers, although I could feel Jo's look on her face was scared I was talking too much to them and they might have not liked it.
-Listen, we don't care if they will enjoy their coffee or not, just call their names and give them their coffee- Azou once told me in response to the fact I was politely saying bye to all customers like I used to at the restaurant.
On the other hand, Lucio, a barista from Naples told me -Jo prioritises the form over the substance- meaning she liked that things were being done according to standards. She claimed speed, but forbade shortcuts.
Jo's success at work consisted of getting good reviews and that happened when we smiled and acted very friendly to customers all the time, making no exceptions.
I was sure that many customers, busy men and women in office clothes who looked rushed and sometimes stressed didn't care at all about our smile and would have probably been comprehensive if we were to serve them with the same face they had given us.

-Never tell her this or you're fired, just like it happened to Maria- Lucio once told me during a quiet moment between the two main rushes of customers of the early afternoon. Maria was an Italian girl with short blonde curly hair and a very angry face I saw during my trial shift. She came outside the shop with me at the end of her shift to have a cigarette and complain about how it was impossible to be friendly in a place like that and that I would have realised it with the passage of time.
-So she got...-
-Fired, yes, Jo fired her last week, you haven't seen her at work at all in the last days, you must have noticed- he added.
-Well, I was assuming she was on holiday, I mean, I haven't heard anything from anyone-
-Nobody really liked working with her, except Lukas for some reason. She wasn't friendly, she often wouldn't say please and Jo had been waiting for an excuse to get rid of her for a while until the last time she was rude with a customer turned out to be the perfect moment for it-
I felt somehow good. The idea of someone from my team being fired meant there was going to be some more space for me and that we were going to hire someone new, someone who, even though I had just finished my training, was less skilled than I was.
Unlike in Cote, where people left the job on a monthly basis, which allowed me to be head runner in about eight months, the possibility for the same thing to happen there were smaller, seeing that we were less people. Apart from that, I was enjoying the lack of gossiping and whining. Everyone was too busy to argue, and the customers were too many to follow all service steps.
In Holborn we were forced to be a team. Two of us were on the till and two on the coffee machines. The guys from the till would pass us empty cups with letters written on them that told us the names of the customers and the drinks they wanted.
Just like in my previous job, I was the one that worked faster than everybody else, but far from being the most accurate, standards-accepting member of the team.

As Jo made me notice, I kept forgetting to make eye contact with the customers and mixing the order of the service steps. It was extremely important for her that I started warming up the milk and then pouring the espresso shots into the cup. I did my best to make this happen as often as I could, but the only way to carry out my duty without complaints and without making people wait too long was to do as many things as I could at the same time. Jo would pick on me anytime this happened, showing some growing frustration each time.

-Look, when she's around, you have to follow the steps, I know what you're feeling, I don't follow the steps either, but pay attention to your priorities, she doesn't have any problems getting rid of people if she has to- Azou once told me.

With the passage of time, I became faster and better at following the steps and I had memorised everything I needed to know about my job within the second week from the date of my employment. Jo called herself satisfied and even called me a genius once when she stated that never before a training had been so short before the staff member was already good to go on his own.

On the other hand, her frustration about me taking shortcuts and showing up either in perfect time or one minute late was getting visible, it was literally on her face.

-It makes me panic that I don't see you until the start of your shift. Didn't you say you live nearby?- she once asked me with a polite tone that unsuccessfully hid the fact she had been thinking about that question a lot before.

-By bicycle, I live three minutes away from here- I said, regretting the fact I looked pleased about that.

My relationships with my co-workers were less intense, positively and negatively speaking, than the ones with my co-workers from Sloane Square. I wasn't going to ever hang out with anyone from my current job outside of the working hours. We were all too different in age, backgrounds and interests, although I had a feeling that sometimes they would go for beers. Maybe not lately, but they did it before as I found out from one of my occasional deep stalking of people's Facebook profiles in my boring sleepless nights.

By the end of May, my bank account was back to the usual desperate situation, not to mention that I still had debts I aimed at paying off as soon as I got paid my first salary scheduled for the first week of June.
My mental situation was very different though. The money problem wasn't affecting my mood too much. It did give me some worries, but I was too busy being happy to care about such details, at least all until the night Rey told me he was going to leave London because he got in some big trouble.
-What kind of trouble?- I asked him when he told me, hoping he wouldn't mention gambling. I would have volunteered to end any other problems on my own if necessary, but there was nothing I could have done about gambling problems, especially in those days.
-Big trouble- he cut it short, very stressed.
-Why? Why do you bet? And how can you lose so much? How much is it?- I whined.
-Look, I don't need you to speak rubbish to me. All I need is money, I need to travel and hopefully some rich dude would fix it all-
-How much is it? Can you wait for me to get paid? I'll pay you hostel and food and you can try to make money here in London, you've always managed to make money here-
-Not anymore, it's not like before. People know me here and they always want someone else, someone new- he said, still looking doomed at the wall and never crossing my eyes.
-How much is it? 3k? 5k?- I said, exaggerating the number just because I wanted him to give me a lower one and be able to see it as good news.
-More, much more than that- he said. If my heart was sinking in that moment, I didn't know what was happening to his.
-Can I see?- I took the papers that were on the table in front of him. He didn't seem to like me taking them, but he didn't move a finger.
Rey had placed several bets worth hundreds of pounds each on football and tennis matches. Every bet had from one to three different games which were relatively likely to be won. Rey bet large amounts on such games, hoping that what was supposed to happen would simply do and he would win

easily. On one of them, he bet 150 pounds for a game where the success of the favoured team paid back originally very little, but in case successful, the return would have been maximised.
-You lost all of them?-
-Yes-
-So unlucky, I can't believe you lost all of them, they're all favoured teams- I noticed, sad for him, but partially cruelly satisfied about the fact that he wanted to escape the working life like that.
-This doesn't add up to the amount of money you said you've lost though-
-I have a betting account online as well. Anyway, I'm going to Paris next week, I've got customers there- he said, but I struggled to focus.

Meanwhile, Lisa and I were talking everyday on skype. Our conversations lasted from half hour to even five hours and we talked about everything, from what happened during our days to the dreams we had. With the passage of time, Lisa became more intensely attached to me. She would smile all the time, stare into my eyes any time I said something, beg me to keep talking when she realised I was trying to end the call and kept in touch with me every time during the day.
On my side, I treated her with respect and showed her I was present any time she wanted to talk.
At the same time, I decided to do my best not to get carried away with that story. If I could have definitely done it in the past, it would have been a mistake in that moment since I didn't have the money to allow myself to think about such thing.
I couldn't believe I used to pay lots of money to fly to Russia to visit my annoying ex and now that there was a girl I liked much more and who lived much closer, I happened to be stuck on the edge of homelessness.
Something that pleased me was that Jemma kept wanting to see me. She asked numerous times for dates which I always declined, still a bit nervous to go and see her.

-I keep feeling intimidated. I honestly can't believe I'm dating this chick- I told Rey once when we were making dinner in the hostel.
-You're overestimating her. She's fat-
-She's not, she's almost as tall as you and she's got a model body-
-You're kidding man, I prefer Lisa, Lisa is more proportioned than Jemma- he said, then covered his eyes with his arm and took a break from cutting his onions.
-I'll have to close my story with Lisa before it's too late- I commented, pensive. Rey ignored me.
After the dinner, I decided I had to tell Lisa how I really felt about that story and that our passionate talks would have eventually just brought us to face the wall of the distance and that the creation of such sweet feelings would have died, potentially with some sorrow.
I asked her for a call and she connected immediately.
-Is everything ok boy?- she said, her voice sweeter than ever made my heart sink.
-Hey, yeah, Lisa, sure, I just...- I stopped when I saw her face, looking at me with her eternally sad and hopeful expression.
-Lisa, I have to be honest with you- I restarted, trying to ignore the evil man inside of me that was enjoying the fear in her face.
-Right, Lisa, I don't have any money. I will get paid at the beginning of the new month and will pay back a few people that helped me, then I'll probably be broke again by the end of the next month so-
-Is this a problem? Is this what you wanted to tell me?- she said, relief appearing on her face.
-Well, yeah-
-Oh boy, I wanted to ask you if you wanted to come to Paris this weekend, there are many cheap tickets, I was checking before- she said.
She was checking tickets. She thought about me and imagined seeing me in person, just like I did.
-Lisa, I think you're missing a point here...-
-I can pay it for you. I just really want to see you- she said, convincing me on the spot.

-Dom, you will never know what happened to me- Rey texted me the next morning while I was having breakfast.
-Do you remember Paul? the guy that Latif caught smoking in the sofas area the other night? We thought he was a fool for doing that, but you have no idea what I found out about him. He's definitely not a fool- Rey went on, texting and sending about one to two words per message, making my phone ring so many times that the two girls sitting next to stared at me annoyed.
-Tell me-
-I can't tell you through phone, I will have to tell you when I see you in person, it's important-
-Ok, now you're making me curious, and you've spoken so far so I guess you can just go on at this point- I typed.
-Five minutes, I'll be there in five minutes-
Curious, intriguing, I'm loving it. What can it be about? Who is that guy?
Rey walked into the common room next to Paul, a man in his fifties with blonde, straight hair pulled back and pretty sunbathed skin.
-Be careful Rey, it stays between me and you- I heard him say when they approached my table. Rey reassured him and then sat down on the bench in front of me while the man went downstairs.
-Dom, I have to tell you- he looked around.
-Paul is a secret agent and he's here to investigate something-
-Rey, mate...-
-I know what you're thinking, but he proved it. We went to the park together and he showed me a lot of papers, you have no idea how many papers he has with a lot of qualifications, and he has huge knowledge about the police and the state and so on-
-What do you mean?-
-He knows a lot, Dom, about what happens in the world, who is making the crimes and how people hide. He knows a lot, I don't know if you will get a chance to talk to him or if he will feel like talking to you about it, but he'll be here for a few days-

-Right, Rey, I don't believe it, the guy's just a fool who almost got kicked out for smoking inside the hostel-
-Exactly, think about why somebody would do something so stupid and what opinion people will have about him, think about it Dom, that's for his job, it's all for his job. Anyway, I've got to go, see you later- Rey sounded very excited. Then he stood up and left me there, now more intrigued.

This is absurd, and beautiful, I thought while, in an afternoon by the end of May, I took a seat on the back of the London to Paris bus in Victoria coach station.
I got three days off in a row from work and I was going to see Lisa that night. The feeling was incredible, the realisation of a recurring and very intense desire that I had dismissed since when it arose in order to avoid emotional pain was actually coming true. The fact that something I didn't expect to happen was going to happen made me feel so good that I had goose bumps for quite a good part of the trip, at times alternated with the annoying feeling caused by the awareness that I was going to miss the final game of the Champions League.
I thought about her a lot since when I met her but never thought I would see her again. Now it was happening and it was her that paid for the tickets, even though I meant to pay her back as soon as I could.
The unceasing rain that travelled with me from London to Dover was replaced by a dark cloudless sky when I entered France up to when I reached Paris in the late evening.
Lisa told me that she was going to be running late because of an accident at work, which was perfect for me. I would have tried to watch the final game somewhere.
I left Porte Maillot and quickly went to grab a seat in the nearest cafe with Real Madrid and Atletico Madrid playing for the trophy in the extra time of a match that had been probably very exciting, especially since I had missed it.
About ten minutes afterwards, Lisa appeared by the end of the road, walking towards me on her denim jacket, dark leggings and white trainers.

She didn't slow down, but walked at the same pace into my arms, then lifted her head up to look at me. We were unable to say a word, or at least I wasn't.
-Hey- I said with a feeble voice.
-Hey boy- she said, excited.
We walked, walked for miles before our conversation started to make sense. Most of the times I tried to say something I would stop to make sure she was listening. The fact that I struggled to fully handle that moment affected my judgement of her focus as well. She didn't seem as excited as I was, but she did smile at me all the time and proved to be paying attention to anything I said. It was me to be overexcited, but she didn't have to notice this.
-Do you want some food? I'm starving- I said when I noticed a fast-food shop that broadcast the game, now at its very final stage. No team had managed to prevail after two extra times and they needed to shoot penalties to determine a winner.
Lisa agreed and we bought sandwiches and a couple of beers, then we sat down on the banks of a canal in Quai de Valmy and talked for a few hours before heading to her place.
Lisa lived in Avenue d'Eylau, straight outside of Trocadero metro station.
-What job do the people that hired you do?- I could see the Tour Eiffel very close to us from the entrance of her building.
-They both work for a television programme and they travel a lot so they need me to take care of their kids full-time- she said and led me on to her room on the top floor.
-Wow, I have never seen anything like this before- I told her, surprised.
Lisa was staying in a tiny room that had a stove, a sink, a wardrobe and even a shower placed all next to each other like in a very weird looking jigsaw with a very tight space that separated everything from her bed.
-It's cute, and it's super central, I really like it- she said, smiling.
It must be a good sign that your face doesn't look sad at all today.

-I would love to have a place like yours in London. I think I may even leave the hostel for it- I told her the next morning

as we walked through the Latin Quarter for a break and some food.
-Are you still living in the hostel?- she asked, surprised.
-Yes, luckily- I said, thinking about the night I almost got kicked out and my bookings cancelled.
-Look, I know it's cliché, but I want to go to the Eiffel Tower and take some pictures, then send them to my parents who never believed I would have been able to make it without them- I suggested then.
-Sure, let's go-
Lisa was lovely, she said yes to anything I asked, smiled every time I made her a compliment and held my hand every now and then.
We walked until we got to our destination and queued underneath the tower, and after about one hour, we were up on the first floor, where taking a picture with her wouldn't have risked to sound anything strange due to such circumstances.
-What a beautiful sight. I love this city- I said dreamily while wrapping my arms around her upper body from her back. I couldn't hold it any longer.
Lisa turned her face towards mine and gave me the sweetest of smiles, blushed and held my arms with hers tighter. Then, she exhaled as if she was tired, and the sadness reappeared on her face.
-This would be a perfect moment to die- she said, serious.
I took a few seconds to process what she said, and a few more before answering.
-No, think about all the people who want to live, Lisa. We're lucky, and we also have a lot of things to do before our time is up- I said, looking at the foggy sky, genuinely happy. I used to be like her when I was younger.
Lisa didn't reply, but rather kept smiling.
Her and Clelia were completely different kind of people. Clelia put her life in the middle of the universe, whereas Lisa had no interest in living her life.
Lisa was lost, maybe depressed and I felt I needed to save her. I wanted her to be happy and I wanted to be the one to lift her up, then be looked at with eyes of gratitude forever. I wanted her to know that I would never let her go, no

matter in which conditions she might have been in the future. I wondered if I was really a hero, or just a very selfish person anytime I thought like that. What I wanted was the possession of a person that was literally too sad to live and be the only reason for her happiness after all.
-You're young, I understand your age, I went through this as well. Trust me, one day you wake up and just feel happy. Your body will stop feeding the tiny part of it that likes it when we're sad and it's all happening sooner than you think- I summed up my thoughts like this, but she still didn't say a word. Nobody likes people who speak like know-it-all.

I kept thinking about her words later on in the evening while we walked through her neighbourhood on the way back to her place in Trocadero.
Every moment I spent with her stored emotions that I couldn't sum up in words. It all felt just easy, sweet, romantic. Her hug and her voice felt tender, innocent, like a girl who had never been hurt before, but her eyes looked for someone that could help her and if she paid for my tickets to Paris, talked to me everyday and told me she could have died between my arms, then that meant that the one she wanted to be helped by was me.
-Lisa- I said, hesitating.
-Mm?- she replied, then held my hand.
-I have to tell you- I said, trying to gather the strength to go on. My heart was pounding and my legs would have stopped moving within the next few metres if I hadn't said something.
-I have feelings of... love, for you- I finally looked into her eyes when I said it.
She stared at me with her smile opening up more, but did not reply.

The next morning, Lisa and I managed to meet up with Rey, who was also in Paris, and we ate a chocolate cake together, counting 29 candles to celebrate his years.
About half hour later, we decided to leave Rey alone, who was trying to be friendly, but still somehow grumpy due to his unhappy economic moment.

Later on, by the early afternoon, Lisa went with me to Porte Maillot, we kissed one last time and then I left the station, looking back at the train where we were sitting taking her away from me.
It would have been much sadder if I hadn't missed London so much anytime I was away from it.

June 2016

When I got back to the hostel, I found the receptionist manager and his supervisors setting up a new, big screen television in the sofas area with a lot of excited people around it. Some of the sofas that were underneath the television were moved sideways so that more people could see the European championship that was about to start the following week.
In the next days, I received good and bad news. Mina was throwing his leaving party that week. He was moving back to France with his girlfriend for a while and then their plan was to move to Madrid.
On the other hand, Rey was going to come back to London.
-Dom, I've been lucky in Paris- he texted me.
-I met a millionaire from Brazil who paid me 1k pounds only for one night and it wasn't even that difficult, we mostly talked, the guy's pretty lonely-
-Rich people are always lonely, that's the side effect of being rich- I said, realising straight away that my statement had no arguments in favour and it made no sense even. Although, I could imagine many people clapping their hands at it in my head.
I also had the impression that the family got bigger those days without me.
I noticed Mina talking to a big guy with short curly dark hair in a blazer at a table with a young girl and a bottle of wine between them.
-Domenico, come here, let me introduce you to a new friend I have, Mario, from Italy- Mina seemed very entertained by him.
-Hi, nice to meet you- I said with no interest. The guy was in his thirties and was clearly hitting on that young girl.

Knowing how Italians are when it came to flirting, I wouldn't have been surprised to find out that Mario was extremely annoyed by the presence of Mina at the same table and especially by the presence of another man as well.

Mario shook my hand and replied with a smile which forced me to show one back to him.

The well-mannered tall guy with messy hair who played a chess game with me was still in the hostel too, sitting on a table with a few other stable members of the family. For some reason, I just couldn't like him. I was hoping he wouldn't become one of us and didn't start hanging out around me, even his clothes were annoying to me, from his colourful t-shirts to his long, large blue jeans. With the passage of time though, the process of his integration in our family seemed inevitably occurring.

His name was Matt, an electronic engineer from Australia looking for work in London. He would usually sit on the steps next door wearing his sunglasses and smoke one cigarette after another before going back inside the hostel to spend the afternoon on his laptop and the evenings between us.

Unlike with Matt, I got to like Mario a lot.

Mario took the game of hitting on girls up to a level I couldn't even imagine possible. He sat down at a table where a girl or a group of girls were and started a conversation, acting polite and easy-going at the same time. Anytime he got rejected he would move to the next table or even just to the next girls that were passing by on their way to the toilet. Many of us would spend time looking at him jumping from one prey to another in an overconfident way and enjoyed seeing him getting rejected because of how close to them he would sit or how he looked at them.

He would have been the best if it wasn't a bit older than us and didn't try to rush to the point all the time. It didn't take him more than five minutes of conversation with a girl before he made an actual move or just said something that was too much and too early for her to hear.

-He's shameless- I commented entertained to Rey, who stated he didn't like him at all.

-I don't like Italians, they're all desperate and misbehaved. They don't know what respect means-

-Rey, I'm Italian-
-You're rude as well Dom, and by the way, everyone in here noticed that you only talk to girls and never to guys-
-What are you talking about? You know that this isn't true- I said, feeling betrayed and red-handed as it was partially true. I was wondering when Rey was going to mention that.
-Not true Rey, I think some of them might be jealous of my success- I said, regretting it.
-You're just arrogant, that's why nobody likes you- said Rey.
-What's up man? Did you lose a lot of money again recently and now you're acting like this with me? Sort yourself out, if you don't like me then hang out with somebody else- I stood up and left.
-Hi Domenico- Victoria greeted me waving her hand and smiling.
She was nicer than usual with me even though I never really saw her that way.
Victoria... was it you that sent me that letter wrapped around my favourite chocolate bar? You saw me eating one of it everyday here, are you trying to corrupt me with sugar?
I had never really had a proper conversation with her alone, but only just been nice because she was always nice to me. On the other hand, this could mean that she was up for it. You've been very far from home for some time after all and the only reason why I didn't hit on you so far is because you look innocent and you're very nice, but how does that have anything to do with how keen you might be?
-Hey Victoria, how are you?-
-I'm good thanks, and you?- she said, a bit surprised I asked her that since we lived in the same building and shared every night together.
-I'm good too. Do you want to go watch a film together? Maybe in our room? I'm also in room 51 right now- I said, shameless, feeling embarrassed at every word, more and more.
Am I just messing up a friendship with someone so nice? What will happen to the family if she tells everyone how cheeky I acted?
-Oh, ok, can you give me about ten minutes?- she said timidly.

-Sure, text me when you want- I said and smiled, trying not to show her I was scared I had gone too far and too fast.
Ten minutes later though, she texted me and told me to go back to the room.
She was standing near the bathroom, silent, a bit confused when I approached her.
-Let's go to my bed- I whispered.
-Let's go to mine actually- she said, taking me to hers. I kissed her straight away and slowly started taking away her clothes when, at some point, she blocked me.
-Domenico- she said, very timidly.
-Yes?-
-Will we still be friends after this happens?- she asked, sounding terribly sweet and cautious at the same time.
-Of course we will- I reassured her.

A few days later, I finally got the chance to sit down at the same table with Paul, the alleged secret agent.
I went to the common room after my usual nap and looked around for him like I did everyday since when Rey told me about him. Most of the times he would sit alone, a dead serious look on his face and eyes constantly checking his phone every other minute. He knew I was friend with Rey and that he could have told me about him, so I couldn't just sit down and pretend I wasn't looking for some more information without blowing Rey's cover.
That night though, the tables in the hostel were busier than usual and Paul had a couple of people sitting next to him, so I pretended to be looking around for some emptier table, but eventually took a seat on the bench in front of him acting as I had to casually pick that with no particular interest in talking to anyone there.
He was staring at me, serious, so I gave him a quick smile and went back to my book. My smile had to prove him I wasn't intimidated by him nor that I wanted to talk to him.
-You're Domenico, right?- he said, still staring at me, a little grin on his face made me wince.
-Yes, I am, and you? How do you know that...-
-You're a friend of Rey, he told me about you the other day- he said.

-My name's Paul- he added and shook my hand.
The couple that was sitting next to us stood up right in that moment, winning my complete appreciation.
Now it was just me and him.
-I heard he's going to Paris soon- he said, still looking firmly into my eyes.
-Yeah, he comes and goes from there all the time- I said.
Paul looked at me, a surprised look on his face. Did I speak too much? How could I say something regarding a friend's life to someone I didn't even know? If I sounded so naïve, there was no way Paul was going to trust me and tell me about himself. -He really likes it there- I added, hoping that he would buy it.
Come on, just ask me why he goes there so I'll tell you I have no idea, then maybe I will stand up and wish you good night, acting as if I'm bothered by the fact that you want to know something about someone I know.
-I respect what he does, I do not approve of it, but I respect it. It's his life after all- he said.
I didn't reply. If he wanted me to betray myself so easily, he should have played a better move than that.
-Rey loves Paris- I said, playing the fool role.
-You must be good friends then. See, I believe Rey might have mentioned you something about me and the reason why I'm staying in this hostel- he said, slowly.
I didn't reply again. If I had said no, he would have considered me a liar and if I had said yes, he would have known he couldn't trust me.
We looked into each other's eyes for about a minute without saying a word when he spoke again.
-I'm a law enforcement officer- he said then, calmly.
I waited for a minute, preparing my best reply.
-I understand- I said, craving for him to say more.
-You might be wondering why I'm here and why I lit a cigarette in the middle of this area to just get spotted by the security guy in front of other people. It's a cover. I'm acting so that no one will suspect of me, I have to look like a fool- he said.

-I understand- I said again and then paused. -Is there something going on around here? A reason why you're needed here?-
-Yes. Lot of stuff goes on in central London. Lots of bad things, lots of bad people, really bad people that have to be stopped and for which the government is willing to spend millions for- he said. To every word I became more and more intrigued. What was going on?
He saw the expression on my face and decided to go on.
-Russell Square is not the safest area. It looks all nice and so on, but it's hell, a real hell-
-What's happening around here?- I started visualising the streets I walked through everyday, trying to remember something wrong I might have seen, but ignored up to that point. What was I missing?
-We'll talk some more tomorrow though, I have to leave now, I'm going on duty in a minute. Have a good night Domenico- he got up and left.

The next morning, I found Matt sitting on the usual step next to the hostel, smoking his usual cigarette. He said hi to me when I passed by and I replied, polite. I couldn't deny that I disliked him less than before, especially since we were now forced to hang out with each other and also because I genuinely had no reason to dislike him in general.
On my way back from my grocery shop I found him still sitting there and decided to stop and try to be friendly, just like he was with me all the time.
-Hey Matt, is it ok if I sit here for a minute?-
-Yeah sure mate, go ahead- he smiled and moved sideways.
-How's your adventure going?- I asked.
-Pretty well, I'm finishing up my cover letter though. As soon as I'm done with it, I'll send my cv to a few companies and if I'm lucky I'll get to start working soon- he said, slow and calm. His voice was deep, on the same frequency of an old black man, but somehow slightly lighter from my personal perception.
-I see. You've been here for some time, I would have bet that you had already prepared your cover letter and everything

before moving here to be honest- I said, trying not to sound provocative, but just friendly.
-Yeah, well, I decided that my first month had to be some sort of holiday, I worked two years in a row in Australia, full-time and without a single break just to save up as much as I could after all-
-What were you doing?-
-I worked in a shop of electronics for the last two years, but I was working as an engineer before until I left that job-
-Why?-
-Oh, long story actually...-
-Don't worry then, you'll tell me another day- I told him.
-Sure. And you? What are you doing here in the hostel?-
-I live here. I live here for the girls actually- I said, and Matt laughed.
-I'm not going to deny I've seen you chatting to a lot of girls since when I'm here. What happened with Molly? The American girl I mean-
-I banged her-
-Oh, really? You... man, I wanted her! I was trying to get her, but you were faster than me and then eventually you guys were gone- he said, having the last puffs of his cigarette and starting to roll another one.
-Sorry about that. Next time call dibs first and I'll leave her to you- I said, unsure if that was going to be the deal with him.
-It's ok man, I guess I'll just have to get faster- he seemed amused. -It's impressive though that you're living in a hostel. How long has it been by the way?-
-About a year actually, except the end of December and the whole January. I wasn't here, I was in a room in Clapham South, then I came back-
-Why did you leave?-
-For a girl. I thought we were going to have a story together, so I left the hostel for her, but she dumped me the next week or so- I said.
-Oh, wow, that sucks. Something similar happened to me, you know- he said, then lit his cigarette and went on.
-I was in a relationship with a girl I met and fell in love with straight away. With the passage of time everything got very

fast and it was just like a fairy tale to me. Her family was perfect, she was perfect, her friends were perfect, but then she just called it over. She met someone else and just dumped me, fast as it all started.
-Sorry man, however you felt- I said, trying to sound supportive.
-It's ok, three months after me it was her boyfriend that dumped her, so yeah!- he lifted up his fist in sign of victory.
-Oh, that felt rewarding, didn't it?- Matt laughed again.
-Right, I'm going to get ready for work, talk to you soon Matt-
-Yeah, we should walk together to Mina's party if you're going- he added.

On Mina's leaving party night, besides Rey and Adrian who found an excuse not to show up, everybody else was there. People from the hostel family, his workplace and the members of the football team he played with sometimes. When Matt and I got there, I felt like we were about eighty people stuck in the basement of the Zoo bar, I place I hated because of the presence of too many Italians and Spanish people, which made the night out less enjoyable than anywhere else I could imagine going to.
-Why do you hate the Italians so much?- Matt asked me when I told him about that.
-I don't hate them, I just don't want them around- I said. -Right, look, tonight you will see that all Italian men will show up with ironed shirts, earrings, finger rings, polished shoes and a crave for fights and desire to prove who's the strongest. Italian girls will act as if they were the prettiest girls in the club and will not talk to any man as long as he doesn't look stunning. On the other hand, Spanish guys are very friendly and always underdressed- I said, but I felt like Matt wasn't taking me seriously.

The next morning, I found Paul sitting on the table near the sofas area with a strange expression on his face.
-Good morning- I sat down in front of him with my cup of milk and four slices of toasted bread with chocolate cream on the side.

-Oh, good morning to you Domenico. It's not a good morning to me unfortunately. I have just come back from my shift and it was a horrible, horrible night- he said, looking exhausted. I didn't have many doubts that he had been awake all night from the look of his face.
-What happened? I hope you're ok?- I asked.
-A very, very long night, but thank God it's all over. The guy is already behind bars now-
-What? Who? What happened?- I asked, craving to know more.
-Right, finish your breakfast, then we'll go for a walk and then, I'll finally get some well-deserved sleep-
I finished my breakfast faster than I had ever done before and joined him outside where he was waiting for me.
-This way- he led from Grenville Street to Hunter Street and we walked a little bit further north until he stopped when we got at the cross with Handel Street.
-Have you seen anything unusual so far?- he asked me. Was he testing me?
Was he trying to see if I was smart enough before confessing stuff? I had to say something smart, but I hadn't seen anything unusual...
-Two military jeeps so far- that came to my mind.
-Exactly- he said. -Do you know what this means?-
-Something is going on around here- I concluded.
-Well said, they're looking at us as we move around this area. They're looking at everyone that lives around here, seeing where they're going, what habits they have and all sort of information that can help them find out how to stop crime-
If he was trying to freak me out, I could say he mildly succeeded.
We went back to the hostel, where he told me he would go rest, leaving me alone at my table, pensive.

That night I had another meeting scheduled with Jemma at her place. I promised her to make her risotto with mushroom and cream with spinach, my speciality as I described to her, but actually just one of the very few things I could cook. The problem was though, that I just didn't want to see her and I was hoping that she would cancel the appointment for some reason.

Instead, Jemma texted me stating she was looking forward to tasting my risotto and that it had been quite some time we hadn't seen each other, which made sense because I only had time for Lisa and I was getting tired of texting two girls at the same time, especially because Lisa took a lot of time from me everyday.
Lisa texted me in the morning and from there she would text me about anything that happened during her day, any time she had a mood swing and needed somebody to calm her down a bit, any time she had to work but didn't want to, and any time she felt like she missed me, everyday. I was talking to her less and acting a little bit colder than usual although still present when she had something serious to say. The fact that she didn't reply to when I told her about my feelings was a turn off for me and I decided not to invest more than the available time I had on her.
For this reason, her messages came more and more often to my phone. Maybe, she was afraid she had lost me and now she was acting desperate, although I couldn't deny that my feelings for her were almost the same, just a bit less intense because she wasn't trying to manipulate me.
Despite the fact that I had feelings for her and that we talked for hours everyday, I had no intention to stop my sexual life in London, especially since it was her that said that we were free to do what we wanted when we said goodbye the first time in Victoria station.
I reached Battersea area and left my bicycle from the furthest corner of the block so that Jemma wouldn't see it, also because of the handlebar that cut in half suddenly when I was riding a few days before. If she had seen me in those conditions, that would have been the end.
-Hi Jemma-
-Hi, how are you?- she greeted me.
-I'm good, I'm good, I've brought food and beers as you can see-
-Thanks, you didn't have to- she said.
Weird, I thought that was the reason why I came here.
Jemma and her flatmates were watching a celebrities tv show and they seemed to be very excited about it.

I was chopping the spinach and some tomatoes, paying attention not to mess up with the moves order when a few negative thoughts came across my mind.
I wanted to leave, I didn't want to be there. Being there was wrong. Why were they watching that stuff? Why did they care about celebrities' private lives? What kind of human being found joy with such thing? Alright, this is what I'll do. We're all going to enjoy our food, then I'll tell her I have to go after washing the plates and everything, it was great to see her and I was looking forward to meeting her another day, a day that would have never arrived.
-Do you need help?- Jemma asked at some point.
Sure, I'm literally done here and now you remember to check if I need help.
-Don't worry, it's all done actually-
I sat down by the sofa in front of the tv and Jemma sat next to me. The smell of flowers from her hair and the legs she shaved prior to my arrival inspired a few thoughts inside my head that I couldn't leave out. I had to hit on her now, she got her risotto, so I'll get my part too, and then I'll leave.
-She looks so gorgeous- her flatmate said for the umpteenth time, looking at the tv screen. I wonder if those people ever said something different.
-Yeah she does- the other two girls confirmed, dreamily.
-Yeah she's cute- I said, not sure why. How wrong could it have been though? It was their language after all.
-How is your business going?- Jemma asked me at some point.
-Well, we're a bit in a bad moment, my partner is having some health problems, so we're stuck at the moment- I said.
-Oh, I'm so sorry, I hope he'll be alright?-
-Yeah, he will, so in the meantime, I'm working in a cafe in central London, just not to be unemployed, I don't like it when there is no income at all and when you own a business, that's your nightmare- I said, getting a bit nervous.
Maybe I can tell her this just to start, then if Lisa breaks things up with me and Jemma buys the story that my business simply had to be dropped because my partner had suddenly died, and if she lowers down her standards, maybe, me and Jemma could be together until I found love. In that

case, I won't be sexually unemployed. Besides, striking Jemma always felt great.
She got silent for a while.
-I'm going to finish this in my room- she stood up and reached her room without even looking at me.
I followed her to find her door open and the bowl on her nightstand.

Just like at work, the hostel also saw some people leaving and some other people taking their places. Sometimes they were lovely people, sometimes they were annoying, sometimes extroverts and introverts. The family who lived stable in Russell Square hostel in June 2016 was almost completely changed, exceptions being me, Rey, Adrian, Joseph, the old man with a suit and the black guy with two laptops. For more than a year though, the family saw people like Mina, Laurine, Carlos, Arlena, Mark and a bunch of others, but with the passage of time they were all gone. However, this wasn't a tragedy, because the current family was also a good one.
I was developing some sort of good terms with Joao based on the fact that he appreciated my interest in football and some closer situation with Adam, who enjoyed partying with the rest of us.
Mario and I became closer too. He loved playing chess and we usually went on with it for entire nights with Matt and Paul who also had their sleeping patterns messed up.
In one of the past nights, Paul was checking Mario's moves on a young girl for the whole evening until the moment Mario followed her downstairs when she said she was going to sleep. Paul ran after him just to find out he was actually joking and making his own way to the toilet, and from that accident, the two became friends, which made me wonder how many people in the hostel knew about Paul's secret operations. I doubted Paul told the others, maybe he told Matt, but definitely not Mario who was just too... extrovert, at least to bear such secrets.

-Guys, where did you find alcohol at this time? I'd love a beer- I asked when I once saw Paul and Mario coming back in

the common room in the middle of the night with some cans of beers and cyders in a small plastic bag.
-Well- Paul said, then waited for Mario to go downstairs and continued, -I know where, but it's under the counter. You're lucky that I know this area very well, come with me and I'll get you sorted out-
Paul and I walked north towards King's Cross station when we crossed Argyle Square and Paul finally decided to be clearer about his job.
-See Domenico, these buildings and these streets that seem so quiet all around here are actually filled with crime- he said.
-What happens here?-
-Human trafficking, mostly regarding the sale of sex, forced and mostly involving minors- he said, a very serious tone.
-Really? Around here?- I looked around myself and imagined some rich fat men having sex with minor aged girls, chained on the top floors of the buildings we were passing by.
-How does this work? And what do you do exactly?-
-It's very simple. Minor people are imported here and constantly drugged so they never get to escape. They are always under control and eventually they lose their minds, then they get killed. It's not only girls, but also a lot of young men go to the same faith. My duty, Domenico, is to try and stop these bastards from doing this, and that's what happened last night for example-
-How did you find them?- I asked, trying to contain the disgust and rage I was feeling for whoever was in charge of such dirty business.
-That's why I live in the hostel. I have to operate in this area and the hostel is located in a perfect place for me. I go out, look for some people, study their movements and come back at them to arrest them. Last night, I caught a man we were looking for a very long time. He was involved in human trafficking, but he won't do it for many, many years now-
-What happened?-
-I pointed my gun at him and he shitted into his pants, he literally did. I can't say it was easy but oh, the satisfaction of getting him behind the bars...- said Paul, enjoying looking at my face, now totally absorbed by his story.

We reached an off-licence in Pentonville Road and got our drinks. I had been living in the area for about a year and never known about that place, but Paul found out about a week after moving in the area. The guy seemed to be very sharp.
We got a couple of beer cans each and walked back to the hostel. We sat in the common room and Paul told me more about South Africa and its many problems. Then Mario and the guy with red hair and nerdy look joined us drinking.
A few hours later, in the middle of the night, we were watching the big tv in the sofas area when Paul received a message and we all looked at him, not knowing what to say.
-Oh, no, no, please, not now...- Paul seemed desperate, covering his face with his hands, then went on.
-They want me to work now, oh, I'm so tired of this life, and this is a very, very dangerous operation...- Paul hid his phone behind the palm of his hand and put on a very serious expression on his face.
So, everyone knew, it wasn't just me or maybe Rey. Paul told his secrets to more people. Mario and the nerdy looking guy knew, and they were looking at him concerned now. Did they believe him too? I had to find out what they thought about him to have better ideas.
For some reasons though, I started thinking they didn't believe him.

In the following days, Paul approached me more and more often. He once showed me a binder with lots of qualifications, all related to jobs he studied for. All medical stuff.
He said he was working on ambulances in South Africa. I caught him once on the black sofa in the middle of the night watching video of police chasing after cars with suspected criminals in his country.
It all looked real, although Mario once told me Paul asked him for four pounds to do his laundry, something that was in high contradiction with the day he typed a number that was superior to 9100 on his phone calculator, passing it to me, telling me that that was what he made each month working in law enforcement.

Things just started sounding different eventually. A few times while he was talking, I was glanced by other guys who happened to be around in these moments. They looked at me for a second, acted very serious, but I knew that they were feeling just like I was. I was waiting for the moment I could finally dare asking them if they believed him, in private, obviously.

Meanwhile, I was spending a lot of time with Matt. If I initially didn't like him, now I felt slightly different, although I still couldn't be completely matched with him for some reason. He was down to earth though, and I truly appreciated that aspect. I thought he was going to be more politically correct, but he turned out to be just cool. His nice manners tricked me, he was still nice but also easy-going, like a true Australian.
-I have spoken to the police and I am happy to follow the protocol dictated by you. I will have to pick up my suitcase with all my clothes and belongings. Please let me know what time works best for you and we could arrange that- he typed on his laptop and said out loud to Mario, who was keen on the screen.
-Everything ok?- I asked.
-Yeah, I just have to pick up my clothes, I've got nothing left here and I can't even get changed. I wanna take a shower, a proper one- said Mario, sad.
-What happened to your clothes?-
-My ex has them all. She broke up with me two weeks ago, that's why I'm here bro- he said. I realised I had never tried to investigate on his past as a matter of fact.
-And she won't return your clothes? Why? What did you do to her?- I said, trying to be funny.
-Nothing... I don't know, we were very happy together and now she not only dumped me all of a sudden, but she also drove mad. She won't return any of my belongings and she said I can't get any close to her home because she will call the police- he said, sounding sad.
I regretted trying to joke about it. Deep inside his apparent constant joy and cheerful ways, he was hurt. I knew he was going to do well soon though, he wasn't like me.

-By the way guys, do you believe Paul?- I asked suddenly, looking around me. I always had a feeling that he could hear me. The mysterious ways of that man had affected me a lot and I was looking up to him for that.
-I don't, although he sounds very convincing. I don't know actually- said Matt, looking at his screen, apparently feeling just like I was.
Mario didn't reply, but he looked at me. I recognised they were both waiting for that moment to happen, we were all on the same page on that regard.
-Things are weird, I don't have any proof against this story- I avoided mentioning his name, -but he told me this stuff about becoming a pilot and said he's going to set me up for the RAF, which I don't even know if I can legally join anyway- I said trying to sound sceptical, although I was feeling also excited. What if that was actually true? Paul promised me that he would get me signed up to become a pilot a few nights before.
-It's probably not true- said Matt, dismantling half of my castle in one go.
-Yeah, I guess...-

By the end of June, I was on my way for my second trip to Paris.
I had a feeling of anxiety whenever I thought about the direction of my story with Lisa. I knew it couldn't have gone anywhere because of the distance, that it was going to end eventually, but now it was too late to cut that off because I was in love with her. I thought about her a lot, and the usual feeling of fear to lose something valuable had reached me, and now I was trapped.
Lisa came to pick me up at the bus station. She was wearing her earphones and seemed lost, the usual puzzling expression on her face where I couldn't tell where she was with her thoughts, but I knew that she was sad.
-How are you?- I got off the bus, walked towards her with normal pace, and did my best not to seem unbalanced. Not too fast, too sweet or too cold, I wanted her to feel comfortable. I was an addition to her life, not someone who needed her or anything like that.

I was standing in front of her, not kissed her yet, but slowly moving my arms around her neck. She put a smile on her face, but did not reply.
We were walking down a massive ramp of stairs in the middle of a big square near the bus station, holding hands for a bit, and constantly giving each other excited looks and smiles. I felt this was as sweet as it could have possibly been.
-Don't do it- I exclaimed at some point. Lisa had accidentally dropped the unwrapped chocolate bar I bought for her on the ground and was picking it up to eat it.
-It's fine- she said in her usual easy-going voice tone.
-It's not, it just touched the ground, rats are walking on the ground everyday, especially in Paris-
-Not enough time has passed to actually worry. A couple of seconds will not get something contaminated- she said, still smiling. Her voice was sweet, high and warm at the same time.
-What if it was wet?-
-It isn't- she said, now maybe getting tired of it.
-Whatever. Dinner tonight?-
-Yes- she sounded very happy, -I'm taking you to a special place, where I celebrated my birthday last month- she said, holding my hand again.
-Oh yeah, I remember you texted me about that. Right, I'm not a fan of tiramisu, but I'll eat something else I guess- I said, just to say something. I wasn't a fan of tiramisu, that was true, but it wouldn't have been a problem at all to have some.
The time with Clelia increased my insecurity about entertaining girls. I felt like I had to make an impression on them, as if they were a prize that a man could get by being amazing, while all they had to do was absolutely nothing. I found girls were overrated, but I was never going to say this out loud, especially to her.
You are genuine, so lost in yourself. Where are you right now, Lisa?

In the afternoon, I left my suitcase at her place and then, when night came, we walked to her favourite pizzeria, few blocks away from the Eiffel Tower.

The place looked very Parisian, had tables outside and French music inside. It was expensive, but not too much. The prices were high because Paris allowed it, but the atmosphere wasn't the fanciest. Lisa was a down-to-earth person and cared nothing about the look of things outside of the realm of arts.
-You know Lisa, the music you listen to, the frequencies that you mostly send to your brain are what can cause you a mental state of sadness-
-Yeah, you told me this already, in Primrose Hill- she cut it short, not willing to listen to that again.
I looked around, slightly embarrassed.
Lisa was wearing a white linen top that looked really good on her. The food was good and I was taking pictures of her. She was pulling out silly faces, enjoying the moment. Tiramisu was good too, I had to admit.
Lisa and I walked careless near the fences that surrounded the area of the Eiffel tower. At times we danced, at times just acted silly.
We talked a lot about our past too when we were in bed. I was shocked, but not truly annoyed about her stories. I liked to listen to such stories from her. She clearly thought I was nuts, or that I didn't care enough about her since I had no sexual jealousy on that regard.
-It's weird that you like to listen to this- she said whilst looking at me, speaking slowly.
-It's just a perversion I have, and also, I try not to be sexually jealous of people, it's the best thing to do. One's sentimental life would be miserable otherwise-
-I couldn't listen to a story from you or see you with another girl. I'd be jealous- she said, giving me an unexpected and pleasant feeling.
How could you think I'd do that? I mean, I do that, but you know, I would never do anything to hurt you.
-Don't worry, I'm not very focused on that. I like your body a lot- I looked at her, naked in bed with me. The lights were still on that night in her room.
We smoked weed by the tiny window and were now able to carry on. Weed made all more relaxed, but it also made me

unable to have a grown-up conversation since it made me completely dumb.
-I'll have to think about what to do tomorrow- I said at some point, slowly, looking at her blue eyes. The lights were now off and Lisa couldn't take her eyes off of me, and neither could I.
-You're leaving tomorrow!- she said, amused.
-What? No I'm not- I replied, thinking she was joking.
-Yes, you are, check the date- she said, laughing now.
With a growing feeling of terror, I scrolled my tickets online to realise I actually did make a mistake with my booking. I thought I had booked a two days trip to Paris, but I completely left out the fact that one full day of trip would have been spent on the bus the way to France and back to England, and I couldn't believe it.
My usual way of doing things without thinking too much had punished me again, this time badly. I had waited a month to see Lisa again, I could have even stayed an extra day and yet I booked it wrong. On top of that, what annoyed me was also that Lisa didn't seem to mind that I was leaving that soon.

The next morning, I packed my clothes back in my suitcase. Lisa wore a long red and black squared coat whilst we were leaving her flat together. She was on her way to work, and I was on my way to the bus stop, painfully sooner than I thought. One of the stupidest mistakes that my constant distraction had caused me.
If she was lost, and she definitely was, I probably wasn't the right person to put her back on track. Together, we were even more lost.
I haven't told you anything lovely though, and I'm happy about it. Besides, you gave me a great feeling yesterday when you told me you'd be jealous if I slept with someone else. Well, you know what? I'm glad to go back to London anyway. My best friend is back at the hostel, and besides that, nothing else matters.
Actually, you do, you do matter, but it's all less intense now.
-This is a classy coat- she told me, genuinely looking happy on the stairs the way down to the courtyard.
-It is- I said, winking at her.

I don't know if I will see you again. Probably not. This has been great though.

July 2016

I had to speak to Jemma. I had a feeling that my body spoke entirely differently, but I just couldn't keep it any longer. It was a weird moment.
Her tall and fit body, typical feminine presentation and care to the details of her look caused a premature end of our intimate moment together. I was too attracted to her and that was why I failed, at least that time.
She told me I was the first man to have slept in her bed since she had moved to Battersea, about six months before, which I initially didn't believe, but now I was feeling more and more prone to do so.
She gave me the impression to be a smart, committed and mentally very sane person, a bad target for my goal. I was wasting her time and I was sorry about it.
I could have kept pretending, keeping the game still on to enjoy what she had to offer. But what she had to offer was not for me, she was slightly taller than me, her salary was about four times as high as mine, and the effort she made for the sake of her look was by far superior to the one I made. Breaking up with her would have been the most ethical thing to do, and I wanted to be a good person. I wouldn't have used the joy of my pleasure at the cost of a person's heart.
-Jemma, I have to tell you something. This will sound weird, but to be honest, I don't think I can be in a relationship with anyone. I just want you to know, I think you're brilliant, but all I can do is try not to be in relationships. I know we haven't really talked about this anyway, so I don't know where you stand, but yeah, I had to tell you- I said one morning after sleeping at her place. I was still in bed, too tired to stand up. She was coming from the bathroom back towards me, then stared at me, silent for a couple of seconds.
-Take off your pants- she told me with a smile.

Perfect, I thought. Maybe I could even continue this. Maybe I can keep banging this babe and focus my heart aims on Lisa. I

can keep Jemma on the side, that is just a golden position to be in. What else could a man want?
I wasn't very sure about Lisa's feelings, but I also knew for sure that I wasn't ever going to act again as I did in the past. I wasn't going to talk, text or think desperate anymore.
I felt relieved I said that to Jemma, my conscience was now fine, I could keep walking with my head held high. If you have a problem with that Jemma, know that I never meant to use you, I never misled you. If your expectations were higher, it was your fault and I call myself innocent. I'm cycling the way back to the hostel now, I feel good, but I also feel like I might have made a mistake.

In the next days, Molly texted me again. We had reached a point of apparent stalemate with our plan of meeting up again. She was still travelling with her American group and they were in Italy now.
I was pressuring my manager about when I was going to get paid, since the fact I got paid monthly was very annoying. After the apparent end of the plan, Molly's message was just a pleasant surprise.
She said she was going to make it, but that would have been expensive. I promised to help her out with the money, which didn't sound too much of a problem. My race for financial improvement and the development of a healthy attitude towards my own preservation would have started a month later, although I had been postponing this for about two years now.
I rented a single room for a couple of days in Mapesbury Road, near Kilburn. That would have been the nest of our two days of passion. Molly was nice, friendly, and she fancied me a bit clearly.

Molly arrived in London at the end of the first week of July. I asked Matt to come meet me in front of Kilburn station, from which we could have walked there and maybe had a threesome with her.
Molly and I reached the tube in Kilburn and found Matt on his phone, tall figure leaning lazy on the black rail gate in front of the station.

-Yo guys- he said with his usual low tone.
We started walking through the Shoot-up-Hill when I finally got notified I had been paid about 1.5k by Starbucks. The two of them looked happy about it and congratulated me. Eventually, we reached the venue. I checked in and got a set of keys from the reception, a lock case hanging on the left side of the door. I picked up my keys and together we found the way to our room on the top floor. Matt took off his sunglasses and lay down in bed. I followed him after putting my suitcase away.
Molly seemed shy, but then followed me into my arms. Matt was slightly distant from us, but I was trying to encourage him to get closer, without success though.
He told us a story of brain surgery that a friend of his had to go through in Australia. A young girl who had been disabled her whole life after this revolutionary science was officially recognised.
He was very knowledgeable, always had a story to tell about something, and it was always inspiring. Molly and I were listening, keen. That took a bit of the sex atmosphere away, but it definitely increased the intellectual one.
-Anyway guys, I have to go. Stepan and Chloe bought me a concert ticket and I'm going with them, I promised them- he suddenly stood up.
-Matt? What? Stay with us!- I said, caught by surprise.
-Yeah, stay...- said Molly.
-I would love to guys, but I can't break the promise. Next time maybe- Matt looked disappointed. He probably regretted saying yes to them and now was keeping faith to his word.
Matt left, and me and Molly were now looking at each other, both feeling a bit shy for some reason.

Me and the American spent hours in bed before we finally decided to take a break and go downstairs to check out the kitchen.
I prepared my special plate of risotto, then we had a pool game and a couple of beer cans.
Molly deserved the best out of me, both in mood and performance in bed, and I was being as active as I could.

I wasn't like that all the time though, the ghost of depression could have taken me away anytime and given me a relatively long period of emotional stagnation. The effort of being full of energy didn't cost me much, but it constantly felt unnatural. The longer I spent like that, the longer being happy became a habit. The longer I spent away from people, the harder it became to see myself being able to be happy again.

Molly and I enjoyed the rest of the time we had until eventually we had to stand up in the middle of the night so to get to her bus stop. From there, she would have reached her stop towards the airport.

I was happy that she made it to me, happy also because I could have continued dedicating time to myself, but also slightly sad for the umpteenth time I saw somebody physically leaving my life. We would have stayed in touch through social media, but for how long?

-I'm happy to be here with you. I'm glad you've decided to stay a little longer, apparently?- I asked Matt one afternoon, unsure on how he would take the question. I was not the only one who enjoyed making more bookings and keep living in the hostel, but I was the only one who didn't plan to leave eventually. However, I didn't want Matt to believe I was trying to recruit him into the team of "those who stay and don't progress in life", team of which I was indeed the captain.

-I won't be moving to any place until I find a job- he said, having a puff of his cigarette. His sunglasses looked good on him, but now that I knew he was a harmless engineer, he just couldn't look as cool as he already was for me on a personal level.

We were sitting on the usual step three doors down on the right side of the hostel in Guilford Street.

-How's the job hunt going?-

-I'm still working on my cover letter. As soon as it's ready, I'll start sending my cv to everyone- he replied, usual low voice tone, as if he had throat issues.

-You've been here for months by now, you still haven't finished your cover letter?-

-Right, I've heard this before- he suddenly seemed annoyed.
-Look, this is not like your Starbucks job, where they hire people more because they need them than by how qualified they are for the role- he looked at me firmly.
-Sorry, don't get offended- he added.
-I couldn't care less. You run no risks of offending me. I'm just asking how perfect you want your cover letter to be and why didn't you prepare one before moving to England anyway- I said, trying not to sound unpleasant, as if that depended more on my tone than on the content within my words. Matt sounded really annoyed now, but kept his tranquillity untouchable as usual.
-I need to look perfect to them- he concluded after a few seconds. He had just rolled another cigarette.
-I understand-
-How did things go with Molly?- he said, changing topic.
-Good, and you should have stayed with us-
-Oh man, don't tell me this. I regretted leaving as soon as I was outside the building. Also, the concert where we were going to got cancelled, can you believe it? Molly got a great body, although she's not fat- he lit his cigarette and chuckled.
-Not fat? I mean, yeah, but...- I was surprised.
-Well- Matt took a pause. I looked at him for what seemed to be half minute in complete silence.
-Right, here is my type, if you really want to know- Matt nodded his head towards a passer-by.
A black, very fat girl was crossing the street right in that moment. She wasn't the average level of fat. She was clearly sick, way too fat, American fat.
-Wow- I commented, slowly, knowing he was kidding, but suspecting that he might have had a little fetish for something like that. It wouldn't have been very uncommon nor wrong, I assumed.
-I'm serious- he said, chuckling.
-Yeah, sure, I mean...- I started chuckling too until I had to stop.
-I'm serious man- said Matt, calm, amused, but now starting to sound serious. The muscles of his face were slowly

returning to his typical serious, and slightly careless aspect of his.
-You see, more meat, more pleasure. Also, better sex, in general, in all aspects- he said, briefly pausing after every statement, pronouncing them very fast.
-Better sex. How- I asked without the question mark in my voice.
-You don't understand because you're not there yet, but you'll get there eventually. At some point, when your brain will be where mine is, you'll understand- he seemed to be leading me on a joke. Lying to me, but I couldn't be sure. Matt didn't act like that at all in general, he was too genuine.
-What do you mean? You mean the number of girls you had sex with?-
-Well, besides that, I think I've masturbated way too much in my life- he finally came to a conclusion, now sounding much more relaxed than before, as if admitting that liberated him from something heavy. He felt relieved, I could see that.
-You can't. It's impossible, you can't have done more than me. I'm way too much of a wanker- I replied. Was I really in a challenge with someone about how much of wankers we were?
-You don't know. I have hard disks full of porn. In fact, this thing of fat chicks happened like that. I just needed to see something different, then it sucked me into it- he chuckled once again.
-I understand what you mean, but have you actually slept with someone that looks like the one who just passed by?-
-Oh, I wish. Unfortunately, not that fat, but I've had pretty fat ones before, sure-
-Right, but it can't be as good as with skinny girls- I said slowly, staring into the car park entrance in front of us.
-Oh, and this is where you're wrong. Skinny girls suck- he said.
-Ok, look, Matt, I'll never judge you of course, but you cannot tell me you can do with a very overweight girl the same number of things you can do with a skinny one. It's a matter of physics-
-Yeah exactly, you can do more with a fat one. The fatter, the better- he said, now clearly making fun of me.

-You can't lift her up against the wall for example- I said, mentioning something I never thought of doing anyway.
-Have you ever put your dick into a couple of fat rolls and lost sight of it?- he asked, serious.
-No, and I have to say, it's not in my bucket list-
-Then you don't know what you're missing out. Look, I was just like you before, but then it all changed. I was exploring more porn and couldn't find anything that inspired me. It was a crisis, but then I tried fat porn out. At first, I was like, eew, and then I was like, eew, but then I was like, eew, and then eventually I was like, yes-
Matt was literally reproducing a gradually improving facial expression for every single noise he made, from disgust to pleasure, all whilst moving his hands as part of the acting. I stared at him, unable to say a word, then burst out laughing with him.

Working at Starbucks started giving me the same type of feelings that I had in Cote after the initial stage. When you're new, everyone treats you nicely. Then, once you're part of the team, the brutal war over where you are going to be placed in the social pyramid begins, and only a tough attitude can save you from reaching the bottom of it. Talent and skills can take you quite far, but without a bossy attitude, you're vulnerable against the least talented and often the most self-centred members that will try to undermine your position.
My first phase for Starbucks was over and everyone was happy about me. Then, my nice team-orientated attitude was starting to cause me some headache.
The woman from Ethiopia was acting nicely to me and speaking Italian anytime the manager wasn't around, but as I found out one morning, she had filled a complaint about me.
-Dom, I need to talk to you- said Jo with a serious tone once.
I wasn't happy about it, since my money situation was terrible, and I couldn't have afforded to lose that job and find another one with the current expenses of the hostel and basic needs until my first payment.
I went downstairs at the end of my shift and waited in the small staff room.

Michail's book by George Martin was on the table. He loved reading it during the breaks. I felt like I had lost my lifelong passion for books. I read many books in Italy, but none in London.
-This is a letter. Please read it- the Ethiopian woman gave me a letter that stated a warning for me. The complaint was about the fact that I kept speaking a foreign language at work after being previously told more than once that it wasn't allowed. She looked at me with a cautious face, speaking slowly, backed up by Jo who was sitting in her office, listening.
I stared at her, furious but acting calm. I couldn't react. In any other situation, I would have, but not in my current one. I couldn't believe it. My madness reached a peak but then gradually faded, replaced by the relief that I hadn't been fired. I wouldn't have spoken Italian any more behind the till with my co-workers, but I was outraged by the act of my shift leader. I stared at her, who now had a guilty look on her face, but certainly no shame whatsoever.
Then, unable to resist, I spoke.
-You speak Italian too, all the time- I said, hearing Jo's chair moving at the sound of my voice.
-I only reply to you because you speak to me, but I don't start it- she replied. Again, I didn't even know what to say.
-Right, Dom, this is a warning, let's not discuss this any further- Jo came by and the Ethiopian showed an expression of relief. I put a calm expression on my face.
-Yeah, ok, I'll make sure this doesn't happen again- I said, then I left.

Luckily, the hostel could make me forget about all the dirty things that people tend to do to other people at work. The hostel threw me in another world, where everyone was better than they were outside and at work. The hostel was people's home after all, and few people wanted problems in their homes. I believed that the same people that happily shared life with each other in Russell Square would have potentially been terrible co-workers, but there simply was no social pyramid in there, so nobody acted according to it.

I tended to believe that, anyway, that wouldn't have happened, and that we all would have been good co-workers, but my judgement was biased, not taking into account that we were already friends.

This made me think, workplaces need to increase the number of staff parties. Wouldn't creating a good atmosphere between co-workers be the key to improve things at work? You would be doing less evil to your teammate at work if he was the one that helped you crawl safe at home the previous night after all.

-Dom, I'm going to see a girl tonight, I already talked to her. She's French- Rey told me, standing by the entrance door, visibly excited.

-Who's the girl?- I made my way in, leaving my backpack on the first table before me.

In that moment, a girl came by with her eyes directed at Chloe and Stepan's table in front of mine.

My relationship with Chloe, a friendly French girl a few years younger than me who was living in the hostel, was close to becoming alright, but the one with her boyfriend was more based on respectful lack of hostility. He seemed disgusted by me.

He was Asian, although pretty tall, his skin was quite dark and he was always dressed impeccably. All his clothes were expensive branded, and he was studying to become a lawyer. Clearly from well-off families, him and Chloe made a good couple, and due to their higher status, they were probably unhappy to have me around.

I felt sure of this anytime I happened to be close enough to their table. Stepan would even stand up and move to another table, making it look like it was just a random choice, but there were too many coincidences for me not to suspect that the reason was me. And to be fair, people like him were repulsed by the way people like me lived their lives. I was shabby, my clothes were often used more than once before they were discarded in the dirty clothes bag, my shoes always had a hole somewhere and I would never buy new ones until the ones I had were literally destroyed.

The repulse I had for people like them though was similar and different at the same time. I didn't feel disgusted by their

clothes, but rather by their personalities and clear incompatibility. In their case, they felt disgusted both by my personality and by my presentation.
The girl I saw approached the table and Chloe asked her something in French. She had a cigarette between her fingers, straight long dark brown hair and circled small earrings. Then, a bull earring that connected her nostrils as a cherry on the cake to show the perfect prototype of the French, alternative-looking girl. Most French girls looked exactly like that. Cute, aware to be cute, skinny, petite and smokers, so that they could look cooler. I saw so many of them and they were all French.
-Her name is Charlotte, come meet her- Rey invited me to her table.
-Nah, not the kind of people I want to meet- I said, then opened my chess book and dug myself in, alone at my table. I was definitely not keen in joining a table with that girl, Chloe and Stepan.
-You're so shallow, Dom- said Rey, disappointed, making a move to her table.
I stood up and went to make myself some food, then left again for the supermarket and bought a few cans of beer.

I loved finishing work in the afternoon and being able to spend the evening in the hostel. I just had to resist the temptation to take a nap, which would have messed up my sleeping pattern. Even one hour nap could have broken the routine successfully.
Hours later, Rey was gone. Was it for business?
I had a feeling that he wasn't very happy. I saw him standing up and making a move outside with an annoyed look on his face. He wasn't wearing any jacket, so I thought he was going to go back inside soon, but then I remembered that Rey never wore any jacket, not even when we went out at night.
I sat down next to Matt, who was now talking to Charlotte, alone at the table. Her thick French accent started irritating me the moment I sat down.
-Hi- I said, politely, not keen on continuing.
-Hi- she said, shy, a very high-pitched voice. She was very pretty, and so were her dimples.

-What happened to Rey?- I asked looking at Matt.
-He's gone. Don't know where to- he replied, quickly.
Something must have happened between him and Charlotte. I texted him.
-What's your name?- she asked me.
-Domenico. Nice to meet you- I said, trying to smile to cover my prejudice based on the look, which made me feel ashamed once again. It wasn't the first time.
-Where are you from?- I asked then. She looked and acted very shy, as if she was scared but also very keen on talking. She gave me a big smile. She trusted Matt, and the fact I knew Matt was for her a reason to trust me, I assumed.
-France- she said, blushing.
-Yeah, I knew that already, but where exactly in France?- I said, trying to smile again. I had the feeling that girls that looked like Charlotte just wanted attention, but she was giving me a different impression. She certainly wasn't arrogant.
-Toulouse, south- she said, barely able to look at me, still very shy. Matt was looking at us with his arms crossed.
-Wanna play a game?- I asked him. He accepted.
-I'm busy with my business. I will come back later tonight I think- Rey texted me in the meantime.
Matt, Charlotte and I spent the next two hours just chatting. Matt tried to focus and do his best to beat me, but he blundered too often and I went on to win all games.
Charlotte was simply next to us the whole time and acted very nice.
She was often going for cigarettes, and so was Matt. Was he going for it?
Difficult, I thought, since his prototype of girls was much fatter than Charlotte, who was actually more petite than the average girl.
At some point, Matt suggested I went outside to smoke with them during breaks. Yeah, he probably wasn't planning anything at all.

Darina was working in Pret full-time and living with an older woman who hosted her in exchange of taking care of her house and her old dog.

I once visited her in mid-July. She told me that she was going to prepare a great dinner with some proper Italian specialities. The old woman was clearly wealthy, owned a shop in Regent Street, according to what she said.
She lived in a place in north Wembley, a beautiful house with a big garden. A quiet street with other houses from well-off people too, badly lit, but probably pretty safe.
About a week after the dinner, she had contacted me again, telling me she was going to visit me at the hostel for an afternoon together.
I accepted, I loved her presence after all, although I wished I could have rested instead. I realised then, that the necessity of accomplishing the social duty of meeting up with a person I hadn't seen in some time could have been fulfilled twice in the same occasion. In fact, I did promise Andrea to meet up and postponed a lot over time, so why not call him and ask him to come over? The three of us could have met, and then I would have enjoyed a long time on my own, trying to finish off my things.
Andrea accepted, and we all met up in Soho Square.
We were walking together, me and Andrea sipping some Carling cans, when I just couldn't help asking them for a break to have a quick nap.
-You mean, you need to nap? Like, here, for real?- Andrea was surprised.
-Yeah, I just need a quick nap, I'm suffering- I said, too ashamed to even look at him in the eyes. He had come from Forest Gate to visit me and now I was ditching him like that. He had company though. Maybe they could have just chatted, but I didn't know how that was going to end. I needed more than a nap. I needed it all the time, and that moment was one of the many moments that got me thinking, what was my problem? Was I healthy or not? Why was I tired all the time? Why was I bored with everything except chess or chasing after girls? Why were Rey and Matt the only people which I could be next to without feeling like sleeping would be a better option?
I was feeling terribly sorry in seeing Andrea's disappointment in his face.

I'll sleep only half hour, but I have to, I'm in pain. I promise, half hour and then I'll give you my best until you leave the way home. Regarding you, Darina, I visited you last week, so we're even. My effort of visiting you is nullified by my disappointing act of napping before your eyes.

I fell asleep in the middle of Soho Square with my arms and legs crossed. I didn't wear a jacket and July in London could still surprise you with some slightly cold wind hitting your neck.

I slept half hour, then I woke up through my alarm, and suddenly felt very awake, which was perfect.

Eventually, I invited them for dinner at the hostel. I would have cooked to compensate for the fact that my sleeping urge had sucked me away from them for some time during the time we were meant to just be together. This was the plan until we arrived in front of the hostel though.

-Excuse me!- the voice of Adam the security guy was loud and aggressive when he saw Andrea.

-You can't come in. You are not allowed here, I remember you- he said to Andrea and got closer to him with a threatening look on his face.

Andrea got red and also closer to him.

-Guys, what's happening?- I asked, half worried and half amused, I couldn't deny.

-You know what he did. He once tried to stay in without booking. He didn't have a key card that night and we kicked him out. Next time I see you with him, I'll come to you, and you'll be out too, then, you can't come back- he went on saying louder and stricter.

-Oh, actually, I didn't know it. That's very bad- I said to Adam, pretending to be offended by what he had done. I genuinely didn't know about it, but from Andrea, I wasn't very surprised to find out he did something like that.

Rey greeted me from a table near the windows when I entered the common room. Darina sat down next to him and the two, no matter how different they were, developed a bantering confidence straight away. By the time I came back from the kitchen, Darina was red in her face for laughing hard at Rey's jokes.

A fun evening ended, and when the young girl left, only Rey and I were left for some chess before bed.
We ended up sitting by the table near the sofas area.
Rey and I used to move around the common room a lot. I wondered if the reason behind it was that we wanted to mark control of the hostel, to feel more at ease in the place we called our home, like dogs.
-You guys are playing chess!- someone exclaimed and sat next to us. A man probably in his early forties and with a very friendly face smiled at us.
He had some short beard and short dark hair, slightly chubby but well connected with his good height. Besides, his confidence with us made me want to introduce myself with pleasure.
-What are your guys' names?- he asked us, and we introduced ourselves.
We started playing some games with each other. He was pretty much at our level. I managed to win a game I was completely losing. I put my poker face on, although I was shaking out of fear for most of the game. Rey used to comment my moves a lot and making negative judgements, which I found very annoying, although he wouldn't stop, no matter how many times I asked him to.
His name was Cosimo, and as I found out, he was from Trani, literally the town next to my native one. I also found out he was drinking vodka from his cup, and then the suggestion came out naturally.
-Guys, we should go out tonight- I said, immediately happy about the appearance and open character of our new man. The reply arrived straight away.
-Let's do this- he said.
Rey looked tempted, then accepted.
After a few more games and some vodka, we stood up, and me, Rey and Cosimo were heading out of the hostel when Peter the delivery guy asked us to join.
Peter was an English guy, around my age, generally very introvert. He would usually even avoid greeting me by pretending he didn't see me when I walked past the sofas area heading to the kitchen.

He would usually sit and eat alone. He worked for Deliveroo, and usually left the bag on the floor next to him in the common room after a long shift and just ate bread with some other healthy food. I never saw him drinking alcohol, for example, and neither hitting on girls. The person he mostly matched with was Matt, who was not just too polite and spoke to him, but also, I had to admit, had some compatibility with.
Sometimes I felt slightly jealous that Peter could take Matt's attention away from me, and I was quite possessive when I liked someone's presence near me.
They both were shy though, and I remember hearing from Matt once, that Peter was looking for girls.
-Hey guys, are you going out? Mind if I join?- he asked, politely.
Really? You didn't give me any oil for my bike when I asked you some and now you want to hang out with us just because, unlike you, you know we will talk to many tonight?
-Yeah, sure, we're probably going to a club- I said, hoping he would withdraw his idea.
-Cool- and he went to get changed. Then, he came back still wearing shorts, which Cosimo showed not to appreciate.
The four of us left the hostel and walked towards Leicester Square. Peter clearly wasn't one of us, but he really needed some interaction with girls, and he knew that we could have helped in that case.
-See this guy? You know, how many girls is he going to talk to tonight? Come on...- Cosimo was mocking Peter in my language and made me laugh. I liked him more and more.
We crossed Cambridge Circus in that moment and decided to head to Old Compton Street, looking for a bar.
Cosimo eyed a lot of girls and catcalled a few times, never hesitated. He didn't care.
-Is it free entry?- I asked a big security guy in front of a long queue at Zebrano.
-You got to be on the reservation list- he replied.
-Can you make an exception?- I asked, also because of the alcohol and maybe to make an impression on Cosimo.
-You got to be on the reservation list, especially you with the shorts, double reservation list for you- he chuckled at his own

joke. Cosimo looked unhappy about it and looked at Peter with despise.
We figured it was too late for us to get anywhere that night. It was the weekend and all the small bars were reserved. In a matter of minutes, Peter, disgusted by the aggressive way we were approaching girls in the streets, made his way out of the group and walked back to the hostel.
-Honestly, these people, how are they not feeling shame? Did you see how he was dressed?- Cosimo commented after Peter's departure.
-Yeah, they have no interest in doing any effort to get girls, yet they still want them- I replied.
Back at the hostel, a couple of hours later, Rey and I sat on the table near the sofa, a glance between us to point out we identified a potential target, an Australian who was in room 10 with us.
Blonde, slightly messy hair, in her early thirties, easy going like most Aussies, sitting with her legs crossed on the bench towards the entrance door.
Cosimo sat down in front of her, but he suddenly stood up to follow one of the French young girls which we met a bit before the night began.
Rey and I didn't wait any longer. It was too late to start any work after all, so we jumped quickly to the sex talk, to see if she responded to it.
-You guys are so bad, I thought you just wanted to play chess, but you were just tricking me into this- she replied at first.
We kept it going, and got more and more dirty in the talk. I started to get the feeling that she might have begun to feel uncomfortable when Rey stood up and declared he was going to bed.
Meanwhile, Cosimo had come back and now sat in front of the girl, all whilst looking at me and licking his own lips. He had been in the kitchen with that girl, about twenty years younger than him, for over ten minutes and now she was leaving with just a cup and a smile on her face. I admired him, but now I was scared he wanted to get some kissing with my prey too.

Smoothly, and without sounding any creepy, he managed to ask her for sex without explicitly asking her. It was some pretty good technique.
She smiled, kept the conversation going, but then dismissed it with a good technique too.
-Thanks, but I think I'll go to bed now- she said, not scared nor annoyed. I could see she was truly tired.
I said good night to Cosimo, then followed her downstairs.
I found out Rey was still awake in the bed by the bottom of the room. The Aussie was on the bed next to his, whilst mine was further away.
I walked past her bed to see if she would give me any signals, but she just looked at me with a face that had no expression. Just the usual, calm and easy-going look. She was definitely not scared of allowing people to treat her as if she was family to them.
Rey looked at me and at her bed, moving his eyes, excited.
-I think I'll pull out my dick and see if she takes it- I said to him in Spanish. He struggled not to laugh.
I was in front of her bed now, and I noticed she was looking at me. Same expression, as if nothing could surprise her. I unbuttoned my trousers and checked whether her look would finally change and show me some sort of consent. I was getting more and more excited and also amused by Rey who was probably still peeking.
I buttoned my trousers back up though. I didn't feel I had a right to believe that her silence meant I could proceed. I learnt on my own skin that women certainly weren't the most honest and coherently behaving animals, but recognising appropriate contexts and act accordingly was not a duty I could feel exempt from. It could have worked, but the risk would have been too high.

The next day, I spent another closing shift with Azou, the Algerian shift leader and definitely my favourite one.
We often watched football games behind the counter, chatted about random stuff and kept the bantering up to top level.

-Listen motherfucker, I'm going to smoke a cigarette, don't break anything here- he would say, to which I would respond with a similar manner.

Working with him and with Lukas, the Lithuanian shift leader was very different. They both cared about the job being done rightly, although their mindsets would reflect on the standards they required from the way I closed, which had an impact on my stress.

What annoyed me was not the hard work, but the lack of rationality in the requests that people had at work. I understood where they came from, but I couldn't bear them. If one were to open our shop in the early morning, he wouldn't be able to spot whether I closed it under Azou's or Lukas' supervision. The difference would have been little to the point it wouldn't have even appeared.

I had to sweep and mop the floor upstairs and downstairs, then clean both toilets and finally, also do cleaning behind the counter, this last duty shared with the shift leaders, who had to take care of counting stocks and other stuff. Azou would check my job and make sure the standards were met, but Lukas was clearly looking for perfection, and more than once he even asked me to do some cleaning again from scratch. Alternatively, he was also capable of some really good chats about the Soviet Union and other political topics I enjoyed.

That evening, I was mopping the floor at the end of a particularly long shift when my phone rang.

-Hey boy? How are you?- Lisa's name followed by a small rocket popped up, imposing a pause to my duty.

-What happened to you?- she texted me straight after.

I waited a minute, getting slightly excited. She missed me, I thought.

-Hi Lisa, all good, and you? I can't wait to finish work and get to watch the games tonight- I mentioned the Euro, knowing she didn't care about football at all.

-Cool, enjoy!- she texted back. I put my phone back in my apron when I saw she was still typing.

Another message came out on the screen, and this one was hard to ignore.

-I miss talking to you. Can we talk tonight? I don't know what is happening, but I feel you more distant lately- she went on texting.

I stared at the screen with my heartbeat slowly pacing up to a pleasant but also slightly disturbing feeling. I was confused, unsure on how to proceed.

I couldn't deny I was happy to see her name on the screen. I was definitely leaving her out a lot and she was feeling it. Not only that, she was also telling me about it, which was very unusual from a person of my historical era.

Was I becoming that person? Was I going to play with that girl's heart?

No, no way, although I could tell I was finally getting to know how girls feel when someone shows to be longing for getting them. I was by the other side of the courting now, and something inside of me was enjoying the pleasure of being desperately wanted, but I had to act upon this and do the best thing. Azou was still downstairs in the office, and I didn't really care much anyway.

After thinking about it for a few minutes, I reached the conclusion that Lisa needed a reply from me, and I was going to be honest. I took my phone behind the counter where the camera didn't get and contemplated a proper reply.

-Lisa, sure, we could have a chat tonight, I'll text you when I get home later- I replied.

-Okay boy, but do it, I'll be waiting for your call. I miss you!- she texted back straight away, to which my heart could no longer keep it.

-Are you in love with me?- I texted.

She started typing something, then deleted it, and then typed again.

-Yes- she said, finally.

Lisa wasn't Clelia, nor any other girl I had met before. Unlike many, Lisa was not damaged nor narcissistic. She didn't create any drama and never got angry at me for no reason. She talked to me and asked for support when she was sad, opened her feelings up and never hid anything.

That night, I told Lisa that I was there, present in her life, I wasn't leaving, that she was the one that mattered to me,

and that we should have met up that summer, probably in Valencia at Rey's place.
I thought about Manu's words and my past experience. I didn't speak in a way that could reassure her about my feelings completely, but I made sure she knew I wasn't playing with her.

Matt, Charlotte and I were spending every moment in the hostel together.
Charlotte was in London for an internship and Matt was still unemployed, which meant they were always chilling in the living room.
Every night, we would sit by the steps next to the hostel and just talk about the world for hours and hours.
I started randomly asking for cigarettes, just for social reasons. Matt told me it was getting on his nerves, which I ignored, and Charlotte seemed to have no problems at all with that. She was a heavy smoker too, like Matt.
I initially disliked Charlotte for her typical French fashionable look, but with the passage of time, we were getting along very good. We talked a lot and mocked Matt when we were all together.
There was an atmosphere of great bantering which made me want to stay up all night. We were all very close to each other, but I was curious to see how things were going to go when I was going to be alone with Charlotte, something which was happening for the first time that night.
Matt made a move to bed sooner that night, and the two of us were left on the small alley between Guilford Street and Queen Square.
We kept talking, but I was already planning the moment to hit on her. The usual, exciting but also hard decision on when to hit and also, get ready to face a potential rejection that could ruin everything.
I like you Charlotte, you're fun, nice, and we're very like-minded.
I made a move towards her lips. The second that separated me from her showed me she knew it was coming. I saw her closing her eyes.

My relationships with my Starbucks co-workers went on to become very unequal from one another. They got to become from good to amazing with some of them, and from bad to horrible with some others.

Two of them, Jo and the Ethiopian woman, clearly disliked me. I disliked them too, but we all tried to bear each other's presence. I suspected that Jo, who made up the schedules, purposely put me and her on as less as possible shifts together, which I truly appreciated.

Rey got fired from his job at a pub near London Bridge after only two weeks of work. He said he was enjoying it a lot, but he couldn't bear the attitude of one of his managers, a younger English girl who was, according to him, disrespectful.

-I'm not like you Dom, I don't let them treat me like a slave at work. London managers suck man, I hate them. They think they're better than us, we work hard and they treat us so bad. You need to stop letting them treat you like that Dom- Rey was acting complacent of his own lifestyle tip, although I could see he was still angry about it. On top of that, he was broke again.

-Rey, first of all, I'm not that guy anymore. Secondly, I'm thinking of leaving this job and go on holiday with you. I want to see Valencia and get Lisa to come there too if you don't mind-

-Really? Let's do it! Of course she can come. Quit your job Dom, do it now!- Rey was very happy to hear me talking like that.

-Not now, I'll do it at the end of the month- I said, and I meant it.

By the end of July, Lisa and I had planned our visit to Valencia. I was going to stay nine days at Rey's place, and Lisa just five. That would have been a perfect amount of time to spend with her and also alone with Rey.

Meanwhile, Charlotte told me she was going to leave London soon too.

I was glad that our friendship remained just the same after the night we were together. I was scared that something could have changed in her, but so it wasn't.

Actually, it turned out, as she told me a few days later, that she was seeing someone and that she liked him.
That meant that we either subconsciously used each other because the stories with our preferred ones weren't stable enough yet, or we were both cheaters with no regrets. As for me, I was one, but I thought she was saying the truth, which got me a little surprised. Maybe she knew about Lisa, or simply, the type of guy I was.

August 2016

Jo terminated my work and scheduled my last day of work for the first of August. I was going to get paid that day, and that matched perfectly with the fact my holiday started two days later.
She told me she wanted to keep me just a few days before, and I was quite surprised about it, but with the hassle of covering my time on holiday and making up schedules, she concluded that the best thing to do was to terminate my employment.
She had a coffee during my shift, then left without saying goodbye.
I stressed her a lot during our shifts together. I didn't care anyway.
I left Starbucks and walked to the hostel with a great feeling. I changed, I was different than I was about one year before. I would have never thought that I could have chosen to be unemployed, with no much money on the side, and yet be so careless. Just one year before, I had much more in savings, and yet I was terrified to lose a job where I wasn't even treated as good as I was in my last one. Rey's influence on me was becoming clear, and I didn't mind that at all.

The night before our trip to Valencia, Rey, Adrian, Stepan, Matt, Charlotte, Chloe, Laurine and I headed to the Tiger club. People that crossed their paths with one another and were so glad about it were there all together. We didn't know when and if we were going to see each other again because, at some point, each and everyone of us would have had to leave and go their own ways.

Nights out with people from hostels were the least toxic way to spend time. It was the fact that we weren't a fixed part of anyone else's lives that got the best out of us.
We were all temporary presences for each other. All we were doing was producing memories into other people's heads.
We had no other goals but having fun. That was why I didn't want any friends, but only temporary ones, except for Rey of course.
-Matt, I think I got the right one for you tonight- I was leaning on the counter with my beer next to me. The music was so loud that I had to repeat it for him.
-Which one? Well, it doesn't matter, I'm not going for it. I'm not in the mood, you know I'm shy- Matt was amused, but sounded firm in his decision.
-I'll get her for you then- I said, then walked to the other side of the floor and approached her.
She seemed to be in her early thirties, and was fat, very fat. She was sitting alone and looked very grumpy. The expression on her face would have looked discouraging to anyone, I assumed.
-Hi- I said with a smile, confident also because I wasn't hitting on her by myself.
-Hi- she replied, not looking into my eyes.
She had blonde, long straight hair like a barbie and a very English face. Lot of makeup and long eyelashes. If it wasn't for her body, she would have looked like a model.
-Can I introduce you to a friend? He's a bit shy, but he's been checking you out for a while- I lied.
-Maybe- she replied, surprisingly shy.
In a second, I grabbed Matt and forcefully brought him to her.
The two started chatting immediately at her table. I couldn't believe it though, Matt really was into that size of girl.
The night ended, and we all walked back to the hostel. All except for Matt, who was going back to her conquest's place.
I could have hit on her friend, a truly hot one, but way too hot for me to be bothered wasting time with. I wasn't drunk enough, and also, I didn't want to get rejected with my mates there close to me.

The morning after, Rey and I boarded on our airplane to Valencia.
I was looking forward to enjoying being on holidays with Rey, and I was also glad that Lisa was going to be with me for a bit, and not for the entire time.
She landed in Valencia from Zurich about one hour after our arrival. We were sitting in the airport when we saw her approaching us.
Not a single word, just a big smile on her face. We didn't kiss in front of Rey, I knew Lisa wouldn't have liked it as she wasn't the type and in fact neither was I. We were never going to make anything public, nor mention it on social media for example. Only our closest friends knew we were dating, although we weren't even a couple.
The three of us got picked up by the car of Rey's mum, a woman in her late fifties with long dark hair and skin with a very strong high-pitched voice. The typical Mediterranean mum, I thought when I noticed Rey used to just ignore her when she was talking about how she worried about him a little bit too much.

Eventually, we got to Rey's place, a cosy apartment with a balcony on the outskirts of Valencia.
We were welcomed by Rey's two dogs barking hard when they saw two strangers arriving. A tiny light-brown dog, one of those that bark forever and never give you a break, and the other one was a massive white Argentinian Dogo with a dark brown stain on his left ear.
Lisa and I left our suitcases in Rey's room, then decided to join him and his friends by the beach.
I knew Lisa would have been happy to visit the beach, not only because she brought her swimming costume and pulled it out at her first occasion, but also because she lived in Germany, precisely in Baden-Württemberg, a place where visiting the sea is only possible by travelling away from it. Regarding me, I hated the beach and the sea for several reasons.
I didn't feel any need to be by a beach to start with. Also, my pale skin got burnt very easily and I disliked sun creams, not only because of their smell, but also because they weren't

effective. No matter how much I used them, they never saved me in the past when my parents forced me to go to the beach with them on sunny Sundays during my childhood summers. On top of that, I didn't feel any pleasure in swimming.

I drove a car for the first time in about two years, taking Rey, Lisa and two more guys to the beach, promising myself not to take off my t-shirt once we were there for the whole lasting of that social duty I had to fulfil.

Lisa was sweeter than ever. She held my hand all the time and walked constantly next to me. The disinhibited girl I met in Paris and got to know better in London was now still cool, but also deeply attached to me.

On the other hand, I was managing my emotions in a very mature way, although I feared that the reason behind that, was that I didn't feel the same for her. I knew I cared the world about her, but I couldn't be bothered acting silly around her. Maybe it was a natural reaction to her not making me doubt anything. Anyway, I was going to do my best for her to enjoy her holidays.

The next morning, I woke up in pain. Gradually, the pain got harsher until it stabilised. My calves were red and burning, and I was going to pay for not covering them during the previous afternoon by the beach.

I found out it was Blanco that woke me up through scratching my legs, now sitting next to me in bed, keen on playing more. The huge dog was unable to rest, and he would follow me everywhere I went. He thought that my good spirit for playing with him I initially showed him meant I could have become his new friend, but he certainly didn't have any idea of the difference in energy between us, not to mention that his paws were weapons to my burnt skin.

-See, this is why I hate going to the beach. Every time, it happens every time- I complained out loud with Lisa, now awake too, worried about me.

-You should have told me, we wouldn't have gone there- she said, nicely.

The pain was so hard I had to visit a pharmacy that afternoon and buy myself a relieving cream to calm it down.

Besides that, we enjoyed the specialities cooked by Rey's mum and her kindness. We ate a lot and well.
It was all very different than how we ate in London, as Rey liked to point out, all because of me.
-Domenico cooks really bad. He is the least talented cook I've ever known, really- he said, looking at me with the usual provoking face.
-You don't even cook at all. You literally wait for me to prepare stuff for you and then judge it- I said irritated, but he wasn't listening anymore.
His mum smiled, knowing him better than I did. She would never allow me or Lisa to take care of the plates or wash anything. She found her biggest pleasure in being nice to her guests, a pleasure I couldn't take away from her, since I knew my mum would have done the exact same.

Over the passage of days, Lisa and I were inseparable. We were finally physically together again and we couldn't stop talking about all sorts of things.
-I've never cheated on my past boyfriends- she said one night, but I suspected she said it for the obvious reason that I was there with her, and I knew she was doing her best to make a better and better impression on me.
-Except once, I was dancing with this guy in a night club in Switzerland. I was there with my friends and I knew he was throwing a stag party. He was going to get married the following week and we were kissing like... madly, and I thought, poor his woman, with a guy like this- she said, looking sorry for her.
I decided not to tell her that the reason why that woman wasn't marrying the ideal man was related not only to the behaviour of her man, but also to her decision to interfere when she could have chosen not to.
Lisa always had boyfriends, and when she didn't have any, she would have no problems having one night stands with guys met at concerts, parks and other random places.
It was one of those conversations that inspired me to ask her something me and Rey had been thinking about quite a bit.
-We should have a threesome. If you fancy Rey, we could do this- I suggested her there, feeling a growing excitement all

over my body. I did already tempt her with past conversation through the phone into stuff like that, to which she responded timidly just to show me she cared about me and put me on a pedestal, but I also noticed she never rejected the idea. Her past and sexual appetite, in addition to the fact ours was a distance relationship meant for me a good chance to do something I had been trying to do for years.
I noticed she was looking at me in the dark, excited as well. I texted Rey right then, and asked him to come to his room.

Days went by pleasantly. Mornings and afternoons were unbearably hot, but Lisa was enjoying the sun, and I was taking care of myself as good as I could.
We visited parks and skateboard rinks, drove a car and took buses, from green grass to small canals, a perfectly cloudless sky all the time and warm nights, Valencia appeared to be a very good place for living.
People were easy-going and did their best to speak English when Lisa was around, although they weren't that good.
People working in hospitality were way kinder than they ever were in Paris, although Lisa didn't like to hear that, she didn't accept any criticism of Paris.
It was in one of Lisa's last nights in Valencia though, that she spoke clear to me about our story, and I could finally start becoming responsible for my actions without doubts.
-By the way, I wanted to ask you whether we are a couple or not- Lisa asked me whilst we were away from the rest of the group. We spent some moments apart by the darkest side of the beach just to be on our own after dinner at a restaurant. Rey and his friends were chilling by the beach and the two of us were walking back to rejoin the group when Lisa spoke to me with an insecure tone, very unusual from her.
-Well, we're not a couple, but if you want to know how I feel, don't worry, you're special to me. You mean more than any other to me- I said.
-I see, but I just wanted to know whether we are a couple or not- her voice was very soft, so soft I couldn't ignore her.
-Does it matter?- I replied, maybe sounding a bit harsh.

-No, it doesn't, I guess, but I think about you all the time like a boyfriend, so that's what you are to me already- she was walking faster now to step up to me.
-Well, I mean...- I kept walking.
I looked at her, and then back at the direction of the group, standing and chatting happy next to a massive castle made of sand with the name Valencia sculpted on it and lit by many red candles. Then, I looked at her eyes, now staring at me, begging for an answer, hoping that her heart goals were mutual, and not being wasted.
-Fine then, you can call me like that- I said.
She jumped out of excitement, just like she did when she met me in Russell Square the night of the dinner at the hostel.
I wasn't going to be the one to disappoint her, and besides, our feelings were indeed mutual.

The night before her departure back to Germany, I caught Lisa crying in bed, lying down towards the wall, trying her best not to show it to me.
-Hey, what happened?- I asked her, half hurt and half amused by her tears, like it often happened to all narcissists like me.
-I'm disappointed- she said, panting hard.
-What happened?- I asked her again, confused and getting slightly worried now.
-You said you were coming to Germany, and then you changed your mind about the dates- she struggled to talk whilst sobbing.
-And? What do you mean? Of course I'm coming to Germany, I just changed the dates because they were best suitable for my plans. I've been taking advantage of Rey's family's kindness so far, so I'm going to spend a few more days with Rey in Barcelona, I think I owe it to him- I said.
Actually, I was planning to party with Rey in Barcelona for a few more days without Lisa. The trip to Germany was also going to be the end of my holidays and from there, I would have had to go back to London, also forced by my economic situation.
In the morning, we took Lisa to the airport, from where she flew to Stuttgart.

We didn't kiss goodbye. Sometimes I thought she did it on purpose, a voluntary challenge to the system, sometimes I thought she just couldn't be bothered.
I was happy to be with someone like her. A very low-maintenance girl.

I spent a few more days in Valencia with Rey, his mother, her man and the two dogs. Blanco was not giving me a break yet, but at least the burning pain on my legs faded off, although my new skin was very red and still sensitive, and I wasn't keen on having his ravens anywhere near them.
Eventually, our days in Valencia ended. Rey and I decided to reach Barcelona by jumping in a car with a stranger from an internet application for people who shared their routes in exchange of some affordable sums of money. A few hours under the unbearably hot highway that connected the two cities, and finally, we reached our destination.
What I didn't like about Rey at that time was his abuse of his phone, and that was something I was constantly telling him about, without being heard apparently.
-Are you betting again? I knew you couldn't resist that- I provoked him once we were checked in our hostel near the Rambla de Catalunya.
I mostly received no reply, and sometimes he would just grumble back at me some undistinguished words just aimed at silencing me.
-Right, I've just uploaded a new status on Facebook, now we'll just have to wait for the likes- he said that evening, smiling and proud, making a German girl sitting next to us laugh.
We were on the terrace of the hostel, and I was getting more and more frustrated about Rey not taking his eyes off his phone at all. He hadn't spoken to me at all, except for communicating about necessities such as "give me the key for the locker" or "where is my water". Rey was not keen on any type of conversation, ever.
-Rey, you're out of your mind, stop being on your phone. What is it that interests you so much by the way?- I peeked to find out most of the times he was just either on Facebook or Tinder. He was good at hiding his gambling activities from me

though, and the fact I hadn't caught him yet didn't mean he wasn't doing it.
-Leave me alone man- was his usual response.
I knew that girls were the only ones that could get him to put his phone away in a moment of such addiction. The girl that was sitting next to us was a perfect target, I thought.
She was German, quite tall and also pretty chubby, which combined with her big glasses, messy curled up hair and unnaturally pale skin, made her certainly not the most desirable target. Anyway, I was hoping that she would get into me. I knew Rey was listening.
-Hi, do you want to go to the magic fountain with me? It shouldn't be that far from here-
-Yeah sure, why not- she said, friendly.
-Ok Dom, I'm coming too- Rey finally stood up.

The night before flying to Germany, I met up with Sandra in the city centre.
Meanwhile, Rey was on a Tinder date with an Asian woman somewhere by the Montjuic hill.
Sandra was a girl Rey and I met in London a few months before and spent a night with in the city centre. She was naturally very attractive and extremely extrovert, typical of a Spanish girl after all. I initially tried to get her but had no success at all.
To that day, Sandra was the only girl that managed to successfully friendzone me whilst still being part of my life on my own will.
She looked radiant when I saw her on the Rambla, entertained by three guys that stopped her to introduce themselves.
-Domenico!- she jumped on me, very happy to see me.
-Alright bro, take care of her, she's truly amazing- one of the guys said to me, maybe embarrassed. I wasn't going to tell him we were just friends, but I needed him and his friends to leave. Besides, that was going to be my second night out with her after the one in Embankment.
Sandra and I spent the night drinking and visiting a few of her favourite spots in town.

After visiting several bars, we finally got to a night club, the one where she wanted to take me.
She chose well, the music was awesome, and I was dancing unstoppably for the first time maybe in my entire life. That was what it felt like, to actually enjoy going to clubs, I thought. I never would have thought that clubs could have had attractive girls and good quality music at the same time. I promised myself to come back to Nasty Mondays sometimes in the future.
-Sandra, I can't make it anymore, I'm too drunk, I'm going home. I'll see you next time I guess- I told Sandra at some point.
I couldn't handle it any longer. The amount of alcohol we had drunk that night passed over two bottles of vodka each and some more beers. Dancing hard made it all worse, and I was feeling that things had to end right there.
-Let's go together then- said Sandra to me.
-Right, I'm feeling better now- I said after walking and taking fresh air for almost half hour. She seemed to handle alcohol better than me, although she was strangely silent, probably hit hard by it as well. She was way too skinny to bear that much after all. Or maybe, could it be that she was waiting for me to make a move?
-Here I am, this is my hostel. Come upstairs?- I asked her.
-Fine- she said, with a tone of resignation.
-Walk behind me, hopefully they won't ask to see your key card, they don't always ask- I instructed her whilst we were in the hall. I had no idea if what I said was true or not though.
I passed through the reception, glad they didn't ask for my card. I kept going up and entered the elevator, ready to text Sandra where to go next, realising only then that I should have told her before.
Right then, I noticed they were holding her. The receptionist had just called the security guy and, as far as I could see, Sandra was being escorted out.
I ran downstairs, tried to convince them to let her in, failed, then met her outside just to say good night.
I had to let go, and to be honest, I wasn't even sure of why we were doing it.

The next morning, I was sad to leave Barcelona, but also looking forward to seeing Lisa in Germany. Besides, Rey wasn't the best company anymore, still obsessed by his phone and social media in general.
We agreed on meeting up soon, although I had never felt less keen on that.
I reached the airport, and texted Lisa I was on my way to her. She was also acting distant from me in the last days, which was an annoying feeling I did my best to ignore.
I landed in Stuttgart in the late morning. The connection between the capital of the region and her town wasn't the best, since I had to change trains a few times.
I arrived at the train station, and decided not to waste any time. It would have still taken me a few hours to get to the destination.
I had to wait one hour for the train to Offenburg to come, and from there I would have had to get to Lahr, which was actually pretty near, or maybe I could have asked Lisa to pick me up from there. She mentioned she would have done that without problems already, but I didn't want to bother her too much. The main reason maybe was that I enjoyed finding my own way and feel lost for a bit.
Finally, I was in the train on my way to Offenburg. There were a few German girls there, sitting on random places, old people, some foreigners, clearly middle eastern, quite a few actually, but mostly German looking people, way less diverse than it was in Berlin for sure.
That region was a very German one, the views outside my window couldn't be more stereotypical. The voice in the train repeated messages both in the local language and in English, but I had a feeling nobody needed the latter.
I could tell how people were all relatable except the foreigners. It was like being in my town in Italy, except this area was in Germany. I got so used to diversity of races and cultures in London that I had completely forgotten about the fact that towns weren't in general diverse, not much at least, yet it all seemed weird to me.
I found it cute in some ways, the fact that one could still find such place in this century. It felt like going back in time and

visit a particular time in history where societies were still forming up.

I woke up to the sound of the loudspeaker.
Apparently, we were few minutes away from Rottweil.
The name of that town surprised me. Why didn't it ring up any bells? I had memorised all my stops by the time I got in the train...
Far, I was pretty far from Offenburg. How long did I sleep? Maybe not that long.
It was afternoon already though, and I didn't want to be that late. I even planned to take some proper rest before meeting her friends for dinner, and on top of that, my phone was off.
I left the station of Rottweil, angry about the fact I had to wait about three hours for my train the way back.
I was hungry but I had no food, and I was too broke to pay for any of the over-expensive sandwiches in the station, which wouldn't have filled me up anyway.
I decided to walk up a hill and chill out a bit.
It was very peaceful, clean and green.
I found the first shop after about half hour walk. The sun was strong, but I had seen much worse than that.
Three hours, three long hours to go though. Having a book with me would have been perfect, but I just wasn't the same guy anymore. I couldn't even bother opening the first page without starting to space out. My explanation for the fact I needed less escaping from reality was that my pleasures, alongside worries and pains in life were too real, and as a consequence of that, I was too busy feeling stuff, which was what the readers try to do by reading, but that was just a potential explanation. The truth might have been that I had become a shallower person, so attached to the physical aspect of life to have forgotten what the dreamy one was about.
Later that afternoon, I got back to the train station, this time determined not to fall asleep again, although a headache was already kicking in.
By late afternoon, I finally made it to my destination. I asked a girl outside the station to make a phone call since my phone was off, and she replied surprisingly available to do

that. She didn't even ask to hold my phone in her hand in the meantime. I hoped she wouldn't do anything like that in London.
Lisa picked me up from the station with a blue Golf, a car I truly liked.
-Hey princess- I greeted her, taking a seat. We hugged for a second, her big smile and sunglasses gave her a fun look.
She didn't say a word, but she handed me a bottle of coke, she knew I was a big fan of it.

Lisa's place was fabulous, I loved it straight away. On top of the highest hill of the town, it was a massive cottage house on two floors, a basement and a balcony that leant on a beautiful garden with lots of plants that her family was growing. She once mentioned to me that her parents earned well, but I wasn't expecting that.
Lisa had already planned our schedule for the four days I was going to be there. To start, that night we were going to have dinner with her friends at her place.
She looked at me slightly worried when I told her I needed a nap, probably scared that my long naps were going to be part of the daily routine.
Unlike what happened in Paris once, I didn't fail her that day. I woke up two hours later and met the first friends that showed up. Three girls of about her age, all truly attractive and in great physical shape too. I had to act good though, for too many reasons, the main one being respect for her, but I had to initially struggle to take my eyes off them. By the time I sat down, I concluded that my girlfriend was still the prettiest in there anyway.
Later on, we were joined by a sociable skater guy and his girlfriend, who unlike him was very reserved.
The sceptical look I was given by her friends whilst I took the lead in the kitchen, cooking my usual risotto, were now changed and everybody seemed to be enjoying my recipe. Lisa looked at me proud, sitting next to me on the bench outside the garden.
A long dinner was followed by a card game inside her living room. A game based on knowledge, and completely in German. I was paired up with Lisa, and together we did

surprisingly well. Once I knew the meaning of something, I was actually quite good. Knowledge didn't really have a language after all.
Eventually, one by one, all her friends started getting on their ways home, until only Lisa and I were left.
We tried to listen to some music together on the balcony again, but stopped when it got too cold.
Before going back inside though, I gave one more look at the dark sky, her garden, the peaceful hills and thought about the well-hearted people around her quiet town.
I was where I wanted to be, with who I wanted to be.

Over the next few days, Lisa and I were spending every minute together, and I was doing my best to sleep as less as possible. Lisa was shocked to know that eight hours sleep to me were not enough to start a new day, which pushed her to offer me more and more coffee.
My worry that my rest hadn't been long enough before the beginning of a new day was subconsciously generated by my inhuman work shifts at the restaurant in London. The fact that I didn't know when I was going to sleep properly again, between sleepless nights and nights that simply were too short for that, I had developed a new lifestyle that was mostly focused on storing as much as possible rest inside of me, so to be ready for whatever shift was going to be necessary. I needed to store as much sleep as I could in my body so that I could sell energy without collapsing anytime soon.
Working for the minimum wage forced me to put work on top of my priorities, but now, my relationship with work was completely different, and I owed it all to Rey's absurd approach to life. Now, I was again going to be broke soon, but prioritising the things I loved over the things I thought I had to do had made me happier than I had ever been in my entire life.

Lisa and I visited a small and beautiful square in town, cycled around and even ran some errands together. We visited her grandparents downstairs everyday, and I played chess with her grandfather, a very enthusiast player, which I defeated

easily on my first game, but to which I lost miserably the following day, due to a blunder of a piece that compromised my position until I decided to resign. The look on his face when he immediately communicated his victory to his wife was so sweet that it made me feel almost happy. I would have had another match the next day, and I didn't need to beat him three to nil after all.
The following morning, we left to Oppenau.
Lisa drove for 40 minutes until we reached the Allerheiligen Wasserfälle, waterfalls located in the middle of the Black Forest. The weather was cloudy, my favourite one, but it wasn't too cold since it was August.
As we walked in the nature, I was presented with something that not only I had never seen before, but that was also objectively stunning. No one could be there and not appreciate it in my opinion.
The more we ambled around the tight paths, the thin and long stairs up and down all around the place, the more it looked like a paradise, unpolluted and untouched by people who, aware of the beauty surrounding them, acted at their best to keep it that way.
The sound of the water that poured on the rocks and the smell of nature around us threw me into another world. I was as far from London as I could possibly imagine, yet still being in the middle of the European continent.
That day, Lisa was acting even sweeter than usual. She would keep her eyes on me and I knew she was checking about my reactions, as if the main goal taking me there was to make an impression on me, giving a gift to my eyes.
-I hope this will stay like this forever, it will be the symbol of our love- she said whilst looking at the pile of small stones we put on top of each other, building up some sort of a tower. Other people had done that too a little bit everywhere.
-Many people do this, couples mostly- she added. That was something I never expected to hear from her. A girl that was lost, depressed for most of her teens, who used to live a hedonistic lifestyle trying to crush her existential problems, now committed with me. She saw a hope in me, since I never

judged her for anything. Besides, we were made for each other, clearly.
-Yeah, maybe one day we'll come back here and still find this stone tower standing- I said to her, hopeful that it was going to be the case.
She looked at me, touched, and smiled.

The next day we were scheduled to visit Europa-park in Rust, not too far from her hometown.
We reached it in the early morning. A massive theme park with focus on European countries and their touristic attractions, all built in great style and excellent similarity, although in miniature, to real symbols of these countries' cultures.
A double deck bus and a merry-go-round in the English area, the streets of Mykonos and the ruins of Ancient Greece, with the roller-coaster that inevitably got you wet at the final sprint that ended up lifting up the waves of the massive pool behind the construction. A satellite to represent the space achievements of the Soviets in the Russian area,
accompanied by theme music that brought me back in time to when I visited Moscow. A small Paris and Moulin Rouge in the French zone and a beautiful area with the canals of Venice, much cleaner than the real ones.
From Switzerland to Scandinavia, Iceland, Spain and other areas, by late afternoon, Lisa and I had visited them all, including rollercoasters and merry-go-rounds in all countries except one, the highest and fastest one. I made sure that we took the day so slow that we wouldn't have been able to get there too, which amused Lisa, who was conscious of the fact I couldn't handle that any longer. I wasn't a big fan of rollercoasters.
In the evening, we were driving back home, tired but still excited.
I had never seen her so thoughtless and relaxed before. I felt important and in control of my emotions like that. She made me feel helpful, even necessary in her life, and that made me want to do my best to pay attention to her and work on that.

I was looking forward to going back to London, but for the first time since when I was living in England, I was feeling also sorry that my holiday was going to end.
I did enjoy every moment of that, and definitely changed my views on relationships and how healthy and easy they could be. There was no secret between me and her, but just a desire to face life together.
Driving to Stuttgart was somehow sad as a matter of fact. I said goodbye to the warmest looking house I had ever been to, and enjoyed the pleasure of driving on a no speed limit highway to the airport, impossible in my country, but legal in hers.
We promised each other to meet up again. She didn't look any sorry that I was leaving, but rather keen on enjoying time on her own. I knew that a girl with that mindset would have been able to be loyal and committed for some time, but I also knew she was weak.
Sooner or later, our relationship was going to end. Her mechanism of defence built against the possibility of experiencing emotional disappointment was painted on her face. She was clearly putting up an extra effort to not get carried away and still be in control of her mind and body.
She did the right thing.
We kissed one last time, and then I boarded the plane on my way to England.

By the end of August, Adrian told us he was leaving London too.
Another member of the family on his way to experiment something new. He wanted to move to Spain, clearly a better environment for him, I thought.
We had spent a night together with Alessia, two random guys of which I didn't even learn their names, and two girls from Austria, of which one was very easy-going and one was initially pretty snobby, but eventually got to relax and act friendlier too.
Anyway, Adrian and I decided to have one more last night out together. We didn't have many of them actually, and we weren't either that compatible nor great friends. But we paid great respect for each other, and our night started out as a

polite way to show each other we cared, rather than a spontaneous event sparkled by a mutual desire to actually go for it.

We walked to Soho and entered a bar together. The type of bar someone like Adrian was suitable for. No dance floor, but loud music, fancy looking people and sofas, with buckets of white wine opened in most tables and girls taking pictures in all poses for so long it felt like their posts on social media were the only reason why they went out in the first place, whilst the fact they were with each other was of no importance.

Right when we were about to finish our wine and we were going to probably suggest getting home, two young girls sat on the table next to us, giving me a chance to buy some extra respect from Adrian.

-Girls, what are you up to?- I waved my hand, showing them the free spots at our table.

-Hi- they replied together, friendly, and slowly taking a seat next to us. Adrian was amused, his English wasn't any good. The two girls were English, one was black, chubby and wore a bright pink dress, the other one was a typical white English one, with some reddish hair and a fringe, wearing a black top, acting and talking as if she was older than her actual age.

In a matter of minutes, the girls and us turned our main topic of conversation to sex, and they seemed to be quite comfortable with that.

-So, what is the naughtiest thing you've ever done?- the black girl asked me at some point.

-Well, let me think...- I started, then stopped.

Just a few days before, I received a message from the escorting website and went for a business in Brixton. A German guy who had a foot fetish asked me not to shower for a day and paid me 70 pounds to go to his place and lick my feet for about half hour before he called himself satisfied. The week before, straight after returning to London, an old man in Battersea contacted me and paid me a similar amount of money to rim my arsehole in his place, but she certainly didn't need to know any of this.

-I had a foursome a few months ago with my best friend- I came up with. The girls looked very excited to hear that, and at some point, we managed to convince them to go to Adrian's friend's place in Brent Cross.
-We'll pay your way back later- I said when the white girl started looking a bit suspicious of us, walking on the dark streets towards Brent Cross area at night.
We were finally at his place, and the girls had taken a seat on the sofa in the living room, when Adrian went to look for some more alcohol in the kitchen.
Right then, I slowly noticed that the girls weren't feeling at best ease. Didn't they like the place?
It wasn't the best, and neither in the best area, but we definitely gave the impression of being safe guys, even they were young, maybe too young.
-We need to use the toilet- the white girl said suddenly, supporting her friend who was now looking sick.
-Yeah sure- I asked Adrian for the way to the toilet and escorted them upstairs, where they entered together, although I couldn't help staying for a minute behind the door and trying to hear their conversation.
-We should go... I'm not sure... Yeah...- I grasped some words but couldn't really follow what they were saying since they were almost whispering to each other.
They didn't want to stay, they wanted to leave clearly. I recognised that, and my adrenaline met a crush in that moment. Close, we were close from a binding experience that I was really looking forward to achieving.
I heard the noise of the black girl from the toilet, now faking to vomit with a sound that just didn't seem any real, and then I walked down the stairs before they could see me or hear me.
-They're going, they're not staying- I told Adrian, who just laughed. He didn't seem to care too much about it, and was already preparing his mattress on the floor for himself.
-Guys, my friend is feeling sick, we should go home, sorry about it- the white girl helped her friend to the living room, and asked us to go out together.
We walked towards the bus stop where they could have taken a bus to the place where they said they were staying.

-You promised you would pay for our ride the way back home- the white girl said at some point.
Yeah, I did, but I didn't have any money and I didn't get anything from any of you. Besides, my newly developed policy towards people who lied and faked drama imposed me only one type of reaction.
-Here is your bus, we'll wait for you here until it comes- I cut it short. I ignored the rest of the whining, and whilst Adrian was silent, I could see he was still amused by all of that and also pretty tired.
We said goodbye the next morning. I did hope to see him again one day.

September 2016

By the beginning of September, a trial shift with Pret a Manger in Lower Regent Street was scheduled.
Unlike my first try at the recruitment centre in Victoria in the first days of my arrival in London, this time I paid attention to do the most important thing one had to do at a job interview, to lie about their life's plan.
When they asked me how long I planned to work for the company, I said I had no plans to ever leave, and a trial shift got arranged at the start of the following week. Early morning was the only slot available for me and, according to how the company worked, so it was for most others.
Pret was a cafe that served coffee just like every other, but mainly sold food, quite expensive for me, but affordable for office people who jumped in during their breaks from work.
Everyone in the hostel told me they believed in me and that I could have easily got the job when they saw I was slightly anxious about it.
I wasn't scared about the trial shift nor about getting people to like me. Working hard and learning new skills were not at all a problem to me, but rather key features that made me happy at work.
I was also happy that now Stepan and Chloe were closer to me than they ever were before.
I enjoyed the pleasure of talking to Stepan and Matt a lot now. Stepan was highly educated, and now that the sense of

repulse he felt towards me was somehow vanished, or maybe he had just become able to live with that, we were spending a lot of time sitting on the step next door and talking about all sort of subjects, from science to politics, from serious to more shallow topics.
-You know, if men got to space at some point, we all owe it to the Germans, it all started with von Braun- Matt said that morning.
-Yeah- Stepan agreed. Matt had previously told me that he had talked about it with him in the past already. Matt often repeated things he really liked to point out, such as the fact that apparently, central London councils removed most bins from the streets following the London bombings in 2005, of which I didn't have any prove against.
Another point he often made was that fat women are the naturally most attractive ones, and that the only thing that made skinny women attractive in the last century was related to the way beauty was portrayed by influential stylists who had changed what was beautiful to the eyes of the public through the media.
-All men are supposed to see a fat woman and feel like there could be many kids popping out of her. All men naturally always believed that. When you like a skinny woman, you're a by-product of what they created- he was really getting confident once, as we were letting him talk without interrupting him, since we were too busy laughing.
-You'll be alright, don't worry at all- Stepan told me later that afternoon. I had the impulse of quickly checking my clothes and make a self-analysis on how scrubby I looked. Chloe was smiling. She enjoyed the fact that we were closer, I thought.

The good thing about the cafe being in Piccadilly Circus area was that at least I didn't have to pay for transport to get there on my trial shift. They would have given me 30 pounds anyway, but I was broke again, and I needed to save to the last penny anytime I could. I would have cycled to work with my new companion, a dark pink mountain bike that Darina gifted me in exchange of my help with her moving to England.

We had responded to an internet ad and got the bike for a cheap price. Not my favourite colour, and I neither could say I liked the butterfly-themed drawing on its down tube frame, but it worked well and I appreciated her gesture a lot.

I got to the cafe the next morning. The guys had already opened up everything, food on the shelves, customers queuing up, busy employees at the tills, managers rushing back and forth.

I was a bit intimidated by the fact I knew nothing about that, but also keen on showing I was going to do well, as I always did at any job.

Over the course of four hours, they taught me how to cut bread, prepare sandwiches by reading the instructions on papers and lots of other things. Every sandwich had its picture and description, although I was supposed to memorise it at some point, the sooner the better, I realised.

I had to go up and down the stairs taking with me a tray with food and place it on the shelves, then run downstairs to prepare some more. We were all timed and were supposed to finish the preparations of each product in a specific quantity in a specific time.

At first, I thought the timings were unreal, but I also saw how someone was able to finish in perfect timing on the quick productivity check the managers held at some point during the shift.

Besides all other many small things, I concluded that working in the kitchen would have been hard, but not new. Boring, but at least there was loud motivational music in the background.

In the second part of the shift, I was put upstairs, working at the till, followed by my manager, a woman from Lithuania with a tough approach to explaining stuff, although I couldn't say she was any rude to anyone.

I had to learn a lot if I wanted to get fast at that, with all the names of the products on the screen and no bar codes.

Eventually, I was told my shift was over and I took a seat by the front side of the cafe, waiting for a response about that. The first thing I saw when I checked my phone was a message from Lisa, which gave me an unpleasant feeling going through my throat.

I recognised it, I felt it before, but it was less intense, although still annoying.
I didn't want it. I knew I felt it anytime I thought I was about to lose something. At times, I knew it was all in my head and was just produced by my own insecurity based on craving for possession, but I also knew that people were sometimes able to change their mind from one day to the next one with no forewarning. Lisa and I weren't talking much lately.
-So, I've asked everyone, both downstairs and upstairs and... congratulations, you got the job!- my manager sat next to me, then firmly shook my hand and smiled.
-Great news then, thank you- I replied with a smile. That was a relief at least.
I left the shop and cycled towards Russell Square. Getting 30 pounds right then instead of getting the job would have also been fine, I thought whilst checking my banking app. I was in trouble, but I didn't want to ask money to anyone.
I made some mental calculations whilst leaving my bike in front of the hostel and greeting Matt, as usual sitting on our step. I figured out I should have made it to get paid right before my account touched zero.

Part of the family in the hostel were now Tomas and Diego, two guys from Argentina who didn't know each other before getting to Guilford Street.
Tomas was in his early twenties, had dark short well-combed hair and a neat goatee. He had a fit body and a very decent look, the typical well-mannered guy that gained everybody's respect in no time. He was socially open, although his default mode was quite reserved.
On the other hand, Diego had just come of age, and had a scrubby and completely careless look.
We often saw him lying down in the sofas area with his phone on his hand, not moving his head for hours and hours. His shaved head gave some neat impression that challenged the otherwise clearly messy approach to life he had.
Both guys had Italian passports and were staying in London, applying for work from the first day of their arrival.
It was no surprise that Tomas got hired as soon as he tried, and was now stable and fully focused on his job in Pret

somewhere near Waterloo. He was discipline made person. It was also no surprise that Diego still didn't have a job, and neither an interview planned anytime soon.
I was glad though, that soon enough, the two of them decided to stay longer. They fit well in the group, which was now larger and more complete.

By the end of my first week at work, I learnt as much and as fast as I could, but still, I was surprised when my manager asked me to stand by the counter and take a picture of me holding a big box of candies as a reward for being the worker of the week.
I was already happy with my job, just as I also was to enjoy free coffees and two free sandwiches on every shift, which allowed me to save some money in a moment where every little saving was crucial to survive until my first payment. Something that also helped me with that was the attitude of the people in the hostel.
We had all become so close to each other that some sort of race to kindness had begun between all of us. Whether it was a subconscious desire of self-promotion in the social pyramid, or a natural impulse of showing gratitude to the people that were part of their lives, everyone did their best to take as much food as possible from their workplaces and bring it all to the hostel.
By the nights, one or sometimes two tables were full of food that was otherwise destined to wastage, brought there by all of us who had a chance to. The major two contributors though, were Tomas and Enzo, a guy with Brazilian and Japanese origin who happened to work for a Japanese style food chain and brought delicious sushi to many.
On top of the many long talks and consolidating friendships, the nights in Russell Square included everything from chess, poker and all sorts of games, all in their drinking version, to chasing after girls and organising group dinners.
The arrival of Samir, a man in his forties from Sudan, latest member of the family, the return of Rey to London and the regular visits of Mark in the visitors' time made the hostel a friendly, loud, peaceful and socially open home for the enjoyment of those that happened to be there.

It was a nest in the heart of London, a loud place in a quiet street, a home to people who constantly wrote us back about how much they missed it. It was all just perfect.

Rey's presence in all of that was the cherry on the cake of my social life. We were ready to hit the clubs again, hopefully using some extra help from his businesses.
He did well each time he landed in London. In fact, every time he upgraded his profile on the website, potential clients were able to see his pictures first on the research, which helped a lot. With the passage of time though, this would fade, and the sex addicted rich people that scrolled through the profiles of escorts online began to look for someone new, someone different, and that resulted in a decrease of Rey's daily income.
Even though this still allowed him a monthly earning that was by far superior to many of us ordinary workers combined in the hostel, he suffered from panic attacks that made him lose control of himself at the first negative moment.
The hundreds of pounds he so carelessly gave away even in just one night out with me caused a sense of regret and sorrow in him as soon as he began to realise that the work calls were becoming more and more seldom.
The fact that he earned so much in so little time and was unable to save anything was of no help in his personal growth and maturity. He was as happy as one could possibly be in good times, but tremendously worried when things just didn't look as good as in the very previous day. The final touch to his fall occurred with his compulsive need to gamble in order to maintain debauchery at the same pace as it was in his top earning days.
The inevitable result of this was his development of debts towards people that sent him money to bet, a wave of depression and obviously, his return to his home in Spain.

-Hi Rey- I greeted him one afternoon after work. He was sitting at the table nearest to the sofas area with Matt on his side, playing chess against a tough looking guy in his thirties with dark skin and very short dark hair. He had a very serious expression and was listening to music from one earphone. A

guy with a friendlier face was sitting next to him, probably his friend.
Both players seemed to be focusing at the best of their possibilities, taking their time for moves that, as I had time to figure out, were good, solid. The game went on for about ten more minutes when Rey's position slowly decayed, forcing him to resign, reason why I felt I had to ask the guy for a game.
-What's your name?-
-Emil, nice to meet you- the guy shook my hand firmly and looked into my eyes, then set his side of the board up, all whilst keeping a very serious face on.
-He's from Bulgaria, rated 2200- Rey commented loud, squeezing next to Matt so to look at my game.
-I haven't played in a very long time though- the guy commented, humble, still not a smile on his face.
I was excited to hear that. If his rating was true, I should have had no hope to win at all.
From start to end, I played a very good game and focused on each move. We played without clocks, but we were obviously meant to not take too long to play our moves to prevent boredom.
Eventually, I got to a losing endgame, discovering the harsh way that my opponent wouldn't fall for any traps I tried to create.
I shook my hand with his when the right time to resign came.

I was finally enjoying the comfortable normality and beauty of living in the hostel back again, and it all was happening unexpectedly.
I didn't ask for it, nor I thought I would have ever happened to experience that again. A similar feeling I had the previous September had returned, but this time with a family I was fully part of in every aspect, with a job that allowed me to not waste a single evening in company of everyone else, family members and especially tourists.
Charlotte was gone now. I personally reached Victoria Coach station the night of her departure. She chose to spend as much time as she could with me and Matt, which I was glad for.

I slept with her only once, but got rejected when I tried again though due to the fact she told me she had met a guy she liked, a blonde guy from Slovakia who once showed up at the hostel in a striped shirt and an unfriendly, but yet polite attitude towards all people at the table.
The grievance lasted a few nights, where we kept calling each other, but the distractions and possibilities of interaction that the hostel and Rey together offered were way too many for me to lie in a state of nostalgia.

I once reached the common room and found Rey talking to two girls at the table near the stairs the way down the basement.
-Hey Dom, come here!- he stood up and shouted when he saw me, happy to have a wingman available.
-Hey guys, how are you?- I joined the table and asked friendly, with a purposely tired-looking expression on my face.
The two girls were young, probably in their late teens or early twenties. One was skinny and quite tall, had long brunette hair and a mildly attractive face.
The other one was in good shape too, although slightly shorter. Her wavy hair was somewhere between brown and red and was wearing a light-coloured top with some laces connecting the sides of the cut in the centre of it, showing quite a bit of her breast. They were both from Argentina.
Rey and the girls were already at the banter time of the conversation. They had just met, but they were part of the southern world after all.
We were enjoying the conversation and the easy-going atmosphere, but just like it started, it seemed to end. The focus on sex slowly but cleverly got taken away from the table, mostly by the brunette girl, who at some point stood up and left us for few minutes, stating she would come back, which made Rey give up on the spot.
He eventually got up, moved to the table next to ours and just dove into his phone.
Meanwhile, the other girl was still sitting in front of me. Some drinks and empty cups were on the table.

I realised she was talking to her boyfriend when she said good night to him and put the phone down, so I didn't wait any longer.
-Wanna go outside?- I asked her. We hadn't spoken that long and neither I was paying much attention, but it was worth trying.
-Yes- she said, distracted. Rey was still sitting on his phone, probably checking football odds online.
-What's your name?-
-Lucia- she told me when we sat on the usual step. That night, Matt and the others were sitting in the dark alley, keen on sharing joints with others.
We talked about a few shallow topics just to get things going, and then I found my way to get to talk about music. From her look, I guessed she was into rock music, old one in particular, and I knew some stuff too after devoting my teens to that genre.
-I have a feeling that we have a lot in common- I said, with a growing feeling of excitement inside of me.
-Really? Well, I have to say, I have that feeling too- she said, leaving me a bit surprised and pleased to hear that.
-Hey Domenico- I heard Matt shouting from the distance in mocking tone. He knew I was hitting on her, and so did the others who laughed along.
-Your friends?- she asked, amused.
-Yeah, don't worry- I said, a bit nervous on how she was going to take it.
-I don't worry- she smiled and kept looking at the height of my lips.
-Yeah Domenico, yeah!- Matt was laughing hard, and so were the others, all looking at us now. Lucia and I were kissing hard now and I went on to find out she never rejected my hands no matter where I put them, which forced me to take advantage of that moment.
-Follow me, I know a place where we can be alone- I suggested her, and took her hand walking through the guys in the dark alley, all very high and cheerful now.
I took Lucia down the black stairs that led to the basement of the Great Ormond Hospital, opposite Queen Square, a perfect place to smoke weed or just be alone. Lucia was wild

and did nothing to stop my barely under control groping. She was enjoying it.
The look on the face of a disinhibited girl who was taking what she wanted was driving me insane. I loved that look, and I was going to interpret it as a permission to go further. If she wanted me to stop, she could have said it anytime, but this wasn't happening. I took off her trousers right there and she didn't even look around.
-You have to be quick- she said whilst muting the calls she was receiving from her boyfriend on her phone.
-You have a boyfriend- I commented, smiling and making sure she didn't think that was a problem for me.
-Yeah, a rugby player from Wales- she said. I couldn't tell whether she was happy or unhappy about it from her tone. We walked up the stairs and then made our way back to the hostel. She had one hand into mine and one hand on the phone.
She was lying to her boyfriend about where she was and what she was doing with tranquillity and some experience. I was thrilled and felt excited I had done the same thing.
We were both able to still hold a unique feeling for our favourite person, and yet not waste a chance when it occurred.
Things between me and Lisa weren't great. She wasn't happy about the distance between us, and I knew that our story, no matter how beautiful I felt it was, was going to end soon. Actually, I thought, I guessed I would have done that in any case.

With the passage of days, I started to notice that my situation at work was going to be shaped through the usual mechanism of dominance that characterised most, if not all, workplaces in the world. Soon enough, I began to identify the personalities of the people around me.
Having always been employed since the age of 16 developed in me great working skills, from bearing hard situations and rude bosses to not complain and do what was needed silently, not looking for the sympathy of anyone. At the same time, my natural kindness and team-orientated spirit often

made some people feel entitled of exploiting it, all until I met Rey though.

Rey's mocking words over the time penetrated my mind and influenced me a lot. Anytime someone acted rudely at work with me, I pictured how he would react to that and began to act alike.

Rey had a special job and this allowed him to be out of the poisonous working cycle though. He didn't have to bear any of that, anytime ever, and I knew that I could have left the working cycle too.

I could have become self-employed, worked on my own, maybe teach Italian to people, that would have been an easy job for me, and I wouldn't have had to deal with anyone except for paying customers. Also, maybe a trader, or an investor of some type. I thought about this whilst I crossed Herbrand Street on my way to the hostel, when I suddenly noticed Tomas on his bicycle carrying a squared box behind his back.

-Tomas?- he stopped.
-Hey Domenico- he approached me with his usual smile.
-How are you man?-
-Good, good, just finished work, another long day at the cafe- I said. He also worked for Pret.
-What are you doing? You work for Uber too?- I noticed his black t-shirt with the white and green mark of UberEats.
-Yeah, although today wasn't really great. I've been cycling for over one hour but received no calls from anyone- he said, not sounding any worried. If there was a person in the hostel who was mature and in full control of his plans in life, that was him.
-How is it like?-
-Oh, it's great. You go online and offline whenever you want, and they pay quite well. Yesterday I worked in the afternoon and I made about 50 pounds in less than three hours of work. I enjoy it a lot, I get about the same amount of money I make over the whole morning in Pret just like that- he said, a satisfied tone.

He needed to say no more. I was feeling my blood reaching a boiling state.

-Well, that's fantastic! That would be the perfect job for me! What do I do to apply?-

By the next day, my appointment with UberEats was already scheduled, and I was looking forward to the most important interview of my London life.
I didn't know much about it yet, but the fact I was going to work on my own and never deal with any superior rank was going to be the real deal. It would have been perfect even if I was going to make less money than in Pret. Working with music in my ears and having no bosses would have counterbalanced against anything.
By the day of the interview, my mood and attitude at work started to slowly decline, excited by the potential change of lifestyle that was going to take over soon, although I couldn't hide some anxiety about getting the job for real.
I was having problems with a manager from Portugal, a young woman who was quite attractive, who made compliments to me when she realised I took care of the delivery faster than anyone else, but shouted way too bad when things weren't being done the way she wanted to, which happened a lot considering my ideal of following the standards.
Just like in every other job, Pret needed its workers to follow standards that were justified for lots of good reasons, but also unreal when such standards had to be met together with the required timings. In my view, it was either I did it fast, or I did it well.
I couldn't deny that it was basically possible to do it all fast and well, but I wasn't capable of that yet, since I hadn't yet memorised the recipes by heart like my co-workers did. I was new though, and that made sense, I thought.

The day of the interview, I sat slightly nervous in the waiting room of a fancy building in Piccadilly that happened to be literally in front of the cafe where I worked.
I was called straight away and got ready to lie to them about having worked my whole life on a bicycle, or even won some competition. Anything, to get the job.
Oh, the irony, I thought whilst leaving the building and passing by my cafe. I was successful, and my appointment

with the guys who were going to install the big, squared box on my bike was set for the following week. It was easy, much easier than I thought it could possibly be. All I needed to do was sorting out some stuff with the revenue and customs and declare myself an independent worker.

I would have slept whenever I wanted to, worked and spent each evening in the hostel, never missed a Champion's league game, planned and went on holiday anytime I found some cheap offers. The visions in my head were priceless, and if that was all real, and it had gone well, I would have left Pret in about a couple of months or so.

Because of Pret's early morning schedules, I took the decision to sleep all afternoons for as much as I could, stay up the whole night and go straight to work in the morning. It didn't matter that my sleeping pattern was messed up for as long as I got some rest everyday after all.

In one of my nights out on the step that week, Matt and I met Shelby and Molly, two American girls who were travelling around Europe to celebrate their graduation from university that year.

Shelby was a cheeky banter, she had straight brown hair and a provocative expression constantly on her face. She was quite under my height, which I appreciated, together with the fact that the atmosphere got easy-going as soon as she sat with us.

-Will you stop playing with this God damn cube?- she said, half pissed off and half provoking referring to me and Matt, who were losing our heads whilst trying to solve the Rubik's cube.

-Shut up, I used to know how to do it and finish it in less than a minute, I just forgot the strategy- I said, honest. I spent my teens dealing with that cube and only managing to solve it through tutorials on YouTube eventually.

Matt didn't know how to do it either, and that was puzzling us in those nights.

We were committed not to use any external help though, and my memory on how to solve it was tricking me, leaving both of us frustrated and often spacing out.

-You guys are boring- said Shelby, which activated something in my brain.
-I'll take you out then, let's go to dance, I know a place in Embankment, free entry if we get going now- I said with a tone that admitted no rejection.
-Mm... fine, but we'll have to go now- said Shelby, looking at Molly.
-Forget it, I'm not going anywhere- Matt hated clubbing. He was a great company for me, and together with Rey, my favourite person in the hostel and in London, but he was no wingman to me, ever.
I could have talked about any topic in the world with him, but he was too nerdy to do anything shallow. He did enjoy lots of nights out, but he didn't do much to make them happen anyway. I needed him to entertain Molly now, who was not my target that night, both because I was already flirting with Shelby and because Molly was taller than me. At some point, we stood up and headed to Soho to pick up the bracelets we needed so to get into the club, all without Matt.
The girls were fun, but I wasn't sure I was getting anywhere that night. Fun didn't mean they were into anything after all. We reached the club before midnight and I wasn't any drunk, which was a problem to me. Being sober created in my head fears that didn't exist on any level if not in my personal habits.
The girls were having fun and were more naturally disinhibited than me. Molly's height and curves were already attracting lots of candidate dancers that she was quickly rejecting each time.
Meanwhile, I observed the situation from the low of my sobriety and suddenly got shyer. What was going on with me? I was a doer, or at least I liked to think I was one. Shelby was looking at me and smiling now. It was just a matter of time before someone took her. Girls didn't have a second on their own in London clubs before someone hit on them. Shelby was literally getting closer and closer to me while I thought that. Molly was looking at us then, and from Shelby's look I realised I wasn't getting anything if Molly didn't get anything either.

That was the moment I took the first good looking guy that appeared in front of me and introduced him to her.

The guy looked Arab, with a properly fixed beard and a good height. He looked a bit insecure at first, but then contracted his fist as he was ready for a fight and manned up for the moment, just like Arab men usually do in any situations.

I felt like I could see the process through his head. He needed to prove a point to himself, and he started dancing with Molly, who now wasn't rejecting anyone since her friend was doing some kissing and she needed to equalise that.

-Let's go to the hostel- I told Shelby at some point when I noticed she was getting less interested in me and I was fearing she might have decided to go for someone else.

-First, we have to make sure Molly is fine- she said. I wasn't expecting that answer, but it was great news.

-Can we all go to this guy's place?- I asked Molly. I didn't even know what her plan was, and I suddenly feared that she wouldn't have liked my assumption that she was keen on having sex with a stranger just met.

-I cannot take anyone else- the guy said, his eyes desperately stuck on Molly's face the whole time. God knows how badly he wanted it to happen.

After a few minutes in which I slowly began to feel resigned, the girls swapped something from their purses, and they looked at us, agreeing with the plan.

Excited, I led Shelby out of the club hand in hand and I called a cab to get us to the hostel as soon as possible.

-I'll take you to the park, Russell Square looks great at night- I told her in the cab, hoping that she would see that as an extra reason to be looking forward to that.

-I don't care- she bantered, then looked at the screen of her phone.

-All good here, no red flags- Molly had texted her.

-Right, looks like you're lucky enough tonight, but you need to get a condom before I change my mind- she said.

-I don't have any on me, we'll have to go and buy some at the supermarket, there's one open all night right behind the hostel- I said.

-You know I can change my mind anytime I want it, right?- she said, probably able to read my mind and pushing a delicate button, girl's favourite activity in the world.
-You'd miss out the night of your life- I joked back.
-Nah, I'm a girl, I can get it from anyone and anytime I want it- she said, now maybe being serious. She was right, and I couldn't deny it.
-You're ok though, take me to the park- she said eventually, satisfied about the mental torture she gave me before allowing me to get her.

The girls left London two days after. I managed to get Shelby back to the park the following night for a second round, then making sure to be back at the hostel before 4.30 am to get ready and cycle to work.
I was missing Rey to some degree, but the presence of Matt was definitely compensating.
We were closer than ever, and I was enjoying that Matt's company was also perfectly suitable for me too. He had a much better talent than me in selecting people.
Samir, the man from Sudan, was a great conversational presence together with Sean, a very knowledgeable Welsh guy with a huge beard who played the guitar in the common room and annoyed some snobby guests who complained to the reception more than once.
-How's it going guys?- I asked after taking a seat on our step one night.
-You know, at the end of the day, attraction can be broken down in scientific terms as well, just like everything else- Sean was saying, with Matt agreeing.
-What do you mean by that?- I asked, intrigued.
-The brain identifies all connotations that a person presents and examines whether they're healthy or not. That's how we decide whether someone is attractive or not- Matt explained whilst Sean looked at me with his big eyes, probably quite high by then, although both of them handled weed good enough.
-Oh- I replied, unable to go forward. How could I not think about this? That made sense after all.

-See guys, I remember how, many years ago in my country, a guy I used to know once wrote a thesis for his uni, claiming that what makes people attracted to each other was a proof of the existence of God. The fact that the connection between humans was magic basically, and not explicable in any other way than through love- I said, thinking about a guy that reminded me of Salvatore. They also looked very similar to each other.
Matt and Sean burst out laughing uncontrollably.
-What a fucking idiot- Matt managed to finally speak clear. I loved it how he was capable of debunking anything said by spiritual people simply by keeping his eyes on physics, which made me feel worse about how my ignorance often trapped me and made me more vulnerable to lies.
-It's all about health. Your brain notices that the chick in front of you has a regular bone structure, no deformities, a clean skin, long healthy hair that doesn't look like it's going to fall anytime soon, good sized breast that contains calcium for the bones of your baby, fit body, young age that indicates that she's likely to be a mother for a long time before she dies, long enough to ensure the care that your baby will need to grow up mentally sane- Matt was listing, but from his voice, I assumed there was much more to that.
-I guess even just logically speaking I could assume the rest of all other things that could be part of the list- I said, now embarrassed for not figuring it out before, although I never really cared about it too much.
-Exactly, you're a smart guy, it's a shame you gave up on education- Matt often pointed that out. He really wanted me to progress on that.
-So, the same works with love then. They must be connected- I began to rationalise.
-Dopamine, norepinephrine and a bunch of hormones, can't be exact in this right now, but that's what it is. Love is just a combination of chemicals being released by your brain to make you feel so energetic towards a person that you will go on to reproduce. It's just nature compelling you to procreate- he continued.
-Evolution made sex enjoyable also as a way to push you to reproduce. Knowing that you're going to die one day, all you

can do to keep surviving is to pass your genes to a new human being that will carry the struggle for you, and for that, your brain constantly looks for matches for reproduction. So, there you go, now you know that the reason why younger women are more attractive than older ones is not bound to any magic- Matt ended, simple and polite, although still managing to make me feel envious of the times he, unlike me, had spent learning stuff.

That night, I was wandering around the common room until I saw a girl eating on her own from a Pret box.
-I wouldn't eat it if I were you- I said and sat down in front of her, confident after the two successful nights before that one.
-What do you mean by that?- the girl seemed a bit scared. She was chubby and had an innocent look on her face, wavy light brown hair with blue coloured tips.
-Well, I work for Pret. We do things well, but not all of us. Some of us, me included, avoid caring about standards in order to do the job faster and go home at the end of the shift. They keep you working on your section until the job is done, you probably didn't know that. I always end up working up to forty-five minutes after my shift is scheduled to be over- I spoke as if the topic of standard avoidance was to be taken for granted and remain unquestioned.
-What exactly do you mean?- she repeated, her hands away from the food now. She even stopped chewing.
-Well, personally, many people don't wash their hands that regularly, unfortunately- I lied. In reality, they treated the hands-washing process very strictly.
-Oh my God- she said, wincing.
-Nah, I'm joking, go ahead, eat, you'll be fine- I feared I had spoken too much. It was all just an excuse to get the chat going after all.
-What's your name? I can't even trace where you're from by your accent to be honest-
-Paula, I'm from Argentina-
-You're here to work?-

-No, just travelling for the moment. I'm going to apply for work in Ireland actually, I might be moving there in a week or so- she said.

We kept chatting and found out we had a lot in common. To me, that was the usual chat now. Every time I met someone new, I went through the same topics, starting from where she was from, to the music she liked and other random stuff, getting an idea of the type of person I was dealing with and getting ready to say we were on the same page at some point, either it was true or not.

I often shaped my opinions about life, from politics to social issues, according to where I though she stood by, often helped by the clues the conversation gave me up to that moment.

With Paula, it was all easier than ever, and in a matter of minutes, we were sitting on the step, and I had introduced her to Matt and the others. Half hour later, I invited her to follow me to the steps behind the dark alley before Queen Square.

Over the next days, Paula and I spent a lot of time together. Subconsciously, I felt like the more company I got in general, the better I could have dealt with the imminent breakup with Lisa.

I knew my story with her couldn't last any longer, and our chats and videocalls online were getting more and more problematic.

We were both still in love, but she was suffering the distance a lot, and eventually, she told me that she was no longer going to be loyal to me, and that if a chance had occurred, she might have gone with someone else.

-Really? Wow, so glad to hear that- I told her on call, extremely hypocritical.

-Can't you just sleep around if you really can't help it? Why do we need to break up?- I asked her at some point during the fateful call.

-I'm just saying, I'm not in the mood for relationships- she cut it short, trying to sound comprehensive of how I was feeling.

-Right, look, I'm off to bed. Good night-

-Are you crying?- she asked me.

I wasn't, but the muscles of my face probably tricked me. What she was telling me was making me terribly sad. I loved her, much more than anyone else before her.
-No, good night Lisa-
-Good night- she said, pleased by the look on my face.
-Hey, where have you been?- Matt popped up out of the blue, carrying his usual water bottle with his little finger.
-Yeah, all good. I'm going to sleep Matt, sorry, see you tomorrow- I didn't look at his face whilst I crossed the street and entered the hostel.

October 2016

To actively fight against what was happening, I convinced Matt, who was still unemployed, to go to Oktoberfest in Munich with me.
We found a cheap last-minute offer and booked a tent in the city centre for two nights. My request for days off from work was accepted without problems, although I was ready to simply quit in case they had rejected it.
The morning of our departure, Matt was waiting for me in the common room with his backpack ready.
-Hey, look who is here- Rosa and Lupe greeted me in the middle of a very crowded breakfast area.
Lupe was a Spanish girl who worked in Sevilla Mia, a small club in Tottenham Court Road with traditional Spanish live music on the weekends.
She was very attractive, had dark skin, dark long hair and a cheeky expression on her face. She was great banter, although I had given up trying to get her after several failed attempts.
-Good morning girls- I greeted back in Spanish.
-Things are getting pretty hot in here- Rosa commented, amused.
Two girls were sitting on one side of the sofas area, with Matt in front of them when Lupe sat down crossed legs on the table after the cleaner had got rid of the breakfast stuff and the tablecloth.
-What's the issue, girls?- I stood up in the middle of the room, perceiving the topic of debate was hot because of the tones.

-They're talking about women at the workplaces, and I think they're right- Matt explained. He was sensitive of women's issues, a true leftist.
-Yeah, it's probably nonsense- I commented, to which Lupe responded with widening of her eyes.
-Are you joking, you don't even know what we're talking about! Typical behaviour of men, you think the world is yours, right?-
-I never said that. Tell me then, what's the problem you have?- I asked her, enjoying the topic.
-It's sexist that women have to wear a tight skirt as part of the uniform at work whilst men don't have to. It's the patriarchy, objectifying women in every moment of their lives- one of the girls sitting comfortably in front of Matt replied in Spanish, knowing I could speak the language from my chat with Rosa and Lupe.
She had short straight brown hair that barely touched her shoulder with her light, blonde-coloured tips. Her tanned skin and the unusual hair contrast made her look bright. I felt it was strange I hadn't noticed her before. She was looking at me with a serious and challenging look. For the next few seconds, I couldn't keep my eyes off her dark eyelashes and big eyes.
-That's not true, you're not forced to do this. You don't even have to wear make-up, it's all your choice- I replied, still pleasantly impressed by her look.
-I've heard this before- she replied with a mocking tone and turning to her friend for support.
-We have to, it's part of the uniform, we don't have a choice about that, do you understand?- her friend replied. She was quite tall like the one who replied before, and also pretty attractive too. She had long dark curly hair and pale skin with dark penetrating eyes.
-Right, I understand of course, but the reason is not this so-called objectification of women. It's just a strategy to attract more customers. Everyone enjoys going to shops and places where the person who serves you looks good- I replied, confident.

-Then they should also force men to the same strategy. They should make you work with your shirt opened up, women would love to see more skin than clothes- she replied, firm.
I felt like she already had that conversation before, and her answer was pre-set.
-Alright, we don't have time to argue about this now- Matt stood up and spoke loud, although still low key as usual.
-We have to go to the airport, come on-
-Right, bye- I said to the girls, respectful, and then giving one more look at the angry looking girl who spoke to me first. She still had a challenging face, but then turned to her friend and smiled.

On our return to Germany, I was pleased to see that the Spanish girl was still at the hostel. We were missing only three days after all.
That morning, I saw her at breakfast again and wondered whether she remembered me.
She was taking some slices of bread from the toaster and talking loud with Rosa. I sat down next to her seat after realising where exactly she was heading to.
-How are you Rosa?- I asked Rosa in Spanish, just to let that girl notice I was there.
-Hey young man, good to see you again. How was the trip?-
-Lovely, we had fun- I replied.
-Good for you, back to work now- she mocked me. I didn't even think about that. I was scheduled to work in Pret the next morning, but I was going to finally be online on my bicycle that night, and I was very excited about it.
-Are you ok?- I asked my target.
-Well, not really- she replied.
-What happened?-
-I'm having problems at work, today they sent me home because I argued with a customer- she said. She was still wearing her Pret tight uniform. As I thought, she had a challenging attitude with everyone.
-It's alright, this stuff happens to all people-
-Well, I got fired from my other job the other day, just like that- she said, still frustrated about it.

-Then maybe you're not a very good one- I bantered. She appreciated it for a second, but then went back to being upset.

That night, I jumped on my bicycle and got ready to go online. I opened the UberEats app and the map of my surroundings appeared in a blue background, sort of dark mode.
I made sure I was ready to go and clicked on the online button, then, all I needed to do was wait.
In less than two minutes, a request reached my phone. I looked at it and read it twice. I didn't want to fail my first delivery ever.
According to the app, I had to pick up food from a restaurant in Bloomsbury, few minutes cycle away from me, but it didn't tell me where I was going to go afterwards.
I reached the restaurant as fast as I could, and grabbed the food after a couple of minutes waiting, checking my bike was still outside the shop whilst the south-east Asian man who managed an Italian restaurant announced the food was ready with some joy in his voice.
I put it inside the box and clicked further on the app to find out where I was going.
Essex Street, Aldwych, not too far at all, I reckoned I could have been there in less than three minutes.
I was there in four. A friendly young girl came down the building when I called her and tipped me one pound, then wished me good night. It was late in fact.
I went offline straight after ending the delivery on the app and seeing I had been credited five pounds, which meant six including the tip.
I reached the hostel when I realised it was already midnight and I was scheduled to work in the early morning in the cafe. After taxes, Pret paid me per hour the same amount I made in less than fifteen minutes on my bicycle, I calculated whilst in bed. If that was how things really worked, I would have quit Pret straight away, but I needed some other days of work to find out more about it.

Over the next days, I found out that Alba and Angela, the two Spanish girls, were working in London and didn't plan of leaving the hostel anytime soon.
Just like many before them, they booked there, liked it, and stayed. On top of that, they were also hanging out with us a lot.
We had dinners all together, waited for others to come back from work and kept their food hot, created a group chat to make it all easier, planned stuff, shopped together, suggested recipes, argued about politics, bantered, and cared for each other. We were a family, and the two girls became part of it in no time.
Angela was slightly more reserved, and way more respectful than Alba, who was on the warpath anytime she heard a different opinion than hers about what she considered important matters.
I was doing my best to get her, but things weren't progressing, I noticed at some point.
She once mentioned that she had recently been dumped by her ex-boyfriend, but I quickly led to a change of topic. I needed her not to think about him if I wanted her to move past him.
Meanwhile, my work for UberEats was going well, although I was working only in the evenings, since I hadn't quit Pret yet. Having two jobs meant to get two salaries, and by the second week, I calculated I was going to finally have over 500 pounds stable in my bank account, the highest since January. What I didn't consider though, was that this was doable, but it couldn't last. The more the time passed, the worse I slept, the more my body and legs complained, the less I could focus on anything.
My presence was becoming dumber, as Matt noticed. I was boring, unable to keep up with the conversations and falling asleep for quick naps between one work and the other, which not only didn't give me the energy I was trying to get, but actually made me feel worse.
-I thought you wanted to bang the Spanish girl mate. You're not even trying though, she won't be interested in you if you keep living like a ghost- Matt once pointed out to me whilst we were sitting on our step.

-Yeah, I lost focus on that, I lost focus on everything, I don't even know why I'm still working two jobs, I should quit Pret- I said, struggling between one statement and another.
-Seriously? Is UberEats even better?- he was surprised.
-Much better, being self-employed is the best thing in the world, and it's perfect for me. I'm just addicted to the double salary I'm getting at the moment, but I need to quit soon-
-Do it- said Matt. Always caring.

The next day I finally spoke to Rachel, the head manager.
-Rachel, I'm really sorry, but I am forced to leave this job at the end of the week. I hope the short notice doesn't put you in too much trouble- I told her beofre the end of my shift. Rachel looked at me and spoke with a surprised tone, almost disappointed, which I didn't expect.
-Are you sure? You know, we can actually fix your schedule... Would you like evening shifts maybe? You'd be home by 8 pm- she tried.
-Oh really? I mean, oh, actually, I'm leaving London soon. You know, I loved life and I was a sociable person before moving here, but the chaos and the stress just really made me hate it, and besides I'm planning to study at a university in Italy- I gave her no chances of reply with my half lies. She looked at me and smiled, comprehensive.
-It's fine Domenico, you can go and finish your shift now-

By mid-October, I was finally going to meet up with Sabino, my cousin, on his first night out after a while.
He came from our hometown in May the same year, and yet I saw him only a few times. He was working as a chef in a pub in Wandsworth and barely had a social life. He wanted to pay off a few debts he had before dedicating some time to debauchery, in which he was quite committed back in the days.
I met him in Soho, dressed up impeccably from his hair to his shoes as usual.
-Cousin, finally we see each other again- he greeted me.
-You're the one that never goes out- I replied, shaking his hand, glad to see him.

-Yeah, I made an exception though, my friend Miky is here on holiday and I promised to spend some time with him.
In that moment, an exceptionally tall guy came out of the bar in front of us.
-Hey, I was just talking to this chick in there, you guys should come in- he took a cigarette off his packet and lit it.
Confidently, without too much hesitating, he shook my hand, somehow looking unhappy to see me.
-Nice to meet you- I said, to which I got an unenthusiastic reply.
Over the night I got to realise that Miky was not just a man that hit on all women like me and Rey. He was even beyond our level.
If Rey and I had no fear of rejection, Miky seemed actually amused by it. He would stop every woman who was walking in front of him and just ask random questions, standing still in front of them and giving them a firm films-like look and trying to make an impression. Either they stayed or left, said they were flattered or made a rude comment, he would always laugh with us about it straight after the talk with them.
I also had to notice though, that he might have been even taller than Rey, and also had better clothing style. He looked very vain.
-Do you know how much this belt cost me? Almost 200 euros- he said, as if there was a reason to brag about spending that much for a belt.
Over the night, Sabino's mood also got influenced by the shameless ways. In no time, we were attracting attention from the people who were passing by, especially men, those many who were brainwashed by society into being decent and spending a miserable life, jealous they weren't like us and especially like Miky, and left out with the only option of looking at our brutal approaches and judge us.
-What's the worst thing that could possibly happen? That they say no. That's the worst thing, so there's no reason to not try- he said later on in the night in a more philosophical mood after some more alcohol.
Meanwhile, I did all I could to step up to his game. It wouldn't have been a mask anyway.

I was that kind of guy, but spending time without Rey and surrounded by normal guys affected my attitude in general.
-Move to London, I'll help you out with everything you need- I told him at the end of the night.
-Oh, I wish, I'll think about it, not sure yet, I have a shop to manage- he seemed really tempted.
We met again the next few days before he went back to Italy.

Claudio was back at the hostel once again, and I was looking forward to playing chess and get better at it.
We were sitting by the sofas area, taking a break after food and chatting with Giuseppe, a man in his early forties from Naples.
-This one is way too hot. I love it when they wear those black tight trousers- I said to him in Italian, referring to a girl sitting in front of us.
-I knew you were Italian- a guy I didn't notice before spoke. He was sitting on the sofa next to the girls with his legs slightly opened up, comfortable. His messy dark hair wasn't very long, but I could see he hadn't had a haircut in a month or two.
-Well, yeah, I guess it's not difficult to recognise it- I said, not sure if I wanted to continue the conversation. I liked to avoid meeting new Italians. Those I knew were enough already, and I felt like I could only be introduced to new ones under some trusted people's recommendation.
I stood up and invited Claudio for a game by the bottom of the common room when Mark phoned me and told me he was on his way to the hostel too.
Half hour later, the guy approached again.
-Can I have a game with the winner?- he asked, serious, but friendly at the same time.
-Yeah sure, Claudio, play with him- Claudio had just beaten me.
In a matter of few moves, Claudio's position against the new guy was much better, although it was taking him some time to finish him off.
-What do you guys do?- the guy, called Luigi, asked us after the game.

-Delivery guy, just started- I said.
-McDonalds. You?- Claudio asked him.
-I arrived today. I need to apply for jobs as soon as possible- he said.
-You'll be alright, it's London- I added, glad to see my comment relieved him from some anxiety he had in his face.

By the end of October, delivering food was my only job. The switch from being an employee to a self-employed person was not only successful, but extremely rewarding under both economic and social aspect.
I tried to work all day as often as I could, but I stayed home whenever I was too tired, worked longer whenever I wanted to, took several breaks throughout the day, never argued with anyone, heard no rude words at all from anyone, went offline when Mark suggested me to watch the football at the pub, back online if I wasn't too drunk, stayed offline I was.
It was a dream, and it was always there to be found, it never hid from me.
I concluded that the reason why I was trapped into a one-direction path up to that point in my life was because of my luck of strong internal desire for improvement that made me work underpaid for two years for other people instead of working for myself.
So, this is it, this is my life now, I thought whilst cycling the way back to Russell Square after a particularly good shift.
UberEats rewarded you if you went online during very busy times of the day, sometimes even contacted you and offered extra money when it was needed that badly.
Employees with their ironed shirts outside offices had no idea that people cycling and delivering food to them were sometimes making 20 to 30 pounds per hour, probably more than many of them.
-Poor you, delivering today and it's cold, I bet you want to go home as soon as possible- a very kind but truly unaware British woman once told me after I handed her a bag from a pastry shop.
-Don't worry, I'm having a great time. Enjoy your food- I said with a smile, and left her with a puzzled face. She had no idea I felt everything but envy towards her.

Working on my bicycle also allowed me to space out and discover new music, although I had a tendency to play music I already knew to be safe.

Meanwhile, Luigi also took the decision to stay and extended his reservations in the hostel for at least another month. He was working as a barista for Caffe Nero in Green Park apparently.

He was 22, same age and unfortunately same attitude as Alba. In fact, in a matter of few days, the two of them had arrived to saying words to each other already.

Their personalities, often arrogant about their skills in the kitchen, at times decent and at times very rude when it came to defending their points of view in the debates, were causing some drama within the family, although they always ended up calmed down by the benevolence of the rest of the group.

Matt, who was certainly the most peaceful and mature, would often say what he thought during dramas and then leave to Queen Square to smoke for the rest of the night. I spent almost every night with him after work, also because I just wasn't getting Alba.

I would usually hit on her, try to get the atmosphere going and create some banter, to which she replied with passion, but we just weren't getting there. The main reason though, was that I hadn't even tried to kiss her yet because I was afraid to fail, and failing in that case wouldn't have been a simple rejection, but the rejection of someone I was getting terribly into, both physically and socially.

I loved having her around, insulting each other for the smallest reason, dodging her slaps whenever I crossed the line, siding with Luigi when he argued with her and Angela, defending her when she argued with anyone else. A failed kiss would have led to things getting weird between us, and I wouldn't have wanted that at all.

Luigi got quickly well integrated in the family too. He told me he was shy at the beginning, but with the passage of days, he was getting more and more extrovert and talking to tourists on his own initiative, often leading them outside for a cigarette, the usual move to be alone with girls.

-I have a feeling he imitates you- Matt once told me during one of our usual long night chats in Queen Square.
-When are you going to get a job? Did you finish your cover letter? Are you aware that weed is what keeps you down? That's an evil substance, a brain killer-
-Alright, stop it now. Do you think that yelling at me will be of any help? I don't need this mate-
-You don't need weed either-
-Just this one. As soon as I finish this bag, I won't buy anymore, I promise. And oh, by the way, you'll need to get your own tobacco for when we go to Norwich- he added.
He was right. After the many talks with him and Luigi at night time, my random cigarettes ended up giving me a proper addiction, although I tried not to buy tobacco.
The two of them, heavy smokers, never really denied me a cigarette whenever I asked for one, and now they were paying the consequences of having a scrounger friend, and so was I, developing an unhealthy habit.

In those days, something very unexpected happened to me, to which I initially thought it had to have been a mistake.
I received an email during one of my early shifts on my bicycle, which said someone was looking for chess coaches for kids. After reading that email a few times, I found myself in the middle of an internal struggle.
Part of me, in fact, wanted to believe it, and that I had to at least try to respond to it, and if it was just a joke or some spam of some kind, that would have caused me no damage, because on the other hand, if that was true, it was safe to say I was thrilled at that idea.
Then, I did something I should have done before the internal struggle arose. I checked their name on google and found out they were a real thing, which put a lot of pressure on me.
Now, I had a chance, with development of great desire and some degree of expectation, both easily transformable into disappointment in case my interview had gone badly.
I thought about it for a couple of more minutes. No one had called me for a delivery yet anyway.
-Hello, I am happy about your interest in me- I hadn't sent any applications, but I suspected they found my cv online

somewhere in some job search websites, and read that I liked chess in my personal interests section.
-I only have a rating of about 1450, are you sure it would be enough for the position?- I said, being honest since the very beginning. There was no need to keep that going otherwise. Their answer arrived within the next hour. They told me they were ok with that, and asked me about my availability for an interview.

Matt and I spent the Halloween weekend in Norwich. Matt got in a few arguments when Emma, the woman I introduced him to at the club in Piccadilly few months before, proving he wasn't lying all the times he told me how unbearable she was. Emma found every excuse she could to fight with Matt, and the only reason why he kept being with her was that she was one of those few people that were so overweight to actually please his particular taste. Emma understood this and acted accordingly, proving how the value of anything in the market is based on how badly it is wanted, regardless of its usefulness.
We had a great time, and I had to say that she was just lovely with me. Norwich gave me a good impression, there were lots of actual English people, which I liked to see.

November 2016

By the beginning of November, I organised a paintball day for the hostel family. I met some people at a stand near the supermarket in Bernard Street who were advertising it, and after a bit of thinking, I decided to let the impulses win. I always wanted to do something like that after all.
-It's totally a swindle, they took your money, and now you won't see it again- said Sean one afternoon by the step, with Matt laughing with him in agreement. The light of the sunset made his big ginger beard look even brighter.
-How do you know?- I asked him, slightly scared he might have been right.
-You know how these things go. They put up these stands, make some money over people who fall for the stuff they're claiming to sell, then disappear- said Matt.

-I'm not such naïve person. It's not the case, they're a fully registered thing, I checked them online, it's a real thing. Come on, join please!- I said, now scared I had lost my money for real. I should have checked with the guys whether they wanted to participate before buying the whole package with my own money.
-If this thing won't happen I'll reimburse you, I promise- I told Matt, who eventually got convinced. He wasn't in the mood for something like that. If it was for him, he would have never left the step.
On the other hand, Luigi and Diego declared to be very keen on that, whilst Alba, Angela and Tomas told me they would let me know.
-Worst case scenario, it'll be the four of us and I'll lose some money, but at least not all of it- I once told Luigi.
-Don't say that, I'm sure others will show up. You should finally make a move on Alba by the way, I still can't figure how things are between you guys. Also, I don't even know what you see in her, she's not that good-looking- he seemed to be serious.
-She's pretty hot. If she wasn't that level of hot, I would have been more explicit with her already. Now, on another topic, do you want to play football? We're playing on a small pitch with some friends of mine in Canary Wharf- I would have enjoyed talking about Alba, but I realised I was feeling quite resigned about it when he mentioned her.
-Sure, I'm your man- he replied.
I didn't do much for us to become friends, but Luigi had beaten all records about his timing in becoming attached to me, and I was feeling just the same. He was about my height, few years younger than me, handsome and quite active, easy-going, left-wing, but not very politically correct, which was perfect.

By the weekend, Tomas finally managed to get a day off from work and Alba also confirmed she was going to join, which meant we were six instead of eight. Angela couldn't make it because she fell sick the night before.
We managed to get Ariel to join too as a last-minute recruited soldier. He was a Spanish man in his early thirties

who spoke almost no English at all, although he was very friendly and agreed on being part of the team almost instantly.

On Sunday morning, we were all together on our way to Upminster.

It was fun to notice who between us was a morning person and who wasn't. Tomas was active and full energetic, Diego was sleepy, but looking forward to playing, Alba was just cool with it, she never lacked any energy, Ariel seemed misplaced in there since we didn't really hang out that much with him, but he looked cool too. Matt was grumpy, still upset with me for calling him into that. Luigi was still sleepy, but on his way to get active.

Right the night before, we burnt all we could find in the streets in Coram's field to celebrate along the 5th of November, then we stayed up longer when we found out I lost my phone, which was luckily recovered by Samir on his way back to the hostel.

We finally made it to the venue, late, and our promised extra 100 bullets each for booking in advance were cancelled, as stated by the receptionist I called when notifying him we were going to be late.

-Right, Matt, this is because it took you ages to get ready- I blurted out.

-Alright, you know what? Next time don't even think of calling me- he said, now sounding mad. His sleeping pattern was upside down, he lived like a vampire and I should have thought about that.

The base was placed by the countryside. I could tell we were far from central London.

It looked great, a typical military looking place to the very details.

We queued up, followed all instructions and dressed up with military uniforms.

-Choose a colour between the ones that are left guys- someone asked us out loud from a wooden pedestal, next to a big blackboard with the names of the teams and their colours.

-Red please!- I shouted.

-I knew it- said Luigi, sneering. We had lots of heated debates about communism back in Queen Square.
After half hour of listening to instructions given to all teams around, about six of them, we made a move inside the battlefield.
We had to wear a helmet at all times, whenever we got shot and ink was visible on our uniform, we had to leave the battle.
We always faced one team in several different scenarios, all built quite good. A forest, a military airbase, a fortress, even London in ruins and more.
At the end of each battle, we all got back to base, checked our scores and took a break.
We started off quite slow, with Matt who was reluctant and Alba who fell on her knee at her very first step in the first field.
With the passage of time and some battles with positive outcomes, we were third when we entered the second-last field. I was having a good time, and so was everyone else as far as I could see. Surprisingly, Matt became actually engaged in the fight.
-Right Domenico, listen, I'm going to walk around that side so they'll start shooting against me. Meanwhile, you run to the other side and grab the flag so we can get out of here, ok?-
-Matt? Really? If you actually sacrifice, you'll be our most...- he was already walking in the mentioned direction. Did he change his mind about all of that? Or did he just want to leave so badly?
It worked though. Matt got the attention of our opponents, who shot him from the distance whilst thinking he was going for the flag, not realising I was running to the destination from the other side.

We were on our way back, winners of the battle, but not of the war yet.
-Alba, jokes apart, you know I mock you and insult you a lot, but I have to say you're a great contribution to this team today, you're a fighter- I said, hoping I hadn't gone too far. Thinking about it, I never really made a compliment to her. I

wanted her, thought about her and also hit on her with my usual ways, except I lacked something.
She gave me a long smile and we just stared into each other's eyes through our dirty helmets for a few seconds before reaching the base once again.
-Well, now that I've done it, I'm finally able to say this is not something I'd like to do again- Matt's comment came out at the end of the war.
We ended up second for a matter of one point eventually. We removed the red bands from our arms and threw the uniforms in the boxes, then made a move out of the place, tired, but still very excited.

Few days later, Tomas, Luigi and I played football near Canary Wharf with Matina, an Aussie I once met in a pool room near Kilburn and another girl from New Zealand. Andrea and Simone from Hyde Park hostel were also there.
-So great to see you all guys- I was happy to see us all together once again.
Andrea and Simone weren't going to stay in London for too long. They both lived their experience and were planning to leave England at some point. I never knew when it was going to be the last time I was going to see them there. London brought people together in short and intense ways, then suddenly split them since no one could really live there for too long and keep up with the stress.
We lost the game, but it was fun. No goalkeepers, just players running around attacking and defending whenever it was necessary. No quality, but fun like a game between children.
We said bye to Andrea and Simone after hanging out a bit and having a couple of beer cans, then took our train back to Russell Square.
-Domenico, why did you give up on Alba?- Tomas asked me, making my blood boil all of a sudden.
-What?-
-I asked her what was going on between you guys, but she didn't really reply. She thinks you don't want her, that you're just leading her on-

-What? What makes you say this?- I hated he was doing that chat. His optimistic views risked to making me feel good for nothing.
-She was weirdly silent, but then she told me that you wanted to follow her into her room and that she said yes, but you didn't do it- he said with his usual high-pitched slow voice.
Was it even true?
I started thinking about it hard, trying to recall a missing clue I didn't catch. I did stay up with Alba in the common room the previous night, but there were other people with us.
She was helping me to edit a picture of us at the paintball on my laptop, then she called it a night and... yes, I did ask her if I could follow her downstairs, but it was the usual banter with sexual allusion... did she reply yes and I didn't hear her?
-I actually... Well, never mind, I don't really care anymore- I wasn't sure on how to go on. Tomas would have kept the secret, but I preferred to not say anything. If Alba had found out that I just didn't hear her, she would think I'd be hitting on her confident to win, and I didn't want this. Actually, a little bit of doubts in her mind could only help.

That night, I got into the hostel, excited to see my family as usual. Trump was officially the new president of the US, and the hostel reacted in different ways.
Some laughed, some got worried, some were just speechless. Matt hated him, Diego liked him, I knew he was joking and considered him not a threat at all to democracy as he was pictured by mainstream media. Alba didn't care much about politics, but she was a tough feminist, so she clearly didn't like him either.
-He's the guy that is going to push the button- said Matt, standing on the step, passionate and worried later on the night.
-No he's not. The president of the US is just a puppet. He doesn't have any decisional power- I said.
-Yes he does. You may be right, but he can still authorise a nuclear war to start, and by the time his administration will get rid of him, it will be too late- he continued.

Then, we sat down, chilled all together, and one by one, everyone was gone to bed, except me and Alba.
-How are you doing at work? All good?- I asked her once we were back inside sitting on a central table of the common room.
-It's fucking shit- she replied loud.
-The way you speak is disgusting, and you're a girl, which makes it even more disgusting- I mocked her with my eyes still on my laptop, working on Paint.
-I'm going to slap you so hard now that your ears will get to smile- she said, threatening.
-What? What the hell is this even supposed to mean?-
-It's a Spanish expression. We say it in my region-
-I still don't get it-
-Basically, I'll slap you so hard that your ear will get to the other side of your face, creating the shape of a smile on the trajectory- she explained in a serious tone, which made it even weirder.
-You come from a region of psychos then- I said, and finally looked at her again.
I was nervous as I rarely was before. I thought I was over that type of moments, I didn't know I could still fear a kiss, a pointless fear. She had her knees on the bench, her body was more directed at me than at the table itself.
Then, I knew I had to go for it. Positive or negative, there was not going to be another chance like that.
Then, a quick move towards her, and I kissed her.
I figured it could have happened before, I thought, that she was waiting for it too.
The passionate voice of the news reporter from the tv behind us was the only thing I could hear in the whole common room.

-Damn Alba, she's so stupid- Luigi complained the next afternoon whilst we had lunch in the common room.
-What happened?-
-I couldn't sleep last night. She was shaving her legs in the middle of the night and that thing was noisy. Why couldn't she do it any other moment of the day?-
-I see- what was that supposed to suggest me?

-What room are you in?-
-13. It's a small one, nine people only fit in there, and it's five of us between me, Angela, Alba, Diego and Tomas-
-That's nice-
-No, it's not, I didn't have a good sleep-
-Eh, Luigi, are you still talking about that? Why don't you talk to me in person then?- Alba came out of the blue and spoke aggressively. She always heard us speaking Italian with each other and tried to guess the meaning of what we were saying, often failing at it.
-Shut up Alba-
-No, you shut up- Angela was looking at Luigi in a threatening way now. She looked as if she was even going to hit him.
-Ok, everyone calm down now. I already have enough of this- it took me a while to actually make them stop shouting, but eventually they all seemed to have found an agreement, which consisted of silence.
The two girls and Luigi were way too defensive to actually listen to the other side of the debate. Luigi could be unbearable sometimes, but he would at least try to use some logic, whereas Alba was uncontrollable all the time. She just couldn't accept people questioning her views.
-Right, let's just all play some board games tonight and be friends once again, ok?- I tried, looking at them one by one. Flamed glances followed.

That night, things actually seemed to be doing fine between them. The atmosphere in the hostel wouldn't allow any such moments to last.
We often played games, and Monopoly was the newest arrival in the closet of the reception, which made it quite popular in those days.
-Where are you going?- I asked Alba when I saw her getting up.
-My laundry should be ready- she said, and smiled excited. That had to mean something.
-I'll help you- I said, and walked downstairs just behind her. We picked up her clothes from the laundry room and brought them to room 13, not far at all from it, still in the basement. Slowly, without turning the lights on, we hanged her stuff to

the window and to other available spaces, and then she turned towards me after kneeling down for a bit too long to fix something in her suitcase. I was staring at her, preventing her to get to the door now.
She had a grin on her face she couldn't hide.
Alba was sultry, just as tall as me, very skinny but with a massive butt, her breast wasn't the biggest, but it was acceptable. Her face was perfect, and I liked everything of her, from her bone structure to the darkish colour of her skin, her black tight dress, her big eyes, her over offensive language and her sweet smile.
-How was the sex?- Matt asked us when we got back upstairs about half hour later.
-What are you talking about?- I couldn't help smiling, still fully satisfied about my success.
-It was good- said Alba, then laughed and took a seat.

Few days later, I decided that my trip to Leipzig was actually going to happen. I did book a trip to Germany for three days to both spend them with Lisa and also to get informed about my university prospects.
My relationship with Lisa was officially over, although we were still in touch.
I wasn't thinking about it too much, but anytime I saw her name on my screen I felt a mix of emotions, something between nostalgic to slightly annoyed and definitely a bit sad.
I didn't know why I was taking the breakup so good though, especially compared to my previous one. I guessed my body was developing antibodies against breakup pains, some sort of immunity after getting a disease once and becoming stronger to face it when it appears again.
I was in touch with Lisa mostly to get help regarding my application for Berlin university. In fact, unlike in the UK, universities in Germany were cheap, just like they were in Italy.
Lisa's contribution though, was slow and not very helpful. She was clearly doing it against her will, moved by the honesty and fairness that always existed between us.

-Alright, so, you just need to pass a language test where you prove you can speak German, and then once you get a job you can just sign up- she cut it short. I expected the phone call she promised to make for me to a Berlin university with all my questions didn't last longer than a minute.
My trip was booked though, and I was totally going to Germany to find out if I had some actual chances to make it. I had called a sudden leaving party the night before and received some lovely requests to stay by everyone. I told them not to worry, I would have come back to fix my last things before moving to Germany, that they were going to see me again soon before the final goodbye, but I wasn't even sure that was going to work anyway.
-Domenico? You have mail- Francesca stopped me by the reception right when I was on my way out to Victoria.
I opened the mail that Francesca handed me and found out with disgust that it was a fine I had to pay.
I looked twice before actually digesting what it said. The sum amounted to 327 pounds to pay as soon as possible so to avoid increases that could have easily reached, according to the letter, a sum beyond 1000 pounds.
-What the hell is this?- I said out loud. Francesca and Turkey, the manager, looked at me.
The fine referred to a day in March when I got stopped by a police officer on my way to Sloane Square for crossing through the red traffic lights with my BMX in Trafalgar Square before entering the mall. The officer told me I would have received a letter soon and that the fine was going to be about 50 pounds worth. This letter though, said that there was an increase because I missed to pay at the first advice, which I didn't, since I never got that letter in the first place. What was I going to do with that? I was gradually getting angrier by the time I reached Victoria, unable to stop thinking about the injustice.
I needed to take that to court, solve that issue. I didn't want to have any problems with justice in Britain, I wanted the country to be always available for me just in case I screwed things up in another one.

I got to Leipzig in the late afternoon. My heartbeat wasn't racing out of excitement and love like it always did before meeting up with Lisa, but rather an annoying doomed feeling, something I just wanted to get rid of.
-Hi Lisa- I greeted her when I got to the train stop she instructed me to go to before landing.
-Hey Domenico- she greeted, apparently happy to see me, her usual smile on her eternally sad face whilst she softly hugged me.
Lisa told me she was going to spend her evening working in her pub after letting me in her place, a flat with big rooms in the eastern side of the city.
Quiet, Germany always gave me that impression every time I was there on my own.
I loved the chaos and crowds, and I knew I certainly wasn't going to be happy in a place like that. In fact, it was to Berlin that I was going to, and Berlin definitely wasn't that far from London standards.
Lisa was into cinema and had a passion for visual arts in general. She wanted to become a film producer and was now living in Leipzig, where the best German university for such subject was. Her parents didn't have any problems in paying her expensive course and accommodation. They even offered her to just focus on study and not work, but she really wanted to contribute as much as she could, reason why she got hired in a part-time job.
By the evening, I got up from her comfortable big bed at some point, having had enough of spacing out and scrolling social media through my phone.
I looked around her room. There were drawings, small paintings a little bit everywhere, including a small map of central London that barely covered zone 1, one of those maps they gave you at the stations so you could walk around, perfect for elderly tourists with no smartphones.
"Let's run away together" was written on it with giant bold black capital letters, repeatedly marked by a pen out of an emotional moment.
I felt my heart getting warmer. She never told me she did that.

I decided to go visit her at her pub in the city centre. My long walk in the silent evening through the empty street lined with a massive park on the left indicated me it certainly wasn't a very rich city, or at least it didn't look like it.
Lisa looked very pretty on her uniform at work. Her white shirt and black trousers were way too fancy for a simple girl like her. Her blonde hair tied up nicely and her lack of experience in working in hospitality was giving her a fun look. Thinking about it, I couldn't recall a single time Lisa didn't look somehow clumsy and adorable at the same time since when I had known her.
-It's good that you're here- she told me later on when we were walking home together.
-I'm glad to be here too, but I have to tell you that I'm going back to London in three days, I have to fix a fine to pay and I don't really want to pay what it says on the bill. I want to take that to court and see what happens-
-It's ok- she didn't look very sorry to hear that.
-How is life here? Are you enjoying it? I don't think I could possibly live here. It would bore me to death- maybe I was overtalking.
-I know what you think about it, but I love it, and I love the place where I study, I'm definitely the most beginner in there, everyone else knows so much...- she said, a bit discouraged.
-You'll be just fine. You're very talented and smart, you'll be the best, I'm sure about that- she seemed very pleased to hear that.
One great thing about Lisa was how healthy her relationship with men was. I related this to the fact that her parents were still together and were described by her to be the nicest parents on earth, although I had never met them. Her grandparents were awesome, I remembered that though.
Lisa smiled at each compliment I ever made to her. Unlike most girls of her generation, she was turned on by kindness and support rather than by lack of attention and emotional abuse. She appreciated who appreciated her and didn't give love to who didn't give it back.
-I know this is over, and it's sad, but I wanted to tell you, that you have been the best girlfriend I could have possibly

got. This was great, from its beginning to its end- I said, unable to handle my sadness at some point in the night.
I was in bed, closed in a tight hug with her. She looked at me and seemed really sad too. She didn't reply, but we simply kept cuddling until we both fell asleep.

Two days later, Lisa took me to the airport.
We spent the previous day just as if nothing between us had happened. We talked, laughed, discussed, confessed our dreams and been intimate with each other just like in summer in her hometown, just like in Valencia. Every minute with her was as sweet as her personality, every other minute I felt the clock ticking, telling me she was gone, and that those moments with her were the last ones ever. She was my soulmate, but we had to part because of the distance between us.
Our different life purposes took us to different directions, but we would have never forgotten our story.
-So, you lied to me- she said the day before after starting some sort of investigation about my sexual life in London. She sounded terribly cute, asking questions in casual voice tone whilst trying to find out more.
-You said that you never slept with anyone else, but now you mentioned this Australian girl- she said.
-No, we weren't together then. We got together in Valencia, and since then I never slept with anyone else until we broke up- I said, confident.
I didn't want her to suspect.
-But you said...-
-No, you said it. You said it when we were in Victoria Coach station. You said we could do whatever we wanted- I interrupted her, and I was actually right.
After some quick calculations in my mind, I figured I actually hadn't cheated on her at all.
Or had I? Whatever, it didn't matter.
I was looking at her now, I wanted her to feel I was grateful for what she gave me and to feel I respected her to the best of my possibilities.
She seemed happy, I reckoned, she believed me, I was happy to confirm that at least.

We kissed once again, then we hugged. I saw her looking at me by the time I entered my gate in the airport. She was standing behind, waiting for me to be gone.
I gave her one more look, smiled, and then boarded my airplane to London.

Back at the hostel, I found out that Joao had planned to stay for some more time, whilst Adam was just regularly visiting. The poker nights between all of us had become a daily thing, sometimes even with some money on the table. I never really learnt nor liked poker enough to become competitive at it, which caused me to lose the earliest in every game.
Meanwhile, I was looking forward to having another chance to get Alba. I wasn't being very explicit about it after our first and only time together. I wanted to take it easy and show her no pressure at all, although the vision of somebody else taking her away from me was kind of rushing me into making things clear.
-You're so beautiful- came out my mouth once when we were having dinner together with the rest of the family, to which she responded by just looking back at me, blushing. The next moment, our kiss at the table was welcomed with mocking noise and grimaces from all others, which she seemed not to mind at all.
Alba had the capacity to be extremely aggressive, both with her words and body language, but she was also very sensitive, and sometimes she would also show it.
One more proof I was overthinking it all came the next day, when Alba and I happened to be together in room 51. I was pleased to see her name on the tag on top of my bed by the bottom side of the room, just as I was to recognise her bags spread around, which confirmed it wasn't just another Alba. That night, I did my best to get home as soon as possible from work.
If it was true that I could have chosen when to finish, it was also true I couldn't choose where. Sometimes my last delivery brought me over half hour cycle away from Russell Square, sometimes even one hour away.

I needed to be home soon enough though, probably before 11 pm just to make sure she wasn't already in bed. I wasn't going to open the curtains of her bed and neither text her.
The best scenario was, I thought, to randomly meet her in our room and take advantage of the dark to inspire her.
I got home late though. Work took me all over central London the whole day until the last delivery called me towards south and I had already accepted it, which meant I couldn't reject it anymore, or maybe I could, but I didn't want to be unprofessional. Besides, I loved my job as much as I needed money after all.
I wasn't going to make any change of plans because of her, a stoic thought crossed my mind that night whilst I walked through the common room to reach the kitchen and drink a full bottle of water.
I quickly said hi to those that were awake and noticed that Alba wasn't between them, which forced me to head even faster the way to my room, hoping to find her there.
A few negative thoughts came into my head. What if she wasn't there either? What if she was with someone else?
Then, I saw her lying down in bed, scrolling news on her phone.
-What the hell happened to your hair?-
-Hi- she replied and turned her head towards me, smiling. She was waiting for me as well, I reckoned by the way she was staring at me now.
-You painted that?-
-No, my hair is naturally very dark. This is how I look normally- she said, amused.
-Mind if I come there with you for a bit? Just to talk?- I suggested.
-Yeah, come- she whispered, then made some space for me.
-How was work today?- I whispered and closed the curtains. Her bed looked cosier than mine. Unlike me, she had a few things spread around, including an extended plug for her devices and a small blue lamp next to her pillow.
-I hate my job. I hate everyone- she replied as if it was the most natural way to continue the small talk, although her sweet expression was slowly turning to upset.
-You're not a pleasure to be around of, so I'm not surprised-

-Listen, get out of bed, I don't want you here- she sounded almost serious whilst she said it.
I loved how rude we were to each other.

Few days later, it was finally time for my interview with London Kings, the chess company, scheduled for the early afternoon in a small venue somewhere near Baker Street. There were me, two Spanish guys and a Lithuanian one, all pretty much my age, candidates for the same position.
The two directors and their personal assistant were there already, and after a brief introduction of each other and a few moves played on friendly mode over the boards, a big demonstration board was brought to our room.
Then, one by one, the four of us had to give a few minutes lesson about some basic chess and talk as if we were talking to kids.
Strange, just very strange, not an everyday thing to do, but fun. I enjoyed it a lot.
The guys and I exchanged numbers outside the venue at the end of it, promising to meet up one day and play some friendly games, although I doubted it was going to happen.

Meanwhile, I was looking forward to the surprise party I was organising for Alba's birthday. I had created a Facebook group and got everyone to pay five pounds each, then had already handed the money to Angela, who was in charge of choosing the present. She knew her the best between us since they were best friends in London.
By the night of her birthday, Rey called me and told me he was coming back to London.
-Dom, this is it, this is the last time I'm travelling. I'm coming to you, we'll be back, I'll get a job and live a stable life, far from gambling and all other problems. Just me and you Dom, and Angela, my new love- he added when I introduced the two girls on camera.
-I don't like him, he's too Spanish- said Angela after the call. She had a boyfriend and wasn't really giving herself to anyone as far as we knew.
That night, I bought two small vanilla cakes that I knew Alba liked, together with candles. We organised the table for it,

now not only packed with beer cans, but also crisps and other small things I though the others would like.
That was something I would have never done if I hadn't already scored with Alba and also felt something for her. Alba looked good on her new black dress that night. She really loved dresses, which was probably why Angela bought five of them with our money, picking very different colours, just to play safe.
We enjoyed a night without drama, with Alba who was too happy to start any argument with Luigi, Matt patiently waiting inside with all of us, although we knew he was craving to go outside for smokes, Diego looking clueless at some point, sitting by the sofas, Luigi rolling a cigarette and me helping the girls to clean the table.
-Domenico?- Alba was still awake when I came back from a long chat with Matt and Luigi in Queen Square.
-Where do you think we could go? To fuck, I mean- she whispered.
-Well...- I was surprised to hear her saying it that way. She was probably tired of waiting for me to make moves on her just as she was of living a sexual life in a hostel.
-Let's go to a hotel then, next week, I'm very busy this week- I said.
-Cool- she replied, then smiled complacent before closing the curtains.

By the end of November, the hostel felt so good that I often had goose bumps.
I thought that having a group of good friends and mutual genuine affection was generally a great pleasure in life, and the hostel provided me of the best version of it in those days. Claudio, who met Emil in Caffe Nero round the corner of Russell Square once, was spending more and more time between us. Matt, Luigi, Tomas and Diego all loved to play chess and often stayed up all night until breakfast the next morning.
I felt both homeless and in the best of homes at the same time. Homeless because I had to change bed every two weeks and I had no stable flatmates, and in the best of homes because, unlike so many people who lived in actual homes, I

had real friends. This didn't mean that I assumed all people's lives were socially miserable, but they certainly were compared to ours.
In a flat, or at work or at uni, one got the same people to hang out with. Some great bounds could be created, but at the same time, the natural toxicity of humans would go on to play its role in creating problems.
People got attached to someone and then eventually lost them. They could get into fights over bad habits others had towards them or even just in general. They would rarely hang out with each other, usually once or twice a week and for a couple of hours or more, some small talk, then move on with their lives, just using each other's company in the moments of need.
The hostel worked the opposite way though.
I could get attached to someone, but it was only in my head, since tourists were there for just a week, or a few days, or even just one.
I never got into fights, because tourists and people who lived there just wanted to have a good time. I hung out with my friends all the time, especially since they surrounded me, spread between different rooms, meeting in the common room every night.
By reserving privacy only for sleep and intimate moments, the hostel automatically eradicated privacy everywhere else, and consequentially, also the need of it.
People who never lived in hostels often told me they couldn't even imagine how it would feel to live without privacy, just like those who couldn't imagine life without conversing with God.
Privacy was made necessary by fair reasons, but it had gone too far. Society felt like everyone was shut in their own cages, living a fully employed life whilst desperately paying with time, money and effort to get to live those moments we were living everyday. One had to pay for transport to get to the city centre, pay for a drink or two to get in the mood, search for new people in a bar once a week, getting lucky about once a month.

I was in the city centre, didn't need to go out to meet girls, and got laid at higher rates than average, and it was always a different one.

Unlike others, I wasn't living in a fixed reality designed by the system and fed the media with the cooperation of the people themselves. I didn't have to stick to one girl and get her emotional abuse, her lies, or whatever it was necessary for her to achieve the best result with her life. I didn't own nor I was owned by anyone. I was a passer-by in tourists' and people's lives just like they were for me. There was no toxicity, no jealousy, no secrets in my relationships with people. You couldn't hate someone you didn't know. Privacy was a social construct, a need they needed us to have, but that we didn't naturally have.

-This song is beautiful. That's a nice pick, I must admit-
-It's from my favourite album by this band-
That night, Alba and I were lying down together in a hotel room in Roman Road, East London. The music she chose was from a rock band, although it was quite slow and romantic, an unusual piece from their repertoire.
Under the lights of the night coming from the window, I could see her face, switching from rude expressions to sweet looks at any moment, amusing me each time.
-You're beautiful- I repeated. I loved to see her blushing whenever I said that.
The album sounded different now. The romantic introduction had given space to a more traditional type of rock, although it still sounded somehow light.
That morning, we took a bus to the hotel I booked, spent the whole day together, had some wine and talked a lot. Nothing about us specifically, although we both talked about our past and found out we were also connected on lots of points.
There was, and I was certain at that point, some unquestionable proper chemistry between us.
We stayed up all night until the next morning, when we went downstairs for a breakfast that, compared to the one in our hostel, was luxurious.

-Don't you have to work?- she asked me whilst we were at the table, interrupting my chat with a family of Italian tourists sitting at the closest table.
-No, I don't have to. I should, but I don't have to- I said.
I felt like a king, only exception being my economic conditions. Poor, but still a king.
-Imagine working in hospitality on night shifts and not being able to spend the night the way we did, or having to wait for a day off to find out you're working the next morning, which means your day off isn't really a day off, since you have obligations for the next day that affect the previous one. What a miserable fucking life- I said, loud and ending with a laughter.
-Domenico, I work in hospitality- said Alba, annoyed.

December 2016

By the first days of December, Rey was back in London.
From the day of his arrival, he started pushing me towards our usual plan for the nights.
We would drink the usual bottle of vodka before getting into clubs, and then hit on everyone in there. I would have loved to take his suggestions anytime, but back then, I was genuinely struggling to feel any particular desire for them.
-Definitely, let's go out, we're back!- I replied, excited, although I felt something really weird.
How would Alba have taken it? What would she have thought if she had found out? Besides, I didn't even want it.
-You know Rey, I have to tell you, I'm having a nice thing with Alba, so I don't think I'll be doing anything with anyone, but I'll definitely be your wingman as usual- I told him once in the common room.
-Yeah, sure Dom, sure. Like I don't know you- he said and laughed.
-I'm serious man-
-Come on man, stop playing with me. You might feel something, but you'd still cheat if you could. I know you would do this- he commented. He didn't like the idea of losing me. Not that he was ever going to, but maybe he feared losing his best wingman.

He seemed pensive for a minute, then he spoke.
-Alba is not the right girl for you. I identified her straight away. She might be a good friend, but not a good girlfriend. She's a rat-
-You don't need to speak badly about her. I'm telling you, you're never going to lose me anyway-
-And I'm telling you that this is a mistake. You really suck at choosing people, Dom. You always do-
-Alright, enough now. I don't need your advice, I thought you came here to play chess. Play in silence- I ended the conversation.
He didn't seem to like that situation at all.

Most arguments between Luigi, the girls and I, were about feminism, or at least random theories that derived from it. Luigi couldn't help pointing out statistics that showed the harsh reality of men, calling out the hypocrisy of feminists who, like Alba and Angela, constantly stated that women were having it harder.
All conversations started with the girls pointing out some stereotypes with a light tone, eventually escalating into political discussion and ending with insults and rage. We often had to calm them down, sometimes even separate them. Once Angela told him he deserved to be punched in his face for the way he spoke to women, which I found ridiculous. If their cause was righteous, and I had no doubts about it, their interpretations of reality was very biased and gave no space to discussions, but rather to challenges.
It was about winning or losing, more than it was about actually listening.
Sometimes you gave them advice about something and they thought you were doing it because you thought you were superior, but it just wasn't true. Some of their assumptions came from understandable places, but they were exaggerating it all.
-Want women to make more money? Then change your subject from psychology to engineering- he once said with a grin on his face, giving birth to a furious debate within the group.

-Don't you think that women make specific choices because of how they are raised? This is a man's world- said Matt once in Queen Square.
In my case, I agreed with both views to a certain degree. I thought they all had points, but they were too stuck and incapable of any flexibility, which made the whole thing hysterical.
-Women choose jobs that pay less, and this is a thing. No one takes their right to sign up for harder subjects at uni, therefore there is no reason to complain about money. Besides, I also believe that it is not true that they get paid less for doing the same job. I've been researching this stuff all day- Luigi replied to him.
-Where? On conservative websites?- Matt was definitely by the side of the girls.
-No, it's also illegal to pay them less for doing the same job. There is just no such thing, at least in the UK-
-That's because they're more agreeable, we raise them to be submissive and then they end up paying the consequences- Matt's logic made sense.
As a left-wing on every aspect, he tended to always look at the historical background of any group of people and explain their success or lack of it through that. Luigi was also a left-wing, but totally insensitive to the feminist matter. His judgement was more rushed, less deep and articulated, although he proved to be very knowledgeable and open-minded on other topics.
-So we can agree that the pay gap between men and women doesn't exist, and that the problem is mainly cultural?- I said, noticing that Matt contradicted himself.
-Right, I'm done discussing this. Let's talk about something else- he said, losing his patience.
-What about this?- Luigi showed a picture he googled from his phone to both of us, a war scenario, with hundreds of dead bodies on the ground.
-Where is my privilege?- he said, passionate, to which Matt didn't reply. Luigi was lacking the skills to think the way Matt did, but he was right in pointing out the fact that the girls kept talking about gender inequalities, but never mentioned wars.

However, the worst conflicts usually occurred between the two girls and Joseph.

Being an African man in his eighties, his views on women were comprehensible for his age and place, but simply deplorable for our times.

-See, you cannot give power to women. They cannot use it, they would use it for themselves only, because they have no ideals- he shouted from the other side of the room once, his hands on his wide stomach, laughing after he had said that. His bushy moustache made it hard to understand him sometimes, but we had got used to that.

-During wars, one of the best strategies after invading a territory is to kill all women, so they don't reproduce. It's a very clever strategy- he burst out laughing at his own words.

-What does this son of a bitch want? Somebody tell him to shut up!- Alba and Angela were the only two people that always challenged him loud, never scared of him.

Joseph was an all-mighty and all-knowing presence in the hostel. His obsession for order and aggressive ways imposed stability within the guests. Without him, there would have been anarchy, we all believed at least.

He would often chase after people who didn't wash their plates just to take them back to the kitchen. Men or women, he allowed no excuses and treated everyone equally.

That evening, Alba got so angry at him that she started crying.

-I hate him! I hate this bastard!- she was sobbing hard.

-Don't listen to him. Try to understand where he comes from, a totally different reality...-

-I don't care!- she shouted, out of control.

-Well, he didn't really mean that he likes to think of doing something like that. He just stated it would be a great war strategy to secure victory, and to be fair, he's probably right. I mean, if you prevent your enemies to reproduce, you should probably...-

-Fuck off Domenico!- furious, she dismissed my arms from her shoulders and left.

I hadn't picked the right words.

In the meantime, the hostel had increased its average chess level by far.
Connected through the chess board, a net of passionate players was formed over time, which, I was sure, was the main reason that convinced some of them to extend their bookings.
By then, two new quite skilled players had just moved to the hostel. One of them was called Becks, or at least that was how we called him due to his passion for such beer. He was a man in his early forties from Kosovo, or, as he liked to nostalgically point out each time, Yugoslavia.
-Yugoslavia was the best country in the world. We had everything, we were rich, and then they burnt it all down one day- he found his chance to say this everyday, especially when he was tipsy enough.
Claudio beat him more often than I did, also because Becks and I were on a very similar level. The other guy was slightly younger than me, from Algeria, and his name was Zak.
He was very handsome and in great shape. Besides, he was also very polite and had an eye that was constantly focused on girls. I caught myself thinking a couple of times whether he had already made a move on Alba or not, but I felt like I had to keep an eye on him anyway.
He was good at chess, slightly better than me I had to admit. If it was unquestioned that Emil was superior to everyone, the place for the worst player of the hostel was still contended, and I was doing my best not to be labelled as such. I felt it frustrating when Emil and Mark mocked my skills for losing against them when I was in winning positions, and I didn't want this mockery to come from more people.

-Hey Alba, how are you?- I once asked Alba, who was alone in the kitchen at night, looking totally absent-minded.
-Fine, you?- she was standing with her arms crossed, her usual position. Something was wrong, again.
-What happened this time?-
-Nothing- she said, sour.
-Tell me-
-Nothing, Domenico!- she was on her way out before I stopped her.

-Alba, I wanted to hang out with you- I said. I was staring into her eyes when I thought about it. I was never explicit about sex until my doubts were cleared by her, but I also wasn't explicit when it came to something I never mentioned to her, something I had learnt to keep for myself with experience. I couldn't deny that the more the time passed, the more I thought about her, but I definitely wasn't going to tell her this.
What I knew for sure though, was that I kept most of my thoughts inside and never showed what I felt outside, except for very few compliments, alternated by horribly rude and more frequent bantering. Acting uninterested and evil was the key to get a damaged one like Clelia, but the same treatment would have only hurt someone like Lisa, for example. I realised I had developed a tendency of playing uninterested and keep my feelings for me, and now I had to unlearn it anytime I was dating someone new, or at least shaping it according to their level of mental derangement and narcissism, which was getting higher and higher with the newest generation of girls.
-Wanna hang out? I want to be with you- I said, glad to have finally let it out of my mouth.
-Me too, but we never do anything on our own. You always call Luigi and Rey. We are never together, alone I mean- she said, sad.
-Right, I understand. Tonight I'm yours though, let's go grab a coffee, come on, it's on me- I said. Alba was extremely stingy, and coffees were expensive.
-Ok- she said, now smiling finally.
Was she actually sad because she was lacking attention? Were we at that stage?

Few nights later, Rey and I were planning to go to O'neills, our favourite place to party, an Irish pub with both live bands and contemporary hits over three floors.
-I was missing this. I can't wait to do this with you, my blood brother- Rey often called me like that.
-Right, I'm glad to go out too- I said. The chemistry that attracted me to Alba was trying to force me into a different

direction and I was facing a struggle now. Was I really going to hit on other girls? Alba and I weren't a thing after all.
Did I have to please Rey? Make an impression on him? No, of course not. I never needed to hide anything from him.
-Sorry guys, I'm just trying to...- my thoughts were interrupted by someone who was literally leaning on our table, her face focusing on the world map hanging on the wall behind us.
Rey and I looked at each other instantly. The girl was blonde, with a very curvy body and a tattoo over her naked shoulder. We could see almost all of her breast whilst she leant further.
-I'm just trying to find Poland on the map- she said.
-Here- I pointed out in a second, realising only afterwards how weird it actually was, that somebody could struggle to find Poland.
-Oh, thanks- she said with an American accent, justifying her ignorance about Europe.
-Where are you from? Texas?- Rey didn't hesitate a moment.
In a matter of minutes, the girl and her friend who was sitting behind her moved to our table, with Rey preparing to get flirty as soon as the small introductory talk was over. The girls were both very attractive, the blonde one could have easily been a model, and the brunette was also very attractive, but slightly more petite.
Meanwhile, Alba was talking to someone from the family by the sofas, unsuspicious.
Inevitably, just like it usually happened with Rey, pushing the girls to go out wasn't very hard.
His friendly ways rarely got a rejection, at least when it came to just going out together, since girls took it in a "nothing is meant to happen" way before we offered drinks. Within half hour, the girls had gone and come back from their rooms, ready to party, and Rey was on fire.
-This is going well Dom, this is going to end up well, I know it. We're banging them together probably- and then he laughed at his own words. What he didn't know though, was that this time I didn't feel like even trying to make that happen.

I gave one more look at Alba, who was still talking to Rosa and a girl I didn't know now.
Where were we? Did I need to say I was going out for party? We never really got to that point.
No, who cares, that's pathetic, I thought.
We left the hostel and walked towards Embankment until we made it to Heaven, the gay club.
By the time we got in the club, the two Texans had revealed to have deep Christian beliefs. They were both in their early twenties, and one of them, the brunette one, said she was a virgin.
-Are you for real?- I felt very surprised, but I did my best not to look disrespectful of her choice.
-Yeah- she said, whilst lifting up her t-shirt to show me some bible-related tattoos.
Slowly, I got to believe her, that she was actually being serious.
-I don't want to sound rude but I want to ask you... do you never feel any desire? How do you turn it off? You don't know when your marriage is going to happen after all- I realised alcohol was kicking in, and that I couldn't stop looking at her exceptionally well-shaped body. To be religious, she was dressed very slutty.
-It's weird, you know, because you're such an attractive girl- I said, now going for it. Alba wasn't there, and Rey wouldn't have said anything. I felt warmth all over my body suddenly, excited at the idea of hitting on someone else.
I wasn't sure I was doing the right thing though. Apart from countless dramas and arguments in the hostel, she never really treated me wrong.
-Thanks, you're lovely, like most Italian men I should say. This is the guy I'm dating by the way, we've been together for about a year now, and he understands I can't have sex before the marriage. He is bearing it all with so much patience, he's so adorable- she said with dreamy eyes, losing me. She was showing me a few pictures from her phone where her and a guy were close to each other, hugging or at dinner, clearly looking like a couple. She wasn't just lying to reject me at least.
-He's been ok for over a year without sex? A real keeper- I said, now hopeless to get anything from her.

-He's Italian like you, from Naples though- he zoomed on a picture where I could see him better. He looked fit, and also like a nice guy. I didn't know if I could really say that that guy made a great catch in his life. The loyalty and integrity of his girlfriend was impressive, not to mention her look, but if it was true that he had been a year without sex, I also had to admit I didn't envy him to the slightest.
I met Rey a few minutes later, realising he hadn't had any luck either.
We walked home.

In the next days, the hostel was looking more and more christmassy, with a small fully decorated fir by the corner and lots of bright coloured balls all around the walls. Even the background music in the loudspeaker was playing the usual commercial music with some Christmas versions, just like in cafes all over London.
One afternoon, I was walking through Endell Street, near Covent Garden running some errands when I was surprised by Lisa's name appearing on the screen of my phone.
I hadn't deleted her, but at the same time, I had almost forgotten about her.
A strange feeling I didn't fully comprehend took over me right then. Did I really want to take that call?
-Hello?- I picked up.
-Hey Domenico- her voice sounded very shy.
-Hi- I decided to just wait for her to speak.
-Did you decide what to do? Are you going to Berlin?- she asked me.
It didn't make any sense, the fact that she was calling me after about a month at least. She probably just wanted to hear my voice.
-Oh, well, you know, I've actually managed to take that fine to court, so I'm going to have to wait for that. My hearing is in January, so it can't be before that at least. I think I'll be able to get them to reduce my fine since I'm right and they're wrong- I stopped. I didn't want to talk too much.
-I understand- she sounded bad, worse than the usual bad.
-Are you ok Lisa? Is there a reason why you called? You can tell me anything if you need- I replied. I owed it to her.

-I'm feeling like dropping uni. It's too hard, I'm struggling too much and I don't want to tell my parents about it. They paid for it and I'm so sorry to fail them... I also know my mother would immediately drive to visit me, they would both worry, I don't know what to do- she sounded desperate. Probably one of her extreme lows that threw her in devastating mental conditions, at times making her wish to die.
-Ok, look, calm down please. I know how you feel. I know you struggle, but think about it, everyone struggles too. You have less knowledge than others right now, but they all started from scratch and now they're good. There is no reason to believe you won't be just as good as them- I hated to hear she was in such state again.
-I know, but I also feel lonely. I feel like I've lost you- she added with a very weak voice.
-What? Well, yeah, you are the one who left me, and it was about a month ago, just in case you don't remember it- I said, maybe too harsh, although I tried to sound just factually cold.
She didn't reply for a minute, but I could hear she was still there from the sound of her breath.
-Are you dating anyone?- she asked me then.
-Lisa, it doesn't matter. I'm not going to disappear from your life if you need me. If you need to talk to someone, I'm here, you know that-
She sighed, then spoke again.
-But you are with a girl now?-
I stopped for a second. I had to be honest with her.
-Yes, I am. We're just dating, but then again, if you need to talk to someone, I'm here Lisa, so this doesn't matter-
-But you don't have feelings for her, right?- she asked, hopeful, especially since she knew me quite well.
-Yes, I do- I said. I was sitting by a small step by the pavement now, rolling a cigarette, when I finally realised it. The fact that somebody asked me about it triggered my answer. I did have feelings for Alba, and that was the reason why I wasn't thinking almost at all about Lisa. Besides, life in the hostel in general was so good that it was hard to ever get negative thoughts, the atmosphere within the family simply killed any sort of negativity that could have arisen in my life.

-Lisa, I'm sorry- I said then. Her voice was freezing me, it was painful to hear.
-It's not like before- Lisa managed to say whilst sobbing hard.
-What? What is not like before?- I was getting a bit upset. -It was you that left me!- I exclaimed. A part of me was enjoying it, but I was committed to challenge that, and let kindness win.
-I didn't know you were going to move on so quickly- she said, desperate.
-Well, first of all, I live in London, and secondly, it could have happened to you before, don't you think? It's just a coincidence- I tried to calm her down with logic.
-I just...- she suddenly stopped, unable to talk.
We waited one, or maybe two minutes in silence, before I spoke again. I could hear she was still there.
-Look, I can stop dating her if you want. If that can make you feel better, I'll do that until you move on too. Then, we can let this go together- I said, without meaning it.
I certainly wasn't going to, but she could have never found out after all, and the thought of being able to help her as much as I could was good to me.
-No, well, you don't have to do this, but I'm glad you're there for me- she said eventually, relieved.
-Of course I am. Now, you should try to relax- I said, and she chuckled.

One of those nights, I found my way to introduce myself to a French girl who had just arrived at the hostel.
She was tall with dark long wavy hair, quite pretty, although not my type. I noticed she was sitting alone at a table behind one of ours, and I was the first one to talk to her.
I didn't like seeing people alone, and I knew how difficult it could have been for many, to introduce themselves to a table full of people who were already friends with each other.
-What's your name?- I asked in French, also because her English was terrible.
-Ella, yours?- she replied, shy.
She sat down at our table, next to Adam, who was now back at the hostel after having problems with his previous home,

and all the others. Meanwhile, I noticed Alba eyed her real badly.
Ella's integration in the group that night was very quick, and her confidence in speaking English seemed to be growing. She was there for that reason primarily after all.
Later on, Luigi and I, followed by Ella, were going outside for a cigarette when I heard Alba running towards me all of a sudden.
-Domenico?-
-Yes?-
-Kiss me- said Alba, sitting on the central table of the common room, the nearest one to the exit door.
I felt like Ella could have been a potential target for the future, and I wanted to start working on that. Alba was going on holiday to Malaga for about three weeks over Christmas time, which would have left me some time to maybe achieve something, but I had to be careful.
I didn't have my mind clear on that anyway, although I certainly appreciated that Ella was very friendly. For all I knew, I wanted Ella to know I was available, just in case, even though I didn't think anything was going to happen.
-What?- I replied, unhappy.
-Kiss me Domenico!- she insisted, Luigi and Ella were looking at me now.
Alba got her kiss and gave Ella a satisfied look.

It wasn't just then though. Alba often showed insecurities and jealous attitude about our story. Once, Luigi and I were talking to two German girls in the hostel, which we then invited to have beers with us in the common room, with Alba looking at us the whole time until she made a move to the table and required to help us pour the beers.
-That's not how you pour beer into a glass. Let me show you- she said whilst trying to take the beer can from my hand.
-Don't worry Alba- I was there mainly to be Luigi's wingman since he still wasn't as skilled as someone like Rey, for example.
-Domenico, let me do this, I work in a pub- her and Angela had been working in a pub in Covent Garden for about a week by then.

-It's ok Alba, I know you work in a pub, but the girls here are Germans, they probably know better than you how to serve a beer- I said, making the girls laugh.
I was glad to see her, but I needed her to go so that Luigi and I could work on that, for him, and maybe even for me too. Visibly angry, she ran to the kitchen where she met Angela, busy with her usual vegetable mix salad.
-Do you know what happened this time?- she shouted to her friend in the busy kitchen. Angela wasn't surprised to see her upset apparently, and I appreciated she only got mad at Luigi and never at me. Whether that was related to the fact I had a story with Alba, or to mutual genuine respect, I didn't know and couldn't figure it either.
-What is wrong with you? See how crazy this looks? In front of those girls?- I followed her and I was also shouting.
I was slightly amused by all of that, appreciating her jealousy, but I also recognised that what was happening was insane.
-Do you know what respect is?- she shouted at me, her face was red out of fury.
-Right, I'm out of here- I said, and went back to Luigi's table, still hearing her shouts from the kitchen.
I saw her few minutes later by the sofas area, crying with Angela who was trying to calm her down. Alba often proved to have no mental stability. She was smart and sensitive, but had little to no mood management whatsoever. The smallest sparkle could inflame the whole room in a second anytime she was around.

Meanwhile, the conversations between Matt, Luigi and I had become so good in quality that our nights together in Queen Square became a routine, forcing me and Luigi to adjust our day clocks to the one of Matt, which was completely messed up.
-Germans are the best at building trains, well, not only them, but everything in general. The world owes them a lot. Did you know that London's tube trains are built by German engineering experts?- he mentioned Germany and engineering at every occasion, as if such statements were requested during each break and changes of topic. Luigi and I

were too polite to tell him that yes, we knew that well by then, but we listened to him with pleasure.
-The Germans dropped silent bombs over London during the Second World War. Doodlebugs, they were silent, you wouldn't hear a thing until they touched the ground- Matt always found a way to put engineering in between our history conversations. We often ended up talking about the Second World War, one of the greatest pioneers of engineering of all kinds.
I was also enjoying Samir's presence a lot. He would often drive his car from his place near Argyle Square to Russell Square, picked us up and brought us somewhere dark where we could be covered from the cold and just smoke weed all night. Socially speaking, they were very fulfilling times, although I was unhappy I picked up the habit of smoking weed again.
Regarding me and Alba, we were back to normal after the episode of the beers.
-We should do that again, just like last time, before I go to Spain- she suggested once.
-Yes, that works for me. Hopefully a closer hotel this time- I said, then figuring that the only ones affordable for us were in East London for that moment.
We were sitting together by the sofas that afternoon. In the meantime, Rey was with us and was now very good friend with both girls, and they were enjoying a lot of talks together, since they were well connected with him. His and Luigi's attempts of getting Angela were to be considered failed though, just like it was everyone else's case. Angela was just impossible to get.

By mid-December, Alba was leaving England to spend Christmas with her family in Spain.
Her flight was in the late evening, and we all decided to spend our day with her, who unsurprisingly became very emotional about it and cried a few times.
The hostel was a great place when somebody was leaving. We did our best for someone to feel loved until their departure, although to different extents. It all depended on how much people liked you, and drama was not uncommon within the

family, especially after the recent arrival of more people and their conflictual personalities.
Angela and Alba would often confabulate stuff about people. Things like "Diego never really buys stuff to share with others, but he likes to take ours every time" or "I don't like Ella, I see her offering it to everyone" were normal things I used to get whispered into my ears.
-She has a boyfriend in France- I said to Alba once.
-I don't care Domenico, I'm a woman, I understand- she said, more out of jealousy than anything. In fact, Ella was indeed engaged in visible teasing ways with most guys, but not really allowing anyone in her bed. I often received messages from her in the middle of the night, messages that could have easily been interpreted with flirting, although never explicit enough. I found out later on that she was texting multiple guys at the same time and not just me.
Luigi's attitude would in general cost him some problems with girls.
Ella slapped him a few times for getting a bit touchy, to which he tried to defend himself by blaming it on her teasing habits.
I often defended him too, which started to create some tensions also between me and her, and in response to that, the hostel began to create sides and people started picking them according not only to their ideals, but mostly to the social possibilities and the popularity that some of us enjoyed compared to others.
This though, was a minor problem, since most of the times gossips would just stay harmless and everyone's attitude towards others remained positive overall.
I didn't like to think about what would have happened if the number of toxic people in the hostel was to increase.
All I understood about it, was that a few selfish people could spoil a whole community of generous-minded ones. A bunch of bad actions and evil words could throw plenty of people in an uncomfortable situation, forcing them eventually to either leave or become more reserved, or even to shape their personality as well, deciding to play their game.
The main problem though was that some of us would listen to the gossiper and carefully start making sure to say the right

things, or at least nothing that they might have eventually gossiped to someone else.
In my opinion, the one and only thing to do with gossipers was to kick them out of the family, but most others didn't see it that way. I personally hated to pass by some tables and hear any sentences starting with "he" or "she" with a low, almost whispering voice and heads that had a quick look around before beginning their judgements, carefully heard by a bunch of weak cunts that were afraid of the person who was spitting poison out of their mouth, rather than being indignant.
-How is your friend doing? What are his intentions? What about these two?- lost in my thoughts, I didn't realise I could hear Angela asking Matt and Luigi in a jokey tone about me and Alba, which caused me to freeze instantly.
-Well, I wouldn't say he's always the same person. I think he's actually ready for a relationship- I heard Matt replying with the same jokey tone that hid a truth.
In one of our night chats, the guys asked me whether I was just playing with Alba as I did with others, when I decided to tell them the truth, that I wanted Alba and that I didn't need anyone else. Now, Matt was communicating it to Angela.
Later on that night, Matt and I took Alba to the same bus stop where we took Charlotte the day she left.
Alba and I kissed one last time before she got on her bus, and then she left on her way to Victoria Coach Station.

Over the next days, I managed to increase my working activities, becoming more and more active and serious about my job.
-Good, I'm glad to see some more discipline from you- said Claudio, to which I had told how hard it was for someone who could choose his shifts to actually choose any shifts at all.
I was working during breakfast for a couple of hours, typically between 7 and 9.30, then back to the hostel to either take a nap or get food, depending on how I had treated myself the previous day.
I would get back on my bicycle for lunch time and office breaks, then back to the hostel to work on my chess

studying, and then dinner time at work, my favourite and also most profitable time to be online.
I was determined to earn 100 pounds per day, which was basically possible, but quite hard actually.
Sometimes I did earn that, but that affected my next day, since my legs started complaining for the mistreatment. Eventually, I decided to call myself satisfied with making about 400 pounds a week, the maximum I could get if I wanted to keep my social life standards high enough.
What was making it harder though, was that in those days I wasn't really in the mood for anything, since I was experiencing a low due to the fact that Alba wasn't talking to me at all.
I wrote her about once a day and tried to have conversations, but she always dismissed my attempts with a quick reply, which reminded me of what I used to do with Jemma, and within days, I ended up in the same vicious circle that trapped me each time I had an unhealthy management of my feelings for my dates.
I checked when she was online the last time, questioned what reasons there could have been for her not texting back, felt relieved each time I saw her name on my screen and disappointed when I realised her words didn't encourage any conversation to start.
I began thinking about what could have been my best strategy to deal with that.
Unlike in the past, this didn't hit me that hard, although I couldn't deny my frustration was growing, also because I felt that Alba was with someone else. More often than not, in her last days before leaving to Spain, I often caught her chatting with a guy, got his name in my head and found him appearing on her social media a lot. Quite hypocritical, I thought, that she acted very jealous with me when she was in London and now she was doing whatever she wanted in Spain.
I concluded I had to find out.
-Alba? What are you up to? You're not really talking to me, and I was wondering what happened- I texted one morning after finishing a delivery near Hyde Park Corner.
I went offline and parked my bike to have a cigarette. I knew I was going to go on a break soon and I thought that was the

perfect moment for me to finally set myself free from the low of those days.
-Hi Domenico, yes sure, I understand. I'm just very busy lately- she texted one of the world's most popular lies for such occasions.
Busy doing what? You said you're watching Netflix all the time.
I started texting this, then deleted it, and texted something else. I had to be straight-forward and not waste my time. I felt like I was getting old for that kind of stuff, but also too attracted to her to just let it go like that.
-Right, I just wanted to tell you that I'm not sleeping with anyone here and I'm just waiting for you to come back- I was now looking at the screen of my phone, miserably waiting for an answer.
How did I get from someone like Lisa to someone like Alba?
-Domenico- she texted at some point.
I opened the phone right away, needy.
-Do you know that I don't live in England? I have a university to attend here, my future is in Spain- she wrote.
-My plan was to just come back there in January for a few more weeks, and then leave. Forever- she added then. A full minute was what it took me to process what she had written. I was shocked by that. Not only I didn't know it, but I also had to forcefully resign.
-Right, I understand. I didn't know it, or maybe you mentioned it and I forgot it. Well, this changes everything I guess- I wrote down, hoping to bring the conversation back to normal. I felt like something inside of me was boiling cold somehow.
-You are crazy, only few days that I'm gone and you've totally lost your mind- she texted then.
I thought about it for a minute, then replied.
-No, I'm not, I just didn't know you were going to live in Spain- I was feeling annoyed by her words.
-I couldn't think of anything different with you, I can't start something if I can see the end of it- she wrote. I could see the app was indicating to me she was typing constantly.

-It's ok Alba, you don't have to say this. I appreciate it, but let's drop it here, since it's pointless- now I just wanted her to stop texting.
-No, now we have to talk- she texted. I had a feeling that she was enjoying it.
-You're crazy, I can't believe what you've told me- she wrote once again. I saw she was still typing when I decided I had had enough of that.
-You don't need to insult me- I texted. -I made a mistake, I thought I felt something and I decided to let you know. I thought this stuff could happen, but I don't really believe it anymore- I added, only reading my last message after sending it and regretting doing it straight away. It didn't make much sense.
-Well, it's over now- she wrote back, leaving me fairly disappointed.
-And see you in January- she finished it.
The cloudy sky didn't promise any improvement for the following hours, and I was sure it was going to rain soon. I headed home.

On Christmas day, Claudio, Luigi, Riccardo, Leonardo and I were hanging out in the common room. Some family members were in their own countries, some had other plans outside of the hostel for that day. All of us were doing our best to make it a proper dinner, spending some extra money and taking extra care about the look of the table, taking all wine glasses available in the kitchen for ourselves, chatting and taking it easy.
That was when Luigi and I noticed a girl who was working on her laptop by the sofas area and decided to approach.
-Hi- we sat down at her table. The girl replied politely and with a friendly smile. She had some olive skin tone and was wearing a wool blue hat that covered most of her very short hair.
-What are you up to here on your own?- we asked her.
-Just trying to finish some stuff on my laptop. I'm actually supposed to be enjoying a few days of vacation- she added and chuckled.
-You should join us, we're having dinner soon-

She thought about it for a second, then accepted.
After the dinner, Luigi and I got to know her better. She was studying in Belgium and was going to return there soon. She loved weed, could do with alcohol, had a passion for arts and told us about her anti-conformist family in the US. In no time, Luigi and her found out they had a lot in common when it came to music taste.
Personally, I had no knowledge of indie bands since I spent most of my life listening and studying classical music pieces. I suddenly felt like an intruder in the middle of so much knowledge and names of bands I never heard of, nothing mainstream.
The three of us standing in the dark alley outside the hostel were slowly getting high, and with alcohol, also flirty.
I felt that Sami would have considered my flirting a tricky thing to deal with in a dark place after offering her weed, alcohol and greatly cooked pasta.
I didn't want her to think our kindness was transactional, but I was also aware of the fact that within a few minutes, I would have lost both of them.
-Guys, we should hang out in our room- I said at some point.
By coincidence, we were all in room 51 that night.
-Alright, sure- said the American.
She enjoyed our company, especially Luigi's, and I was looking for a binding experience to happen between me and him. We were very good friends since the beginning, our friendship was growing stronger, and I liked it.
We walked to the room, still high when I saw Luigi walking in the direction of his bed. Where was he going?
I knew it, he was too shy, I concluded, now feeling a growing rush of excitement at the idea of getting her just for myself, although I still wasn't sure about her intentions.
I found her next to my bed, standing, still slow in her movements due to the highness. She looked somehow delicate, her flexible curvy body with mine in the dark of the room by the wall. She smiled, seeming perfectly aware of what was happening. I had no doubts she handled weed better than I did, but now I needed to find Luigi, I owed this to him.

-Come- I whispered to her, leading her hand in hand to the middle of the room, where Luigi was standing, getting ready to go to bed.
Finally, he made a move. Behind us, Riccardo was having the time of his life laughing on the floor, looking at the three of us naked on the floor until an Asian guy woke up and complained about the noise.

The next day, I was sitting in the common room with Luigi, recalling the moments of the previous night when I received an unexpected message.
-Ahahah, I hear news- Alba had just texted. My heart pounded when I realised it.
-How are you?- she added.
I thought for a few seconds, then replied.
-What do you want?-
She typed and deleted something a few times before finally sending a message, all whilst I kept my eyes on the screen.
-Well, now I guess it wouldn't make sense to talk about us-
-Who told you? And again, what do you want?- I wanted to be as rude as possible.
-I don't have anything to tell you. Have a good day- I added then.
Two minutes later, she texted back.
-Three days ago you were telling me that you loved me, and now you're already with someone else. This is nothing but funny-
I left it like that, and decided to not text back. Her reaction was childish, and I knew I had done nothing wrong.

By the end of the year, the family in the hostel had reached a great size.
There were many long-term stayers, making up to about one quarter of all available spaces and one third of the people that typically slept there on average.
Rey, Luigi, Matt and I were ready to celebrate New Year's Eve in Primrose Hill, hoping to get more people to join us too. We met two Dutch and one Asian girl who were staying in London for the time being.

Luigi was quickly getting much better at taking initiative and hitting on girls. He targeted the blonde, tall Dutch one, the one that had long straight blonde hair and blue eyes, just like anyone would imagine a Dutch girl to look like. Meanwhile, I was chatting with her friend, slightly shorter and fit brown-haired girl with a tanned skin.
-Maartje? I feel you've just found love tonight-
-Sorry, I prefer guys who wear suits- she bantered back.
The hostel presented some real characters, and all of them gave a unique addition to the family that filled up all necessary requirements for the whole place to be complete. We literally lacked no kind of people.
We had chefs with criminal records, a guy who claimed to be extremely wealthy and worked as a kitchen porter in a place that didn't allow him to be off on New Year's Eve, a bunch of guys who worked on Rick shows during the nights and came back at dawn, satisfied and often shitfaced.
We had chess players from beginners to some that had challenged grandmasters, some professionals, engineers specialised in electronics, computers and construction, hospitality workers, a guitar player and a full-time escort with a gambling problem. We came from all continents, spoke the same language with some differences in skills, had different religious beliefs, from atheists to Muslims and from Christians to a few Jews.
-Multiculturalism just don't work, every culture has a tendency of trying to prevail over the others- said Patrick, a conservative Irish man who defended Brexit against me and Luigi in heated debates almost on a daily basis. He was Joseph's number one challenger in political discussions, although the two tended to get along and proved mutual respect on several occasions.
-Doesn't this hostel prove you that multiculturalism works?- I said, with Luigi crossing his arms and putting his usual grin of debates on his face.
-It's because we're all bound by a mutual reason. We're all here thanks to capitalism. We're all here to make money and that's why we adjust to the British values, but imagine this place without the economic security and employability it offers to everyone. If we weren't all taking advantage of

British welfare and exploiting the NHS, lots of us would focus on imposing their culture on others- he said, the usual calm voice.
He was respectful in debates, never interrupted and always gave a chance to respond, never shouted, not even once.
He made a few reasonable points that often blocked me for a bit, until Luigi, less moderate than I was, would usually come to help me.
The second last night of the year, I spent it with Rey, who had made tickets to watch the Millwall game in the Den stadium in south-east London.
We had fun not only enjoying a game at the stadium, but also analysing the spirit of the fans.
A much less civilised atmosphere than the one at Stamford Bridge, some Millwall fans befriended Rey and I in the half time and told us they were flattered by seeing two foreigners supporting their team for the night.
A very conservative streets-like environment with people that were extremely friendly towards us, but probably wouldn't have hesitated to act the very opposite way if we were to have said we were supporting their opponents.

The last night of 2016 felt like a recap of the whole year to me. All what we planned from the morning to the night had turned out to happen in completely unpredictable ways, ending up chaotic and fun. The hostel was a place where everything moved faster, where even the simplest plan, such as having lunch together could become anything else but that, and if the plan made in the morning concerned an idea on what to do in the evening, chances were, it was going to change by the time evening arrived.
By the moment we had reached Primrose Hill, the group that left the hostel was spread out to the point almost all of us had lost each other, some of us too drunk to even pick up the phone.

January 2017

I was just as happy to be reunited with Rey as I was unhappy to hear that he was going to leave soon.

-Things aren't going very well here, I hate this city- he muttered every now and then.
-What do you hate about this city? Seriously, you've got friends and a huge amount of job opportunities, it's all available here. If you can't make it in London, that's because you're lazy- I often told him.
-That's not true, I hate the people here, they are rude- he always found different excuses to justify the fact that he just didn't want to work.
-It's because you earn so much by doing so little that now you can't go back to work just to earn the minimum wage. You had to know that your work is a temporary thing in life, it cannot last forever. You should have saved everything you made and now you would have been able to invest it- my thoughts always made him uncomfortable to the point he would often stand up and just walk away, at times swearing against me.
-I'm not a slave like you- he said with a grin and loud tone.
-Then stop asking me for money every time- I shouted back, often with people around us turning their heads towards us, wondering whether we were being serious or not and why we were shouting in the middle of the common room.
That afternoon, I was in a break for lunch in the common room when I noticed Matt by the sofas.
-What are you doing?-
-Fixing my shoes- Matt answered without looking at me. He was using tape to fix the sole of his shoes back with their upper side.
-Couldn't you just buy new shoes?- I asked him, amused.
-I'm actually tight on money, I need to moderate my expenses as much as I can if I want to survive. Things aren't looking very well for me. It seems like British companies don't want to hire Australian engineers. I think they're just prioritising British engineers, which is fair enough I guess-
-Are you actually applying for work or just watching stuff on your phone all the time?- I felt compelled to remind him that his attitude wasn't going to take him anywhere.
-Right, if you've come here to just piss me off, I don't need it. I've been awake all night, can't bear you yelling at me now-

-Guys, let's take a quick holiday, all of us- I said all of a sudden just to change topic, getting a completely unexpected response.
Matt and Rey looked at me, not saying a word, but looking very interested apparently.
-I want to go to Denmark. I've never been there and I know that the girls are the best in the world- I said, hoping at least one of them would follow me. I wasn't going to go there on my own of course.
Rey seemed to like the idea, whilst Matt was taking his time before choosing how he felt about it.
I knew that to change his mind, I needed to play with pressure, so I invested my energy in getting Rey to feel even more enthusiastic about it.
-Right guys, I'm just going to go through the tickets offers, and if there are some cheap tickets, well, I'm telling you, I'm going there. Are you coming with me?-
Rey didn't reply, but sat next to me and faced the screen of my laptop.
It didn't take long for things to become interesting.
We figured we could have reached Copenhagen and come back to London for less than 50 pounds right on the closest weekend.
Rey took about a minute and then concluded he was in. Matt was now looking at us, appearing scared to miss out on some fun.
-Are you guys actually not going to involve me? I mean, if you go there, then get me a ticket, I'll give you cash now- he rushed to our table.
I knew it would have happened. Matt wouldn't have moved a finger to get anything done, but if he realised that the people that were close to him were up to something, he would have acted even just out of fear of missing out. I also knew though, that if we had decided to do nothing, he would have been even happier.

And so it was, that the three of us were travelling to Copenhagen after planning it only two days before. Luigi eventually joined too out of the same pressure that Matt felt.

In fact, I doubted he would have booked if it had been just me to suggest that to him.
-Why didn't you say anything? You were going there without me- he felt really worried whilst he sat on his closest sofa and booked a ticket for the same flight from his phone.
We reached Denmark in the early afternoon of the first weekend of the month.
We didn't take too long to reach Handersen Boulevard and check in into our hostel, a massive skyscraper with a very fancy and tidy look.
The hostel looked much better than ours, but that was also because we didn't go for the cheapest, but rather for one that was cheap enough whilst being good and central.
January's weather in Denmark was even colder than I could imagine. We couldn't walk for a minute straight without complaining about it, exception made for Rey, who never felt cold for some inexplicable reason.
Eventually, when we were in, everybody exclaimed how relieved they were to finally feel the indoors warmth.
Walking in those streets and then getting somewhere felt like surviving a blizzard, I thought whilst we got into the elevator and made a move towards our room. In the evening, the four of us left together and reached the closest supermarket by the other side of the river.
Copenhagen felt a lot like Moscow. Tremendously cold, but not unbearable.
-I can't drink vodka, I get very aggressive, let's not buy vodka- Matt was insisting when we were by the cashiers.
I found it funny that he never looked upset even though he often was, which was due to the fact that he was a nerd in the first place, and suffered from epilepsy in the second place. Keeping calm was key for his well-being, and weed and some pills he regularly took were contributing to keep things under control, at least for some relatively long periods of time.
-Who's going to cook? I hope it's not Domenico- said Rey once we were in the huge kitchen in the basement of the hostel.
-Yeah, I should do it- said Luigi.

-Domenico is the worst at cooking, and it's weird considering he's Italian- Rey began the mocking when I called it over already.
-Enough- I look at Rey challenging him.
-But it's true Dom- him and Luigi were now laughing at me again.
-Should I remind you the shit risotto that Luigi made few weeks ago in the hostel? He cooked it with cold water, can you believe it?-
-Yeah, that's how you're supposed to do it in fact, you know nothing about cooking- Luigi was being serious now. He could escalate and get angry very fast.
-Is that why nobody wanted to eat it? Because it was supposed to be like stones and break people's teeth?-
-Enough now, everyone, shut up. I'm waiting for food- Matt was sitting at our table now.
He never made any effort in such moments. Anything that had to be organised for the team always needed to be organised by somebody else.
Since the day I met him, he would always buy two pre-cooked dishes only, tortellini with meat or rice with chicken. He would then go back to the hostel, microwave them for a few minutes and eat them sitting away from everyone, and most importantly from Diego, just to avoid his constant requests for food.
-Right, anyway, we forgot the olive oil, we can't do it without it- I noticed.
After a quick search around, we found no one had any in the shelves.
-Excuse me, could I please ask you whether you have some olive oil?- I asked the only other person in the kitchen, an elderly man sitting by the other side of the massive room.
-Well, no I don't have any, and anyway, you should have bought some if you really needed it, don't you think?- the old man said, sounding very annoying to me.
-Yeah, alright man, listen, I don't need your philosophical comment now- the previous state I was in after the comments I was receiving about my skills in the kitchen paved the way for me to just adjust the way I dealt with

them towards a ruder one, the only possible one in such moments.
The old man stood up and seemed to be coming towards me with a threatening expression on his face when I decided to keep it going.
-Fucking idiot- I called him, now angry.
-Leave it man!- the three of them approached me and separated me from the old man, apologising to him on my behalf.
-You always do these stupid things. You're so rude man- Rey was particularly annoyed about it, as if I did such things everyday.
-You didn't need to talk like that- Matt told me when we were heading back to our room on the eighteenth floor.
-Neither did he- I said, stuck with my opinion.

We were getting ready, one at a time using the bathroom, when Matt claimed to use it before me. I accepted, although I knew he was slow, which was a problem, also considering that there were no toilets outside the rooms.
-Punctually, as it always happens, I need to shit guys, how long do you think he's going to take?- I complained to Rey and Luigi, who were amused by what was happening.
Eventually, after begging Matt to get out and getting no reply, I saw no other options available.
-Right guys, just don't tell Matt about it- I said, and knowing they were laid back people, I took the rubbish basket and placed it underneath me in the middle of the room, with the two of them now bending down because of laughing too hard, although unfortunately, that didn't work well.
I didn't hit the target due to a miscalculation in my position on top of the basket, and as a result, half of my stuff just fell down to the floor.
I began working effortlessly to remove it, with two guys in the room that seemed to be having the time of their lives.
-Can you imagine if another guest was in our room with us?- Luigi suggested a scenario to Rey, who now couldn't control himself laughing.
-Guys, what the hell is this smell?- Matt said as soon as he left the bathroom.

Trying to hide it would have been pointless, which forced me to try and stay serious myself. If Matt had seen that I was taking it seriously, he might have understood, but that also didn't go well.
-What? Are you out of your mind?- in a second, Matt was fuming.
-Matt, calm down, it's not what it looks like- Rey and Luigi were crying now, unable to stop.
-Tell me then, what should stop me from punching your face?- for the first time ever, I saw Matt angry. At least now I knew something that he truly didn't accept.
I stood still, unable to find something to say to defend myself.
Matt swore a lot and confessed to being as disgusted as he had ever been in his life for a few minutes before he finally seemed to calm down and come up with the most mature statement.
-I'm not going out with you. Sort this out immediately, go buy some cleaning product or something, and get rid of this right now-
Luckily, the reception was able to help me, and in less than half hour, the problem was solved and the guys were ready to go out, all except Matt.
-Right Matt, are you coming or not?- Rey asked him when he was ready.
-No, I don't care anymore. I didn't want to travel with you guys. I didn't want to wake up early today, I'm staying here tonight. I may go out tomorrow, leave me alone now- he lay down in bed, firm in his decision, making me feel guilty to some extent, but also already quite drunk and slightly careless.
He overreacted, in my opinion at least. I decided to blame it all on the fact he always woke up grumpy if he hadn't had a good rest.

That night, we walked to Gothersgade, an area of the city centre where, as we were told, there were plenty of open late bars. Within one hour, Matt was with us again, ready to party after agreeing on not talking about what happened ever again.

I was glad to be with them, I felt like I couldn't have had better trip mates.

What I enjoyed the most about them was that they were genuine people, they never acted. Apart from Rey, they never wore fancy clothes, never used skin cream or hair gel, never said things they didn't mean and not really wasted any chance. When we entered the bar, I could tell that the Danes noticed that we were foreigners right away.

-Chicks look stunning here- Matt pointed out, and he was right. They were seriously beyond the average.

If countries were to be ranked by the average female look, Denmark would be first with some distance from the second placed country, whatever that was.

We were between the most stereotyped types of Danish people I could think of. Most men were taller than me and Luigi, some even taller than Matt, some just as tall as Rey. Most girls were blonde, with few brown headed ones, no brunettes as far as I could see in the dark and also because my sight wasn't the best when I was drunk.

-Kissing a Danish one is just as good as banging any other girl in the world. It's the equivalent of it, I would say- I approached Luigi and Matt outside the bar for a smoke and for some fresh air.

-Definitely agree- they seemed sincere.

I couldn't believe how much easier it was to get a bit physical with girls in there than it was in most other places I had ever been to.

-There is an inflation of beauty here. The fact that the average girl looks incredible here goes on to lower the standards in the men they can choose between- Matt observed, nerdily.

-Your observation is right, in fact, I might have just made out with an average one, I haven't seen all of them- I said.

-Exactly, otherwise she wouldn't have kissed you, don't you think?- Matt mocked me.

I was happy that things were already fine between us. I feared I had crossed the line that afternoon, but he had too many good reasons to ignore what happened, at least if he counted on enjoying the rest of the trip.

The next day and night went exactly the same way, and by the end of the week, the four of us were landed back in London. I was fully satisfied by the trip and the fact it definitely constituted a binding experience between me and some of my world's favourite people.
We didn't visit anything, but rather just drank and partied. We all agreed that the terrible cold in the streets of the town was a perfect excuse to sleep the morning off and just wake up in the late afternoon.
What was disturbing the perfection of that moment for me though, was the awareness that soon enough, I was going to see Alba.
When someone from my group in Copenhagen took a picture of me whilst in bed naked and sent it to the Facebook group chat where Angela and Alba were, the first called herself outraged and exited the group, with the second one following a minute after.
This was to me a good reason to believe that things were unsolvable between me and her, although over the following week, I decided to send a message to Alba, letting her know that a pack for her had arrived at the hostel after Francesca had told me.
I noticed then that she didn't sound upset or anything, also because she then mentioned she was looking forward to being reunited with all of us.
I didn't know what day she was going to be back exactly, but that morning, I randomly happened to be the first one she saw.
I was cycling through Brunswick Square when I heard her shouting.
-Domenico!-
She was on the pavement, waiting for me with her arms wide open and a big smile on her face, to which I responded in the same way.
We went through a very quick necessary small talk for such moments, then I left almost immediately, saying I was very busy. She didn't seem any reluctant to see that conversation ending either.

It was clear that we both didn't know how to act in front of each other. I wasn't expecting to see her just like that, and my heart was pounding.
I couldn't even say I liked seeing her at all.

As I expected, having Alba around was unpleasant.
The first night, I got back to the hostel after a long shift at work, hoping that she was not around.
Anything would have worked, I thought, but unfortunately she was there in the common room as usual, laughing hard and loud with others from the family.
-Hi Domenico- she greeted me, adjusting her voice from loud to almost inaudible when I passed by to go to the kitchen.
-Hi Alba- a half smile of my face and rushed pace to show her I wanted to stay as far as possible from her, even though that wasn't true at all.
Within the next days, I gradually realised that for the time she was going to stay around, I had no hope of taking her out of my head.
I knew she was going to leave by the first or second week of February, which meant about one month to go. One month where everything could have happened, from having to see her with someone else, either a stranger or a friend, to just being able to see her and having our future memories spoiled by the last days spent in an uncomfortable atmosphere.
-Does anyone know whether the Spanish girl is single?- Zak once asked whilst sitting at the chess table with all of us.
-No, well, she used to be with me- Zak and I weren't friends, we barely spoke to each other, but I was hoping he wouldn't hit on her. Not that it was going to take that long for Alba to get someone else, but at least I didn't want it to happen with one of the people I had around.

By the second half of January, Luigi and I were the first to notice the arrival of a new girl in the hostel.
Her name was Celia, Spanish, quite petite, with long wavy dark brown hair, and a naturally teasing expression on her face.
Luigi introduced himself the quickest and immediately began his attack on her.

After a couple of hours spent talking with each other, we figured she would have soon become one of us. She was, as we commented, totally aligned with our personalities.
-Right, I'll take you upstairs- he said to her, giving me one of his grins before walking up the stairs towards her room.
He came back after a few minutes, bragging about how he kissed her.
-Cool, you're getting good at this- I commented, slightly jealous for the quick conquest, although I probably didn't feel the same way he did. I had to admit Celia was definitely attractive, but that was Luigi's catch.
Meanwhile, my strategy of hanging out in the common room as less as possible was working somehow well, even though things weren't at all as good as they were during my trip to Denmark or during Christmas time even.
Alba's presence was by default a problem. Bumping into her every now and then was the worst thing, whilst seeing her flirting with guys was what sent me straight outside to wait for Matt on the freezing Queen Square usual bench, or sometimes just to bed.
The reason why I wasn't reacting to all of that, but rather playing passively, was that I knew she was going to leave eventually.
The days were going slow, and Alba, who had no problems in telling a guy she wanted sex, could have hit in any moment. For some reason though, as I was pleased to notice, she seemed to be paying attention not to do this in front of me, although I didn't know why. I often saw her sad, shamefully feeling triumphant about it.

Strangely enough, Luigi wasn't bragging about sleeping with Celia.
I didn't expect him to be mature about it, but he was actually quite cool. He was the kind of guy that bragged about achieving stuff forever, from the way he cooked to his wins in chess.
That afternoon, it was him that pushed me to introduce myself to a girl that was sitting alone by the black sofa. She looked off the clouds, a very pale skin and brunette short hair.

-She seems so depressed- Luigi spoke my mind.
He often made evil observations about people and laughed at his own words, although he was generally a very friendly and well-hearted person.
I introduced myself to her, and found out her name was Laura, from Finland.
She was pretty, although not really in my taste.
She showed me several papers with some exceptionally beautiful art on them, which she claimed to have made herself.
-You're a very talented artist- I said, honest.
Over time though, Luigi's assumption about her was kicking in inside my head and not leaving me alone.
There didn't seem to be anything wrong with her, but rather with her facial expression, or maybe with her voice tone when she told me that her favourite music piece was Beethoven's Moonlight Sonata, which made me feel like she actually was in a not very joyful mental state.
After a polite conversation, I figured she was a brilliant person, talented and smart, and so I decided I wasn't going to hit on her.
That night though, I invited her to have a dinner in the common room with Luigi and Celia.
I was glad when she accepted, also because I kind of felt in debt with her after the interesting conversation.
Later on, the four of us sat together and opened a couple of bottles of red wine. The rest of the family was spread around the hostel, with Rey deep busy in a conversation with others at the Spanish table.
The dinner was pleasant, a nice moment that almost distracted me completely from the low mood that affected most of my thoughts in those days.
At some point, when the food was over and we had drunk a few more glasses, I noticed that Laura was gradually getting closer and closer to me, with Celia and Luigi giving looks at each other amused, and then at me, as to encourage me.
What was happening?
-Are you ok?- I asked her, feeling a growing excitement.
-Yes- she replied, timidly and staring at me. She was drunk already, and I knew exactly what to do.

I couldn't see the other two at the table, but I knew they were laughing silent. Rey started calling my name out loud from the other table, also amused. Something inside of me wanted Alba to see me, something else didn't. If I was happy just as I was anytime I kissed someone new, I was also not in my best mood. I wondered what she would have done if she had found out how I felt about it.
I asked Laura to follow me to the dark alley behind Guilford Street, trying to take advantage of her drunkenness, getting once again a positive reply.
She didn't look perfectly aware of what was happening, but neither unaware, which led me to the conclusion that she was just pretending to get me pushing for it.
I checked with her how she was feeling by the time we walked there, to which she replied to be doing just fine.
I brought her to her room about half hour later.
I was overall satisfied about that night, although not yet in a completely healed state, I thought whilst reaching Matt and the others in Queen Square.

Few days later, Rey, two Spanish tourists we met and I decided to go to a club in Piccadilly area.
Since it was an Italian-Spanish night, the club offered all such nationals to enter for only two pounds, which I was really happy to take advantage of.
Unfortunately, Alba decided to join last minute, saying she will reach us at the club after her shift at a Baker Street pub was over.
-I wouldn't normally go to a place full of Italians and Spanish people, that's like one of the most boring environments I can possibly imagine- I told Rey whilst on the way there.
-The club is connected with the rest of the building. We'll enter from our cheap entry and then reach the other floors, all we need to do is our usual smoke bomb and we'll be gone, they won't notice a thing- Rey winked at me.
He was my best friend for many reasons, and that was one of them. He never cared about girls to the point of giving them a minute of his company if he didn't feel like a sexual reward would have arrived. The two Spanish girls were fun, but we

could tell they were just willing to hang out, and nothing more than that was going to happen.
Eventually, we stuck around until the moment Alba texted one of them saying she was outside the building.
-Right, I'm getting lost, see you somewhere- I said to Rey who, after making sure the girls didn't notice, also left and followed me.
Later that night, after wandering around the streets of Piccadilly for a bit longer and with no success, we got back home and found the girls already in the common room. The night wasn't any great, and the fact I could have caught Alba somewhere in the club made me want to leave earlier.
Alba was now sitting in front of Rey, next to the girls who were talking about the night as I found out after coming back from the kitchen with a cup of water.
-She had something with a guy who looked actually quite handsome- one of the girls was mocking Alba, who was smiling, complacent. She looked very attractive with her uniform from work, a tight white shirt and black trousers. Our eyes didn't cross at all during the whole conversation.
I went to bed.

In the next days, my bad mood was escalating, requiring from me more effort to fight it.
One afternoon, after a nap I took in room 50, I reacted in the worst possible way to the umpteenth call by the chess company as they asked me for some more bureaucratic stuff to fill up the necessary papers so that I could get fully employed as a chess coach.
-Right, you know what? It's been months, but this is apparently not happening. I'm sorry, but I think I should leave this. My apologies, and I wish you all the best with your work- I texted after the call.
That was it, I quit before even starting, although it wasn't my fault. It was the Italian embassy in London to be a non-functioning place where Italian citizens received no actual help from, just like it happens in the greatest majority of administration offices all around Italy.
It took one day for the Russian embassy in Notting Hill to provide me with a paper that stated I had no criminal record

developed through my staying in Moscow four years before, whilst it took about one month for the Italian embassy to even pick up the phone to just tell me they couldn't do it, which left no mystery at all in judging what country thrived more between them and why.

That night, I felt even more lonely, also because neither Matt, Luigi nor Celia were around.
Rey was with me, but he was also spending a lot of time with Alba and Angela, all of them glad to speak their own language anytime they could.
Later in the night, Rey was gone to bed and I was left alone sitting in the bench behind Alba, who was acting overemotional and angry for a reason I didn't know anything about.
-Dom, we need help- Luigi had just texted me right then, finally. I was wondering where he was.
-Latif just trapped me and Celia in the toilet. We can't come out. What can we do? I don't want to get kicked out- he said in multiple messages.
-Ella, we have a problem- I told her, the closest person to my bench.
-No, we don't have a problem- Alba blurted out, angry, to which I almost reacted impulsively and with the same challenging tone.
-Why are you talking to me like that? This is not how I usually talk to you- for some reason, I came out somehow submissive.
-Well, yeah, you don't talk to me at all- she said, frustrated.
I felt there were many things I wanted to say to respond to that, but I preferred to say nothing.
A couple of awkwardly silent minutes later, Luigi and Celia got to the living room.
-It was our first time we got caught, so they forgave us this time, but phew man, I got scared- Luigi said, and hugged me, with Celia next to him, a guilty and at the same time careless expression on her face.

My frustration in those days grew to an unbearable level. Having to see Alba around all the time, failing to become a

chess coach because of the incompetence and negligence of Italian born ambassadors, and a terrible economic situation worsened by my last trip to Denmark, all paved the way for me to accept Rey's proposal of going to the USA with him. He had been suggesting that to me many times in the previous months, but I always dismissed it, and I knew inside of me that it was never going to happen, especially in my circumstances. Those days though, were not normal circumstances after all, and I needed to travel more if I wanted to move past that story and find some balance within myself.
-Are you serious? Oh my God, this is going to be the best thing in the world!- he seemed very happy about it, and that was pleasantly contagious.
-I'll show you how to apply for visa, and hopefully you'll be all good in just few days. Now, we have to hurry though- he said. That wasn't his first time in the US.
His first trip the previous October was successful. He came back with some thousands of pounds gathered in a big sock he hid under his jacket, and now I was wondering whether I could have made some money too. What else could I possibly have to lose after all?

My hearing went much better than I thought in one of the last mornings of January. I had previously showed up at the Bromley's tribunal earlier in January just to find out my hearing had been moved to the previous day, which I found obviously very annoying.
I was looking forward to that and I had also wasted a half day of work in a moment I really needed money.
Luckily, after a phone call and an explanation, I was given another chance and that morning, a nice old judge kindly reduced my fine back to 60 pounds, just a little bit more than the price I was supposed to have paid for the original fine. I wondered if that would have happened if I hadn't immediately pleaded guilty.
Alba was the first one in the hostel to ask me about the verdict at my hearing. It was weird, since we hadn't spoken in a while, but I replied it went good, and she replied with a

smile once again, although I felt she wasn't doing real good from the expression on her face.

Later on that afternoon, I received a call from London Kings once again.

-Hi Domenico, how are you?- it was the boss of the company.
-I'm ok thanks and you? Also, I have to tell you, I'm sorry for how things went between us. Please, take my words from the other day as an act of resignation for not being able to sort out my papers, but I was in general very flattered by your interest in me- I said, hoping he had no bad feelings.
-Oh no, don't worry about it at all, I understand. The reason of my call is another one though. You see, I heard what you said the other day, and you didn't sound to be doing ok, and I also remember you mentioned you had some problems with money lately, so I wanted to ask you, is there anything I could do for you? Or maybe, do you just want to talk about anything?- he asked.

A few seconds were necessary before I could talk again. I felt shocked and had goose bumps. How could somebody be so nice? Why was he doing that?

-Oh, wow, I didn't expect this. Well... No, don't worry, I'm ok, I had some rough time but I'm working hard and I should be able to be just fine soon. I'm... grateful that you just asked me about this anyway. Thank you very much- I said.

I felt pleased. These little things often restored my entire faith in humanity just like that.

-Great! And oh, by the way, if you still need time to sort that stuff out, all I need is just one more reference, and take no rush at all, maybe, just give it one or two months, and then you can give it another try with us? What do you think?-
-Yes- I replied straight away. -It's very kind of yours- I added.

By the end of the call, I was still feeling goose bumps all over me.

-Domenico, why did you break Alba's heart?- Tomas bumped into me by the reception half hour later when I was getting ready to go online once again.
-It wasn't me Tomas, I think it's her ex- I answered. She told me a lot about him, a Spanish guy she was in a distance relationship with since the last time she was living in London,

exactly a year before. Then, after getting back to England in October, she found out he had had a girlfriend all along and kept it a secret, which meant then, that she was using me to move past her ex just like I was using her to move past Lisa. The difference though, was in what grew inside our heads after our story started.
Bad timing, I guessed, I shouldn't have taken it personally. I genuinely didn't want to feel good by seeing tears dropping from her eyes in the sofa, but yet I did, to some extent.

February 2017

With the arrival of February, the fact that my visa application was successful and that I was going to travel to Los Angeles within the first week of the month made my mood both better and worse.
Better, because I was going to finally lose sight of Alba and enjoy a trip with my best friend. Worse, because I realised, up to that point, that something inside of me was still hoping to fix things between us.
-I don't know if I'll be able to enter the US. My passport has been giving me problems for a long time by now, the microchip is faulty or something- I said at our dinner table once.
-You'll be alright mate. How long are you going to stay again?- Matt asked me, visibly concerned about me staying away for too long.
-One month, I'll be back in March- I said.
-Wow, I'm going to miss you around here- he said with a resigned tone.
-I'll miss you too, but I really need this trip to happen now- I admitted. The trip to Copenhagen was perfect, but this one was going to be even better than that.
-We have to say goodbye Domenico. I know you don't like hugs, but I'm going to forcefully give you one- Celia knew me well already. We got to know each other more and more with our countless conversations both in the hostel and in Queen Square.

I looked at the dinner table with affection. The people who were sitting there were all keen on saying bye to me properly.
I wanted to believe that they were all genuinely moved by that desire at least. I could have had lots of flaws in my personality, and I knew that some people in the hostel didn't like me, but still acted nicely out of need to keep the atmosphere within the group to a healthy level.
At that table though, there were only people who liked me, and I was sure of that. I was one of those that never created any drama in the group, and they knew it after all. Some of them liked me more, some less, but they were all genuine friends of mine, and so was I for them.
By the end of the dinner, I stood up and, after saying good night to everyone once again, I made a rushed move towards room 51 where I was sleeping, hoping that Alba, who was staring at the Christmas tree by the corner of the room, would not see me.
-Domenico- she said whilst turning around suddenly, indicating that she wasn't looking at the tree more than she was waiting to do something she would have rather avoided doing, just like me.
-Enjoy your trip- she said, and then hugged me.
-Thank you Alba, enjoy your time too- I said.
I made my way to my room, took my suitcase, checked out and reached Victoria Coach Station in the middle of the night.

My early flight was scheduled a stop in Iceland, a country I planned to visit at some point in my life, although this wasn't the right time yet since my layover only lasted two hours. Eventually, I boarded my flight to Los Angeles and reached the West Coast within half a day. Luckily, also managing to sleep for a couple of hours, which was a great score to me. I didn't have the capacity of falling asleep on airplanes, no matter how exhausted I was or how well I organised my sleeping pattern before boarding.
The queue after reaching LA airport was something unseen before. I assumed that the difference between LA and

London was based on the fact that London had more airports and was generally better organised.
After about three hours, I was finally out in the warm evening. A dark sky without clouds welcomed me in what was doubtlessly the best temperature conditions I had ever experienced in a February.
I grabbed a yellow taxi and asked my foreigner driver to take to me to La Mirada Avenue, where Rey was waiting for me. A long drive and a headache that grew during the long travel finally ended when I saw Rey standing in front of one of the most American looking buildings I could picture in my head after growing up to Hollywood made films.
-Macho!- Rey hugged me, quite unusual from him.
By that time, our only language of communication with each other was Spanish. Rey's laziness managed to lead me to get used to only speak his language, which I was also glad to do, since that was a good reason for me to keep improving.
We reached a flat by the other side of a big courtyard. Walking without jacket and seeing Rey wearing shorts gave me a feeling I couldn't describe.
The flat was small and cosy, and it had a kitchen, an oven, a fridge, a double size bed, a desk, a wardrobe, then a toilet and a shower in what was no different than London studio flats for single use, although it had to have been just as expensive, I thought.
Rey's friend was called Carlos, a south American guy who lived his whole life in the US as I could get from his accent when he introduced himself.
-Hi, nice to meet you- he shook my hand and welcomed me with a smile I was glad to return.
-We should go out tonight- said Rey. -I was waiting for you to be here Dom, I need to go out and meet some girls- he added, visibly happy to see me.
-Couldn't you go out with Carlos these days?- I asked him, joking.
-We don't have the same taste- said Carlos, a natural smile and voice tone commented.
It was taking me some time to understand what he meant, with Rey and Carlos who were now laughing about it.

-Oh, I understand now. Sorry guys, I should go to sleep really, my brain isn't working. I haven't slept properly in some time-
I hoped Carlos wasn't that kind of guy that got offended for no reason.
-It's ok- he kept focusing on his food and laughed again.
I had to relax, he was south American after all, and he probably didn't have time for such kind of drama.
-Come on, just a beer Dom- Rey pushed more and more, eventually succeeding.

The next day, I was still in terrible need of resting, although I wanted to start working as soon as possible.
The night before took a very unexpected turn in fact. Rey and I sat down into a small bar with Miami-looking type of graffiti, with beaches, palms and related stuff.
A couple of minutes later, Rey began chatting to two south American girls sitting next to us, with me making no effort at all in encouraging the conversation. My eyes were in fact closing by themselves. Staying up was almost painful.
At some point though, I decided to try and talk to the two girls, hoping that it could help me keep awake.
The girls, both from Chile, were ignoring the flirts of another Latin guy who just sneaked from behind the table, but kept talking to Rey in a polite way, not very enthusiastic though.
After a quick introduction and some uninteresting talks about ourselves, one of the girls surprisingly suggested to take things to their place. To that, Rey reacted way too keen in my opinion, whilst the other girl didn't seem to be sure it was a good idea, although she remained silent about it.
Later on, we ended up at their address just outside town. That was, as far as I could remember, the only time in my life I didn't feel more in the mood to be at a random girl's house with the possibility to have sex, than I was to just go home and sleep.
By then, the unfriendly one was sitting by the bottom of the table, silent and grumpy, whilst her friend was seriously amused by Rey suddenly pulling out his dick and moving it around in what he loudly called the helicopter move. It was when I took a seat on the sofa, desperately trying to rest for

a few minutes that I realised that the night wasn't going to be over yet.
-I like him because he's shy- I heard the leading girl saying whilst pointing at me.
She was curvier than her friend and had long brunette hair in a thick braid. Her plump lips weren't the type that defined my ideal girls, and I was more than happy to leave her to Rey in exchange of some sleep on her comfortable sofa, but that couldn't happen either.
She insisted on going to her room where we inevitably started kissing and undressing.
In a matter of few minutes, the sex was over, for which I apologised before I began begging to sleep there, which she accepted.
Unlike the typical European woman, who gets furious at those who fail in bed, that one let me in her child's room and wished me the kindest of good nights, as if we had been best friends for ages. Different culture, I assumed.

It took me an entire day to get my escorting profile finally sorted. Carlos took several pictures of me and told me how to pose to increase my sex appeal.
-I'm afraid I don't have that many muscles. I don't think anyone will pick me between all of these huge guys I see- I was scrolling the website, demoralised.
-It's not about that, actually, you'll be successful because you're straight- Carlos commented, loving it that he was taking pictures of me.
He was very attractive, with his thick dark hair, properly shaved face that showed a good bone structure and well-built body.
-Gay men don't necessarily look for muscles, they all have their fantasies- Rey commented.
-Exactly, and also, they love it that you're not gay, I told you already. You have no idea how weird it sounds to me when I sleep with a guy and he moans with a high pitch female voice. I don't find it particularly irritating, but many men do. On top of that, I suggest you don't take showers before going to meeting them- then he laughed.

He was amused by that situation, with me posing naked with a leg on his sofa, my hairy legs and belly that had no fat but neither the slightest trace of abs.

Eventually, it was only on the third day that I got my first appointment. I didn't receive any messages from the website, which was depressing and at the same time annoying. The ad had cost me 100 dollars and it only covered one month.
-Hey Dom, I got a client for you. He saw me a few times already, and I know he probably wants to see someone new now. I told him he can trust you- Rey told me after coming home from one of his meetings.
-Cool- I said, now feeling my heart pumping at the height of my throat. I was almost getting used to not going anywhere.
-I don't know, I actually feel like...-
-Don't say that, I know how you feel. Oh wait, he just replied!- he said, then kept reading from his phone for the longest minute in the world.
-This afternoon. You'll go to his place in the afternoon- he said, then got back to his phone, leaving me very nervous.

Two days later, Rey and I were walking in Venice Beach.
-Nothing special really. If it wasn't the US and this place hadn't been recorded in many films with celebrities walking around it, it would just be an average beach- I said, paying attention not to be too deep in the way my thoughts were elaborated. Rey got bored easily.
-Worse than average. It's like this here- Rey said, but he clearly didn't care about what I gave importance to, which was the subtle way in which the world was tricked by US propaganda through its cinema into believing that the American way was a thing of the average citizen, whilst, to say the very least, it was as far as it could be from being true.
-It's dirty and poor, lots of homeless people, lots of gangster faces around here. I bet Carlos' is one of the best areas, and yet I saw many homeless around home too- I reasoned out loud.

-Yeah, these streets are garbage. Lots of places in LA are just garbage, places to stay away from- Rey wasn't in the mood for talking as far as I could tell.
We were sitting by the skateboards tracks.
-I had a good time in that pub few months ago. A nice woman let me stay in the hostel upstairs for free for one night. I was completely broke- he was saying.
-Why were you broke? Did you gamble everything I sent you, right?- I asked him, still hoping that I could help him by mocking him and making him feel ashamed about it.
-You didn't help me last time-
-Yes I did-
-Yeah, but things don't go well each time Dom, you don't understand. You're stuck in London with a job and a regular life, you don't know what it feels to make a lot of money. You feel like spending more, it's a natural consequence of that. If you earned like me, you'd stop being so stingy all the time, but until then, stop judging me- he said, one of the many times I saw him impatient. That topic touched his nerves every time.
-Alright, let's drop it here. Anyway, you're wrong. If I earned as much money as you, I'd be saving it all and investing it in the future...- I started saying, but then stopped when I realised that Rey wasn't listening.
Up to that moment, I had made almost 500 dollars and that had already paid off for the trip and some of the money we gave to Carlos to stay in his apartment.
My first service was a man originally from Brazil but living in the US for a long time. He worked for a pharmaceutical company, as he told me, and lived in a beautiful multiple floors house. I subconsciously always hoped somebody would reveal to me a way to success that required no high education nor any sort of career, but that wasn't the case. The guy had studied for many years of his life to achieve that.
He treated me very well, offered me some drinks, asked me to shave more in his bathtub, and after less than half hour, I was out with the same money Rey charged everyone.
The following day, a huge black guy from Inglewood requested me, and this time I accepted with more

confidence in myself, also seeing the good job I did the day before. He lived in an apartment in rough conditions, in an area that Rey described as very unsafe, which didn't help me to relieve me from my already pre-set fears of encountering a psycho at some point.
However, all went well with that guy too. He played some straight porn in the television next to his bed and turned off the lights of the flat, packed with many clothes hanged a little bit everywhere. I suspected he was either a retailer or simply a professional thief.
He was so happy about the job I did that he said he would save my number and come visit me in London, spoil me and treat me like a king. I couldn't stop picturing me and him driving a convertible car in Shaftesbury Avenue when I was on my way back to Hollywood.
-Do you want to visit San Francisco? Things aren't going very well for me here- Rey proposed me after we had been silent for a bit.
He hadn't received a single call in a couple of days and for someone like him, that meant he needed a change of scenery.
-Yeah, sure- I answered.

Rey and I reached San Francisco by bus the following night and checked in into our hotel room near Union Square.
At first impact, San Francisco looked completely different from Los Angeles, exception made for the same unmeasurable number of homeless people spread everywhere and walking like zombies or just lying down the pavements, either seemingly dead or mad at the walls of the buildings behind their own tents or cartoon boxes.
The city looked chaotic, crowded and loud like London, but with higher buildings.
A rude hotel receptionist gave us the keys to our room on the first floor, a big bed with a lamp on a small nightstand next to it, a small window that showed the internal side of the construction and a small cupboard on the opposite side. The room was tiny, but it was going to be fine for us.
-Let's go get vodka- Rey suggested, receiving my appreciation.

By then, it was already too late to enter any clubs, as we found out whilst trying to get in somewhere.
Having no other choice than focusing our attention on the alcohol, Rey and I drank the bottle up and, within minutes, we started hunting every girl we met on our way. On that aspect, the place where we were wasn't any different than Europe.
The main cultural similarity between the European and the American world was not only the obvious result of the historical impact made by those who travelled to the new world and exported their ideas, but also by the use, in most cases, of the same social media platforms and therefore the type of news, political ideas, cinema fantasies, pornographic perversions, concepts of freedom, individualism and self-promotion through the look, the signalled virtues or both of them at the same time, in those that were the worst cases.
The reaction of the girls, at times pleased with the compliments, at times disgusted and at times scared, were the exact same they were in London. Sometimes I could predict the reaction of girls based on their backgrounds too. I knew that the blonde chick that curled up her hair and wore a fancy fur was going to tell us to fuck off even if we stopped her to tell her she had just dropped her wallet. The girl with round glasses was going to pace up and run away from us as soon as she turned round the corner because of the edited statistics on sexual assault from feminist websites. The hippie-looking girl was going to give us a look loaded with sexual desire due to her habit of attempting to fill up her lows with constant providing her body with highs of any kind. Between the many types of girls, Rey and I had a great ability to recognise their personalities, often showed by the way they answered to our words or looks. We didn't waste time on someone that didn't play along when we mentioned sex. We weren't geniuses nor particularly brilliant with them, but we tried a lot and got rejected a lot.
-Hey!- Rey shouted to a woman who was standing by the pavement on the nearest point to the massive street. He was way too drunk.
Initially, the woman got apparently scared, since a tall man with no great body coordination was approaching her in the

middle of the night with me getting closer, also uncoordinated.
-Are you waiting for a taxi?- Rey asked her the stupidest question I could think of, to which she didn't reply.
-Don't call your taxi, come to our place, we got vodka back home- I said.
When I got closer to the woman, I noticed that she didn't look scared more than she looked confused about what was happening.
Rey and I stopped when we were too close to her. Both of us were looking at her like two lions at a piece of meat after days of starving.
The woman kept looking at us, still not saying a word, now slowly opening what I considered a smile.
-She's saying nothing, let's continue- I told Rey in Spanish. -We have a hotel round the corner, come on up, forget your taxi- he said.
She stood still and kept an unreadable expression on her face. Then, she followed us.
Rey and I were quite surprised she was walking with us and couldn't hide the excitement from one another. Seeing that she was keen on getting to know us, we gave up our aggressive manners and did our best to initiate some sort of small talk with the nicest of tones, hard also because of the alcohol we had.
She was in her late twenties, had brunette straight hair tied up on a bun with two loose strands on her side. She was about my height, a well-shaped body, quite slim too. Her curves and tan gave her the south American look, yet I was sure she had other backgrounds.
By the time we reached the door of our room, the prey, named Cecilia, had said no more than ten words in total.
When we were in, we could finally see her better through the light of the big lamp. She looked very attractive in her denim jacket and tight dark trousers.
We all looked at each other for a few seconds, still not saying much.
-Right, we don't have any vodka left, I just realised- I said, embarrassed. The other two laughed lightly.

-I prefer we go back to mine- she said then, which I comprehended since our room looked like a rat hole.
We got down the streets, grabbed a taxi and reached her place, about half hour drive from us, towards a lovely looking area with very long San Francisco-looking streets, flanked by buildings that had an English style architecture with big, squared windows on ground floors.
We found out Cecilia shared her big flat with two other people. She had her own room, not particularly big but at least she had access to her own toilet from it.
She told me she worked as an architect and mainly took care of the construction of bridges, mostly working in cooperation with the local administration.
I was expecting someone like her to live in a bigger place and maybe on her own, but I guessed that her very central location compensated for it. Cecilia was still naked when she prepared some snacks and drinks for me, also naked at the table in the living room. Rey was already sleeping in her bed. She told me that was her very first threesome, that she fantasised about them but never really got a chance to have one happen.
Her slim body and voluptuous look were stimulating me again.
We smoked a cigarette together downstairs. The tobacco I bought in LA tasted disgusting, but that was the only one I had then.
Cecilia was talking much more now. Weird, thinking about the fact that she was about to take a taxi the way home without us less than three hours before.

Within the third day in San Francisco, I had made almost 1k dollars and I was now on my way to meet my second client in town, a man in his sixties that was going to pick me up from Castro Street and take me to his place for something soft, apparently.
The day before, I had a successful appointment with a man in his forties, a very masculine and well-built man with short military looking hairstyle in a luxurious hotel room quite near Union Square.

He offered me a drink and acted very polite the whole time. Going back home with the cash felt great, alongside with receiving congratulations from Rey who, by the beginning of the trip, had made less money than me.
-I can't believe you're doing so well- he said, unable to hold some envy.
-I owe it to you mostly. My money is our money in case things go wrong in this trip- I said.
-I'll make a lot by the time I'm back in London- he said, slightly frustrated.
That afternoon though, I had a less lucky meeting with an Asian guy who was waiting for me in another luxurious hotel by the northern docks.
The man, probably just as old as me, insisted on kissing me in the elevator, which I declined to do before receiving my money. He then told me he couldn't pay with cash and that he was going to pay me with a cheque.
After thinking about it for a minute, I decided to drop the whole thing. I imposed him to pay for my trip the way back to him and promised myself to report him to the community on the website, then took the cheque that was supposed to compensate for the taxi the way there and back, and left without saying a word nor looking at his face.
That day though, was going to be the easiest ever, and afterwards, I thought, I was probably going to retire and use that money to enjoy the rest of the holidays, visit Las Vegas, and then go back to LA's airport for my way back to Europe.
Meanwhile, the old man had just driven me to his home, saying he just wanted to rim me, and that it was going to be enough for him.
Reluctant as usual, once we were in his bed, I closed my eyes and imagined a girl, although it was difficult because of his moans of pleasure. I had no idea why he was even enjoying it, but he kept saying he was going to finish soon, soon...
Suddenly, the man stuck his thumb in my hole, causing me a sudden, but strong pain.
-What the hell man?- I stood up, getting nervous.
-We didn't agree to this!- I added, knowing there was no way I was going to allow him more of that, but not knowing how

to say it to him. I was afraid that he wouldn't want to pay me if I had stopped him.
The man said he would be gentler, and I eventually decided to agree, also led by my awareness that what was happening in that moment was the very last one of such meetings. Few minutes later, the man called himself fully satisfied and paid me my fee of 200 dollars plus 40 as an extra because he said he enjoyed being with me.
On the way back to the station near Castro Street, I was considering whether I should have accepted his invitation to meet him again soon or not. I had to admit the guy was harmless and also quite rich, according to the beautiful house he owned.
I met Rey in the evening. He wasn't doing very well and he looked at me slightly depressed.
-Right, we should book our tickets to Vegas now- I said to him, excited about it.
Doing that job gave me a feeling of dirt that I needed to remove from me through fun, alcohol, and most importantly, the touch of the female body, which was supposed to clean me up from the previous shameful context my body happened to be in.
-Tomorrow- said Rey.

By the following morning, Rey's mood was getting worse, causing a silly argument at the table we were sitting at in a breakfast cafe near our hotel.
He kept saying I didn't understand what it meant to be in his place and constantly having to pay debts.
At that stage, I was particularly careful in avoiding talking about the fact that he was the only one guilty of such debts, and that he needed to find a job and change his mindset completely if he wanted to get out of that trap.
A couple of hours later, Rey and I were resting in bed together when I realised something that I had been trying to ignore during the last hours.
A growing and irritating itchy feeling between my legs was taking over me to the point I could no longer ignore, which forced me to go to the toilet and check it for peace of mind.
I entered a bathroom from the hallway, locked myself in and

grabbed the mirror, turned it around and put it in a position where I could have opened my legs and see what was there closer, together with the help of the torch from my phone. I was expecting to see something red, maybe a bruise caused by that man, but the small white bubble I saw shocked me, giving me nausea and a moment of panic.
I winced, stood up for half a minute in complete silence, then decided to check again, as if the first time I saw that thing was just an hallucination.
I told Rey about it when I went back to the room. He was distracted, stuck on scrolling newsfeed on his phone, then dismissed my problem by suggesting to go down to the pharmacy together and just buy a cream for that kind of stuff.
-Tomorrow it will be gone- he said whilst we reached a big pharmacy by the opposite side of the subway station.
-I hope so- I still couldn't calm down completely.

By the next day, the pain had got much worse, and so did the frequency to which the itchy feeling spread around.
Within the early afternoon, I realised I couldn't walk properly, neither sit down in the same position for longer than a minute before having to change it in order to find relief, which only lasted a few seconds before the itchy feeling hit again, giving me no peace at all.
By the late afternoon, the pain had become unbearable, forcing me to almost make a sound a few times. I ran to the bathroom of the hotel again, determined to destroy whatever it was, although I didn't know exactly how, since it could have been dangerous.
What was I even going to use? A kitchen knife?
The sight that showed up in front of my eyes after turning the mirror upside down disgusted me.
The white bubble was now almost as big as a pearl, and its faded white colour gave it a gloomy touch that penetrated my head.
I was so disgusted and scared at the same time that my brain forgot the physical pain for a few moments, as if it didn't have enough space for that.

-Rey, I need to go to the hospital. You can stay here if you want- I said whilst preparing a small bag and making sure I had my passport on me.
-I'll go with you- Rey seemed less convinced of his opinion about the seriousness of my problem now.

The sun was gone by the time we reached the hospital. Rey told me he was going to take care of a business, then he would have come back to me.
When I entered the hospital, I was required to show my passport.
I was hoping they would just treat me and never find me again, but that was just a fantasy.
I was glad that the black woman by the reception didn't ask many questions though, and within minutes, I was already sitting by the waiting area.
My brain was being tortured by the thoughts of the bill I would have had to pay. I didn't know much about how the American healthcare system worked, but all I needed then was to be seen, and then leave as soon as I could.
A couple of hours later, I was allowed in the doctor's room. I was relieved when they started checking stuff and asking me about my pain rather than about my money. I knew that as a foreigner and therefore no taxpayer, I was using their service and I had a legal and also moral obligation to pay, but the problem was that defining the medical services in the US as overpriced was a reductive word that didn't show how unfair things truly were.
One could consider an overpriced expense as something that makes them just frown, maybe get angry and pay, think about a few future sacrifices to do in the everyday life to compensate for the loss, but I knew this wasn't the case. US hospital bills went beyond any logic.
-Just tell me if you feel pain and I'll inject more of this- the doctor was literally cutting the bubble with a sharp knife as if he was cutting a big old loaf of bread.
-It's painful- I found myself saying every other minute, with the doctor injecting more and more anaesthetic inside my butt.

Eventually, when the pain got too high and I was struggling to stay still, the doctor went to get his superior to help him out with the operation, together with Rey sitting next to me.
When everything was over, I was given a paper that stated that they were going to get in touch with me for the payment, which I gladly took, folded and put in my pocket.
The doctors told me I would have needed to go back to visit them if the bubble reappeared, which was quite likely to happen again apparently.
Rey and I got a taxi the way home.
I was relieved from the pain, enjoying the pleasure of being able to use my legs again and think about plans that were not related to my health.
I couldn't believe how quickly a body could enter a state of stress and how badly medical service was needed for the return to normal life. It could have happened anytime, to anyone, and doctors were the ones to take care of the most important of all the jobs.
I was feeling particularly grateful to the world and to all those that decided to study medicine when I went to bed that night.
-My life is characterised by bad timings. It's always been like this. I can't believe this crap came into my ass right when I'm on holiday by the other side of the planet. Why couldn't this happen just... any other time?- I blurted out, terribly annoyed.
-Calm down, it's all over now Dom- said Rey.
I owed it to him once again. It was good that he was with me in there, picking me up and calling the doctors at the end of the operation when I fainted in his arms.

I was feeling much better in the following morning, and Rey and I started looking for cheap bus tickets to Vegas. I contacted a girl I previously met in my very first week in Russell Square hostel who actually came from Vegas, and told her I might have been there soon, to which she responded saying she would have been pleased to show me around, since I did that for her and her friend when they visited London a couple of years before.

It was only in the afternoon that I realised that my holiday nightmare wasn't over at all.
An appalling feeling was taking me over, communicating to me that that bubble was back, and for some reason, worse than before.
The existing pain combined with my mental state regarding my renewed awareness that I still had that problem froze my body to the point I didn't move for an entire minute.
-Is it that thing again?- Rey asked me, concerned.
-I need to go to London, now. Maybe I can book a new flight, but I don't have any money left in my bank account... or maybe I can just change the date from my other ticket- I was stuttering.
I could see the disappointment in Rey's face and I felt truly sorry about it, but I was much more than disappointed with everything that was happening to me.

The next morning, we were both on our way back to Los Angeles. A long trip by bus where sleeping was impossible because of the pain gave me a massive headache. I felt like vomiting for a good part of the trip and really glad when I got to the destination.
Meanwhile, I had successfully managed to change the date of my flight for a not too high extra fee, and it was going to be in two days, which was better than I had expected.
Carlos was super nice when he promised to take care of my wound, removing the soft bandage stick from my hole and replacing it with a new one the following day.
I was trying hard to relax, but I was simply feeling too sorry.
I knew I was angry, disappointed and frustrated, but the overwhelming feeling that I could most accurately use to describe how I felt was sorrow.
I was enjoying being in the US and taking advantage of the fact I was Italian to impress the girls that, over time, were proving to be very keen on that specific feature of my being.
The sunshine that crossed the window and brightened up Carlos' flat was going to be missed, and so were the girls in shorts, the friendly Latinos, the lights of the town and all the things I didn't get to see.

The next day, I was on my flight back to London, although I had to stop in Iceland for a few hours once again.

The day after my return in England, I visited the Royal Free Hospital near Belsize Park and told them everything. My operation was scheduled for the early morning of the following day, resulting in a feeling that was mixed between pleasure and gratitude for being helped so quickly and some stress due to the fact I didn't want to be put to sleep whilst giving other people full availability to any part of my body. It was a silly fear, but I knew that, no matter how rational I could be, I was only going to feel fine when all of that was over and the white bubble was removed once for all.
The next morning, I left my belongings into a small locker, wore the surgical gown and sat in the waiting room.
-What are you here for?- a red haired guy, the only other person in the room just asked me.
-A pilonidal cyst apparently, has to be removed. You?- I asked.
-They'll work on my hand- he said whilst lifting up his right hand, horribly cut in half and held together by a long black thread of stitches throughout the palm.
Not even a Halloween costume with some high level make up could have made that effect on me. It was disgusting, which made me feel better about my operation at least. I always needed to compare my situation to the one of the others if I wanted to make a decision about how I actually felt.
When that guy left, I was alone in the waiting room. I wasn't worrying that much anymore, but I was very stressed. I needed that thing to be sorted out once for all.

Back at the hostel, I found out most members of the family were still there.
Matt, Luigi and Riccardo picked me up from the hospital, and by the evening, I was able to return to normality, or almost. In fact, I still couldn't move properly. I could still feel some light itching whenever I sat in the same position for some time, but I was also told, and I felt it, that my cyst wasn't there anymore.

I sat down on a pink bench with a pillow taken from my room, receiving the attention of the family members, alongside the constant mockery by my closest friends.
-Are you sure you didn't just get fucked?- Matt was the most active in mockery, whilst Luigi was more moderated in that. Matt clearly had no idea about what was going on in the US.
-You know, I don't really know many people that have a second asshole- he kept going, with Luigi who couldn't help laughing about it.
I looked around the crowded common room over my dinner table.
Diego was lying down on the sofa, eyes stuck on his phone, God only knew how long he had been in that unnatural position. Tomas was just chilling, but I also knew he was paying his dose of attention to the social side of life, whilst his brain was working out how to get out of a shallow situation so that he could work on his future. He had many projects in mind, and his ambitions gave him no longer than half hour per day to dedicate to all of us, although he did his best, and that was why we all liked him. Pavel, a Bulgarian guy in his mid-twenties with thick dark hair and his fringe up, was keen on his laptop on his usual table next to the vending machine. He had a peaceful nature and a severe interest for videogames. Besides our polite manners when we were near each other though, I couldn't say we interacted much. Ella was still there, now way more confident than before since her friendship with everyone else had consolidated. I could see a great difference in her attitude from the day I met her to the current one. She was louder now, and I wasn't really sure whether I had to try and interact with her more than I already did, but I couldn't tell why. Adam, just like many before him, had decided to extend his bookings in the hostel because he was enjoying the social life, and even though I knew he was looking for a place, I was also totally sure he was doing it as slow as he possibly could.
Zak was also there, which I didn't really like to see. He was still actively trying to get girls, which was annoying, but the fact that he was friendly with me forced me to do my best to respond with the same attitude, although I had to admit I

wanted him to just leave. Celia was, of course, a stable member of the family.
She enjoyed preparing dinners with others, going out and dressing up with a dark goth style, didn't dislike some social drinks, never fought nor gossiped any more than necessary. She was great, and that was the main reason why I kept pushing Luigi to finally tell her how he felt about her.
-She's too nice, too perfect. I can't be with her- Luigi once said when we were in Queen Square.
-Oh man, I know exactly what you mean, but are you sure you want to blow this chance? A girl like that doesn't happen everyday- I tried to be reasonable, although the idea of Luigi being single and therefore more available for myself was appealing.
Luigi didn't reply straight away, maybe ashamed of the way he treated her. In fact, Luigi literally ghosted Celia all of a sudden. I wasn't sure about when exactly he had decided to do so, but I was very aware of the reason why he did.
It was, in my case and apparently in his too, given by fear to hurt a person that, in our opinion, was too nice to be hurt.
At some point, I also tried to tell Luigi that Celia wasn't into anything particularly romantic, and that he had overthought all of that, to which he simply replied it didn't matter anymore.
-Ok, but I hope you're at least still speaking to her like a friend?-
Luigi didn't reply, but just looked embarrassed.
-Tonight, you'll talk to her tonight- I imposed him.

-We should venerate the sun. The sun is the real God, not like the other fake ones we created because we were scared of death. The sun gave us life and it still does. The Egyptians venerated it, and they were right, they were great, that's why they were the first ones to perform brain surgery, thousands of years ago- that wasn't the first time Matt greeted me like that in the morning.
Actually, after thinking about it for a bit, I realised that those very few times I saw Matt being awake in the morning, he hadn't missed to praise the sun once. He did that every single morning.

-Matt, colour doesn't exist in nature, does it?- I asked him.
-Correct- he said, always glad to reply to anything nerdy whenever the chance occurred.
-I once heard a guy saying that that's the mystery of science, that science cannot explain why-
-What? Who's this idiot?- Matt replied, then chuckled.
-Just a guy who used to act very knowledgeable but never gave any answer. He was very spiritual.-
-Spiritual people- Matt commented, then laughed.
-So, as far as I understand, colour is to be explained by our perception?-
-Yes, everything produces a different effect on the way your eyes interpret it. Your eyes simply see the density of something, and all other things that right now are not on the top of my head but that's what it is. It's the interpretation given by your eyes, how they evolved during the struggle of evolution- Matt said, vague, although I knew he had studied it some time in the past.
We were sitting on a bench in Queen Square when I thought about how stupid I was in the past every time I decided not to do my own research. It wouldn't have taken more than few minutes to get some information about that at least, but back when I was working in Cote, I was doing nothing for my personal improvement, and the random words said by the people around me were sounding much more reliable than they should have. I was easy to manipulate in the past because I knew less.
I was glad that by sitting down next to Matt I always got to feel a great desire to learn and a sense of omnipotence as soon as he explained anything to me.
Matt's sleeping pattern was, as I noticed in the next days, finally almost normal from the first time I had met him.
-You don't look any good man- I told him one morning when I randomly bumped into him in Russell Square.
-It's a pretty good day- Matt was once again appreciating the sunshine London was getting in those days.
-You're...- I stopped. I decided not to stress him about how bad he was looking. Matt was a nerd after all, and maybe, his scruffy face was something that didn't matter to him. I doubted it though.

He was wearing a purple wool hat that made him look like an actual homeless who was covered by the first thing he found in the streets, maybe discarded by someone who didn't want it anymore.
-Look at that kid, figuring out the universe- he said, infinitely slow, with a voice tone that somehow seemed to come from a different place.
A boy, not older than 2, was struggling to move around the grass in front of our bench, with his parents walking close to him.
I realised both of us were still staring at that kid after a couple of minutes, following every single one of his movements.
-See? If I don't hold this anymore it will fall down, everything falls down if I drop it- Matt was talking so low that it felt as if he was talking to himself, although I knew he was involving me.
-Figuring out gravity. It's the first time he experiences it maybe, he's taking mental notes at least-
-Yeah- Matt chuckled.
-You're still smoking that crap?- I asked him when I noticed he was rolling a joint.
-It's the least I can do to keep calm. You know, this is good for me, I had a seizure under the shower recently, you weren't in the hostel that night-
-Right, these are excuses. You're just addicted to it- I said, maybe sounding too harsh.
-It's not. Weed is not addictive, I told you many times already, and if whatever thing helps me to stay relaxed, you should be in favour of it- Matt hated me anytime I tried to encourage him to get rid of some of his worst habits. Sometimes I felt like his laziness was the mental state he chose after working so hard studying electronic engineering for five years, probably as a reward for himself.
Matt's knowledge was just as great as his affinity with us under other aspects of life. For example, I found out that Matt was, just like me, confident in managing his sexual life and hitting on girls all the time, but terribly fragile when it came to love management.

-It took me a year to move past my ex- he said one of those nights, which surprised me a lot.
-Really? That's horrible- I said, although I couldn't deny to myself that that made me feel good, or simply less miserable.
With that declaration, my times of sentimental lows suddenly appeared trivial. How could he have been sad for a year? Regarding Luigi, he stated he understood Matt perfectly, although he wasn't caring about Celia at all, I had to say, but it was a completely different scenario anyway.
I had mentioned to him a few days before that I saw Zak sitting next to Celia and clearly hitting on her on several occasions, to which he responded with a very annoyed look on his face for a few seconds, but then switched it back to normal just as quickly as he had reacted when he heard it. He probably didn't mind it at all, I assumed.

March 2017

Luigi, Matt and I agreed that Celia was the perfect family member because her attitude was what we defined a typical male one, which looked unusual due to her very feminine appearance, but made her the most popular person in the hostel. You could joke with her and never worry that she would overreact.
-I think she's more in control of her emotions than we all are at this bench- I told my two closest friends in Queen Square that night.
Talking to the guys was all I could do to keep my days busy, especially since I couldn't work, go out, dance, or even just chill at the park with the others without feeling the itch intensifying because of my activities. All I had to do was rest and do regular medications to make sure it didn't get infected.
-Guys, it's horribly cold here. How can you possibly stay here all night?- I asked Matt, who would manage to sit outdoors until dawn without going back to the hostel.
He didn't feel the need to interact with anyone, but he would rather just sit silent, smoking one cigarette after another,

rolling one new joint each four or five of them, every single night, without exceptions.
-I'm wasting my life- he said one night.
All the sadness of the world seemed to be hidden in his voice tone. His hands were moving unnaturally slow at each puff of his cigarette.
He truly was wasting his life. He had not only accomplished nothing, but neither had he tried to. It was as if he had been thrown down the bottom of a well and had resigned to try and get out of it.
-There is a lot that I can learn from you Matt, and it's great, but it would be selfish of me to just sit here and enjoy your knowledge. Didn't you study hard to have a better future? Wasn't engineering hard?- I didn't know what to say to make Matt change his attitude towards life, but the problem apparently required much more than what I was doing. Blaming him for his own problem made him angry, and motivational speeches didn't work either. He was a case that went beyond my possibilities to help.
-Studying at uni was hard, tremendously hard. It made me want to quit several times, although I never did, also because I had the luck not to work. I was sitting in my garden, back at my parents' place, studying every single day. Finishing my degree took all of my twenties, and I remember the struggle well, especially the hard boring topics, or just maths in general, and all I can say is that it was a long, long nightmare. Just think about this: by the time I finished my first year, more than half of the students had withdrawn from the course-
-I want to study at uni and get a degree. I made a mistake back in Italy, I should have finished it there and then move to London to work in proper jobs, instead of all the hard work I've been doing so far- I said.
-You should totally do it. Uni is the best thing in the world. When you finish it, you're a smarter person, and it ends up affecting every aspect of your life, from the way you look at the world to the way you are around people. Education is the key to solve all world's problems. Mark my word, if everyone had a laptop and free internet connection with free access to all reliable sources of information...-

-Most men would still search topless women and most girls would still search for makeup products and stuff like that. Your view is very optimistic and doesn't take into consideration the imperfect nature of humans- I completed his sentence. Debates about society and how to improve it were not the only ones between us though. With the two of them, I could talk about everything, and that allowed me to open up sometimes and ask for opinions that eventually I regretted asking about.
-I have to say that at the beginning, having to see Alba around was annoying. Sometimes I just left the common room and went to bed earlier for that, and I'm glad she's gone now- I once admitted to them.
-Alba? Are you joking? Her body wasn't anywhere near how a woman's body should be- Matt replied to that.
We knew he was being serious when he talked about female bodies. Matt often showed us he had thousands of pictures and videos of only massively overweight women in his phone.
-Right, I won't even respond to this- I was glad he often used irony to change the topic.

By mid-March, I was living a passive life for the first time in a couple of years, and I wasn't enjoying it.
I only did about one or two deliveries per day to make sure they didn't block my account due to inactivity, then went back home when I felt my hole was beginning to burn too hard.
As a consequence of having more spare time, I ended up needing more money to spend, eating more to kill the boredom, and drinking more, not to mention the fact that I decided to restart smoking even though I had forcefully put my addiction to an end because of the instructions given by the doctors after the surgery.
-It's silly, you don't have to do it actually. I mean, I'm glad you don't smoke any more, but think about it, the Spanish and Italians smoke in much higher rates than the English and yet live longer than them. Again, I'm glad you don't smoke, but you totally can if you want to- Celia once told me after taking care of the medication I needed to do about four to five times a week.

She had not only taken some equipment from her hospital to help me out, but had also offered to do all of that for free anytime I needed it, which saved me a substantial amount of money.
In fact, the free pass medications from the NHS were over at some point, and continuing for about two more weeks would have cost me some money each time.
-You are an angel, and my gratitude will be forever- I told her, sorry that she had to put her fingers in such part of my body each time.
I spent most of the time in the common room, keeping my interaction with the family very active in the mornings and then turning it off in the evenings so to spend time only with Matt, which led to my own gradual distancing from the other members.
In fact, with the passage of time I realised that my relationship with Celia, Matt and Luigi, was far from the one I had with everyone else.
I liked everybody else a lot and I also felt some unquestionable degree of affection towards each one of them, but the amount of chemistry was lower, which left us to feel mutual respect and share great nights together, but also inevitably divided us whilst we rode towards different directions.
The conversation within me and my closest ones could touch great levels of depth, which didn't necessarily describe them as mentally more capable than others, but rather just more passionate in topics that were usually considered as fun killers and promptly dismissed to avoid embarrassing looks around at an uncomfortable table.
If my guys and I were shouting at each other about which system sucked more between the capitalist one and the communist one, tried to prove the opponent wrong by researching stuff on the internet in front of each other, shared our knowledge and constantly discussed possible aftermaths of wars in made up scenarios from the future, all topics were for sure examined in depth. They were never part of a small talk, never just attempts to show off some knowledge or look smarter, but rather deeply articulated

thoughts where we, despite the arguing, simply looked for truths.

This, together with my reduced interest in doing much under the social aspect of life due to my inability to even move well, led the main family of the hostel to not have me as one of its main characters for the first time in a long time, which felt a bit weird, but also, as I found out, was for the best.

The family had fallen, in my opinion at least, in a different state that had very little to do with what usually happens in hostels.

The net of toxicity was dropped from the ceiling and, silent and invisible, had trapped many in there, creating a situation of social stagnation, increasing the presence of insecurities, ego-centred choices, proper courting with attempts of becoming the owner of someone's freedom of sexual expression, gossiping and the most poisonous one being the invisible pyramid that established people's places in it and determined their statuses.

I used to look at this transformation as an inevitable process that became effective anytime the number of long-term stayers went up and the number of tourists or short-term family members went down. I knew that I would have fallen victim of the same net if I had been a willing part of each family that ever originated in the hostel, and that was why I decided to distance myself from the current one.

The messages that were sent in the group chat on Facebook were proving me right, alongside my already biased standpoint on this matter that was affecting my judgement about it.

I didn't like messages that started too nicely or were meant to flatter someone, I didn't like reading people telling other people they loved them if they didn't say the same thing to others too, the reason being based on the fact that such thing was going to create the basis of inequality of value between the family members.

There was no such thing as a functioning family where the parents only showed love to a child and not to the other, and even though I knew that better relationships are built with people that one truly liked, I still didn't like to see it written down. It was like a declaration of side picking, a non-needed thing to be said.

The fact that Luigi and Matt were two of the most important and favourite people in the world to me was clear to all, but I thought that writing it down on a group chat was firstly useless, and secondly only going to work as a declaration of another hidden statement. "You count a lot to me" would have been a true statement, but detrimental in a place where all had to feel valid. I found this necessary because I related it to the world of politics.

I could see the faces of the people who sat on those sofas everyday and read their thoughts. Some of them were planning, or at least just desiring, to start a purge.

I was spacing out by the bottom of the common room. Joseph was saying something about Ghana, but I wasn't listening. Maybe I was overthinking, maybe being too negative, but I knew I had a point.

I stood up and walked through the sofas area. A bunch of people gave me some of the warmest smiles I could get. Celia, who always invited me to be part of the group gatherings, Adam who always wanted to share a drink, Pavel, Diego and others who were always nice to me in every moment.

I had to admit it was also my decision not to be particularly engaged in the group's activities.

I missed Rey, had a post-surgery injury, I was frustrated for the ruined trip in the US and had no money at all, which got me thinking about going back to Italy for a while. A few more other reasons were causing me to just take it easy and feel no interest for a great social interaction.

I wished the guys good night and I thought none of them was faking their genuine response to that. They were good people, and besides, the hostel had positive impact on people's social mind after all. One had to be an extremely toxic person to successfully mess things up in there.

By the end of the month, a series of events managed to spice things up in the most boring month I had lived in a while. First, I was pleased by Charlotte's visit to London and a night

of pints and dance at the Camden Head with her, her boyfriend and Luigi.
I was surprised to hear she was coming back for a couple of days and even more surprised to hear she had a boyfriend. Not for anything actually, she was naturally very pretty, but I felt somehow weird, and I couldn't explain why.
Second, I enjoyed the trip to my hometown I had booked at the beginning of the month, and third, most importantly, London Kings had replied to my email where I mentioned my return to London and they had decided to hire me back.

April 2017

Within the first week of April, Luigi and I surprised everyone by leaving the hostel and moving into a double room in Brecknock Road, Kentish Town area.
Everything happened very fast.
We contacted the first suitable room we found on the internet and, on the same day, we met the landlord and paid our deposit so to secure the place. Within a couple of more days, we were going to be out of the hostel, and we were very excited about it.
The only moral issue in all of that was that Matt was going to be left out of the plan.
-It's not our fault if he's so demanding- Luigi and I alternately reminded this to each other whenever we discussed about it. In fact, we did look for places to move to with Matt, but he was never satisfied.
-How do you think it could be possible to get a place where you have a single room and pay no more than 400 pounds a month in zone 1? This is never going to happen- I told him once after we visited a place in East London that was, in my opinion, definitely acceptable.
-We need to research more- Matt always dismissed us like this, although he never did any research himself, which left me and Luigi stuck.
Eventually, we concluded that the only way for us to progress with our lives and university ambitions was to do it on our own.

-We'll have to tell him that we're leaving, today, as soon as possible, or he'll think we've been plotting behind his back- I told Luigi.
-He knows already, I think he found out from Celia, or someone else- he replied.
Luigi didn't look very sorry, probably due to his excitement. Actually, he was looking pretty absent-minded more often than usual lately.

A couple of days later, Luigi and I cycled together from Guilford Street, carrying a quite unpleasant weight behind our back and parked the bikes to the massive green gate that surrounded Charlton Court, the block of buildings in which our flat was located.
Luigi and I unpacked our suitcases in our new room and looked at each other, excited.
-We have our own place!- we shouted almost at the same time.
-Right, it's going to be amazing here, we're close to Camden, which means we can go to the Camden Head, pick up girls and take them home, not to mention that we can finally focus on uni and get it done for real- I said, but then stopped when I realised that Luigi was ignoring me. He had a happy expression on his face, yet I felt something was wrong with him for some reason.

With the passage of the days, my enthusiasm about my new life was still stable, and the prospect of becoming a uni student was massively contributing to that.
I spent hours each day surfing the internet and looking for the right uni and the right subject to study, with my choice revolving around subjects such as history, politics or languages.
Eventually, I concluded that the bachelor in history and politics at the Open University was the one I had to go for, which was also due to the fact that neither Luigi nor I had what it took to attend any other kind of university.
The reason why we had to enrol in an online course was primarily based on the fact that we didn't have a certificate that proved our knowledge of the English language as

required by all other universities in London. Our visit to the UCL proved it, which reduced our hopes a lot.
This certificate took a year to be obtained, and us working class people with no other resources to survive than work, came to a conclusion that it would have been a waste of time, not only because our English was probably better than many other foreigners', but also because the road to the degree would have been even longer like that.
-The Open university would still look good on our cv, or at least good enough to escape the kind of jobs we are forced to do otherwise. I know that an office job isn't the dream, but it's still better than working for Pret or Starbucks...- I reasoned out loud, but Luigi wasn't there with his head.
Our laptops were both open, but I was the only one that initiated the chats and made phone calls around, whilst Luigi would spend all his time texting someone on his phone.
-The Polish girl? Is that it? Can't you text her later? We should sort this out first...- I tried to ask him in the kindest of tones, but the result was either to be ignored or just silenced.
Within a week we had been in our new room, we had made no progress in terms of our uni ambitions nor had gone out for a drink at all.
We rarely even talked to each other after work, but rather just shared company for a cigarette after dinner and then get separated once again even though we slept in the same bed.
Within the second week, things hadn't changed at all, and pushing Luigi, or even simply suggesting him to go out together gave no results. He was absent, entirely.
-I think I'm in love- he once finally admitted whilst we were outside in the ugly courtyard, smoking.
-Yeah, I get that, but what about your ambitions? You know, I'm making progress with my application, so now I'm wondering whether you...- I was lying.
I hadn't sent any application anywhere yet, but Luigi was literally just going back inside, his eyes firm on the screen of his phone.
The days in Charlton Court were going terribly slow and boring.
Our flatmates were two young girls from Sicily, a Polish man in his forties and a couple from northern Italy, and over time,

they proved the point I tried to make to all those that asked me why I chose to live in a hostel instead of living in a house. To me, that place proved that the fact that the same people walked around those walls everyday claimed the consequential imposition of their favourite rules as the only accepted ones, just to start with.

At first, we didn't have any problems with them. Luigi had befriended with one of the Sicilian girls and found out he had lots of musical chemistry with, whilst we weren't able to befriend the other one, who was grumpy, unhappy about her work, and generally about her life since she was very unattractive.

The couple was cool since they were in their thirties, well-educated and worked professional jobs, whilst the Polish guy was never to be seen.

On top of that, Riccardo was kicked out from his newest job and was homeless once again, having spent all of his money in gambling and partying.

He used to come back home and loudly knock at our door or simply sneak inside from the window since our room was on the ground floor.

Luigi wasn't happy at all about him at first, but weirdly enough, the two completely different people eventually became somehow friends.

By one side, a knowledgeable, law-abiding working citizen from the north, and by the other, an uneducated, lawbreaking cunning lazy citizen from the south. They had nothing to talk about with each other, but they found out at some point, that they didn't despise the use of some recreational drugs, the common treasure that unites criminals and hipsters.

One night of mid-April, I was walking in High Street Kensington, heading to a date.

Her name was Mia, an American girl I met a few days before in a night out at O'neills with Sabino and some other guys. All I got then, was just her phone number whilst she was outside of the club waiting for her cab to come pick her up.

I got no insight on her availability towards me, since she acted quite distant in that moment.

My suspicion that she only gave me her number just so that she wouldn't have to deal with a drunk guy any longer for the night was not completely lifted up by the fact she agreed on going on a dinner date with me because of two main reasons that, although quite unlikely to come true, appeared and remained stable in my head anytime I was going on one. The first fear was that the person I was going to meet would stand me up, take a picture of me from behind the corner and laugh at me whilst publishing my pointless wait on the internet, maybe captioning it too.

The second fear was that she was just going to be there for the dinner, the bill falling obviously on me for inviting her and for being born with male genitalia, only to then say goodbye and getting an emptier wallet in exchange of nothing.

I had to say that such scenarios were unlikely though, and besides, I never offered anything to anyone that had given me no sexual pleasure whatsoever.

Except for that night. That night it was all on me, and it was my fault if that was happening. It was me that asked her out and shouted the dinner proposal at her face with my cousin behind me laughing at how out of control I looked because of the alcohol.

If it was true that she had accepted just to get a free dinner, it wouldn't have been her fault. It would have actually been a good move from her and I would have respected it.

Later than expected, my date showed up, walking from the main road and coming towards me in the alley where our restaurant was.

She was wearing a black satin top and tight dark trousers that highlighted her curves and was slowly approaching me with no smile on her face.

What I liked about Americans was that they didn't need nor believed in the existence of small talk at all. One could just begin a conversation after simply saying hi, and I appreciated that.

On average, American girls didn't look up to well-dressed guys, but rather preferred laughs and alcohol to elegance and manners.

In my opinion there were just a few American girls that had a shallow taste in men, which one could see in some unwatchable tv series for complexed brain-dead girls, and that was why in the US, an average looking guy could work and manage to score with particularly hot girls at times, something that in Europe was generally harder to happen. The luckiest ones were the Australian men anyway, who had some real gorgeous ones across their country who were, unlike the American ones, also capable of making actual intellectual efforts and give birth to deep conversations that weren't spat straight out of the internet's most popular memes. But I definitely wasn't going to tell her this.
-It must have been cool, growing up in Italy. I mean, it was honestly amazing there, I'll never forget my experience- Mia told me.
We were sitting at a table by the bottom of the restaurant, far from windows and from the entrance door and I was feeling I couldn't breathe well.
-Yeah, growing up in Italy was cool- I lied.
I wasn't a fan of Italy, although I knew it could have been much worse.
-What did you do in Italy?- I asked her.
I needed her to talk whilst I made mental calculations of how much money that dinner was going to cost me.
Luckily, despite her very fancy look, her taste was very humble. She wasn't too bad at all, I had to admit.
Actually, now that I realised that she was humble, I was beginning to dislike her heavy make up less and less.
-I was studying Italian, it was a three months course- her eyes were dreamy whilst she spoke.
-Erasmus?-
-Not really, but something similar. It was a project that was only available to few people, and I was one of them. My university sent emails to some random students giving them the possibility to win this trip to Italy, it was basically like a lottery and...yeah- she said.
-Wow, that was lucky, wasn't it?- I said whilst preparing to swallow a massive goat cheese slice in one go.
-Well, yeah, and no I guess. I mean... I believe in the law of attraction, so yeah- she said.

She was eating very slowly. The way she used her hands on the cutlery indicated that she was the poshest American girl I had ever met, although her easy-going attitude created a contradiction between the way I felt about her from her look and the way she actually was.
-What is it?- I asked, curious.
-It's basically... Well, you see, ok, let me put it this way. See, your thoughts are pure energy if you think about it, and this energy, once you direct it towards what you really want, has the power to take your greatest desire to you eventually- she said.
-Mm... I see... This is very interesting- I commented, pretending to be taking that seriously. She was talking to the least spiritual person in the known world, but I couldn't say it to her.
-So, how exactly does this work? I mean, applied to your trip back when you were in uni, how do you think that your desire to go on a trip brought the trip to happen? I tried to ask my questions in the least arrogant way. I wanted her to think I was actually giving her a chance on that.
-Well, you see, the energy of your thoughts is connected with every other source of energy out in the universe. The way they are connected is through magnetism that brings them closer when they are directed into each other's direction, so if you want something real badly, and I remember how badly I wanted to visit Italy back then, everything can happen, and it happened to me!- she said.
I waited half a minute before talking. I felt like if I had said something right away, it might have been a mistake, even paying the maximum attention to not committing one.
-Interesting, very interesting. I've got to investigate on this. I'm not fully convinced yet because I need more proofs, but I'm definitely intrigued- I said, playing my game. The truth was, that the dinner date I had invited her to because I was drunk was something I had to give to her. I wasn't going to stand her up nor calling it off. I wasn't that kind of person after all and I needed to prove that point to myself. If my initial idea was to just go through the dinner and then politely say good night and go home, now my plan was changing, mostly due to the way she was dressed and the

fact I had her around for an amount of time that was good enough for my urge to rise.
I needed her to believe that I wasn't dismissing her opinion, but actually considering it so to show support. At the same time, I needed her to know that I was intrigued but not fully convinced to show her I wasn't just agreeing with her so to show I treated her as equal rather than as just a piece of meat I wanted to touch after the dessert.
-I've had a good time, thanks for tonight- I said to her once we were out.
-Thank you actually- she said.
I thought she enjoyed the date, although she was very reserved.
-I would invite you to mine, but I've got my roommate being silly and his friends are there too tonight- I lied.
-You can come to mine if you want. I'm staying in an apartment in Bermondsey- she said, a very shy tone.
-Yeah, I guess it's not a bad idea- I said, acting.

April was coming to an end and I wasn't any happy about my situation. None of the things surrounding me fit in my plans. I wasn't signed up for any university, I wasn't reading any of the books I promised myself to read, I wasn't compensating my lack of education with making more money than I usually did, I wasn't enjoying the same standard of social life, and that was all because of Luigi.
I was walking home from Kentish Town station once when the thought came into my head. A suspicion I denied myself I had was now finding its way out from the closet of my brain where it hid up to that moment and was suggesting me to review how things truly were and to look at the facts.
Luigi spent not a single night with me, but stayed in his cafe after work until late night, coming back home when I was already sleeping or going to his current lover's place. He was physically and emotionally distant from me, didn't make any effort to further our plan to become students nor seemed any interested in any other thing except his colleague, which he thought about obsessively.
-He just wants to get carried away. He's busy falling in love, his brain is full of chemicals that identify the greatest source

of dopamine in the body and face of this girl. I'm not surprised about what's been happening- Matt calmly rationalised one night when I visited him.
-I never abandon my friends when I date someone- I said firm.
I wanted Matt to feel the same I was feeling for Luigi. I wanted him to believe I had a good reason to be disappointed so that I could have had a more official reason to leave my place in Brecknock Road and reunite with the family.
Matt took a few puffs of his joint and then spoke, unable to hide his disappointment either.
-He hasn't spoken to me once since the day you guys moved- he said, slowly.
-Exactly, whereas I've visited you everyday. Think about it Matt, and tell me if you recall a single period of time where I was away from you just because I was dating someone, and I had some big crushes some time ago-
Matt didn't reply, but he was happy I was there as I could tell. He had a smile stuck on his face that he eventually put down into words.
-I appreciate it. You know, the hostel without you sucks. It's just not the same. Don't get me wrong, they're lovely people, but you were my favourite, and now you're gone- he said, a tragic voice tone.
-I'm not. I'm coming back actually, I'm leaving that place as soon as possible. I'll see if I can make a booking by the beginning of May and just leave, I'll get Riccardo to replace me, I guess. I need to leave, yes, I'm going to do it- I was feeling so excited I couldn't stop repeating myself, as if that could have reinforced the fact that it was going to happen.
-Would you actually? Oh man, that would save my life really, but don't feel like you owe me anything. You guys left without me, and that was wrong, but...-
-That wasn't wrong Matt. It wasn't our fault if you're the most demanding man I know and it's impossible to please all of your requests. Anyway, yeah, I don't owe you anything, but I still need you around- I realised I had made one of my best manipulations ever that night and felt satisfied about it.
Matt didn't say anything but kept smiling, complacent. I did owe him my return, I thought whilst cycling home.

By the end of April, I told Luigi I was leaving the house and set an agreement with Riccardo on my replacement, which worked perfectly, and the landlord was just fine with it.
On the other hand, Luigi's reaction was unexpected, although I saw that coming because of Matt's way to explain it.
Luigi was surprised, slightly annoyed by the fact I was dumping him, but not in the way he would have been if he had been in a normal mental state. He didn't really want to live with Riccardo, who was dirty, disorganised and stole stuff from everyone all the time.
I could see from his face that he was hit, but not at all injured, which was great for me too.
I didn't want to lose that friendship, but he wasn't the same person I knew and used to hang out with everyday. He was unrecognisable, lost.
-You abandoned me- he once said whilst I was packing my stuff. His voice was so feeble I almost couldn't hear it.
-I didn't. You abandoned me, but let's not talk about it. I've got to go my own way Luigi. I'm not happy like this-
-I knew you couldn't live in a house. Moving in with you was a mistake. If you weren't ready to leave the hostel, then you shouldn't have dragged me into this- his voice was now getting stronger, accusing me.
-I was moving in with you, or that's what I thought I was doing, but then you disappeared, I never see you!- I was getting louder too now.
-Well...- he said something else, but his voice was gradually turning back to normal, and then he started texting on his phone again.

April was a complete waste. I lived like an ordinary citizen for one month and it sucked.
I had sex once and it cost me the money for alcohol that I needed to drink so to hit on the girls in the club and get a phone number, a bit of texting so to get the dinner date set up, the effort to make sure my clothes were clean and ironed, the price of about 40 pounds for the dinner, and over 20 pounds for the Uber ride back to her place to only get a

couple of minutes sex, since she had made me struggle so hard I performed horribly.
In the hostel, I could get laid multiple times a month and still spend less money that any guy normally had to spend for that to happen, not to mention the fact that I didn't have to dress up. Never, and that was the cherry on the cake for me.
My social life also sucked. I had only one person to talk to the whole day and that didn't work out either.
This was, in my opinion, a major mistake that most people make in terms of social life management. They force themselves to a group of people or even just one person, and then put up with them and take all the shit that they give them.
One month, and I was alone, bored, more tired, stressed by the arguments lifted up by the two Sicilian girls who spoke behind their backs all the time when they were with us and behind ours when they weren't. I had spent more money than I usually did and met less people, and all in exchange of what? Normality? Conformity? Who on earth gave these two words positive meanings?
I had a grin of satisfaction on my face whilst I walked back to Guilford Street carrying my two only suitcases.

May 2017

Within the first week of May, my feelings for the family were clearer.
I was Matt's favourite and most needed presence, had a stable very friendly relationship with Adam and Diego, and a relationship of mutual respect with Zak, Pavel, Ella and Ema, whereas regarding the others, there was no hostility whatsoever, but neither a real attachment.
I enjoyed a few days in the hostel when I realised that not only the family was different, but so was the attitude of the staff.
In fact, now that the staff was entirely Arab, the sexual life of people was made harder by the constant checks of the security that used to, sometimes, even follow the actions of those who were flirting in the common room up to when they successfully made it to bed.

Personally, I admitted to having got used to that to the point I used to just take girls straight to Russell Square, or in case they weren't up for any outdoors activity, to plan how it was going to happen in mine or their room.
I used to be happy when me and my target happened to stay in the same room, but that was quite of a lucky coincidence, since there were about fifty rooms in the building.
When we slept in different rooms, I had to make sure that either I or her went to my room at some point, wait behind the door and open when she had knocked at it about five to ten minutes later. This was in order to make sure they didn't see us walking together through the cameras.
-It feels like being in a dystopian reality here sometimes- I commented after talking about it with Celia, the only one at that moment who complained about the struggle.
She once got caught in the toilet with Luigi, and the two were really scared to lose their bookings and having to find a new place to move to all of a sudden, which would have been a problem since we were all working class people. We didn't really have time to deal with too many things at the same time, especially since we might have had a very long shift the following morning, and those people took no excuses for such things.
On the other hand, they would usually give a second opportunity to anyone whose behaviour was good enough. People like me, Celia or Luigi in fact never really created problems, and that was the reason why we were once forgiven, but we knew that the same wasn't going to happen for people who were disliked by the staff.
Basically, after analysing the matter, Matt and I came to the conclusion that the hostel was shaping its rules according to the staff and their ideals rather than to the British values, which were supposed to be present everywhere on British soil, but they struggled to exist in a place where no one could do anything to safeguard them.
Seeing the security guys looking at the lesbian couple with disgust on their faces and looking for any excuse to give them some warnings so to be able to kick them out at some point was truly annoying.

It was a situation that could be compared to the day I got fired from Cote for drinking at work. They guessed it right, but they still had no proofs, and anyway, everyone drank at work, and everyone cooperated with each other so that none of us got into any trouble for it. Drinking at work was forbidden, but yet normalised and legitimised by the happy majority, which ironically also allowed anyone to be fired for doing what everyone else did whenever another reason lied behind the dismissal.
The Muslim staff, including Joseph and other guests sometimes hated to see a gay or lesbian couple holding hands by the sofas, but it was the very fact we were on British soil and British laws applied that forbade them to just kick them out cold-blooded. We knew they couldn't do something like that, although we knew they wanted to.
This, together with my desire to refresh the rusty stagnated situation in the hostel pushed me to plot against it, and start convincing the others to move to another hostel based in King's Cross, a place called Home London.
Within the next few days, many conversations where I subconsciously incited everyone to write down any reasons to leave the hostel and head to Home London gave birth to a movement that most people of the family agreed to follow. Soon enough, some of us simply switched the bookings from the former to the new place, and by the second week of the month, the group was officially split, with some moving to a room somewhere, some staying in Guilford Street, and some coming with me.

Home London was much smaller than Russell Square hostel. It had a small bar underneath with proper pub atmosphere that served draught and bottled beers, sofas, a few tables in the common room, a breakfast area that served pancakes and a cute small smoking area in the basement.
In just a few days, the family reached a new level of harmony, also pushed by the perceived promise of better times that happened whenever wanted geographical changes occurred.

In my opinion, people often changed jobs or neighbourhoods even when things weren't that bad for the simple reason of bringing some changes to other aspects of their lives.
This didn't necessarily make much sense and it only showed one of the imperfections of the brain, that in this case tended to work through connections made by experienced associations.
The brain that requires some changes to a stressed person's situation does whatever it takes to pursue that change, often forcing its body to believe that other changes are needed, such as their home, their partner or their jobs, for the big change to actually occur. In my view, none of these things were related to the change that needed to be achieved, since all struggles should be fought individually, but who was I to ask my brain for full rationality in every moment?
There was only one thing now that ruined the harmony of the family, and that was Zak.
Over time, Zak's successes with girls were multiplying exponentially, and as a consequence of this, someone started speaking behind his back.
After sleeping with Celia a few times and getting rejected by her when he mentioned something in regard of his feelings, the rest of the family took advantage of the breakup to pick sides, with everyone choosing Celia due to her unquestioned popularity, except for me.
The reason behind it was not that I picked the other side, but rather that I didn't want to lose any of them. I cared about Celia, but I also cared about Zak now, especially since I happened to be the only person who actually hung out with him due to our mutual passion for chess. Besides that, I also just wasn't naturally keen on drama, a subconscious strategy for people who wanted to create division so to receive a confirmation that, in case, the others will pick their sides.
I definitely enjoyed being in the middle of the attention, but I never wanted it to rise at the cost of someone else's presence in the family.
Zak's situation was like a way for me to prove a point to myself. I wanted to feel like a good Samaritan and accept him whilst everyone else rejected him. In some cases, this was an act that came from my usual habit of taking those

that are stranded by society and welcome them into my arms in order to develop a great sense of loyalty due to their desperation and subsequent relief for being accepted by someone. That was a pure narcissistic move by me, but I also went on to admit this wasn't entirely the case. In fact, I truly believed Zak didn't deserve any of that.

-So, what happened with the rest of the group?- I once asked him at the table in the common room of the new hostel.

We had just played a few games on the new beautiful exotic chess board with a missing rook, and I had lost all of them.

-I don't know man- he said, trying to sound chilled, but at the same time I could see he wasn't enjoying it at all.

I knew he wanted to fix all of that, but it seemed impossible after the messages I read on the group chat.

The ritual that is usually orchestrated by political parties in order to win the favour of the masses against the opposition was put into place with a magnificence resemblance to the world of politics.

First, someone makes their accusations against someone else in private places, such as the sofas area once in the middle of the night after having a few drinks. The next days, someone that heard about it and happens to agree will find their way to find you and confess to you to feeling the same way, creating a bond between the most mediocre and malicious people of the family, which naturally tend to be the most proactive ones too.

The second step is also cunning, since it consists of purposely concentrating the attention and the praise on one person, typically the most popular, so to lead the rest of the group to do the same by dedicating more of their time around a specific part of the family rather than the other, so that when the moment of the truth arrives, the ostracising part of the family will find itself in the urge of letting their perceived outrage against the defendant, winning not only due to the fact that the victim was caught by surprise, but also to the fact that the rest of the group would have supported the winning side and abandoned the losing one.

When it came to popularity, Zak stood not a single chance against Celia, which made everyone's job very easy to be done. A few words said by Celia, tired of Zak's constant chase after her and invasion of her privacy sparked an outrage from other girls that wanted to get rid of him to support Celia, and by the men that, and I was totally sure about it, all wanted to bang Celia.

The guys and the girls managed to get rid of a guy that slept with at least one or two different girls a week out of jealousy and frustration for his active sexual life, by far superior to those of everyone else, including mine and Rey's.

If it was true that Rey and I scored just as much as him, it was also true that we tried and failed more than he did to keep our statistics high, while Zak didn't seem to fail.

He got rejected very rarely, and the level of attractiveness of the girls he picked was also quite high. He hit on the best-looking ones and often succeeded, although, just like us, he didn't mind settling for a lower level one when the night didn't go as planned.

I could tell the guys would have been happy to get rid of him for that reason. Having a player like Zak around meant tough life for other guys, and to be fair, I understood them. I used to dislike him a lot when he got to the hostel because he showed no respect for the game, jumping in the middle of a conversation between me and a new girl, sticking around and at times literally trying to get her away from me if I was gone for a bit. I had to be careful when he was around and I did hope on several occasions that he would just stop making bookings and leave the hostel.

By May though, our relationship was getting better, and I felt like I didn't have to worry about his opportunistic moves anymore, especially after we talked about such thing and he confirmed to me how important loyalty between friends was to him. In fact, as soon as I told him I was planning to make a move on a very attractive red-haired girl who was living in the new hostel that night, he immediately texted me encouraging words to push me towards it. Not that I needed them, but I was pleased to read them.

Now that the step in Guilford Street and the cafe in Greenville Street were far away, Matt found a new place to go and lie in his sad comfort, a bench in a dark park in Hermingford Road, about ten to fifteen minutes walk from our hostel. Matt would walk there and spend the night

isolated from the rest of the group, sitting in silence for hours and hours, often until dawn.
-I may not be able to see my dad again. He may be dead by the time I get back to Australia- he once said. His father was old and had been sick for a few months, getting worse by the day.
Matt's situation and look were degenerating to the point it became almost painful to even just look at his face. A tall, good-looking, intelligent and friendly man whose unproductive habits and small instinct of survival led him to a mental self-sabotage.
I felt he was misplaced in there. His knowledge was wasted on that bench, much like his relaxed ways were in the UK.
-I hate to say this, but you should go back to Australia man, and I promise I will visit you at some point, sooner than you think actually- I said, conscious that it couldn't have been possible anytime soon at all.
-I regret coming to London. It was a mistake- Matt said, his voice even lower and soarer than usual.
He had been in England for a year, but just like me and like many others, the comfort zone trapped him and forced him into a lifestyle of fixed laziness, a sort of prolonged holiday that got renewed day by day, mostly driven by the fact that most people that surrounded Matt were less educated and ambitious than him, which inevitably slowed him down a lot in general. Combined with his passion for weed and natural nice guy manners, the result was a terrifying waste of time and money, and I felt slightly guilty about it. It was me that spent the most time with him after all, and I knew that I might have been a pleasant company for him, but also useless, if not detrimental.
I was more than happy to finish my day of work on my bicycle and then go back to the hostel. My normality was achieved and fulfilled everyday, with ups and downs surely, but I had to realise that it wasn't Matt's reality at all.
-In my defence, I have told you many times that you were wasting time and that you should have gone back home over the months. It's not too late now, consider this like a very long holiday, I guess- I wasn't sure I was making too much sense.

-Don't worry about it. It could have gone worse, I guess. At least I met you guys- his voice almost faded into silence before he ended his sentence.

With Rey's return to London, things were meant to become much better, at least for me. I was looking forward to going out with him again, although as far as I could tell, Rey's feelings for Zak were also genuinely bad.
-I don't like him. I only have a few friends Dom, and the one that matters the most is you. No one else matters, I never cared about anyone- Rey often said, and I knew that, regarding Zak, he didn't like him for the same reason he said he didn't like anyone, which was a simple lack of interest in the existence of people who weren't very close friends to him. He was sociable and polite with everyone, but only gave his time to those he was highly attached to.
That night, Rey and I were supposed to go out with Zak too, which would have been a perfect chance to try and get him closer to him, until the moment we found out he was late because he was hanging out with the red-haired girl I meant to hit on a few days before, but hadn't really had a proper chance to yet.
Zak showed up outside the hostel and said he was ready to go out when I confronted him, to which he sounded surprised and guilty, admitting to already having done his job on the girl.
-I see- I said, then stayed silent, feeling more and more annoyed each second. That was a garbage move to make without telling me first.
-I was drunk- he replied, trying to put as much sorrow as he could on his face.
-See? I told you, I knew since the beginning that he was that kind of guy- said Rey, feeding my disappointment a few minutes later on the bus.
-Right, so this is what I get for being close to him. I guess I should really try to keep him away and consider him a parasite like everyone else does- I thought out loud, with Rey agreeing with me whilst we were on our way to Camden to meet up with the rest of the family.

We left Zak in the hostel, and I found myself glad to be speaking the worst things behind his back and get full agreement of Celia and the others in the streets before reaching the bar.
-He's an Arab man, like me. I know how they are- said Adam, one of the nicest people I knew and also one of the most active in cancelling Zak together with Ella, who truly hated him.
I wasn't surprised to know that she felt like that also because she was the most emotional and dramatic person in the group. I didn't think she was wrong by default, but I usually assumed that her opinion about people was more often tainted by herself rather than by critical analysis.
Rey and Celia eventually fed my feelings through supporting my indecent words and by offering further examples to rationalise the fact that Zak had to be considered a threat to the harmony of our relationships.
However, all I could think about then, was that he was probably having a better night than all of us.

By mid-May, my feelings for the new hostel were already fading. I still liked it more than I could have liked any single room in a house share, but it just wasn't the same. It wasn't Russell Square, and most importantly, there was really no more family.
The group was now reduced to me, Matt, Celia, Diego and Zak, who now had no friends at all, since Matt and Diego, who might have not had anything in particular against him, still felt like avoiding him anyway. We were still in touch with the others, but the core family that lived around me was suddenly, and also very quickly, meeting its end.
Eventually, life chose other homes for most of us, and with Matt leaving at some point, Celia leaving to her own place by the end of the month, I didn't want to be left alone to suffer from nostalgia until the next family were to originate, if a new one ever were to be.
Coincidence was, that Rey had just texted me that day and suggested me to move with him into a studio flat in Knightsbridge.

That evening, I found the address on my navigator and followed the instructions to reach the new place in Hans Crescent, one of the fanciest areas in London, just in front of the embassy of Colombia and next to Harrods.
The flat was big enough for two or even three people, it had a sofa, a small table, an armchair, a big bed, a kitchen and a toilet in two separate rooms.
-The guy says he's ok with 1200 pounds per month, although this place is probably much more expensive than that- said Rey as I unpacked my suitcase.
-Fair enough, it's a bit more expensive than the hostel, but I like it that we're the only ones in here, we won't have to deal with anyone else- I was sure Rey wasn't listening to me though.
-It's only going to be for two months though, then he's coming back from his holidays-
-How do you know this guy? He must be a millionaire or more than that- I asked him.
-A customer of mine- he replied.
I should have known it. Gay men had a tiny choice in the sexual marketplace when compared to the straight population due to a simple matter of numbers, which massively contributed to boost their money-making skills in order to result more desirable in a market that presented way less opportunities. One was either excellent in as many possible sides such as look, care of it, education, personality and social-economic conditions, or he would have had to settle down for someone who was way below in the pyramid of worth.
This didn't happen in the straight world though. In fact, there were so many potential partners, that one could screw things up in life forever and still find new chances, especially through travelling, for instance.
Pleased about what I saw around me, I decided to spend my last days in the hostel and communicate to everyone that I was leaving in a couple of days.

My relationship with the family and its leader Celia was apparently stable, but I could still find some reasons to doubt of its strength. In fact, I wasn't the family's first choice, but rather an addition that could have helped in the moment the group was acting too adult-like and things were being boring. One night, I was invited by Celia to hang out at Joao and Adam's place in Cricklewood. The two of them had developed a great friendship and were constantly doing stuff together. I often saw them posting on social media and felt somehow excluded from that, although I had to conclude that my feelings were based on my usual crave for attention and lack of initiative when it came to anyone except Rey, Luigi and Zak.

It was true that they didn't invite me to be part of the nights out, but it was also true that neither did I, not to mention the fact that we were different types of people, and that I often rejected meeting up with them due to more hedonistic plans with Rey, who loudly admitted to only needing me in his life, something that got us very attached and distanced us from others.

Anyway, I decided it was time for me to show I cared about the family, and that I genuinely liked both Joao and Adam, even though I felt they were ashamed of having me around. When I arrived at their place in Cricklewood, I brought with me drinks and snacks in massive quantity, in an attempt of increasing my likeability.

Celia gave me a very warm welcome, together with the two guys who were inside. I met Joao's girlfriend, a Belgian, pretty tall girl named Clarisse who rushed to confessing me to loving beers and acted suspiciously friendly.

I had no doubts that I was considered the constantly drunk guy by the group, who had to have given Clarisse some sort of description about me prior to my arrival, but I couldn't feel that bothered. Maybe, a bit of fame, regardless of its nature, could have made them see me under a good light anyway.

Over the night, I got more and more convinced that I was overthinking it, and that my spot in the family was secured by the fact I had an established relationship with most people who were invited to the party, including the highly loved Celia, who eventually engaged with me in the usual conversation where we both showed how concerned we were about Matt's state.

-By the way guys, I just wanted to tell you, in case I sometimes caused some embarrassing situations because of drinking, that's not the usual me. You know, I know when I can cross the line and when I should not, so you don't have to worry, this won't happen when I'm with you- I said loud at some point after the umpteenth beer can.
Celia, who was still talking low-key due to the seriousness of our common topic, looked at me shocked, and then burst out laughing, together with some others. Once again, I had managed to take my surrounding environment from an adult atmosphere to a less mature one with a statement.
As I was suspecting though, some people looked at each other and felt encouraged by my pre-emptive move. They thought the same thing, and that was the moment to speak.
-Yeah, to be honest, I only feel we should invite Domenico out with us when we don't have to worry about being embarrassing to others- said Adam with a jokey tone, although I knew he was dead serious about that and also glad to be finally able to voice it in front of me. Joao didn't wait a second to agree with him, making the rest of the group laugh.
I laughed too, and thought that it wasn't too bad.
I was cycling on my way back to Knightsbridge when I thought that actually worked perfectly for me. I was never going to be a member of a group of mentally sane people that cared about making progress with their lives and act mature, but rather the troublemaker that they called when things were too boring. Besides, there was now more transparency between all of us, since we were finally able to make things clear on who we were for each other.
Clarisse told me it was nice meeting me and that she was looking forward to more nights like that right when I reached Hans Crescent.
I told her the pleasure was mutual. I didn't know when and if I was actually going to meet her again because at first, I thought that her and Joao looked pretty unusual as a couple.

I was glad to be in Hans Crescent with Rey, and I was also enjoying Mark's regular visits, who ended up sleeping on a

pair of blankets on the floor a few times a week, especially because he was broke and had nowhere to stay.
-Can't you stay at your mom's or dad's place?- I asked him once.
-Not really, although I'm going to try and get in there through the window at some point soon- he replied. You could never tell whether he was serious or not, since most of his replies to any questions were just jokes he made up at the moment or recalled from comedy shows and podcasts.
Meanwhile, my feelings towards Zak had become mixed. I was still upset with him for making a move on a girl I found first, not because of her specifically, but rather because that was supposed to indicate to me what kind of friend he would have been.
Eventually, I concluded that I couldn't trust him, and decided to ignore his messages, although I also couldn't ignore that he wasn't doing any good.
He got kicked out from Russell Square in the middle of the night at the beginning of the month, his clothes and belongings were gathered into black bin bags and he was dismissed without mercy for having sex with an Italian girl in one of the hostel's rooms by Latif, who was planning to get rid of him for some time already.
Personally, I had no doubts that the reason of their despise towards him was due to the fact he drank alcohol and regularly ate pork in front of everyone.
On top of that, he was hated by pretty much everyone in the family, avoided by those who didn't mind his presence just out of fear of social exclusion, and didn't seem to behave at best with those that gave him an opportunity to show he was a good addition to their lives.
-He's not a friend, he's just someone I know, and I don't need to see him. If he wants to stay here for a night, he'll have to pay us- said Rey, lying down in bed as usual with his phone in his hands. He never got his eyes off the screen, whether he was playing chess, checking messages from the escorting website or gambling in sport events.
Being in Knightsbridge was great. It had the beauty and quiet of Russell Square by night, a unique level, or at least perceived level of safety, lots of very good-looking people,

was super central and also presented busy demand of food deliveries, which I was glad to take both in mornings and evenings shifts, alternated with my chess coaching.
The proximity with most of the schools I coached in allowed me to leave my oyster card at home and go wherever I needed to by bike, which was necessary to pay the higher rent after all. In addition to that, living with Rey was fantastic, a completely different experience than living with Luigi, although I couldn't deny I missed him.
In those days, I was doing my best to get back in touch with Luigi, who now seemed to have moved past my departure, and was keen in meeting up.
What contributed to this was also the fact that his love story with his Polish colleague didn't go anywhere, since she just called it over at some point, about less than a month from its start, and the good thing about that, was that he was now single again, and that meant he was a completely different person.
Unlike Rey and me, Luigi changed massively when he was in a relationship of any kind with a girl. He focused so much on his relationship that he literally forgot about the people who were closest to him straight after meeting a new partner.
That, to me, was comprehensible but also unhealthy. I knew how he felt, but I didn't accept it, also because it made me feel like the only reason why he used to hang out with all of us before getting a romantic partner, was that he didn't have a romantic partner.
However, we managed to get in touch again, and things seemed to have become all normal in a very short time.

By the second half of May, a message from Matt arrived that paralysed me for a couple of minutes.
He said he had booked his ticket back to Australia for the end of the month. He mentioned he was finally acting to change his life for the better and that he hoped to see his dad again.
I replied saying I understood him and invited him to stay over at ours in Hans Crescent, which he accepted pretending to be surprised about my invitation.
I picked him up the day after and helped him carry his suitcases from the tube exit in Sloane Avenue to our place,

and within a couple of minutes, Matt, another person of unreal physical passivity like Rey, had already grabbed his spot on the bed, leaving me to the only option of sleeping on the sofa.
-We're much taller than you- said Matt, making Rey laugh. None of them could have fit on the sofa to be fair, whilst it was almost perfect for me.
By then, I could tell that Matt's lifestyle was a reflection of his inner state. His dark beard had grown a lot and looked bushy, his slow body movements, his tendency to stay silent and lie down in bed all day combined with his refusal to even step outside the door whilst he asked others to do the shopping for him, all indicated that every extra day he was spending away from his home was damaging him even further.
-It's good that you're leaving soon, and it sucks at the same time- I once commented. A part of my brain was keeping track of how many days were missing to his departure, whilst another part was actively trying to prevent me from thinking about it and just enjoy my time with him as much as I could, and eventually, I concluded that being nice to him was the best thing I could do to help.
Matt was no regular person, no average citizen. Unlike many people, his kindness and fairness towards others was not based on a subconscious attempt to get something in exchange, but rather just his nature, and to confirm that, I had two reasons. The first being the fact I had never seen him taking a single irrational decision, even when people had been unfair to him in the past, and the second being my emotional bias that was based on how loyal, supporting and entertaining he had been for me over an entire year together.

I spent three days of the last week of May in Portugal, where I met Denise, a lovely girl I had a very interesting conversation with during my trip to Krakow with Rey. We had kept in touch a bit, and earlier in May, I managed to find some cheap tickets and booked my trip to Lisbon, where she promised to host me.

The time with her and her sister was great, Lisbon was a great place in general. Anyway, the moment I landed back in London, I felt miserable.
A couple of days to spend with Matt was all I had left. In three days, I thought, he was going to be gone forever. Something inside of me was already gathering emotional disappointments from the past and forcing me to better thoughts, whilst something else was actively engaged in reminding me that I needed to feel bad about it.
Meanwhile, Celia had come to stay in our flat, since she wanted to be near Matt as much as she could as well before saying bye to him.
That evening, Celia, Rey, Matt, Zak and I had dinner at our place.
It was weird to see Zak in the same room as Celia and Matt, who were lying down next to each other in bed now. Zak was doing great with girls, but I wasn't sure he was over Celia, although I assumed he probably didn't like to see her. I didn't like it when something like that happened to me after all, and Zak was very similar to me on that.
After dinner, Rey, Zak and I left to go to a pub and get a pint, whilst Matt said he would reach us later on in the night, which eventually didn't happen.
With the passage of hours, I felt more and more upset with him for not showing up and choosing to stay in bed the whole night.
-I'm sorry I'm not there with you- he suddenly texted me. -I have to tell you something, but only if you promise not to share this with Diego- he added.
-Tell me- I texted back, hoping he would give me a reason that was good enough for me to keep my disappointment growing.
Few moments later, Matt sent a picture of him and Celia naked in our bed doing funny faces, which hit me and left me stoned for a minute. What the hell?

On the way home, I was thinking about it, I was angry, and not because of the pints I had. How could he do this to me? I was probably never going to see him again and he didn't spend his last night in London with me?

When we got into our flat, it was the stupidest side of me that spoke.
-Right, off the bed. I've barely slept on that bed since when I'm here, and I'm the one that pays rent, so if you want to sleep here tonight, maybe get to the sofa or something- I told Matt, slowly regretting the harsh tone and the absurd request I had made. Matt wouldn't have fit on the sofa anyway.
Shocked, he slowly stood up and moved away, with Celia who was paralysed because of that. Maybe, if Celia and I hadn't had a relationship of great respect for each other, she would have told me off, but she chose to stay silent, just like everyone else. There was a drama right there and I couldn't believe it was me that started it, although I was praying for something to happen so that I could just turn around towards Matt and tell him it was just a joke, and that of course he could have slept in bed, especially considering he had often told me it was extremely important for people who suffer from epilepsy to sleep well.
-So, is this how you want things to end between us?- Matt's words and painful tone made me feel ashamed.
I didn't say anything. I wasn't able to make the necessary plot twist, so my brain decided that the only way to coexist with the awareness of having done something wrong was to twist the meaning of reality until it matched with the one where I was the good guy.
Yes, I was upset with him, and he deserved this. Also, I didn't like it that Celia spent so much time talking to Diego, but never making it clear to him that he wasn't going to get her. Why would they need to hide that from him otherwise? Or maybe she actually made it clear, but he was too dumb and needy to let that go.
And then, finally, my brain comforted me and suggested me to sleep so not to think about it any further.

The next morning, Matt took his backpack and suitcase as silently as he could, then left with Celia, all whilst I was pretending to still be sleeping.
That was it, the worst thing I had ever done to a friend. I had enjoyed his presence everyday and I couldn't show him I was

actually happy he had finally succeeded in getting Celia. He did tell me quite a few times in the past that he really wanted to get her, and I had ignored it out of pure selfishness. Now, he was gone though. I had also given him an uncomfortable night sleep, and besides, what was Celia going to do about me now? Was she going to hate me? Was she going to turn the family's machine against me and have me cancelled and exiled?

I was already picturing such scenarios in my head when my brain reminded me that, just in case it was necessary, it could have decided it didn't need to feel part of my family and that I could have just started a new one eventually. However, this process was interrupted by Matt's phone call one hour later. If that wasn't my chance, I would have had no other.

-Matt?- I spoke as nicely as I could.
-My father just died. Can you come to me, please?- he begged. The sound of his voice penetrated me and gave me the feeling of a cold shower.
-I'm sorry to hear that. Give me half hour, I'll come see you- I said whilst standing up, both saddened by the news, but also happy he had called and now I had a chance to fix what I had done.
-Copenhagen Park, or whatever it's called- he added at the end.

Rey and Zak followed me to the tube station and accompanied me to King's Cross. A long walk until we reached the park uphill where we found Matt sitting on his usual bench.

That park didn't manage to replace Queen Square in the slightest. That bench didn't look as good as the one where we often stayed up all night, and on top of that, the park was dark pretty much at all times.

Matt and I hugged, and then I apologised. I wished Rey hadn't told him he saw me crying in the pillow that morning, but it was too late to stop him.

In the afternoon, Matt, Celia, Ella, Rey, Zak and I all sat in Pret, the one in front of Russell Square. Matt and I left the group at some point and walked to Guilford Street, where we stayed for a couple of minutes alone. Then, we reached the tube once again, and right by the entrance, the Aussie hugged each one of us and eventually, he walked away without turning his back.

June 2017

By June, my relationship with Zak was going through a renewed improvement.
My decision to give him another opportunity in building up a friendship was not rational, since I figured it derived from my personal desire to exploit his passion and skills for chess to entertain me, his look and confidence with girls to go hunting together, and his general alignment to my own ideals on how to live a life to receive support in discussing my choices. This situation reminded me of some of my past attachment with girls that showed me some red flags during my development of romantic thoughts towards them that I decided to ignore, fabricating stories in my head just to feel good about it, escaping reality for some short, glorious periods of time just to see it coming back and crash me afterwards.
-What makes you think he might change and become a trustworthy person?- Rey was challenging my thoughts a lot, stubborn when it came to judging him.
-I believe that at first, he was acting like that just because he was trying to get laid, just like we always do, but now that we're friends, he'll behave- I replied, realising only then that what I said not only worked as a reply due to a lack of arguments in my favour, but also that I had done some mental gymnastics in trying to prove he could have been a good friend.

In the morning of the third of the month, Rey, Zak and I headed to Cardiff, where the Champions League final was taking place.
The previous night, the three of us spent it at a bar in front of Home London, eventually joined by the red-haired girl from the hostel and another pretty attractive Russian girl who was staying at the same place.
What started off as a night where we tried to act adult for once, having overly expensive drinks and staying at our table

without introducing ourselves to others, later turned out in the usual unpredictable way, this time funnier than usual, in mine and Rey's opinion.

In fact, it turned out that both girls, who had quickly developed some jealous attachment towards Zak, were there for their own goals. The red-haired, who would act rude towards the Russian girl the whole night, and the latter, who was focusing on him only, trying to ignore the other girl.

-I love Zak- the Russian girl told me when she joined me for a cigarette outside the bar.

-What?- I said, slightly envious of how quickly Zak had managed to conquer a very attractive girl that quickly.

-He made breakfast for me- she added with dreamy eyes.

-Yeah, that's what made you fall in love?- I was beginning to think it was all a joke until she spoke again.

-No one ever did anything like this for me- she said, now sounding completely serious and reminding me of the unsurprising fact that she was Russian after all.

-Right, look, it's actually a pretty normal thing to do here. Guys often do nice things for girls in western Europe- I tried to rationalise to her, but it was a lost case.

-I'm willing to move here and leave my boyfriend in Moscow. I don't care, I never loved him anyway, I'll find a job, I can do anything if necessary- she was raving hard, and her face looked almost scary to me.

It wasn't unusual for Russian girls to feel like the one and only thing that mattered in life was a man, but this one was taking the game up to a new level of lameness. It should have been a pleasure, I thought, for a dominant Russian man to live in such reality, to bend attractive girls to only wish to be with him so hard and with no escape from that.

I had spoken with lots of Russian girls in my life, both when I was studying the language many years before, and also during my long stays in Moscow, and I had to admit that the majority of girls truly were in that state, although to slightly varying degrees.

On top of the insane confession I had listened to, what made the night even more entertaining was the explosion of the red-haired girl that resulted into a verbal attack against the Russian one, her response in suggesting to start a proper fight

with her, Zak's attempt of calming them down, unsuccessful due to the amused expression he had on his face, and finally, a punch he got on his face from the Russian one, who saw her feelings not being requited by her new lover.
Later on, the two guys and I returned to our studio flat, laughing about that evening, although I couldn't deny that in that moment, I wanted to be in Zak's place.

-Dom, man, you're not going to believe what chick I just got a number from- Rey told me one afternoon, visibly excited about it.
-Picture- I lazily asked him from my sofa, still unable to lift up my eyes from my phone.
-She's a good one, one that has money, for sure, at least it looks like. See Dom, this is what happens when you move to a fancy area like this one, everything improves, and now we finally get what we deserve- Rey explained his theory, still very excited whilst showing me the picture of a very attractive blonde woman in fancy clothes, posing near the stairs in what seemed to be a luxurious house.
-Right, don't waste your time, she's full of shit- I said, dismissing the idea of ever trying to get somewhere with someone like that, although still very tempted by keep looking at her.
-See? This is how losers talk, you're a loser- said Rey, who still couldn't sit down, now literally walking around the flat with a dumb smile on his face.
-I met her in an Uber on my way here from one of my clients, she said we're going out together tonight, and she gave me her VIP name to get into a night club here in Sloane Square- he said, as if the hard job was already done, and all that was left then was the enjoyment part of it.
-Yeah, listen, she's just trying to get people to get into the club where she works, she either owns the place or charges commissions when she picks up new goers or something- I was rationalising, or maybe just trying to give myself a reason not to believe that Rey was going to have a real chance with a woman like that.
-Is Zak sleeping here tonight again? Did you invite him, right?- Rey asked me, ignoring my words.

-He's visiting us later, he texted me. We should go out all together tonight, I guess- I said, glad he was coming over, but also slightly worried that Rey might have cancelled that.
-He's coming here to stay over the night, that's why he brings his backpack too, didn't you notice? He's manipulating you, he's making you believe you are friends so that he can take advantage of your kindness. I can tell you that, I'm older than you, and also judge better when it comes to selecting friends. One day you'll realise that-
-Right, enough, I don't want to hear this, you've told me too many times already-
-You are his only friend Dom, think about why it is so- he said, sneering as if he had just made a winning point in debate.

In the following days, Rey had become very active on the Couchsurfing website, where he had created a host profile, offering places to stay to all those that were travelling to London and in need of accommodation, or simply willing to try and save money from that.
The idea felt good since the very beginning, especially after Rey had explained to me that he was only going to let girls in our place, giving no help to men whatsoever.
Living in Knightsbridge did give us some unquestionable advantage in attracting girls to our flat.
By mid-June, we had managed to take home two Spanish tourists from Asturias that we met in O'neills, had a threesome with a black British woman from a dating app for perverts where Rey was signed up in, and got plenty of contacts from girls who were visiting the area right after telling them where we lived.
-All it takes to get girls is to show them you have money, or just tell them actually, even if it's not true, like in our case- Rey once commented when we were walking back home from our local Caffe Nero in Old Brompton Road.
-We used to get many back at the hostel too- I noticed out loud, although I thought I knew what he meant with his comment.
-Yeah, but the quality is different Dom. Now we can get the girls that we couldn't get before, don't deny that-

I couldn't deny he had a point. Whenever we lied to girls about our occupations, sometimes telling them we were working in finance or that we owned businesses in our countries, it was impossible not to notice that their facial expressions experienced a change, sometimes more and sometimes less visible, but always present. There was no girl in the world, no matter what type she was, that didn't find rich guys attractive, and we were rich, at least according to our location, an asset we had that they could never disprove and therefore left them with the only choice to believe us. One of those afternoons though, we had a visit from a Couchsurfing girl that was clearly misplaced in all of that. I was surfing on the website myself straight after creating my own profile when I received a one-night stay request by a Scottish girl who was, in Rey's opinion, one of the ugliest girls he had ever seen.

-Don't let her come here man, come on, she's horrible- he complained, which I ignored, also because I knew that Zak was going to be there too and that we were going out that night.

-Who cares? Nothing is supposed to happen, let's just be kind to someone who needs it, just for a night- I said, actually hoping that something could happen, since I had never slept with a Scottish girl before, and I needed it to happen so that I could mark Scotland with a red pencil in my paper map. Amanda showed up in the late afternoon, and I gladly opened the door of our flat to her, letting her to rest in bed near Rey, who didn't even have the courage to look at her when he said hi.

Amanda looked weird, she was very skinny, had a wide nose and unusually large jaws, not to mention the darkish skin tone that didn't seem neither a part of her racial background nor a tan, but rather a sign of some sickness. On top of that, her bright pink dress gave her an even funnier look.

-Wanna have a drink?- she said after a couple of minutes of introduction, pulling out a bottle of whisky.

-I thought you were probably going to rest, you have a big day at a festival tomorrow, haven't you?- I asked her to pretend I was nice, although I hoped she would go on and drink.

-Hey, I'm Scottish, I can drink much more than both of you together, come on, don't be pussies!- she said, very enthusiastically and referring to both of us. Rey though, would still not move from his bed, keeping his eyes on his chess games online.
-Right, I'm in- I gave her my warmest of approvals also in the attempt of counterbalancing Rey's rudeness. That girl's only fault was to be ugly, but she didn't deserve to be considered any less than other company. If she had been any prettier, Rey would have been acting different.
-You always call me rude for the way I talk to people or to customer service, but here's the thing. You are the real rude person, because unlike London's customer service, this girl is actually nice, and she deserves you at least to be friendly, whether you want to try and bang her or not- I told Rey in Spanish, hoping that Amanda didn't speak any, which was quite likely due to her British origin.
-Keep silent please- Rey replied. There was no way he could have chosen to be rational if that involved admitting to being wrong or that I simply had a point.
A few bottles of spirits later, Zak had arrived at the flat, and Luigi with some other members of the family had agreed in going to O'neills together.
-It's so good that we're all going to be there tonight, a family reunion- I couldn't help commenting at some point.
-They're not my family- said Rey.
-Yeah, and in my case, I don't think I can call them that either- Zak commented, chuckling afterwards.
By then, the time spent together had brought Rey closer to Zak. He still wasn't any passionate about having him around, but he no longer complained nor tried to sabotage my attempts to let him sleep at ours.
Kicked out from both hostels he could call homes and that were both affordable and dignity-ensuring places, he was completely broke, had nowhere to go, no friends since after the group's mutiny against him, and he was even unable to get an ordinary job because of some issues with his student status. We didn't know what he was doing to survive, but we couldn't leave him in the streets.

That night, we left our place with a drunk Amanda, an apparently tranquil Zak who, in my opinion, was actually pretty nervous to be facing the rest of the group after what had happened, and Rey, Luigi and I who were just pretty excited and tipsy, looking forward to another night out at our favourite pub-club in the whole London.

-We should have got a cab or something, I don't think we're going to make it there- I commented to Amanda, who was now gradually doing worse and worse because of the alcohol and, some meth she smoked before leaving.

-Do we know the effects of meth on the human body? Generally speaking, I mean, I know nothing about drugs- I asked around the group whilst we were walking through Hyde Park Corner and our way to Piccadilly.

-Well, she shouldn't be like that actually, but I guess that combined with alcohol, the effects could be...- Zak began telling me, but then stopped because of arising uncontrollable chuckles that took over him and Luigi. Rey, on the other hand, still wasn't comfortable about having her around us.

By the time we reached Piccadilly, Amanda's body movements and language had become so weird I decided to stop her and prevent her from joining the queue with everybody else.

-Look, I know you keep saying you're fine, but you're really not to me. Let's take a seat here and then we'll join the rest of the group, I'm not taking no for an answer- I said, firm. I didn't want to carry her around like that, and I was already regretting inviting her.

-You guys go ahead, we'll come back soon- I told the others, who left me with her, now slightly concerned, but still amused as I could tell.

I made Amanda sit on a stone bench in the middle of Leicester Square and told her we wouldn't move until she was showing to be better, although she kept saying she was fine.

-Excuse me? Are you ok?- suddenly, two women appeared and were now talking to Amanda, worried.

-Yeah, she's with me, don't worry- I said, which they ignored, still focusing on her.

At first, I felt disrespected, but then I realised it made sense that they didn't trust me. Why should have they after all?
-Look, I'm going to take you home. Can you tell these girls you know me?- I asked Amanda, now worrying too. God knew how bad things could have got if she were to say the wrong things.
-Yes, I'm with him- she said, still shaking hard, and moving weirdly.
-I'm actually calling a cab now- I said, which worked to reassure the two women about everything apparently.
-We'll be home in just few minutes, and then you'll sleep, ok?- I told her whilst our cab drove us the way back to Knightsbridge.
-Yes, alright, I really like you- she said, still sounding in a confused state, but somehow improved, I guessed from her voice, which now sounded stronger than before. Besides, her body movements were almost under control now.
-Right, here we are- after some help through the stairs to the first floor, we were finally in our flat. I turned the lights off, and put Amanda to bed, brought a glass of water, left it on the nightstand and wished her good night. I wasn't going to pay for a cab to take me back to Piccadilly, and that meant I had to almost run if I wanted to still enjoy the night with my friends.
I had almost left the flat when I thought about her words in the cab, when she said that she liked me.
-Amanda? Do you want me to lie down next to you for a bit?- I asked her, not knowing exactly why.
-Really? Yes- she said.
Works for me, I thought, now undressing and going close to her.
She didn't sound completely fine though, and she didn't even look at me.
She might not be drunk any more, her body has stopped doing those weird movements and she's just tired, but still needs to rest before getting better. If I do anything to her now, her yes might not count in the future, although I have to say that she ruined my night and cost me a cab fare to come back home. It was her choice to drink and smoke that crap at the same time. Her choice, but it was a mistake, and

judging or acting on her mistake would have been the move of a vulture.
This is weird, it's a clear chance to have sex, maybe she's just playing with me, acting like she's slightly unconscious so that I could do my job on her, or maybe she'll call the police tomorrow if I do anything. I really need that cross on Scotland though.
-I want to be with you right now, do you want me too?- I whispered.
-Really? Yes- she repeated, now moving her head around, apparently still confused, responding unnaturally fast.
She did hear my question and she did say yes, but I wasn't recording it, and since she was a girl, her word would have counted more than mine in tribunal.
I thought about it for a few more minutes, my heart pounding both by excitement and fear, but then concluded it didn't make much sense to take that risk, also because I remembered how Alba once told me that such scenario could have easily be defined rape.
I went to sleep too. Going back to the guys would have been pointless by that time.

July 2017

July arrived, and Rey and I were inseparable as usual. We played chess whenever we were at home, discussed plans for future travels, scrolled the Couchsurfing page offering girls a place to stay, and partied every other day.
I loved my working situation at that time. I was working both delivering food and teaching kids in after school chess clubs. Overall, the pay for doing delivery was twice as high as the minimum wage, and the pay for London Kings was about five times higher, which allowed me to work about two to three hours per day everyday to make sure I could pay rent and have as much spare time as possible.
I loved it that things were stable, and in that situation, stable meant perfect.
I used to constantly state how much I hated the comfort zone and how ruthlessly I dismissed people who complained about it whilst taking no action against it, but I had to realise that I

was also a fan of the comfort zone myself, just in its positive meaning, if there really had to be one.

In my first year in London, I lived in places I didn't like, surrounded by co-workers I didn't like in a job I had neutral feelings for, victim of the negative type of comfort zone, the one where people live only to get paid at the end of the month, enjoying life as much as possible with the tiny amount of time and money available to them. I considered that lifestyle miserable, and I proudly bragged about having left that mindset and having acquired one of constant self-improvement.

If you don't like your job, change it, if you don't like your managers, shout at them and get fired, if you don't like coping with frustrated flatmates, move somewhere where you have no same people hanging out around you, taking only the best of them and avoiding the trap of them getting too familiar with you.

I acted like a stoic philosopher that knew how to live better than others, and I was right, but only to a certain extent.

In fact, it wasn't my mindset to be better than others, and it wasn't even near to be true that I constantly worked on my self-improvement. The only difference between me and others, was that I had become intolerant towards even the smallest things that didn't fit in the way I was building the reality around me to the point I dismissed and even fought against anyone that was on my way to my comfort zone, different from the average one, which is based on ordinary citizens' feelings of resignation.

I was rude, as Rey and pretty much everyone else in the family told me, more or less often. I was kind to baristas when they made coffees for me, but called them shit and wrote bad reviews when they forgot to give me my coffee and didn't apologise for it. I thought I was kind to Uber drivers even when I was drunk but I also got reminded by most of my friends that they never wanted to share a ride with me. I immediately deleted phone numbers of girls that didn't reply to my messages about two hours after I had texted them, not giving them a chance to believe them when they said they were busy or that they were sorry and they wanted to get in touch or meet up again. Lack of patience mostly characterised my mindset, and I had begun to consider every single act of any person towards me as their personal responsibility, taking no excuses because, in my opinion, disrespectful behaviour was a subconscious attempt of such people to test whether they could transform their relationship with me into a toxic one, with them being dominant and me being submissive.

To feed my personal sense of coherence, I liked to think I wasn't a rude person at all by giving good tips to nice hospitality workers, stand up for elderly people and women in the tube, helping them out carry suitcases up the stairs each time, always greeting people with a smile whenever I met them whilst internally hoping that they would do anything slightly acceptable for me to have an excuse to talk to them in a verbally abusive way.

I was much happier than I ever was when my attitude towards people was agreeable at any time. I realised that my former attitude was such because I was hoping that people would understand how better life could have been when deciding to act in a civil way and eventually choose to respect me, but I had lived too many scenarios that proved that it just wasn't the case, that it just didn't happen. A life being agreeable wasn't worth it, and now I was enjoying my new way of being me.

My new mindset was proving to be so useful that it often reminded me of my past and produced thoughts of shame about myself, desires of revenge against those that acted wrong towards me, or even desires to go back in time and deal with the same events of the past in a different way, the new way.

An example of that happened one night of mid-July in our flat, on the fourth day of staying of two Latvian girls who were visiting London.

Rey had invited them over, and they had accepted and brought us a small basket with some fruits and sweets from their country.

At first, I thought they were nice, and that something could have happened, since they were both in their early twenties, blonde, mildly attractive and most importantly, tourists. Unfortunately though, Rey had to go for a quick trip to Nice,

paid by a millionaire who wanted to see him urgently and was willing to pay much more than Rey's usual fee for that, which was a chance he obviously didn't reject.
With Rey being gone and me being particularly busy in those days, both on my bicycle and in schools, the girls were left to enjoy sleeping in bed and having the flat all for themselves most of the time.
On Rey's return though, we were willing to give it all a try.
-We should go out together tonight, maybe get a drink or something- I claimed, getting up from my lazy position on my sofa and throwing my phone on the nearest pillow.
-We're actually already going out with two guys, and we probably won't come back before tomorrow morning- one of the girls commented. They both met with two guys from Tinder in the previous days and were spending each evening with them.
-Right, I understand-
There was nothing I could do about it. Rey seemed to have my same opinion about the fact that hosting those girls was a waste of time.
-They are keeping their stuff in our place, but sleeping at another place. Why can't they just stay there at this point?- I asked Rey in Spanish, right in front of the girls, and he replied with a shocked expression on his face.
-One of them actually speaks Spanish fluently!- he texted me a few seconds later, to which I replied out loud.
-I don't care. Who's next? Anyone?- I asked him, still in Spanish, but tempted to even speak English then.
-Shut up, stop being rude- he texted whilst looking worried in the direction of one of the two girls, the one that could speak Spanish, who was now looking perplex, whilst her friend was just confused because of my voice tone.
-Look at these ones, they come to London tomorrow afternoon. I have invited them already, they're pretty hot, both from Australia- Rey was texting me almost one word at a time as he usually did, sending me pictures of two new girls from the Couchsurfing website, both very attractive.
-Fine, get them here tomorrow then. These ones are leaving tomorrow, right?- I texted back.

-They're leaving in the night, which is a problem. What should we do?- he texted.
-Girls, so, tomorrow morning you're leaving, right?- I asked them. Rey was staring at me, interested now.
-Oh, yeah, well, we are leaving in the night, so that we don't have to take our suitcases around the whole day- one of them replied very slow, now scared that there might have been a change of plans.
-Can't you take the suitcases at these guys' place tonight? That would make sense after all, then you can hang out with them tomorrow too instead of coming back here to take your stuff- I was explaining in my nicest of tones, even though I was sure I didn't manage to hide it was a demand.
The girls were both looking at me now, clearly disappointed with that.
I assumed our location, which was about fifteen minutes walk to Victoria Coach Station, would have made it ideal for them to leave their stuff at ours. Rey was literally paralysed, not willing to say a word about it, probably annoyed by my rude ways, but unlike any other time, he wasn't challenging me at all.
The next morning, the girls returned to our flat, took their suitcases and left just in time for the new girls to come up, literally meeting them on the stairs.

The two Australians were only staying two nights, and in the first one, they were offering drinks, which we gladly accepted.
Hannah and Jess had both just turned twenty and were travelling around Europe. Their first stop was Amsterdam, and the next one was going to be Italy.
Hannah had short curly hair and a very curvy body, just like Jess, who also could have been a professional model, but was slightly taller than her friend and her hair was long and straight of the same dense brunette colour.
The two girls were actual babes, I could tell from the way they moved, spoke and constantly checked their looks through their phones, added lipstick or wear perfumes.
Stunning looks, not a good sign, I thought, but at least they

were friendly, much friendlier than the two eastern Europeans we hosted up to a couple of hours before.

With the passage of time and alcohol, Rey and I, seeing that the girls didn't mind we were getting handsy, eventually began making moves on them whilst they put little resistance, although enough to keep rejecting us.

We kept going anyway, closing the curtains to make the room darker and suggesting the girls to drink more, who were then becoming keener on doing something with us.

It was about one hour later, that I was the most grateful to myself for not caring about the problem of the Latvian girls, their damn suitcases, my supposed kindness towards them or some sort of loyalty I had towards the word I gave them about their staying.

I was on top of Jess, enjoying everything of her, from her smooth dark skin and her teasing facial expression to the curves of her body. I had never got to be with a shape like that before, and if it was happening, I owed it to the fact I listened to what I wanted, and not to what I was morally meant to do.

I didn't do anything wrong by kicking those girls out earlier than agreed. They didn't even say hi when I came in, they chose to sleep with someone else that wasn't me, so they had to take their stuff away from me.

My life was better, and I owed it also to Rey. Sometimes I had a voice inside of me telling me that I needed to care about what was morally fair more than what was best for myself, but I learnt to silent that voice because I came to the conclusion that it lied to me each time.

It was the society, the agreeable person I used to identify myself with in the past, that gave me a place to stay and a list of guidelines to follow so to have the feeling of perceived coherence. Then, obeying the rules and staying in line went on to provide me with a sense of righteousness that I confused with goodness, whilst it was actually just a selfish desire to feel morally superior to others. A desire that never made me truly happy nor allowed me some rest, since the cunning people around me always made me work for them, and I always needed to obey just to get that feeling.

Meanwhile, exception made for very few days, Mark was literally staying at ours full-time, often withholding the only keys of the flat we had and working as some sort of receptionist. Reluctant, I had to admit this was actually working fine, since Rey and I were having problems at the beginning because of that, but now that Mark was staying there literally without ever leaving home, we never had to worry about taking the keys and leaving anyone else outside for a long time, especially if we were at work.

Zak was also a regular. Unlike Mark, he often brought us money to contribute to our rent expenses, which worked to function as the very last piece of the jigsaw that Rey needed to get to finally not only be cool with him, but also even like him.

Regarding Mark, he was no part of any family nor cared about anything outside of his own world. Mark was socially very valuable, willing to laugh all the time, extrovert, easy-going and anti-conflictual, but he also had no interest in dealing with others whatsoever. He just preferred to be on his own, checking football news, studying chess endgames or just endlessly watch stand-up comedy and podcasts, at times writing jokes down into some random papers he would leave all over the place.

-Guys, something great happened. I banged this woman, the wife of some guy living nearby, look at this- Zak showed up one late afternoon, looking pretty excited. He sat in bed next to Rey and showed us the picture of a seriously attractive woman, which caused a silent reaction from Rey and me.

-How did you do this? You can't be serious- I asked him a few seconds later, when envy had decreased enough to let me talk.

-I was introduced to this guy by a dude I met in the streets the other day who was selling weed. This guy likes to see you banging his wife, can you believe it?- Zak sounded pretty happy about his catch.

-Look, I'll give you his number, maybe send him a dick picture, you never know- he added, and then laughed.

Immediately, Rey and I took care of this, and sent him a picture each from our phones, hoping to get a reply, or even better, to find out it was all a joke. I wouldn't have liked it to find out that that guy let Zak and potentially also Rey do that to his wife without including me.
Half hour later, I received a reply, which made my heart pound.
-Mate, I can't believe it, you weren't lying then- I told Zak whilst feeling my adrenaline rush rising.
-He hasn't texted me back, that's weird- Rey couldn't believe it. I assumed sometimes people wouldn't believe his dick picture could have been real.
-Right, he wants to see me tonight- I told them after the guy had given me his address, somewhere near South Kensington, and a time for the meeting.
-I don't care- Rey blurted out and turned his body by the other side to face the window, then returned to playing chess on his phone. Zak and I looked at each other, resisting the temptation of laughing.
Later on that evening, both Zak and Rey had received a message from the same guy, who now wanted the three of us to get there all together and to which he received a positive reply straight away.
In no time, Rey and Zak took a quick shower, whilst I waited for them in the hallway. Fifteen minutes later, we were at the guy's place.
-God knows what these people do for a living- my usual question whenever I was about to meet someone who lived in our area came out loud.
-Who cares- Rey commented, now very excited after finding out he wasn't cut out from the plan.
The three of us reached the third floor of the building, and by that time, I was very nervous.
-Hi- we said to a naked man who opened the door for us without replying.
He was tall, in his mid-thirties and had dark hair pulled backwards. He looked very handsome, like one of those celebrities that acted in mafia Hollywood films.
We were led to the hallway and Zak was told to go first. The man hadn't spoken yet, but he somehow looked friendly. I

assumed there was no need to do any small talk in such occasion.
Few minutes later, Zak came out, looking embarrassed.
-Right, I'll meet you downstairs- he said, and walked away, sad.
-You want to come?- the guy asked me, making me even more nervous. What went wrong with Zak? Was there a test first? Hadn't he previously met him anyway?
A woman was naked in a white sofa on my left, as I had the chance to notice. She was very attractive, had blue eyes, wavy long blonde hair and a great body. Meanwhile, the naked man was staring at me, sitting on a smaller sofa in front of it, his hands shaking it in to get things going.
The woman replied friendly to my greeting. By that moment, realising it was all true and I was about to get someone so attractive with no effort whatsoever had brought me to a peak of nervousness that almost immediately vanished, now replaced by a feeling of absolute ease.
-Do you need help?- I asked the stupidest thing I possibly could to the man, who slowly replied -No, just her- still serious, but not at all rude.
He was a pervert, a real one, more than me and Rey. I had done the exact same thing a few times with Rey and Lisa in Valencia, but now that I was seeing another man doing it, I just felt it crossed a line.
-Make sure you don't finish inside your condom- he said, to which I really hoped to be able to obey without problems.
Half hour later, Rey was over too and the three of us left towards Knightsbridge.
-She was hot. You lasted more than anyone- said Rey then referring to me.
-I know- I replied, glad. -Did he ask you your phone number?- I asked Rey.
-No. Did he ask you?- Rey sounded disappointed.
-Well, yeah, he did- I replied, slow.

Sooner than we wanted it to be, the day we had to leave our flat arrived.
Meanwhile, Mark had found the way to get into his mom's place in Holborn from a window, Zak had decided to move to

Brighton, and Rey and I had made some bookings in Russell Square hostel.
-I'm going to miss this place. This is actually the best place I've ever been to so far- I looked at my back, towards number 18, Hans Crescent. A beautiful building in an area that was completely safe from London's rampant criminality. A well decorated jewel in the middle of a massive urban sewer, I had to admit, although Russell Square wasn't too bad either when it came to safety.
-I guess I'll have to go visit you in Brighton sometimes then. Enjoy your trip Zak- we gave a warm goodbye hug and promised to see each other regularly. Rey's bye was not as warm, but there was no hostility whatsoever.
-He must love you a lot, you really are the only close person to him right now- he said once the other two were gone.
-He has you too now- I replied, looking at him whilst we walked towards Knightsbridge station.

August 2017

In the first days of August, I was trying to enjoy being with Rey as much as I could, bearing the awareness that any day for him in London could have been the last one. In fact, as soon as he had lost all his money in gambling, he would have needed to go back to Spain, move past the grief, and then plan his next trip to meet customers around the world to recover from the massive losses.
Being back in the common room of Russell Square hostel was a pleasure. The feeling of being surrounded by strangers rather than by known people carried within the usual virtual promise of the unpredictable. The lack of expectations and the conveniently sped up process of getting to know someone provided us with the feeling of adventures that we were enjoying simply by sitting next to new people from table to table, often uninvited.
-By the way, I wanted to ask you, what's with you and Joseph?- I asked Rey one afternoon. This question came out of me unexpected. I had a feeling I hadn't thought about it, but that my brain had been working it out on its own and

then given voice to it. In fact, I felt I hit a spot when I saw Rey's face.
-Yeah, we don't talk- he cut it short.
-Why? He's friendly with everyone. He actually speaks too much with everyone, all the time, and I remember he used to talk to you a lot too at the beginning-
-Yeah, that was until he found out about my job. He doesn't approve of that- he said and sneered.
-Oh, I understand- that just lit a bulb inside my head. I should have thought about that before. Joseph was an old man from Ghana, and even if his views regarding pretty much everything that stood away from traditional peoples' roles in society were slightly improved by his many years living in London, he was still stuck on several issues, especially when it came to Rey's lifestyle.
-I have a good relationship with him, very good actually, and it's good to have him as a friend also because of his influence in here. I bet he could get anyone he doesn't like kicked out just like that. They take his opinion here- I commented, even though, to be fair, Rey had no power on that.
-Play- Rey didn't want to talk about it. His eyes, now looking very serious, were focusing on the chess board. Rey and I had been visiting the pervert guy from South Kensington a few times already, and Rey, who managed to get his number, was visiting him almost everyday due to his insistence. In fact, Asco, or at least, how both of us had decided to name him since, would usually reply and sometimes even arrange meetings when he had initially not planned any.
-I bet he's a pilot, a wealthy pilot. I saw the miniature of an airplane once in his flat- I commented out loud, but Rey couldn't care less about it.
-Let's go out tonight- I suggested at some point. Rey often had changes of plans, and getting him to say yes to that kind of suggestion was very hard, although we often ended up going out anyway.
-Did you see that one?- Rey replied like that, looking at a blonde girl that just passed by on her way to the kitchen.
I had already noticed her the day before. She was a very attractive blonde girl with blue eyes, just the way I liked,

but I decided not to make a move on her because I knew she was French.
-French- I cut it short.
-I see- Rey felt just the same about them.
In that moment though, I stood up and made a move to the kitchen. Knowing that she was French and also very attractive, meant that she was certainly going to be unbearably rude, or at least so it was in most cases.
-Hi- she replied to my greeting in a surprisingly shy tone when I bumped into her in the kitchen.
Few minutes later, Juliette, the French girl, agreed on joining the table with me and Rey, who was also surprised to see her.
Juliette had a friend as well who joined us from the table where they were sitting before. This one had dark skin and dark curly hair, probably mixed race.
After spending the evening with the girls and receiving no messages from Asco, our plan to go out on our own had changed, which got us to tell the girls we were up for theirs. The two of them were going to a massive nightclub in south London that played my absolute least favourite music genres. One of those places I not only hated for the music they played, but also for the kind of people that usually went there. Guys looked repellent with their ridiculous earrings, weirdly shaped t-shirts, colourful socks and other gadgets to identify themselves within a group of entirely useless people whose lives were mostly focused on stimulants. Girls who went to such places also looked like clowns whose abuse of all pleasure-centred activities such as sex and drugs had turned into zombies.
That night I was heading there though, and the least I could do, I thought, was trying to get the blonde girl drunk, also seeing that her friend wouldn't drink at all.
Now, my plan had initially, and surprisingly worked, because the blonde girl was acting in a submissive way to me, giving me a few sweet glances every now and then and laughing loud at my jokes. Then, I took her outside and kissed her, to which she responded passionately, although I could see the influence of alcohol. She had drunk a lot of vodka and way too quickly, which was now playing in my favour. I was

enjoying what seemed to be going to be an easy win when Rey sat in the back of the Uber by the other side, and with Juliette in the middle, Rey was now having his way with her as well, all whilst her friend, sitting next to the driver, was pretending that nothing was happening, although she was looking very annoyed about that.
What I noticed then bothered me though. Juliette, who was initially allowing both of us to do whatever was possible in the car, gradually rejected my hands on her until she was only for Rey.
The pathetic trip ended when we got off in Elephant and Castle. The darker girl was looking very impatient now and was doing her best to get her girl away from Rey. In my case, I didn't know what to say.
I felt annoyed at the girl for a minute back in the car, but I had to admit that she hadn't done anything wrong. What I didn't like was Rey's move, sneaky, unexpected from him.
-Right, I'm off- I announced, then walked a minute and turned towards the tube station, leaving the three of them behind me. At least, I thought, I got to save 20 pounds or more that now I could use for my Uber to take me home.
Few minutes later, my driver had arrived, and I made sure to sit in the back of the car since I saw a girl on her own there.
-Hi, where are you heading to?- I asked her as soon as I sat next to her.
-Hm... King's cross, why?- she said, hesitant.
-Me too- I said.
-You live there?-
-Closer to Russell Square actually, but I like to take walks before getting home. You're a student, right?- I asked because of her apparent age.
The girl was in her early twenties, Middle Eastern and was studying in London. Probably from a wealthy family, I supposed.
I liked that I was usually able to show people some level of knowledge about pretty much every topic, making it seem better than it actually was and pretending I had some related interest just to get the conversation going.
The talk with my new target went great, and eventually, she accepted my idea of taking her to her door. I kissed her, but

she said nothing was going to happen that night and rejected my self-invitation upstairs.
Resigned, I left Pentonville Road, turned on Gray's Inn Road and kept walking, heading to Russell Square, now slowly sobering up.
Right in that moment, I spotted a girl with brown hair and a black leather jacket standing in front of the entrance of a hotel.
She smiled at me, so I smiled back and kept walking, pretending I believed in a world where women could smile to men without them having to misinterpret it before turning back and walk towards her.
I didn't have any actual excuse to start a conversation, but I knew I didn't need any, since it all depended on her feelings about my face.
-Hi. Hm.. do you speak English?- I asked. No was the only answer that could have made me walk away without trying further. If she didn't speak any English, but was still intrigued about my face, she would have said she did a little bit.
-Yes- she replied, not sounding any scared of me. We were on a high road and even though it was the middle of the night, there were lights on and cameras.
-I've had a long night, just been at a party, too boring. What are you doing here? You're tourist, right?- I stood in front of her now.
-Yeah, I can't sleep actually. I'm leaving tomorrow, but the people in here are too noisy- she said, still smiling at me. She was very attractive, and now that I was closer to her, I could see her hair was actually more red than brown.
-Don't tell me about it, I'm staying in a hostel round the corner these days because I had to leave my house. It's terrible there- I said, making her chuckle.
-Where are you from?-
-Switzerland-
-What part of Switzerland? French or German? By the way, let's sit here, shall we- I said whilst already making a move towards the nearest step, making sure it didn't sound like a question.
-The French one- she said, following me.

-Oh I see, so do you like London so far?- I asked her in French, to which she replied surprised about that.
We talked about the usual stuff, our countries, what we did in there, what we studied and what we planned to do in the future, all whilst I tried to make her laugh and subtly inserting compliments about her.
-You know, I studied German and Russian when I was younger and I also lived both in Germany and Russia for long periods of time- I said, less than half true.
What I enjoyed about her was that we were alternating the languages we were speaking during our conversation, since I found out she was a polyglot like me, although unlike me she actually had proper fluency in speaking all the languages she did.
-You know I have a thing for ginger girls-
-I'm not ginger!- she said, enjoying the banter. I could tell she appreciated that I was sitting there with her and was clearly making a move, but I was afraid this wasn't going anywhere.
-Listen, at first, I was glad you came and talk to me, you're a very handsome man, but you're too smart. I'm attracted to smart men of course, but not the too smart ones- she said with a jokey tone, but I knew she hid some seriousness behind that statement.
-Listen, I'm as dumb as you could possibly imagine- I said, then tried to kiss her, but got rejected.
-No, I've just met you!- she said, enjoying that situation, with her head now facing the other side to prevent me from trying again.
-Come with me, I'll get you a drink and we'll have it in the park, in less than half hour you'll be back here and I'll leave you to sleep, deal?- I suggested.
She thought about it for a minute, then agreed.
I had to thank Paul the law enforcement officer for showing me the shop in Pentonville Road that sold alcohol at night for that.
Later on, Lauren and I were heading to St. George's Gardens in Sidmouth Street, a former cemetery closed by a high black gate at night, although it wasn't hard to break into due to the presence of a small wall and a metal box next to a bin that

allowed us to jump on it and cross the wall to reach the other side.
-So, this is it, this is where I take my victims- I said after sitting on a bench.
-Do you get paid for this?- she asked, visibly happy that I was making such kind of jokes. Girls love the idea of danger, and I had learnt not to question why anymore, although I concluded that the reason was probably bound to evolution. After ten full minutes of kissing hard and seeing no prospects of actual joy due to firm resistance from her side, I decided that my only option left was to pull down my pants and see if that helped.
-Oh my God- she said, shocked, then burst out laughing. I wouldn't have done anything like that if she hadn't smiled to me, encouraged the conversation, replied to my questions, said no to my flirting whilst still smiling, breaking into a park at night time and removing my hands from her body whilst still keeping her tongue with mine. She knew what I wanted from the very beginning, and acting like a nice guy or even resign wouldn't have given me any results anyway.
-I wouldn't do something like this with anyone, but you're so hot you're inspiring me this- I said, hoping that she would believe me. She looked at me for half minute, not saying anything, but still laughing. I was standing in front of her now, she was still sitting on the bench.
-I'm not going to have sex with you- she said, unable to control her chuckles.
I didn't say a word, but kept looking at her, firm. She looked back at me, appreciating I wasn't retreating.
-It was a fun night. Give me your contact, so that if you come back to London one day, I'll take you to dinner- I said half hour later when I dropped her at her hotel.
-Right. Thanks for the night- she said, then said bye. I walked back to the hostel, happy I was able to offer my night such event, and secretly hoping Rey hadn't succeeded with the French girl. I didn't care about her anymore, Lauren was just as much as a catch as Juliette in terms of look, although definitely funnier, smarter and curvier, but at the same time I wasn't happy about what Rey did to me.

One hour later, I was still struggling to fall asleep when I received a message from him.
-Dom, they're kicking me out. I don't want that- Rey began texting me the usual way, one word after another.
-What happened?-
-Joseph, I'm in his room. 108. He caught me taking the French girl to bed. And he's furious. This is unlucky. I don't want to get kicked out. From here. This hostel is my home- he seemed desperate, and I understood perfectly why.
-Ok, calm down, I'll talk to him. He usually listens to me, maybe he'll make an exception this time-
I reached Rey's room to find out he was at the reception, downstairs, talking to the staff. I stood up by the bottom of the room, although they could all see me. I wasn't the right person to go and defend him, since half of the staff was willing to get rid of me and the other half had already been nice enough to me by forgiving me when I did the same thing they were scolding Rey for.
I couldn't hide I was happy that Rey didn't manage to finish his night properly, but I also hated to see him under stress, as if his debts and problems weren't enough. On top of that, leaving the hostel would have forced him away from me, and he couldn't bear it just as I couldn't.
-He is your friend, tell him! Tell him!- Joseph shouted at me, although I could feel that the worst part was gone, and that he was slowly calming down already.
The staff didn't seem to be taking any rushed decision, and Rey's face didn't look much worried.
-I will, Joseph, don't worry, I'll take care of this guy- I said. Getting defensive would have been a mistake, and my perception of the tranquillity of the situation proved to be right a minute later, when we all were going back to our rooms, wishing the staff good night.

September 2017

By the early days of September, Rey and I had spent every moment together.
Juliette texted me the day after her departure, telling me that she was sorry about how things turned out eventually,

and that whenever I happened to be in France near her region, she would have been glad to host me and show me around. I told her off.

Rey's stability had lasted no more than three weeks before he messed everything up through gambling once again, and soon enough, he came up with the usual suggestion.

-Let's travel, that's what we need to do, for the rest of our lives Dom- he tried to push me with that, just as if I had got the same problems he had.

-I can't. I'm done being broke, my uni course starts next month, and I'm going to need some money saved in my account for emergencies. I'm going to work hard for a while. Besides, I'm receiving more and more offers from clubs in schools, which means I won't be able to take holidays on demand-

-So, you're going to be trapped and live like that? Once again? I thought you had changed, Dom- Rey was giving me his usual talk.

-We've travelled a lot together, even when it was my least rational option- I stopped typing on my laptop when I told him that.

We looked at each other for a moment. Even the thought provided by what I just said was enough for both of us to stop for a moment and smile.

-Let it be the last, come with me for a week, then you'll come back to work, and I'll keep travelling around for a bit. I promise I'll meet you back in London at some point, although I don't like it here anymore- he said, pensive at the end.

-A new chapter of my life has started, and I've got to stay here and take care of myself for a bit. I promise to travel with you at the beginning of next year. Deal?-

Rey agreed.

A week later, Rey was gone. I wished him luck with his business and for the future in general, even though I was certain we were going to meet again.

The night of his departure, I felt different than usual. I looked around in the crowded common room, not that different from the one I had come across to when I arrived in London, and just spaced out for a bit.

It felt like I was on my own once again, even though I had many friends now, some still living in London, some far from me, but we were all connected, and I knew they were going to visit at some point. Everyone did eventually.

That night, for instance, Sandra was there with me. She was visiting just for a few days, and she had previously told me she had no doubts about where she was going to stay. We sat down at the table near the sofas, my favourite one, and just chatted until I noticed a girl with long, curly brown hair sitting in front of me. She said she was Australian.

As usual, what started off as a catch up with a friend ended up involving more and more people, forcing me to stay up much later than I had initially planned.

Printed in Great Britain
by Amazon